RAINTREE
ATLAS
of the
WORLD

Written by
Keith Lye

RAINTREE
STECK-VAUGHN
PUBLISHERS

A Harcourt Company

Austin   New York
www.raintreesteckvaughn.com

ABOUT THE ATLAS

Maps are essential tools for anyone who wants to understand the planet Earth. Their use goes back several thousand years. For example, in ancient Egypt, officials used maps to calculate taxes on property. From the days of the ancient Greeks, maps were a way of summarizing information about the known world.

Topographic and thematic maps

Topographic maps incorporate many features, including the height of the land, political boundaries, and cities and towns. They are a form of abbreviation. One map often contains such a vast amount of information that it would take an entire book to put it in words. Today, maps that portray one particular aspect of the changing world have become increasingly useful aids. These thematic maps help us to compare information about one place with that of another.

Flat maps of a round world

Because most maps depict the earth's curved surface on a flat paper surface, no map can be completely accurate. For this reason cartographers have devised different map projections – mathematical ways of projecting the earth's curvature onto a flat surface. Each projection preserves accurately some of the following features: shape, size, distance, and direction. Only a globe can preserve all of them accurately at the same time. But even the largest globes are far less detailed than most maps – and less convenient to carry about.

World maps

This atlas is a collection of up-to-date thematic maps based on the latest available data. It consists of two main parts: world maps and regional maps. Some world maps present information about the natural world, including physical features, habitats, climate, resources, plants, and soils. Other maps reveal how human activity is increasingly modifying natural environments through the exploitation of the earth's dwindling resources, through farming, the building of cities and roads, and industrialization. The world thematic maps, therefore, give an overview of the extent to which natural and human factors are interrelated around the world. They increase our awareness of the dangers inherent in interfering with nature, pinpointing many dangers that the world faces.

Regional maps

Following the world overview, the atlas then takes an in-depth view of the world, which for this purpose is divided into 23 regions. These regions and the countries included in them are listed below. Each regional section contains topographic and political maps, other thematic maps, and climate data, all of which are interrelated. The maps are supplemented by ready-reference fact panels with data that adds to the information on the maps. Basic data and flags are also provided for every independent country in the world, taking account of the many changes to the world map that have occurred in recent years.

Abbreviations	
'000 = thousands	Int $ = international dollars
C = Celsius	m = metric
cm = centimeter	mi = miles
F = Fahrenheit	mil = million
ft = feet	mm = millimeter
GDP = Gross Domestic Product	mil m.t. = million metric tons
GNP = Gross National Product	sq km = square kilometers
in. = inches	sq mi = square miles
	n/a = not available

REGIONS OF THE WORLD

Canada and Greenland Canada, Greenland (dependency of Denmark)
United States of America United States of America
Mexico, Central America, and the Caribbean Antigua and Barbuda, Bahamas, Barbados, Belize, Costa Rica, Cuba, Dominica, Dominican Republic, El Salvador, Grenada, Guatemala, Haiti, Honduras, Jamaica, Mexico, Nicaragua, Panama, St. Kitts-Nevis, St. Lucia, St. Vincent and the Grenadines, Trinidad and Tobago
South America Argentina, Bolivia, Brazil, Chile, Colombia, Ecuador, Guyana, Paraguay, Peru, Suriname, Uruguay, Venezuela
Nordic Countries Denmark, Finland, Iceland, Norway, Sweden
British Isles Ireland, United Kingdom
France Andorra, France, Monaco
Spain and Portugal Portugal, Spain
Italy and Greece Cyprus, Greece, Italy, Malta, San Marino, Vatican City
Central Europe and the Low Countries Austria, Belgium, Germany, Liechtenstein, Luxembourg, Netherlands, Switzerland
Eastern Europe Albania, Bosnia and Herzegovina, Bulgaria, Croatia, Czech Republic, Hungary, Macedonia, Poland, Romania, Slovakia, Slovenia, Yugoslavia
Russia and Its Neighbors Armenia, Azerbaijan, Belarus, Estonia, Georgia, Kazakhstan, Kyrgyzstan, Latvia, Lithuania, Moldova, Mongolia, Russia, Tajikistan, Turkmenistan, Ukraine, Uzbekistan
Southwest Asia Afghanistan, Bahrain, Iran, Iraq, Israel, Jordan, Kuwait, Lebanon, Oman, Qatar, Saudi Arabia, Syria, Turkey, United Arab Emirates, Yemen
Northern Africa Algeria, Chad, Djibouti, Egypt, Eritrea, Ethiopia, Libya, Mali, Mauritania, Morocco, Niger, Somalia, Sudan, Tunisia
Central Africa Benin, Burkina Faso, Burundi, Cameroon, Cape Verde Islands, Central African Republic, Côte d'Ivoire, Democratic Republic of the Congo, Equatorial Guinea, Gabon, Gambia, Ghana, Guinea, Guinea-Bissau, Kenya, Liberia, Nigeria, Republic of the Congo, Rwanda, São Tomé and Príncipe, Senegal, Seychelles, Sierra Leone, Tanzania, Togo, Uganda
Southern Africa Angola, Botswana, Comoros, Lesotho, Madagascar, Malawi, Mauritius, Mozambique, Namibia, South Africa, Swaziland, Zambia, Zimbabwe
Indian Subcontinent Bangladesh, Bhutan, India, Maldives, Nepal, Pakistan, Sri Lanka
China and Taiwan The People's Republic of China, Taiwan
Southeast Asia Brunei, Cambodia, East Timor, Indonesia, Laos, Malaysia, Myanmar, Philippines, Singapore, Thailand, Vietnam
Japan and Korea Japan, North Korea, South Korea
Australia and Its Neighbors Australia, Papua New Guinea
New Zealand and Its Neighbors Federated States of Micronesia, Fiji, Kiribati, Marshall Islands, Nauru, New Zealand, Palau, Samoa, Solomon Islands, Tonga, Tuvalu, Vanuatu
Antarctica

Published in 2002 in the United States of America by:
Raintree Steck-Vaughn Publishers
10801 N. MoPac Expy., Bldg. #3, Austin, Texas 78759, USA.

AN ANDROMEDA BOOK
Copyright © 2002 Andromeda Oxford Ltd; first printed 1994, updated 2001.
Devised and produced by:
Andromeda Oxford Ltd, 11-13 The Vineyard, Abingdon, Oxfordshire OX13 5BL, England.
Editors: Ruth Hooper and Jenny Fry.
Design: Craig Eaton.
Cartography: Richard Watts and Tim Williams.
Flags produced by Lovell Johns, Oxford, U.K. and authenticated by the Flag Research center, Winchester, Mass.

Library of Congress Cataloging-in-Publication Data

Lye, Keith
    Raintree atlas of the world / written by Keith Lye.
        p. cm.
    Rev. ed. of: The complete world atlas / written by Keith Lye. 1995.
    "An Andromeda book"--T.p. verso.
    Includes bibliographical references and index.
    Summary: A collection of world and regional maps which present information about the natural world, including physical features, habitats, climate, and more.
    ISBN: 0-7398-4891-7
    1. Children's atlases. [1. Atlases. 2. Geography.] I. Title: Atlas of the world. II. Complete world atlas. III. Title.
    G1021 .L87 2002
    912--dc21
                                                                    2001048142
Printed by Ajanta, India.
1 2 3 4 5 6 7 8 9 0 AI 05 04 03 02 01

CONTENTS

THE WORLD

PHYSICAL

Land covers about 57,259,000 square miles (148,300,000 sq km) of the earth's surface. The land can be divided broadly into physical regions that are distinguished by the topography (surface features) and the climate.

The changing land

Land features such as mountains are constantly changing. While earthquakes and volcanic eruptions cause sudden and catastrophic change, other forces, such as weathering, are slow.

Worn fragments of rock are removed by the forces of erosion. These include running water, particularly in wet regions; glaciers (moving bodies of ice) in cold regions; winds, especially in deserts; and sea waves along coasts. Much of the worn rock is dumped onto sea or lake beds, where it piles up and eventually over many years forms new rock layers. This is part of the rock cycle, which has continued throughout the earth's history.

The changing map

Other forces operate inside the earth. Movements in the partly molten mantle affect parts of the overlying lithosphere, the planet's hard outer shell. As these huge blocks, or tectonic plates, move, they cause volcanic eruptions, earthquakes, and mountain building. New rock is formed from molten material from the mantle.

Around 280 million years ago, all the world's land areas were joined together in one supercontinent, which geologists call Pangea. About 200 million years ago, this super-continent started to separate, and the continents we know today gradually drifted to their present positions. Along the ocean ridges on the deep sea floor, plates are moving apart. These slow but unceasing movements continue today.

POLITICAL

While natural forces constantly change physical maps, human factors, such as wars, change political maps. For example, the world map in 1946 was substantially different from that of 1939, when World War II began. Another upheaval occurred in the 1950s and 1960s when many European colonies in Africa and Asia achieved their independence. Many of the independent nations adopted new names for cities and even physical features.

New nations

An upheaval occurred in the early 1990s, when the collapse of many communist governments changed the political map of Europe and Asia. For example, when in 1991 the Soviet Union was dissolved, 15 separate nations were born. The former Yugoslavia also has split up into five new nations.

Sovereignty

By 1999 the world contained 192 independent nations. Despite boundary disputes between some neighboring countries, each nation has a defined territory, which is recognized internationally, and a government that is responsible for making and implementing laws. The independent nations are often called sovereign states, because, unlike dependencies or states and provinces within nations, they recognize no authority higher than their own.

Sovereignty has nothing to do with size. The world's five smallest sovereign states have a combined area of about 42 square miles (110 sq km) and a population of about 72,000. Yet they are all sovereign states, unlike Texas, a state within the United States, which covers 267,340 square miles (692,407 sq km) and had a population of 20.85 million by 2000.

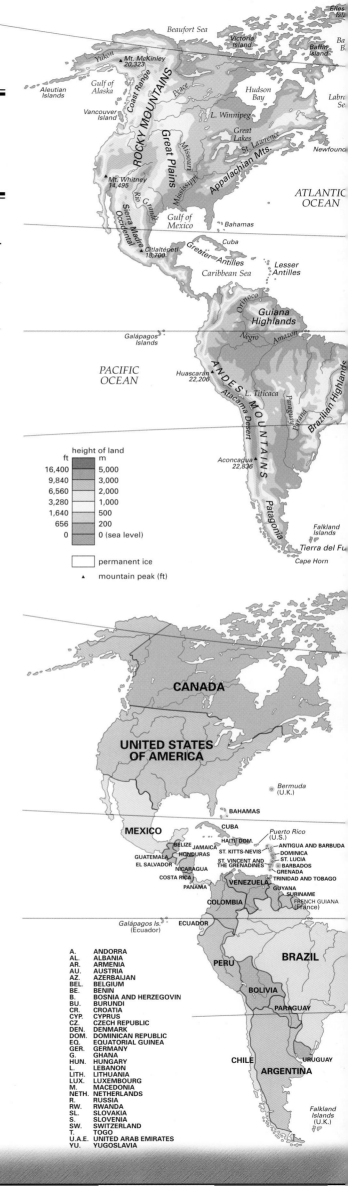

height of land

ft	m
16,400	5,000
9,840	3,000
6,560	2,000
3,280	1,000
1,640	500
656	200
0	0 (sea level)

permanent ice

▲ mountain peak (ft)

A. ANDORRA
AL. ALBANIA
AR. ARMENIA
AU. AUSTRIA
AZ. AZERBAIJAN
BEL. BELGIUM
BE. BENIN
B. BOSNIA AND HERZEGOVIN
BU. BURUNDI
CR. CROATIA
CYP. CYPRUS
CZ. CZECH REPUBLIC
DEN. DENMARK
DOM. DOMINICAN REPUBLIC
EQ. EQUATORIAL GUINEA
GER. GERMANY
G. GHANA
HUN. HUNGARY
L. LEBANON
LITH. LITHUANIA
LUX. LUXEMBOURG
M. MACEDONIA
NETH. NETHERLANDS
R. RUSSIA
RW. RWANDA
SL. SLOVAKIA
S. SLOVENIA
SW. SWITZERLAND
T. TOGO
U.A.E. UNITED ARAB EMIRATES
YU. YUGOSLAVIA

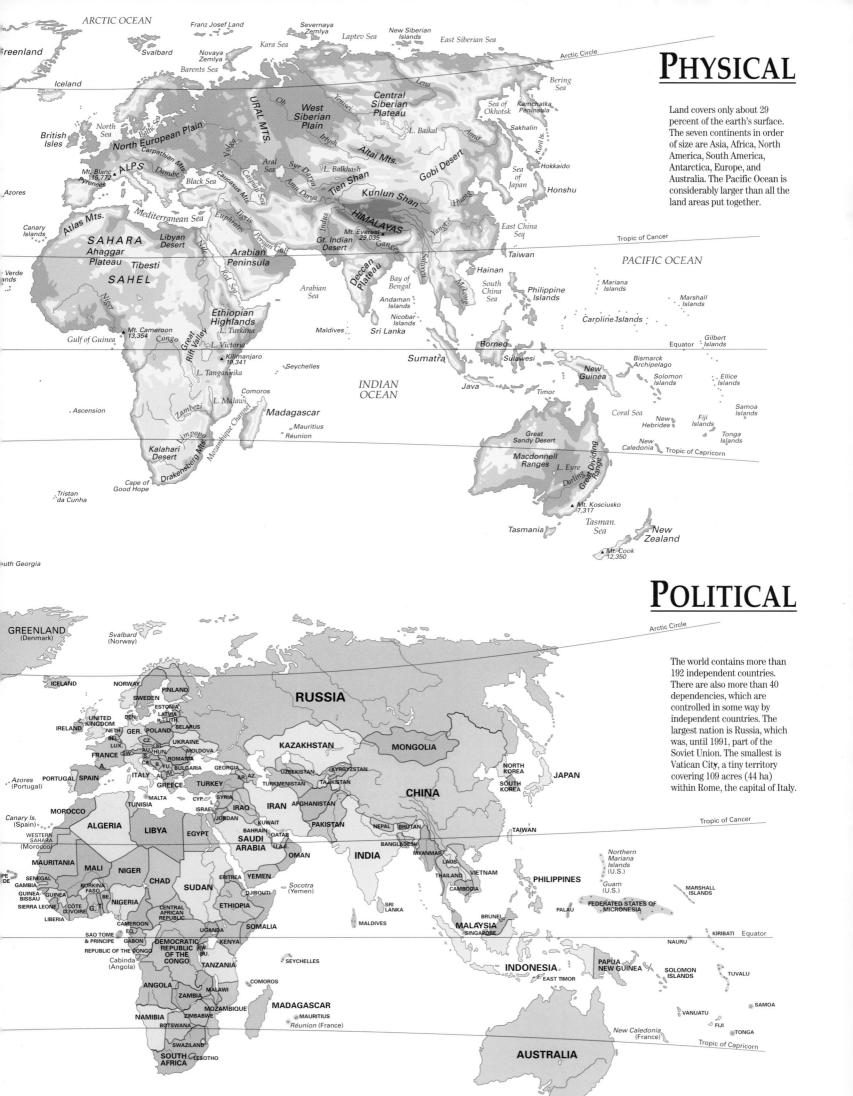

PHYSICAL

Land covers only about 29 percent of the earth's surface. The seven continents in order of size are Asia, Africa, North America, South America, Antarctica, Europe, and Australia. The Pacific Ocean is considerably larger than all the land areas put together.

ARCTIC OCEAN

Franz Josef Land · Severnaya Zemlya · Laptev Sea · New Siberian Islands · East Siberian Sea · Arctic Circle

Greenland · Svalbard · Kara Sea · Bering Sea · Kamchatka Peninsula

Iceland · Barents Sea · Novaya Zemlya · Lena · Sea of Okhotsk · Sakhalin

British Isles · North Sea · Baltic Sea · North European Plain · URAL MTS. · Ob · West Siberian Plain · Yenisei · Central Siberian Plateau · Amur · Kuril Is. · Hokkaido · Sea of Japan

Azores · Pyrenees · ALPS · Mt. Blanc 15,772 · Danube · Carpathian Mts. · Black Sea · Caucasus Mts. · Volga · Aral Sea · Syr Darya · L. Balkhash · Altai Mts. · Tien Shan · Gobi Desert · Huang · Honshu

Canary Islands · Atlas Mts. · Mediterranean Sea · Euphrates · Tigris · Caspian Sea · Amu Darya · Kunlun Shan · Yangtze · East China Sea · Taiwan · Tropic of Cancer

Verde Islands · SAHARA · Ahaggar · Plateau · Libyan Desert · Nile · Red Sea · Arabian Peninsula · Persian Gulf · Indus · HIMALAYAS · Mt. Everest 29,035 · Ganges · Deccan Plateau · Salween · PACIFIC OCEAN

Tibesti · SAHEL · Arabian Sea · Gt. Indian Desert · Bay of Bengal · Mekong · South China Sea · Hainan · Mariana Islands · Marshall Islands

Niger · Gulf of Guinea · Mt. Cameroon 13,354 · Ethiopian Highlands · L. Turkana · Andaman Islands · Nicobar Islands · Maldives · Sri Lanka · Philippine Islands · Caroline Islands

Congo · Great Rift Valley · L. Victoria · Kilimanjaro 19,341 · Seychelles · Sumatra · Borneo · Sulawesi · Equator · Gilbert Islands

Ascension · L. Tanganyika · INDIAN OCEAN · Java · New Guinea · Bismarck Archipelago · Solomon Islands · Ellice Islands

Zambezi · L. Malawi · Comoros · Madagascar · Mauritius · Réunion · Timor · Coral Sea · New Hebrides · Fiji Islands · Samoa Islands

Limpopo · Mozambique Channel · Great Sandy Desert · Macdonnell Ranges · L. Eyre · New Caledonia · Tonga Islands · Tropic of Capricorn

Tristan da Cunha · Kalahari Desert · Drakensberg Mts. · Cape of Good Hope · Durling Range · Great Dividing Range · Mt. Kosciusko 7,317

South Georgia · Tasmania · Tasman Sea · New Zealand · Mt. Cook 12,350

POLITICAL

The world contains more than 192 independent countries. There are also more than 40 dependencies, which are controlled in some way by independent countries. The largest nation is Russia, which was, until 1991, part of the Soviet Union. The smallest is Vatican City, a tiny territory covering 109 acres (44 ha) within Rome, the capital of Italy.

GREENLAND (Denmark) · Svalbard (Norway) · Arctic Circle

ICELAND · NORWAY · SWEDEN · FINLAND · RUSSIA

IRELAND · UNITED KINGDOM · DEN. · EST. · ESTONIA · LATVIA · LITH. · BELARUS · KAZAKHSTAN · MONGOLIA

FRANCE · NETH. · BEL. · GER. · POLAND · UKRAINE · NORTH KOREA · JAPAN

LUX. · SW. · S. · A. · HUN. · ROMANIA · MOLDOVA · UZBEKISTAN · KYRGYZSTAN · SOUTH KOREA

Azores (Portugal) · PORTUGAL · SPAIN · ITALY · B. · YU. · BULGARIA · GEORGIA · TURKMENISTAN · TAJIKISTAN · CHINA

MALTA · GREECE · TURKEY · AR. · AZ. · MOROCCO · CYP. · SYRIA · IRAQ · IRAN · AFGHANISTAN · Tropic of Cancer

Canary Is. (Spain) · TUNISIA · ISRAEL · L. · JORDAN · KUWAIT · PAKISTAN · NEPAL · BHUTAN · TAIWAN

WESTERN SAHARA (Morocco) · ALGERIA · LIBYA · EGYPT · BAHRAIN · QATAR · SAUDI ARABIA · U.A.E. · BANGLADESH · MYANMAR

MAURITANIA · MALI · NIGER · CHAD · SUDAN · ERITREA · YEMEN · OMAN · INDIA · LAOS · Northern Mariana Islands (U.S.)

SENEGAL · GAMBIA · BURKINA FASO · BE. · NIGERIA · CENTRAL AFRICAN REPUBLIC · ETHIOPIA · DJIBOUTI · Socotra (Yemen) · THAILAND · VIETNAM · PHILIPPINES · Guam (U.S.) · MARSHALL ISLANDS

GUINEA-BISSAU · GUINEA · SIERRA LEONE · CÔTE D'IVOIRE · G. · CAMEROON · SRI LANKA · CAMBODIA · PALAU · FEDERATED STATES OF MICRONESIA

LIBERIA · EQ. · SAO TOME & PRINCIPE · GABON · UGANDA · KENYA · SOMALIA · MALDIVES · BRUNEI · MALAYSIA · SINGAPORE · KIRIBATI · Equator

DEMOCRATIC REPUBLIC OF THE CONGO · RW. · BU. · TANZANIA · SEYCHELLES · INDONESIA · EAST TIMOR · PAPUA NEW GUINEA · SOLOMON ISLANDS · NAURU · TUVALU

REPUBLIC OF THE CONGO · Cabinda (Angola) · ANGOLA · ZAMBIA · MALAWI · COMOROS · MADAGASCAR · Mauritius · Réunion (France) · SAMOA

NAMIBIA · ZIMBABWE · MOZAMBIQUE · VANUATU · FIJI · TONGA · New Caledonia (France)

BOTSWANA · SWAZILAND · SOUTH AFRICA · LESOTHO · AUSTRALIA · Tropic of Capricorn

Kerguelen Islands (France) · NEW ZEALAND

South Georgia (U.K.)

THE WORLD

CLIMATE

While weather is the day-to-day, or hour-to-hour, condition of the air, climate is the long-term pattern of weather of a place.

Latitude and climate

The earth's atmosphere is always on the move. The reason for the movement of air is the sun, whose rays are most concentrated in tropical zones and least concentrated at the poles. The difference in temperature is mostly responsible for the planetary winds – the trade winds, westerlies, and polar easterlies – which constantly exchange air between hot tropical and cold polar regions.

Terrain and climate

While latitude is a major factor affecting climate, several other factors determine the pattern of world climates. First, winds are affected by the terrain. Warm, moist winds from the ocean pass over a mountain range and are chilled. Because their capacity to retain water vapor is reduced by cooling, the water vapor is turned into tiny droplets, which form rain clouds. It rains on the side of the mountain where the clouds rise. Beyond the mountain peaks, the winds become warmer as they descend, picking up moisture and creating a dry region, called a rain shadow.

The influence of the sea

The sea often has a moderating influence on the climate, and moist winds from the ocean usually bring plenty of rain. These moderating effects are felt less and less the farther one travels inland. Warm ocean currents, such as the Gulf Stream and its extension, the North Atlantic Current, have a warming effect on northwestern Europe. By contrast, eastern Canada in the same latitude is chilled by the cold Labrador Current.

HABITATS

The type of climate a region has determines broadly the kinds of plants and animals that live there. But many factors influence a species' habitat – topographical features, soil, and availability of oxygen, water, and food. A species' total physical, biological, and chemical surroundings make up its habitat. Similar habitats have like temperature and precipitation ranges, and can be classified into zones that follow lines of latitude.

Rain forests and savanna

Tropical rain forests flourish where it is hot and wet all year. They occur around the globe mostly in areas close to the equator. Savannas occur in tropical regions with a dry season.

Arid regions

Deserts are places with an average annual rainfall of less than 10 inches (25 cm). Deserts cover about one-seventh of the earth's land surface and center on a zone between the tropics and middle latitudes.

Forests and grasslands

In the latitudes on either side of the tropics are the temperate zones, or middle latitudes. Deciduous forests of maples, oaks, and beeches give way to grasslands. In North America and Eurasia, coniferous forests grow in the higher latitudes.

Cold zones

Cold zones include the ice sheets of Antarctica and Greenland and the treeless tundra regions, where plants grow only during the short summer.

Mountain habitats

Mountain habitats are determined largely by altitude rather than latitude. The difference in habitats is caused by temperature differences, which decrease by $1°F$ $(0.55°C)$ every 300 feet (100m) in altitude.

CLIMATE

Hot tropical climates are hot and wet all year.	tropical
Tropical monsoon climates have wet and dry seasons.	
Tropical steppe has a short, unreliable rainy season.	
Summers are wet and warm; winters wet and mild.	subtropical
Summers are dry and warm; winters wet and mild.	
Desert areas have little rain and no cold season.	
It rains all year with no great temperature variation.	temperate
These climates have warm summers and cold winters.	
Little rain with no great temperature variation.	
Subarctic winters are very cold; summers are short.	cold
Arctic or ice-cap climates are freezing all year round.	

The world's climatic zones are affected by latitude, prevailing winds, terrain (especially high mountain ranges that lie in the path of winds), distance from the sea, and ocean currents.

Surface currents have a marked effect on the climate of coastal regions. Onshore winds passing over cold currents are chilled. Winds passing over warm currents are warmed.

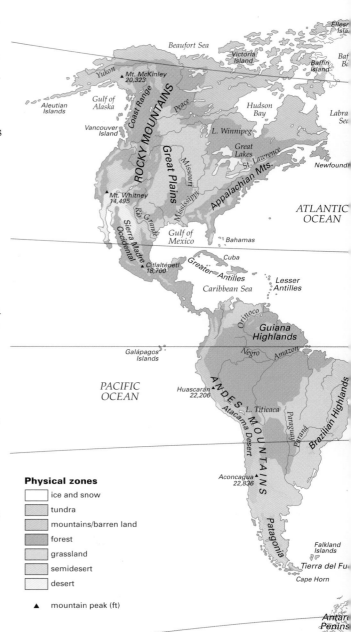

Physical zones

- ice and snow
- tundra
- mountains/barren land
- forest
- grassland
- semidesert
- desert

▲ mountain peak (ft)

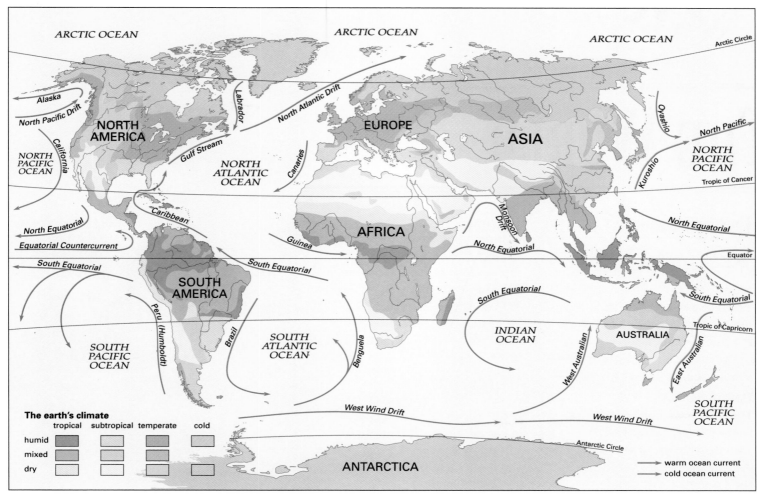

The earth's climate

	tropical	subtropical	temperate	cold
humid				
mixed				
dry				

→ warm ocean current
→ cold ocean current

ARCTIC OCEAN · ARCTIC OCEAN · ARCTIC OCEAN · Arctic Circle

Alaska · North Pacific Drift · Labrador · North Atlantic Drift · Oyashio · North Pacific

NORTH AMERICA · EUROPE · ASIA

NORTH PACIFIC OCEAN · California · Gulf Stream · NORTH ATLANTIC OCEAN · Canaries · Monsoon Drift · Kuroshio · NORTH PACIFIC OCEAN · Tropic of Cancer

Caribbean · North Equatorial · AFRICA · North Equatorial

North Equatorial · Guinea · North Equatorial · Equator

Equatorial Countercurrent · South Equatorial · South Equatorial · South Equatorial

South Equatorial · SOUTH AMERICA · South Equatorial · INDIAN OCEAN · AUSTRALIA · Tropic of Capricorn

Peru (Humboldt) · Brazil · Benguela · West Australian · East Australian

SOUTH PACIFIC OCEAN · SOUTH ATLANTIC OCEAN · SOUTH PACIFIC OCEAN

West Wind Drift · West Wind Drift

Antarctic Circle

ANTARCTICA

HABITATS

The different types of habitats around the world reflect diverse climates, physical features, rock types, soils, and plant and animal life that exist in these areas. A change in any factor, such as climate, leads to changes in the types of living things that populate an area.

ARCTIC OCEAN · Franz Josef Land · Severnaya Zemlya · New Siberian Islands · East Siberian Sea

Greenland · Svalbard · Novaya Zemlya · Kara Sea · Laptev Sea · Arctic Circle

Iceland · Barents Sea · Lena · Bering Sea

URAL MTS. · Ob · West Siberian Plain · Yenisei · Central Siberian Plateau · Sea of Okhotsk · Kamchatka Peninsula

British Isles · North Sea · Baltic Sea · North European Plain · Carpathian Mts. · Volga · Irtysh · L. Baikal · Amur · Sakhalin · Kuril Is. · Hokkaido

Azores · Mt. Blanc 15,772 · ALPS · Danube · Aral Sea · Syr Darya · L. Balkhash · Altai Mts. · Tien Shan · Gobi Desert · Sea of Japan · Pyrenees · Black Sea · Caucasus Mts. · Caspian Sea · Amu Darya · Kunlun Shan · Honshu

Mediterranean Sea · Tigris · Euphrates · Persian Gulf · Indus · HIMALAYAS · Yangtze · East China Sea

Canary Islands · Atlas Mts. · Libyan Desert · Nile · Arabian Peninsula · Mt. Everest 29,035 · Gt. Indian Desert · Ganges · Salween · Tropic of Cancer

SAHARA · Ahaggar Plateau · Tibesti · Red Sea · Deccan Plateau · Taiwan · PACIFIC OCEAN

SAHEL · Arabian Sea · Bay of Bengal · Hainan · South China Sea · Philippine Islands · Mariana Islands · Marshall Islands

Verde ands · Niger · Andaman Islands · Mekong · Caroline Islands

Ethiopian Highlands · L. Turkana · Nicobar Islands · Maldives · Sri Lanka · Gilbert Islands

Mt. Cameroon 13,354 · Congo · Great Rift Valley · L. Victoria · Borneo · Equator

Gulf of Guinea · Kilimanjaro 19,341 · Seychelles · Sumatra · Sulawesi · Bismarck Archipelago · New Guinea · Solomon Islands · Ellice Islands

L. Tanganyika · INDIAN OCEAN · Java · Timor · Samoa Islands

Comoros · Ascension · L. Malawi · Zambezi · Madagascar · Coral Sea · New Hebrides · Fiji Islands · Tonga Islands

Mauritius · Réunion · New Caledonia · Tropic of Capricorn

Kalahari Desert · Limpopo · Mozambique Channel · Great Sandy Desert · Macdonnell Ranges · L. Eyre · Darling · Great Dividing Range

Tristan da Cunha · Drakensberg Mts. · Cape of Good Hope · Mt. Kosciusko 7,317

uth Georgia · Tasmania · Tasman Sea · Mt. Cook 12,350 · New Zealand

Weddell Sea · Enderby Land · Wilkes Land · Antarctic Circle

Queen Maud Land · Antarctica

Coats Land

THE WORLD

ENVIRONMENTAL ISSUES

Natural habitats around the world are always undergoing change with variations in climate. These changes occur gradually over hundreds of years. In addition to natural changes, however, many habitats are being greatly modified by increasing human activity.

Deforestation

The temperate middle latitudes were once largely covered by deciduous forests of ash, beech, elm, oak, and maple. However, much of the original deciduous forests have been cut down to provide fuel, timber, and farmland.

Perhaps the most serious environmental issue in the world today is the destruction of the rain forests in South America, Central Africa, and Southeast Asia. These forests contain more than half of the world's species of plants and animals, many of which are rapidly becoming extinct. Rain forest destruction may cause climatic change and contribute to global warming.

Desertification

Soil erosion often occurs when deforestation, overgrazing, and poor farming lays the land bare to wind and rain. In arid regions, soil erosion can turn fertile land into barren desert. The desertification of semiarid grasslands, such as the Sahel region south of the Sahara, is another major environmental issue.

Other problems

Many environmental problems arise from pollution. Major issues include smog, caused by industrial smoke or motor exhaust fumes, acid rain, the pollution of rivers and lakes by industrial wastes or untreated sewage, discharges of nuclear radiation, and the depletion of freshwater resources.

POPULATION

In 2000, the world's population reached 6.055 billion. It is estimated that this total will reach 7 billion in 2013 and 8 billion in 2028. Predictions show that by 2050 the world population could reach as high as 9.3 billion.

The population explosion

Around 10,000 years ago, when people began to grow crops and live in permanent settlements, the world was thinly populated. From around 5 million people in 8000 B.C., the population increased steadily to reach 500 million in A.D. 1650. The population then doubled in only 200 years, reaching 1 billion in 1850. The acceleration of population growth continued. By the mid-1920s, world population had reached nearly 2 billion, and it passed the 4 billion mark in the 1970s.

The increases in the last 200 years occurred first in nations that were industrializing. But the rates of population growth in the developed industrial world have recently declined. Today, the highest growth rates are in the developing world.

Where people live

At the turn of the twentieth century, about half of the world's people lived on only 5 percent of the world's land area, while about half of the world's land area contained only about 5 percent of the world's population. The population explosion in areas attractive to settlement and the consequent expansion of city populations have all contributed to pollution, while urban living has contributed to many of the environmental problems that exist today.

Population pressure also affects rural areas, where the increasing demand for land to grow food has led to the destruction of natural habitats.

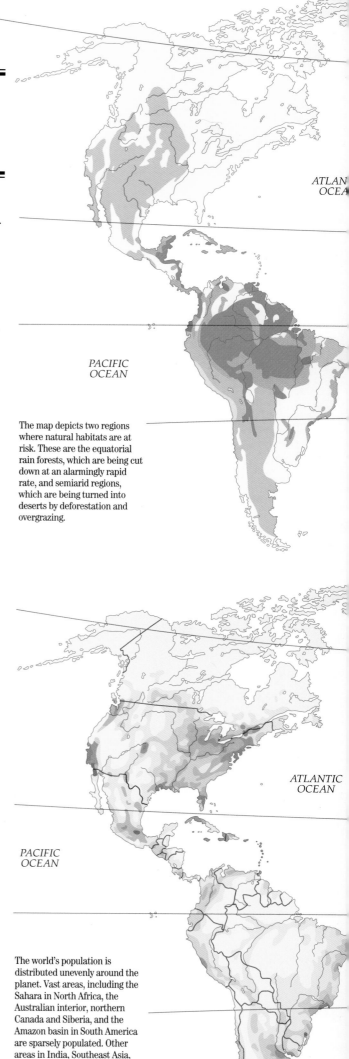

ATLANTIC OCEAN

PACIFIC OCEAN

The map depicts two regions where natural habitats are at risk. These are the equatorial rain forests, which are being cut down at an alarmingly rapid rate, and semiarid regions, which are being turned into deserts by deforestation and overgrazing.

ATLANTIC OCEAN

PACIFIC OCEAN

The world's population is distributed unevenly around the planet. Vast areas, including the Sahara in North Africa, the Australian interior, northern Canada and Siberia, and the Amazon basin in South America are sparsely populated. Other areas in India, Southeast Asia, Western Europe, and the northeastern United States are extremely crowded.

Environmental Issues

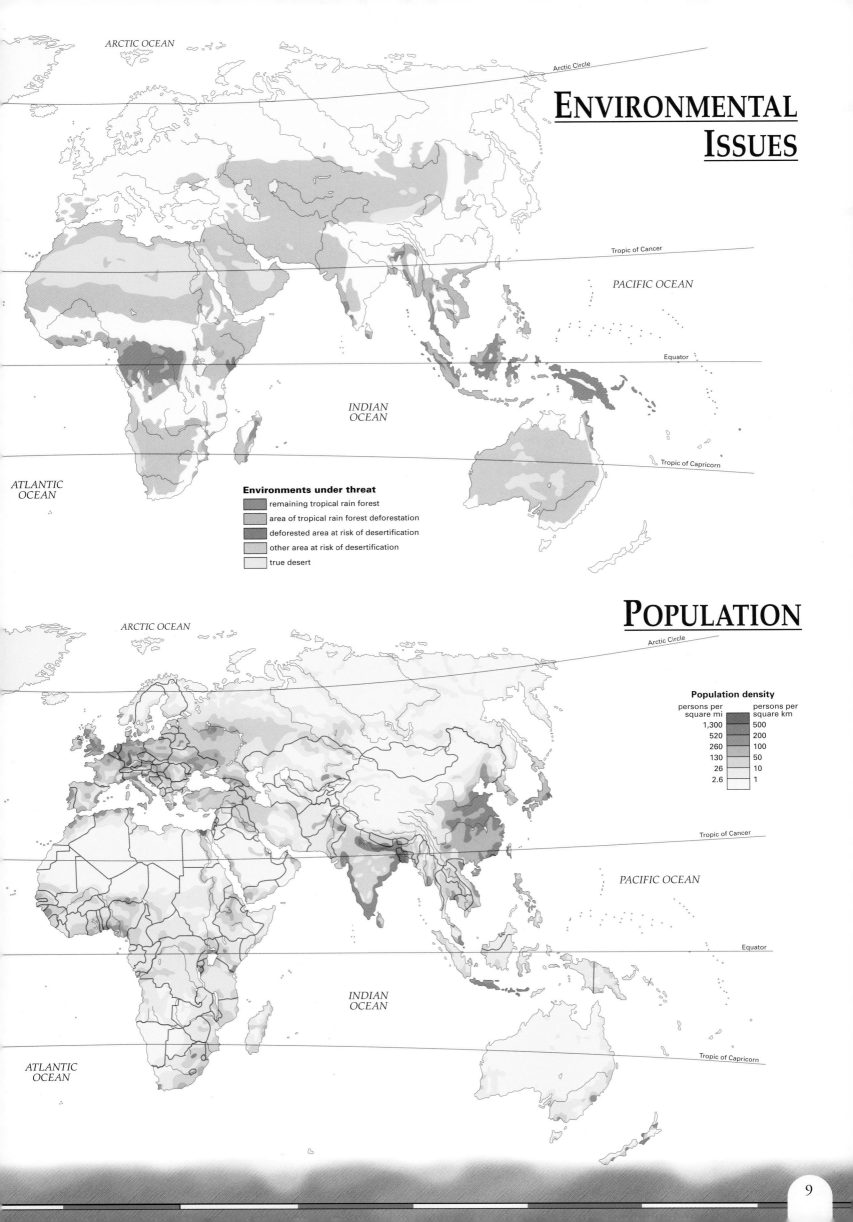

ARCTIC OCEAN

Arctic Circle

Tropic of Cancer

PACIFIC OCEAN

Equator

INDIAN OCEAN

Tropic of Capricorn

ATLANTIC OCEAN

Environments under threat

- remaining tropical rain forest
- area of tropical rain forest deforestation
- deforested area at risk of desertification
- other area at risk of desertification
- true desert

Population

ARCTIC OCEAN

Arctic Circle

Population density

persons per square mi		persons per square km
1,300		500
520		200
260		100
130		50
26		10
2.6		1

Tropic of Cancer

PACIFIC OCEAN

Equator

INDIAN OCEAN

Tropic of Capricorn

ATLANTIC OCEAN

THE WORLD

RESOURCES

The world's leading resources include those that provide fuel, together with metals and nonmetallic minerals used in industry.

Energy resources

Coal, oil, and natural gas are called fossil fuels because they were formed from once-living organisms. Coal was the main fuel during the industrial revolution in the nineteenth century. Today, however, oil and natural gas provide about three-fifths of the world's energy.

Fossil fuels are nonrenewable resources, and some experts estimate that, at present drilling rates, the world's oil reserves will run out by 2035.

Nuclear power continues to be controversial, and so it seems likely that such renewable energy resources as water and solar power will be increasingly used in the future. Also important is the fact that the use of water and solar power, unlike that of fossil fuels, does not cause pollution.

Mineral reserves

Most metals are extracted from ores, which are combinations of minerals. Iron, which is used to make steel, is the most widely used metal. Other major metallic minerals include aluminum, which is obtained from the ore bauxite; copper; lead; tin; and zinc. Uranium is also a metal. It has become important because of its use as a nuclear fuel. Nonmetallic minerals include some building materials, diamonds, phosphates, and sulfur.

Metals are also nonrenewable resources and some are becoming scarce. As a result, recycling is becoming increasingly common. About half of the iron and one-third of the aluminum now used by industry comes from scrap.

AGRICULTURE

Agriculture is the world's leading industry. Not only does it provide food, but it also produces those materials used to make clothing, prepare paints and inks, or make soaps, for example. Forestry and fishing also produce materials used in industry as well as provide food.

The development of agriculture

The deliberate planting and harvesting of crops began around 10,000 years ago, and, soon afterward, farming communities began to displace the traditional hunting and gathering economies. Other early developments were the domestication of animals and irrigation. As of the eighteenth century, farming became increasingly mechanized and scientific. Today, agriculture employs only a small proportion of people in the prosperous developed countries. For example, the United States leads the world in agricultural production, yet agriculture employs only about 3 percent of its work force. By contrast, a high proportion of people in most developing countries work on the land. Much of the agriculture is carried out at subsistence level—that is, farmers produce enough for their families, with comparatively little left over for sale.

Modern transportation methods, especially the use of refrigeration, have made it possible to move perishable goods around the world. Agriculture is big business.

Forestry and fishing

Forests cover about 30 percent of the earth's land area. Forestry is the commercial utilization and management of forests. Wood is a major raw material in industry.

The fishing industry is particularly important in countries such as Japan, where other protein-rich foods are in short supply.

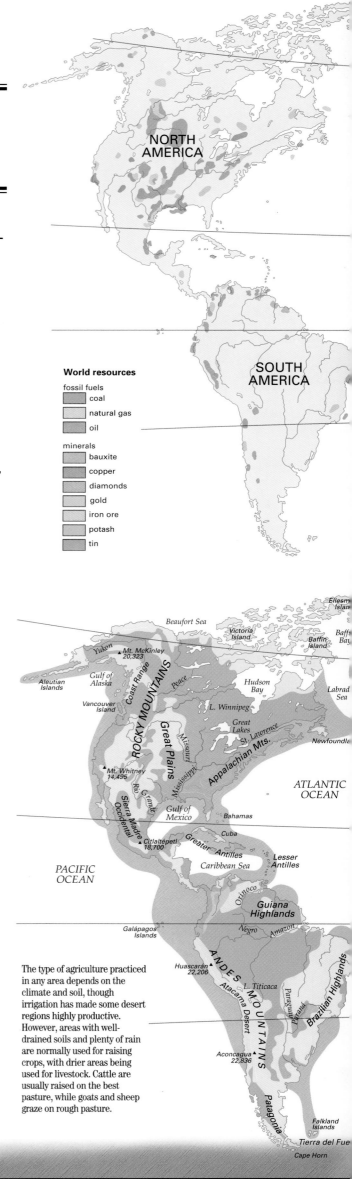

World resources

fossil fuels
- coal
- natural gas
- oil

minerals
- bauxite
- copper
- diamonds
- gold
- iron ore
- potash
- tin

The type of agriculture practiced in any area depends on the climate and soil, though irrigation has made some desert regions highly productive. However, areas with well-drained soils and plenty of rain are normally used for raising crops, with drier areas being used for livestock. Cattle are usually raised on the best pasture, while goats and sheep graze on rough pasture.

RESOURCES

The map shows that fossil fuels, particularly oil and gas, are concentrated in the Northern Hemisphere. North America is especially rich in energy reserves. On the other hand, reserves of metals and other minerals are spread far more evenly around the world.

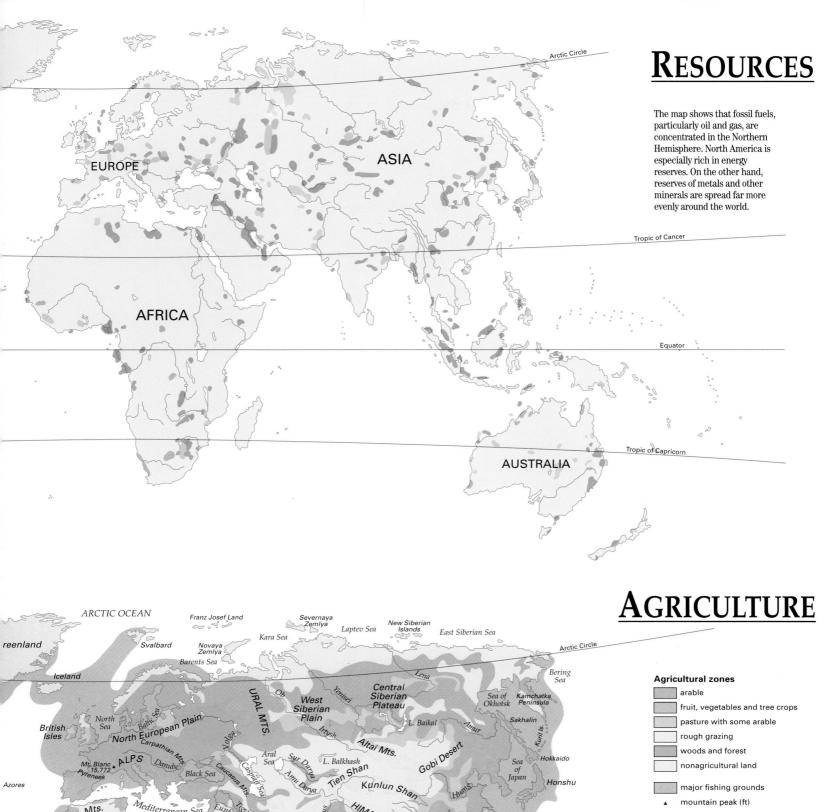

EUROPE

ASIA

AFRICA

AUSTRALIA

Arctic Circle

Tropic of Cancer

Equator

Tropic of Capricorn

AGRICULTURE

Agricultural zones

- arable
- fruit, vegetables and tree crops
- pasture with some arable
- rough grazing
- woods and forest
- nonagricultural land
- major fishing grounds
- ▲ mountain peak (ft)

ARCTIC OCEAN

Franz Josef Land

Severnaya Zemlya

New Siberian Islands

Laptev Sea

East Siberian Sea

reenland

Svalbard

Novaya Zemlya

Kara Sea

Bering Sea

Iceland

Barents Zemlya

Lena

Sea of Okhotsk

Kamchatka Peninsula

Central Siberian Plateau

British Isles

North Sea

Baltic Sea

URAL MTS.

Ob

West Siberian Plain

Yenisei

Sakhalin

Kuril Is.

North European Plain

Carpathian Mts.

Volga

Irtysh

L. Baikal

Altai Mts.

Amur

Hokkaido

Azores

Mt. Blanc 15,772

ALPS

Danube

Pyrenees

Caucasus Mts.

Black Sea

Aral Sea

Syr Darya

L. Balkhash

Tien Shan

Gobi Desert

Sea of Japan

Honshu

Canary Islands

Atlas Mts.

Mediterranean Sea

Caspian Sea

Amu Darya

Kunlun Shan

Hums

Azores

Euphrates

Tigris

Indus

HIMALAYAS

Yangtze

East China Sea

Verde nds

SAHARA

Ahaggar Plateau

Libyan Desert

Nile

Arabian Peninsula

Persian Gulf

Mt. Everest 29,035

Gt. Indian Desert

Ganges

Taiwan

PACIFIC OCEAN

Tibesti

Red Sea

Deccan Plateau

Hainan

Mariana Islands

SAHEL

Arabian Sea

Bay of Bengal

South China Sea

Philippine Islands

Marshall Islands

Niger

Mt. Cameroon 13,354

Ethiopian Highlands

L. Turkana

Andaman Islands

Caroline Islands

Gulf of Guinea

Congo

Great Rift Valley

L. Victoria

Maldives

Nicobar Islands

Sri Lanka

Borneo

Equator

Gilbert Islands

Kilimanjaro 19,341

Seychelles

Sumatra

Sulawesi

New Guinea

Bismarck Archipelago

Solomon Islands

Ellice Islands

L. Tanganyika

INDIAN OCEAN

Java

Timor

Samoa Islands

Ascension

Zambezi

L. Malawi

Comoros

Madagascar

Mauritius Réunion

Coral Sea

New Hebrides

Fiji Islands

Tonga Islands

Limpopo

Mozambique Channel

Great Sandy Desert

New Caledonia

Tropic of Capricorn

Kalahari Desert

Drakensberg Mts.

Macdonnell Ranges

L. Eyre

Great Dividing Range

Tristan da Cunha

Cape of Good Hope

Darling

Mt. Kosciusko 7,317

Tasmania

Tasman Sea

New Zealand

uth Georgia

Mt. Cook 12,350

THE WORLD

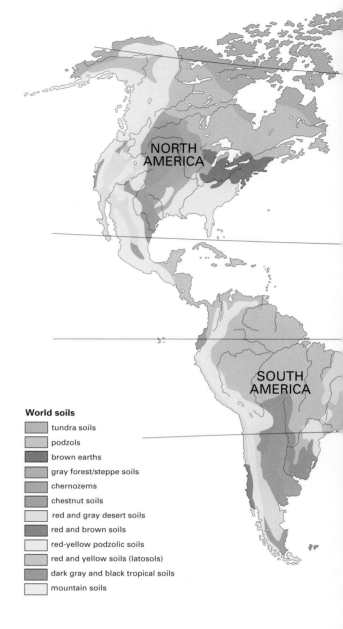

SOILS

Soil is one of the earth's vital resources. Most living things on land could not exist without it. Soil is a complex mixture of worn fragments of rock, humus (the decayed remains of plants and animals), water, air, and living organisms. All the living organisms, together with the roots of plants, contribute to breaking down the soil into smaller and smaller pieces.

Soil formation

The character of soil is affected by the parent rock on which it forms. For example, soils that form on shale, a soft rock, usually have a finer texture than those that form on sandstone, which is composed largely of hard grains of quartz.

Soils are usually thin on sloping land, because soil particles tend to move downhill. But they may reach depths of several yards in hollows. In waterlogged areas, dead plants may accumulate to form peat.

Soil types

The most common soil classifications are based on climate. In wet equatorial regions, the heavy rain leaches (dissolves) minerals from the top layers, leaving a red or yellow soil, latosol, which is rich in bauxite.

Brown forest soils are not heavily leached. Their color comes from the large amount of humus in the top layers. Desert soils are often red and sandy, because they are low in humus. Dark-colored chernozems are soils rich in humus, formed from the remains of the plants that grew on temperate grasslands. By contrast, podzols, the grayish soils of the northern coniferous forest zones, are low in humus. They contain a thin acid layer, overlying a heavily leached layer. Tundra soils are often waterlogged and often remain frozen just below the surface. The frozen subsoil is called permafrost.

PLANTS

The vegetation in any area is governed by three main factors: present climate and geographical conditions, past climate conditions (such as those of the ice ages), and geographical changes (such as those caused by plate movements of the continents).

Botanists have divided the world into six floristic kingdoms, where the major plant families have distinct characteristics in common. These kingdoms are divided into regions.

Boreal kingdom

The Boreal ("northern") kingdom includes the cold temperate and subtropical lands of the Northern Hemisphere. One reason for the similarity between the plants in this kingdom is that the land masses were joined together in recent geological times.

Tropical kingdoms

The Paleotropical ("ancient tropical") kingdom includes most of Africa south of the Sahara and tropical southern Asia. The Neotropical ("new tropical") kingdom in Central and tropical South America has distinctive vegetation, which evolved differently from that of Africa after South America began to move away from Africa about 140 million years ago. South America was also isolated from North America until about 2.5 million years ago.

Southern kingdoms

The southern kingdoms include the South African kingdom, with a climate similar to that of the Mediterranean region, and the Australian kingdom, which evolved its unique and diverse species in geographic isolation from the other continents. Finally, there is the Antarctic kingdom, which includes southern South America and also New Zealand.

World soils

- tundra soils
- podzols
- brown earths
- gray forest/steppe soils
- chernozems
- chestnut soils
- red and gray desert soils
- red and brown soils
- red-yellow podzolic soils
- red and yellow soils (latosols)
- dark gray and black tropical soils
- mountain soils

PLANTS

Plants are found everywhere on earth, with the greatest number of species in hot and wet tropical regions. The map shows the six main floristic kingdoms, which are further subdivided into regions. These kingdoms and regions reflect both the climate of the areas and the factors that governed the evolution of plant communities over millions of years.

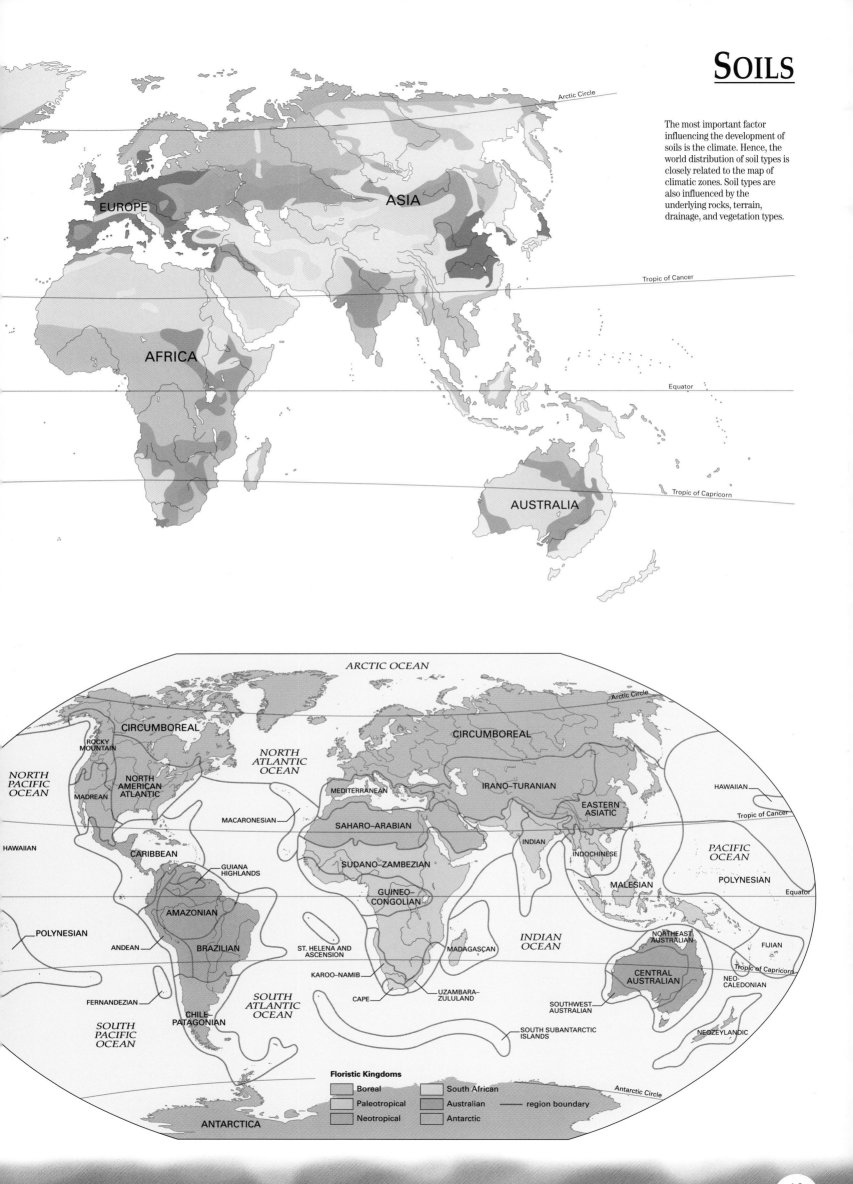

SOILS

The most important factor influencing the development of soils is the climate. Hence, the world distribution of soil types is closely related to the map of climatic zones. Soil types are also influenced by the underlying rocks, terrain, drainage, and vegetation types.

EUROPE

ASIA

AFRICA

AUSTRALIA

Arctic Circle

Tropic of Cancer

Equator

Tropic of Capricorn

ARCTIC OCEAN

Arctic Circle

CIRCUMBOREAL

CIRCUMBOREAL

NORTH
PACIFIC
OCEAN

ROCKY
MOUNTAIN

NORTH
ATLANTIC
OCEAN

NORTH
AMERICAN
ATLANTIC

MADREAN

MEDITERRANEAN

IRANO–TURANIAN

HAWAIIAN

EASTERN
ASIATIC

Tropic of Cancer

MACARONESIAN

HAWAIIAN

CARIBBEAN

SAHARO–ARABIAN

INDIAN

PACIFIC
OCEAN

GUIANA
HIGHLANDS

SUDANO–ZAMBEZIAN

INDOCHINESE

POLYNESIAN

Equator

AMAZONIAN

GUINEO–
CONGOLIAN

MALESIAN

POLYNESIAN

ANDEAN

BRAZILIAN

ST. HELENA AND
ASCENSION

MADAGASCAN

INDIAN
OCEAN

NORTHEAST
AUSTRALIAN

FIJIAN

Tropic of Capricorn

KAROO–NAMIB

CENTRAL
AUSTRALIAN

NEO-
CALEDONIAN

FERNANDEZIAN

CHILE–
PATAGONIAN

CAPE

UZAMBARA–
ZULULAND

SOUTHWEST
AUSTRALIAN

NEOZEYLANDIC

SOUTH
ATLANTIC
OCEAN

SOUTH
PACIFIC
OCEAN

SOUTH SUBANTARCTIC
ISLANDS

Antarctic Circle

ANTARCTICA

Floristic Kingdoms

▢ Boreal	▢ South African	
▢ Paleotropical	▢ Australian	— region boundary
▢ Neotropical	▢ Antarctic	

THE WORLD

BIOMES

Wilderness areas around the world are amazingly diverse. However, they can be divided into a few general types, which are characterized by the dominant plant communities, such as grassland, tundra, coniferous forest, or deciduous forest. These broad regions are called biomes.

Major life zones

Biomes are defined as major life zones that are characterized by their vegetation and climate. Biomes can be changed by both natural factors and human activities. Lakes, for example, are silted by rivers flowing into them. Eventually, the lake becomes a marsh, and the marsh in time becomes dry land. Many dry, flat areas in the western United States were once lakes.

Over longer periods the erosion of mountains changes landscapes, and the movements of continents change climates. Species of plants and animals respond to these changes. Some adapt to the new environment, some migrate, and some become extinct.

Biodiversity

There may be as many as 30 million plant and animal species on our planet, even though 98 percent of all the species that have existed are now extinct. Plant and animal species are the basic units of the rich biodiversity on our planet. But human interference is now threatening millions of species, especially in the tropical forests where biodiversity is at its greatest. Experts predict that one-fourth of all the world's plant and animal species face extinction in the next 25 to 50 years, mainly as a result of changes humans cause to biomes. The future well-being of the earth may depend on preserving biodiversity.

CLIMATIC CHANGES

Several ice ages have occurred during the earth's long history. Geologists have found evidence of five major periods of cooling beginning around 2.3 billion years ago, 670 million years ago, 470 million years ago, 300 million years ago, and 2.5 million years ago.

The Pleistocene ice age

The last ice age, in the Pleistocene epoch, was a relatively short one. There were periods of intense cold, called glacial periods, when ice advanced over large parts of the earth, and interglacial periods, when the climate was warmer than it is today. The ice sheets then melted and retreated. The Pleistocene ice age was at its height between 15,000 and 20,000 years ago. At that time, thick ice sheets covered about 30 percent of the earth's land surface, spreading over much of the Northern Hemisphere. In North America, the ice reached a line between the present-day locations of Seattle and New York City. Ice sheets in Europe reached southern England, the Netherlands, and southern Germany.

Ice ages and vegetation

The effects of the last ice age altered all the earth's climatic and vegetation zones. The middle latitudes developed great areas of tundra, while the tropics became much drier. Huge deserts were formed. About 10,000 years ago, the climate became generally warmer, and plants recolonized the barren tundra zones. Since then, there have been minor climatic fluctuations, such as the "Little Ice Age" in Europe between the fifteenth and eighteenth centuries. These natural fluctuations give some idea of what may happen if global warming, caused by human activity, is allowed to continue.

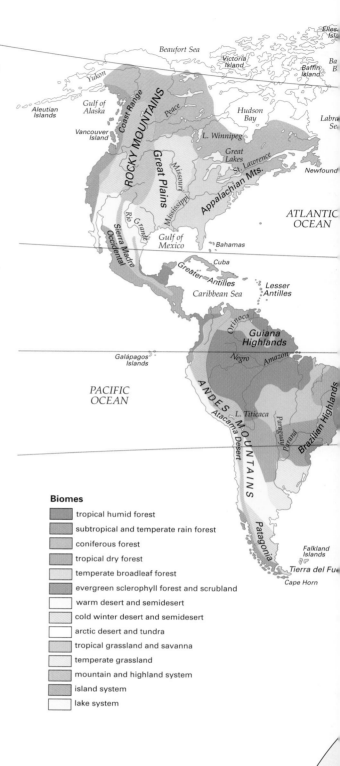

Biomes

- tropical humid forest
- subtropical and temperate rain forest
- coniferous forest
- tropical dry forest
- temperate broadleaf forest
- evergreen sclerophyll forest and scrubland
- warm desert and semidesert
- cold winter desert and semidesert
- arctic desert and tundra
- tropical grassland and savanna
- temperate grassland
- mountain and highland system
- island system
- lake system

BIOMES OF THE PAST

The map shows the world's vegetation about 18,000 years ago, when the last ice age was at its peak. The positions of coastlines were different from those of today, because so much water was frozen in the ice sheets, lowering the sea level. This influenced human development. Dry land bridges were created, enabling early people to migrate from one area to another.

BIOMES TODAY

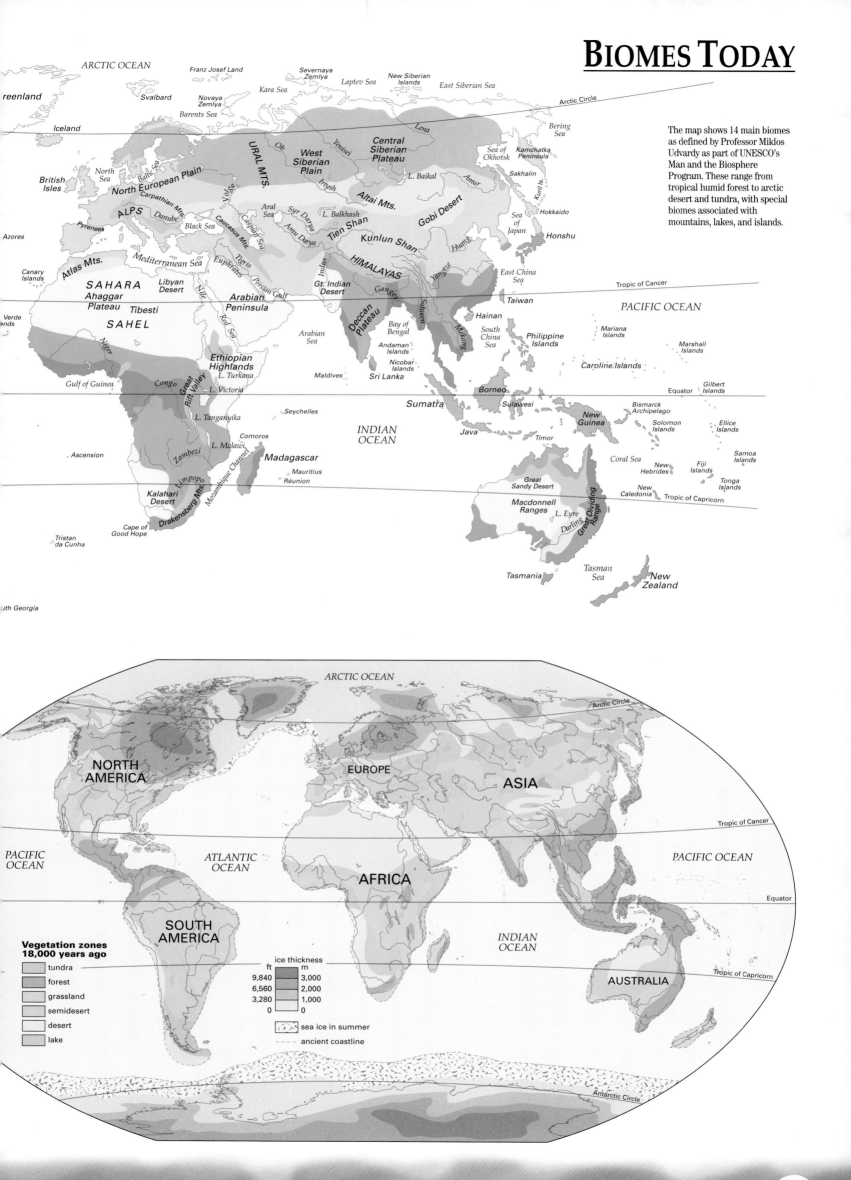

The map shows 14 main biomes as defined by Professor Miklos Udvardy as part of UNESCO's Man and the Biosphere Program. These range from tropical humid forest to arctic desert and tundra, with special biomes associated with mountains, lakes, and islands.

ARCTIC OCEAN

Greenland
Franz Josef Land
Severnaya Zemlya
Laptev Sea
New Siberian Islands
East Siberian Sea
Svalbard
Kara Sea
Arctic Circle
Novaya Zemlya
Iceland
Barents Sea
Bering Sea
British Isles
North Sea
Baltic Sea
North European Plain
URAL MTS.
Ob
West Siberian Plain
Yenisei
Central Siberian Plateau
Lena
Sea of Okhotsk
Kamchatka Peninsula
Carpathian Mts.
Irtysh
Altai Mts.
L. Baikal
Amur
Sakhalin
Kuril Is.
ALPS
Volga
Aral Sea
Syr Darya
L. Balkhash
Tien Shan
Gobi Desert
Sea of Japan
Hokkaido
Pyrenees
Danube
Caucasus Mts.
Caspian Sea
Amu Darya
Kunlun Shan
Huang
Honshu
Azores
Black Sea
Mediterranean Sea
Euphrates
Tigris
Persian Gulf
Indus
HIMALAYAS
Yangtze
East China Sea
Canary Islands
Atlas Mts.
Libyan Desert
Nile
Arabian Peninsula
Gt. Indian Desert
Ganges
Tropic of Cancer
Verde Islands
SAHARA
Ahaggar Plateau
Tibesti
Arabian Sea
Deccan Plateau
Taiwan
PACIFIC OCEAN
SAHEL
Red Sea
Bay of Bengal
Hainan
South China Sea
Philippine Islands
Mariana Islands
Marshall Islands
Niger
Ethiopian Highlands
L. Turkana
Andaman Islands
Nicobar Islands
Maldives
Sri Lanka
Caroline Islands
Gulf of Guinea
Congo
Great Rift Valley
L. Victoria
Salween
Mekong
Borneo
Sumatra
Sulawesi
Equator
Gilbert Islands
Seychelles
INDIAN OCEAN
New Guinea
Bismarck Archipelago
Ellice Islands
L. Tanganyika
Java
Timor
Solomon Islands
Ascension
Comoros
L. Malawi
Samoa Islands
Zambezi
Mauritius
Réunion
Madagascar
Coral Sea
New Hebrides
Fiji Islands
Tonga Islands
Limpopo
Mozambique Channel
Great Sandy Desert
Great Dividing Range
New Caledonia
Tropic of Capricorn
Kalahari Desert
Drakensberg Mts.
Macdonnell Ranges
L. Eyre
Darling
Cape of Good Hope
Tristan da Cunha
Tasmania
Tasman Sea
New Zealand
South Georgia

ARCTIC OCEAN

NORTH AMERICA
EUROPE
ASIA
Arctic Circle

PACIFIC OCEAN
ATLANTIC OCEAN
Tropic of Cancer

AFRICA

PACIFIC OCEAN

SOUTH AMERICA
INDIAN OCEAN
Equator

AUSTRALIA
Tropic of Capricorn

Antarctic Circle

Vegetation zones 18,000 years ago

- tundra
- forest
- grassland
- semidesert
- desert
- lake

ice thickness		
ft	m	
9,840	3,000	
6,560	2,000	
3,280	1,000	
0	0	

sea ice in summer
ancient coastline

CANADA AND GREENLAND

Canada and Greenland make up about half of North America. Northern Canada and most of Greenland lie north of the Arctic Circle, while the northern tip of Greenland is about 441 miles (710 km) from the North Pole. Canada's greatest east-west distance is nearly 3,230 miles (5,200 km). This vast distance is reflected by its six time zones. When it is 8:30 A.M. in St. John's, Newfoundland, it is 4.00 A.M. in Vancouver, British Columbia.

Northern North America includes Canada, the world's second largest country, and Greenland, the world's largest island. The Arctic islands of Canada are a cold tundra region that contain many glaciers. Two of these islands—Baffin and Ellesmere—are also among the world's ten largest islands. About six-sevenths of Greenland is buried under a thick ice sheet, the world's second largest body of ice after the ice sheet of Antarctica.

Canada's most prominent features include the western mountains, the interior plains, the Canadian Shield, the St. Lawrence lowlands, and, in the southeast, an extension of the Appalachian region. Canada also shares with the United States the world's largest expanse of fresh water—the Great Lakes.

Because of the climate, about 80 percent of Canadians live within 186 miles (300 km) of their southern border. Canada is one of the world's leading mineral exporters and manufacturing nations. Its farming and fishing industries are highly efficient.

Canada has a diverse population. The earliest inhabitants, the Native Americans, entered Canada about 30,000 years ago. They were followed by the Inuits, whose descendants now also live in Greenland. These two peoples make up a small minority of the population. Nearly two-thirds of the people today are English and French-speaking descendants of European settlers, though Canada also has communities from other parts of Europe, notably Germany, Italy, and Ukraine, and from Asia.

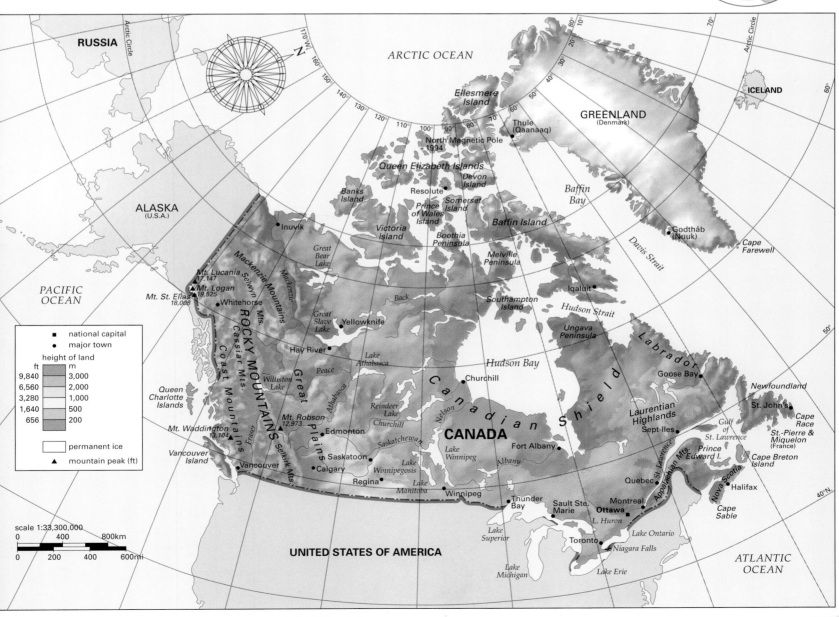

THE POLITICAL AND CULTURAL WORLD

Canada has a federal system of government, but it faces problems arising from its ethnic diversity. One problem is reconciling the aspirations of the French-speaking people, who form the majority in Quebec, with the different traditions of the English-speaking Canadians. Another problem is how to integrate Native American and Inuit peoples in the modern state.

Greenland is a self-governing province of Denmark, though it is 50 times bigger than the rest of the country. To assert its independence, Greenland left the European Community in 1985, though it continued its relationship with Denmark.

COUNTRIES IN THE REGION

Canada (Greenland, dependency of Denmark)

RELIGION

Roman Catholic 46.5%; Protestant 41%; Eastern Orthodox 1.5%; Jewish 1.2%; Muslim 0.4%; Hindu 0.3%; Sikh 0.3%; nonreligious 7.4%; others 1.4%

ETHNIC ORIGIN

French 27%; British 40%; other European 20%; Indigenous Indian and Inuit (known as First Nations) 1.5%; others 11.5%

FORM OF GOVERNMENT

Federal multiparty parliamentary monarchy with two legislative houses

ECONOMIC INDICATORS

	Canada
GDP (US$ billions)	603.1
GNP per capita (US$)	21,860
Annual rate of growth of GDP, 1990–1997	2.2%
Manufacturing as % of GDP	21.7%
Central government spending as % of GDP	20%
Merchandise exports (US$ billions)	214.4
Merchandise imports (US$ billions)	200.9
Aid given as % of GDP	0.34%

WELFARE INDICATORS

	Canada
Infant mortality rate (per 1,000 live births)	
1978	12
1998	6
Population per physician (1996)	476
Expected years of schooling (1995)	16.8
(males 16.5, females 17.1)	
Health expenditure as % of GDP (1995)	9.2%
Adult literacy (1995)	98.8%
(males 99%, females 98.7%)	

Constitutional changes
In the 1990s, Canadians debated the future of their country. Many French Canadians wanted to create a French Canadian state in Quebec. In 1999, the long campaign of the Inuit people for a homeland found success in the creation of Nunavut from a partition of the Northwest Territories.

Area 3,851,791 sq mi (9,976,140 sq km)
Population 31,281,092
Capital Ottawa
Chief languages English, French
Currency 1 Canadian dollar (Can $) = 100 cents

Canada

HABITATS

Canada is a land with many varied landforms. Massive mountain ranges, scenic lakes, great evergreen forests, vast prairies, fertile river valleys, and islands covered with snow and ice can all be found in this second largest country in the world.

LAND

Area 4,691,791 sq mi (12,151,739 sq km)
Highest point Mount Logan, 19,525 ft (5,951 m)
Lowest point sea level
Major features Rocky Mountains, Canadian Shield, Arctic islands; Greenland – world's largest island

WATER

Longest river Mackenzie, 2,635 mi (4,240 km)
Largest basin Mackenzie, 681,100 sq mi (1,764,000 sq km)
Highest average flow St. Lawrence, 460,000 cu ft/sec (13,030 cu m/sec)
Largest lake Superior, 32,150 sq mi (83,270 sq km), world's largest freshwater lake

NOTABLE THREATENED SPECIES

Mammals Vancouver Island marmot (*Marmota vancouverensis*)
Birds None
Others Lake lamprey (*Lampetra macrostoma*), Morrison Creek lamprey (*Lampetra richardsoni*), Copper redhorse fish (*Moxostoma hubbsi*)
Plants *Ameria maritima interior*; *Cypripedium candidum* (small lady's slipper); *Isotria medeoloides* (small whorled fogonia); *Limnanthes macounii*; *Pedicularis furbishiae* (Furbish's lousewort); *Phyllitis japonica americana*; *Plantago cordata*; *Salix planifolia tyrrellii*; *Salix silicicola*; *Senecio newcombei*

CLIMATE

The Arctic has frozen seas and ice caps, with temperatures near the freezing point, and tundra regions with brief, chilly summers. Most of Canada has a subarctic climate, with coniferous forests. Only in the south are there climatic regions warm enough for farming.

CLIMATE

	Temperature °F (°C)		Altitude
	January	July	ft (m)
Resolute	−26 (−32)	39 (4)	200 (64)
Vancouver	36 (2)	63 (17)	0 (0)
Winnipeg	0 (−18)	68 (20)	813 (248)
Montreal	16 (−9)	72 (22)	98 (30)
Halifax	25 (−4)	64 (18)	98 (30)

	Precipitation in. (mm)		
	January	July	Year
Resolute	0.1 (3)	0.8 (21)	5.3 (136)
Vancouver	5.5 (139)	1.0 (26)	42.0 (1,068)
Winnipeg	1.0 (26)	2.7 (69)	21.0 (535)
Montreal	3.3 (83)	3.5 (89)	39.3 (999)
Halifax	5.4 (137)	3.8 (96)	54.4 (1,381)

Highest average annual precipitation in North America recorded at Henderson Lake, British Columbia: 256 in. (6,502 mm)

NATURAL HAZARDS

Cold, snow and icestorms, drought, gales, avalanches, rockfalls, and landslides.

ENVIRONMENTAL ISSUES

Southeastern Canada suffers from acid rain, part of which results from air pollution originating in the northeastern and midwestern United States. Soil erosion, logging, mining, oil drilling, and water pollution are other hazards.

POPULATION AND WEALTH

Population	31,281,000
Population increase (annual growth rate, 1995–2000)	0.8%
Energy use (lbs/year per person of oil equivalent)	17,337
Purchasing power parity (Int$ per year)	22,502

ENVIRONMENTAL INDICATORS

CO_2 emissions ('000 tons/year)	435,749
Proportion of territory protected, including marine areas	9.6%
Forests as a percentage of original forest	91%
Artificial fertilizer use (lbs/acre/year)	55
Access to safe drinking water (% population, rural/urban)	100/100%

MAJOR ENVIRONMENTAL ISSUES AND SOURCES

Air pollution: urban high; acid rain prevalent; high greenhouse gas emissions; transboundary pollution (persistent organic pollutants)
River/lake pollution: medium; *sources:* agricultural, sewage, acid deposition
Land pollution: local; *sources:* industrial, urban/household
Waste disposal problems: domestic; industrial; nuclear
Major events: Mississauga (1979), chlorine gas leak during transportation; Saint Basile le Grand (1988), toxic cloud from waste dump fire

HABITATS

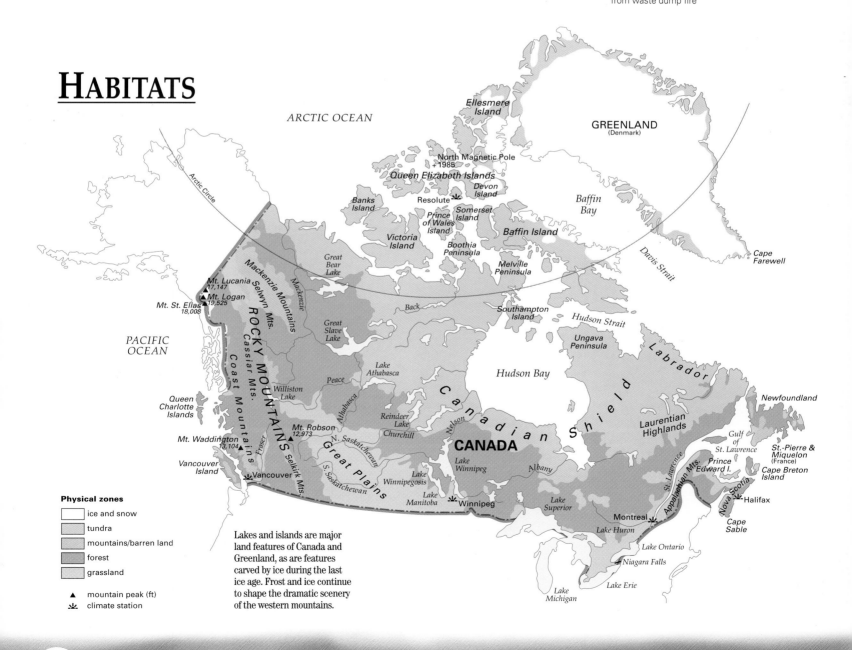

Lakes and islands are major land features of Canada and Greenland, as are features carved by ice during the last ice age. Frost and ice continue to shape the dramatic scenery of the western mountains.

Physical zones
- ice and snow
- tundra
- mountains/barren land
- forest
- grassland

▲ mountain peak (ft)
⚹ climate station

ENVIRONMENTAL ISSUES

ARCTIC OCEAN

North Magnetic Pole 1985

GREENLAND
(Denmark)

Ellesmere Island

Queen Elizabeth Islands

Devon Island

Baffin Bay

Arctic Circle

Banks Island

Somerset Island

Prince of Wales Island

Baffin Island

Victoria Island

Boothia Peninsula

Melville Peninsula

Cape Farewell

Davis Strait

PACIFIC OCEAN

Mackenzie Mts.

Great Bear Lake

Mackenzie

Back

Southampton Island

Hudson Strait

•Whitehorse

Great Slave Lake

Ungava Peninsula

Coast Mountains

ROCKY MOUNTAINS

Great Plains

Peace

Lake Athabasca

Hudson Bay

Labrador

Queen Charlotte Islands

Reindeer Lake

Nelson

Canadian *Shield*

Newfoundland

Fraser

Athabasca

Churchill

Severn

Laurentian Highlands

Gulf of St. Lawrence

St. Pierre & Miquelon (France)

Edmonton• N. Saskatchewan

CANADA

Lake Winnipeg

James Bay

Albany

St. Lawrence

Cape Breton Island

Vancouver Island

Vancouver• S. Saskatchewan

Calgary•

Lake Winnipegosis

Lake Superior

Quebec•

St. John

Nova Scotia

•Regina

Lake Manitoba

Winnipeg•

Sudbury•

Montreal• Saint Basile
Ottawa• le Grand

Lake Huron

Lake Ontario

Cape Sable

Mississauga• •Toronto
Hamilton•

Lake Michigan

Lake Erie

Key environmental issues

- • major town or city
- ↆ polluted town or city
- ↆ major pollution event
- ⌇ polluted river
- ▨ area affected by permafrost
- ▥ area at moderate risk of desertification

acidity of rain (pH units)

- ▦ 4.2 (most acidic)
- ▦ 4.4
- ▦ 4.6
- ▨ 4.8 (least acidic)

Information about environmental damage has alerted many people to the dangers of habitat destruction. In 2000 the Canadian government passed the Canadian Environmental Protection Act, which strengthens pollution prevention measures.

CLIMATE

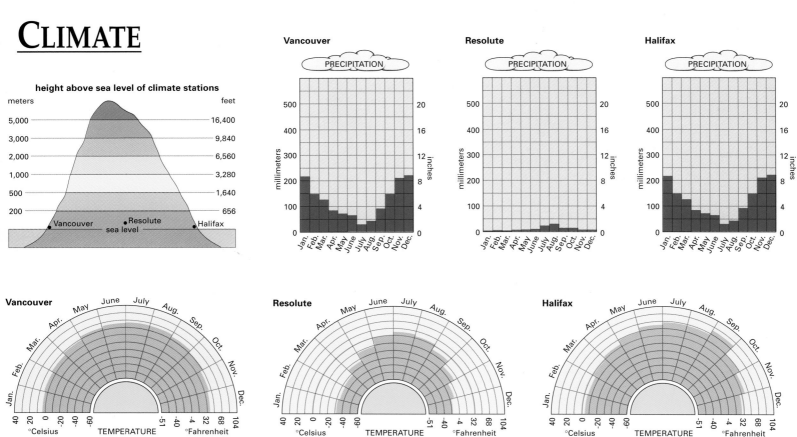

height above sea level of climate stations

meters		feet
5,000		16,400
3,000		9,840
2,000		6,560
1,000		3,280
500		1,640
200		656

Vancouver   Resolute   Halifax
sea level

Vancouver

PRECIPITATION

millimeters — inches

Jan. Feb. Mar. Apr. May June July Aug. Sep. Oct. Nov. Dec.

Resolute

PRECIPITATION

Halifax

PRECIPITATION

Vancouver

Jan. Feb. Mar. Apr. May June July Aug. Sep. Oct. Nov. Dec.

°Celsius   TEMPERATURE   °Fahrenheit

Resolute

°Celsius   TEMPERATURE   °Fahrenheit

Halifax

°Celsius   TEMPERATURE   °Fahrenheit

POPULATION

Although Canada's population has doubled since 1945—the result of immigration and a high birth rate—Canada has one of the world's lowest average population densities. Most Canadians live near the southern border.

POPULATION

Total population of region (millions)	31
Population density (persons per sq mi)	8
Population change (average annual percent 1995–2000)	
Urban	+1.11%
Rural	+0.65%

URBAN POPULATION

As percentage of total population

1960	68.9%
1997	77%

TEN LARGEST CITIES

	Population
Toronto	2,540,100
Montreal	1,035,100
Calgary	847,900
Edmonton	680,300
Winnipeg	632,400
Mississauga	579,700
Vancouver	530,700
London	346,600
Ottawa †	344,300
Hamilton	343,200

† denotes capital city

City population figures are for the city proper.

INDUSTRY

Canada is rich in minerals and is a major exporter of raw materials. Manufacturing industries belong to two main groups: those that process raw materials and those concerned with making products, such as food and vehicles.

INDUSTRIAL OUTPUT (US $ billion)

Total	Mining	Manufacturing	Average annual change since 1960
174	19.7	121	3.5%

MAJOR PRODUCTS (figures in parentheses are percentages of total world production)

Energy and minerals	Output		Change since 1960
Coal (mil m.t.)	75	(2.8%)	+383%
Oil (mil m.t.)	114	(n/a)	+81%
Natural gas (mill terrajoules)	5.7	(6.9%)	+173%
Iron ore (mil m.t.)	21	(2.1%)	–28%
Copper (mil m.t.)	0.7	(2.8%)	+40%
Lead (mil m.t.)	0.2	(5.1%)	–41%
Zinc (mil m.t.)	0.7	(8.2%)	+74%
Nickel (mil m.t.)	0.1	(13.3%)	–41%
Uranium (m.t.)	10,515	(31.8%)	+189%

Manufactures			
Aluminum (mil m.t.)	2.3	(8.5%)	+129%
Steel (mil m.t.)	28.3	(3.8%)	+153%
Woodpulp (mil m.t.)	24.7	(15.9%)	+49%
Newsprint (mil m.t.)	10.0	(31.5%)	+15%
Sulfuric acid (mil m.t.)	3.8	(1.4%)	+45%
Automobiles ('000)	1,150	(3.2%)	+24.6%

AGRICULTURE

Only 8 percent of the land in Canada is used for farming. The best farmland is in the St. Lawrence lowlands and around the Great Lakes. The other main region is the wheat-growing prairie belt—the northern part of the Great Plains.

LAND

Total area 4,691,791 sq mi (12,151,739 sq km)

Cropland	Pasture	Forest/Woodland
5%	3%	54%

FARMERS

Agriculture as % of GDP	3%
% of workforce	3%

MAJOR CROPS

Agricultural products: wheat; barley; oilseed; tobacco; fruits; vegetables; dairy products; forest products; fish

Total cropland ('000 acres)	112,925
Cropland (acres) per 1,000 people	2,842
Irrigated land as percentage of cropland	2%
Annual fertilizer use (lbs per acre of cropland)	55
Number of tractors	711,335
Change since 1987	–4%
Average cereal crop yields (lbs per acre)	2264
Average production of cereals ('000 tons)	53,020
Change since 1986–88	10%

LIVESTOCK AND FISHERIES

Average meat production ('000 tons)	3,320
Change since 1986–88	27%
Marine fish catch ('000 tons)	550.4
Change since 1986–88	–57%
Aquaculture production ('000 tons)	73.7

POPULATION

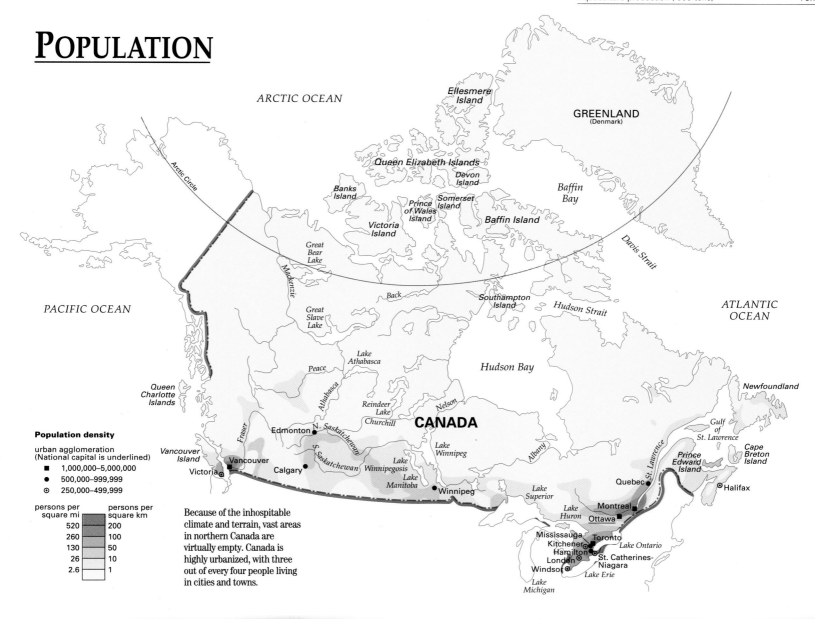

Population density

urban agglomeration
(National capital is underlined)
- ■ 1,000,000–5,000,000
- ● 500,000–999,999
- ◉ 250,000–499,999

persons per square mi	persons per square km
520	200
260	100
130	50
26	10
2.6	1

Because of the inhospitable climate and terrain, vast areas in northern Canada are virtually empty. Canada is highly urbanized, with three out of every four people living in cities and towns.

INDUSTRY

ARCTIC OCEAN

GREENLAND
(Denmark)

Ellesmere
Island

Queen Elizabeth Islands

Devon
Island

Banks
Island

Somerset
Island

Prince
of Wales
Island

Baffin
Bay

Baffin Island

Davis Strait

Victoria
Island

Boothia
Peninsula

Melville
Peninsula

Great
Bear
Lake

Mackenzie

Southampton
Island

Hudson Strait

Back

Great
Slave
Lake

Yellowknife

Hudson Bay

Churchill

Lake
Athabasca

Resources and industry

◆ industrial center
○ port
● other town
— major road
— major railroad

mineral resources and fossil fuels
◆ iron and other ferroalloy
   metal ores
● other metal ores
■ nonmetallic minerals

coal
copper
iron ore
lignite (brown coal)
natural gas
nickel
oil

Queen
Charlotte
Islands

Prince
Rupert

Williston
Lake

Peace

Athabasca

Reindeer
Lake

Churchill

Nelson

CANADA

Newfoundland

St. John's

Vancouver
Island

Vancouver

Edmonton

N. Saskatchewan

S. Saskatchewan

Fraser

Calgary

Regina

Winnipegosis

Lake
Manitoba

Lake
Winnipeg

Albany

Lake
Winnipeg

Gulf
of
St. Lawrence

Port aux
Basques

Port Cartier

Sydney
Cape Breton
Island

Winnipeg

Lake
Superior

Lake
Manitoba

Sudbury

Quebec

Montreal
Ottawa

Halifax

St. Lawrence

Canada's economy has been
based on its rich natural
resources, which have brought
it export earnings and provided
the basis for industrial growth.

Toronto

Lake Ontario

Niagara Falls

Windsor

Lake Erie

Lake
Michigan

L. Huron

AGRICULTURE

ARCTIC OCEAN

GREENLAND
(Denmark)

Ellesmere
Island

North Magnetic Pole
+ 1985

Queen Elizabeth Islands

Devon
Island

Banks
Island

Somerset
Island

Prince
of Wales
Island

Baffin
Bay

Baffin Island

Davis Strait

Cape
Farewell

Victoria
Island

Boothia
Peninsula

Melville
Peninsula

Great
Bear
Lake

Mackenzie

Southampton
Island

Hudson Strait

Back

Mt. Lucania
17,147
Mt. Logan
19,525
Mt. St. Elias
18,008

Selwyn Mountains

Mackenzie Mountains

Great
Slave
Lake

Ungava
Peninsula

Labrador

*PACIFIC
OCEAN*

Agricultural zones

arable
arable and grazing
fruit and vegetables
rough grazing
woods and forest
nonagricultural land

▲ mountain peak (ft)

Canadian agriculture has been
limited by physical conditions,
namely the cold, harsh climate
of the north and the difficult
terrain in the western
mountains.

ROCKY MOUNTAINS

Cassiar Mts.

Coast Mountains

Queen
Charlotte
Islands

Williston
Lake

Peace

Athabasca

Reindeer
Lake

Churchill

Nelson

C a n a d i a n   S h i e l d

Hudson Bay

Lake
Athabasca

Laurentian
Highlands

Newfoundland

Mt. Robson
12,973

Great Plains

N. Saskatchewan

S. Saskatchewan

Fraser

Selkirk Mts.

Mt. Waddington
13,104

Vancouver
Island

CANADA

Lake
Winnipegosis

Lake
Manitoba

Lake
Winnipeg

Albany

Lake
Superior

St. Lawrence

Appalachian Mts.

Prince
Edward I.

Gulf
of
St. Lawrence

St.-Pierre &
Miquelon
(France)

Cape
Race

Cape Breton
Island

Nova Scotia

Cape
Sable

Lake Huron

Niagara Falls

Lake Ontario

Lake Erie

Lake
Michigan

UNITED STATES OF AMERICA

The United States, the world's fourth largest country, is a land of towering mountain ranges and extensive plains. Prominent land features include the Grand Canyon, great rivers that lead into the interior, deserts, explosive volcanoes in the Cascade Range, and wetlands in the southeast. The climate ranges from the icy shores of the Arctic Ocean to the intense heat of the dry Death Valley in California.

The first inhabitants of the United States, the Native Americans, came from Eurasia about 30,000 years ago across a land bridge over what is now the Bering Strait. They were followed about 6,000 years ago by the ancestors of the Inuit. Since the early sixteenth century, Europeans and, later, people from almost every part of the world, have migrated to and made their homes in the United States.

The bulk of the United States, comprising 48 of the 50 states, lies between Canada to the north and Mexico to the south. The forty-ninth state, Alaska, is in the northwestern corner of North America. The fiftieth state, Hawaii, is an island chain situated in the Pacific Ocean.

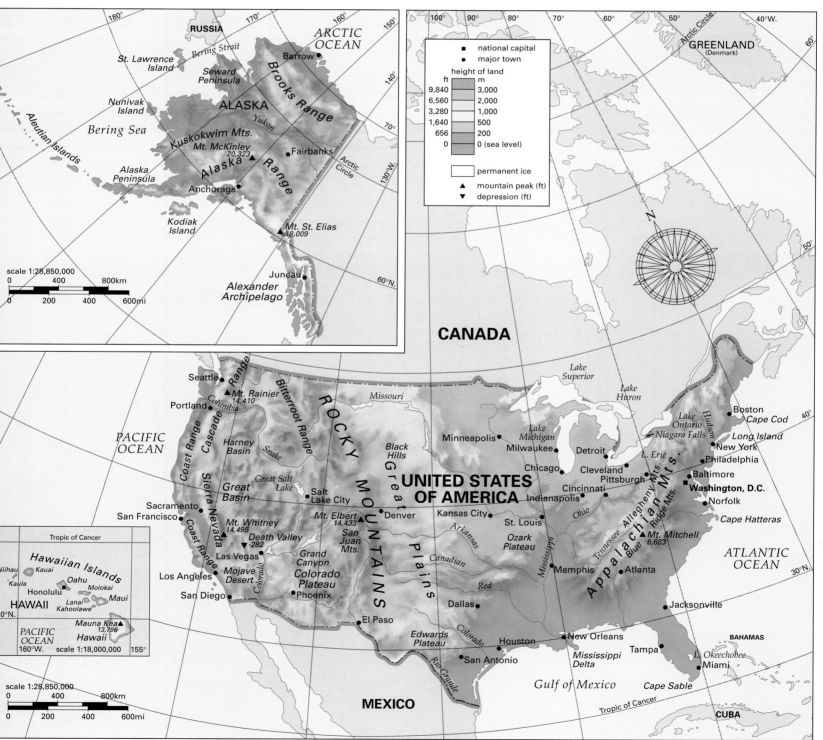

THE POLITICAL AND CULTURAL WORLD

The United States was born during the American Revolution (1775–1783), when the people of the 13 British colonies in the east overthrew British rule. The country expanded westward during the nineteenth century. Alaska was purchased from Russia in 1867, while Hawaii was annexed in 1898. Both territories became states in 1959.

The United States is a federal republic, whose government has three branches. The executive branch is headed by the president, who is also head of state. The legislative branch includes Congress, which consists of the Senate and House of Representatives. The judicial branch is headed by the Supreme Court.

COUNTRIES IN THE REGION

United States of America

Territories outside the region American Samoa, Guam, Johnston Atoll, Midway Islands, Northern Marianas, Puerto Rico, U.S. Virgin Islands, Wake Island, Howland, Jarvis, Baker, Palmyra

The U.S.A. is composed of 50 states, including Alaska and Hawaii.

LANGUAGE

Official language English
Percentage of population by first language
English (79%), Spanish (11%), German (3%), Italian (2%), French (1.3%), Polish (1.2%)

IMMIGRATION

Percentage of foreign born 9.5
Total immigrants (1996) 915,900
Regions sending most immigrants (1996) Mexico (163,743), Russia (19,668), Ukraine (21,079), Philippines (54,588), Africa (52,889), China (50,981), India (42,819), Vietnam (39,922), Cuba (26,166), Canada (21,751), Poland (15,504), Yugoslavia (former) (10,755)

RELIGION

Protestant (56%), Roman Catholic (28%), nonreligious and atheist (6.8%), Jewish (2%), Eastern Orthodox (2.3%), Muslim (1.9%), Hindu (0.2%)

MEMBERSHIP OF INTERNATIONAL ORGANIZATIONS

Colombo Plan
North Atlantic Treaty Organization (NATO)
Organization of American States (OAS)
Organization for Economic Cooperation and Development (OECD)
World Trade Organization (WTO)

STYLE OF GOVERNMENT

Multiparty federal republic with two-chamber assembly

ECONOMIC INDICATORS

	United States
GDP (US$ trillions)	7.819
GNP per capita (US$)	28,740
Annual rate of growth of GDP, 1990-1997	4.1%
Manufacturing as % of GDP	17%
Central government spending as % of GNP	21.1%
Merchandise exports (US$ billions)	681.3
Merchandise imports (US$ billions)	877.3
Aid given as % of GNP	0.12%

WELFARE INDICATORS

	United States
Infant mortality rate (per 1,000 live births)	
1965	25
2000	7
Daily food supply available	
(calories per capita, 1995)	3,603
Population per physician (1995)	470
Teacher–pupil ratio (primary school, 1995)	1 : 21

Area 3,618,770 sq mi (9,368,900 sq km)
Population 275,562,673
Armed forces army 495,000; navy 388,760; air force 390,000; marines 174,000
Ethnic composition White 80.3%; African-American 12.1%; Asian 2.8%; Native American 0.8%; other 3.9% (Hispanics comprise 11% and are included in White and African-American percentages.)
Currency 1 United States dollar (US$) = 100 cents
Life expectancy males 72.9 yrs; females 79.7 yrs

United States of America

- ■ national capital
- ■ state capital
- ● other town

D.C.   DISTRICT OF COLUMBIA
MISS.   MISSISSIPPI
W.VA.   WEST VIRGINIA

The national flag of the United States is popularly called the "Stars and Stripes." The 13 alternating red and white stripes represent the original 13 colonies that declared themselves states in 1776. The 50 white stars on a blue background represent the 50 states of today.

HABITATS

The United States is a region of contrasts. In the east, the Appalachian Mountains overlook the eastern Atlantic plains. This range was formed more than 225 million years ago and has been worn down by erosion. West of the Appalachians lie the interior plains, drained by the Mississippi River and its tributaries.

The land rises to the west to form the higher Great Plains, which are bordered by the Rocky Mountains. Formed within the last 65 million years, the Rockies are higher and more rugged than the Appalachians. West of the Rockies lies a region of basins and ranges formed by upward and downward movements of blocks of land along huge faults (cracks) in the earth's crust. In the far west lie the Pacific ranges and lowlands. The country's highest mountain is in Alaska.

LAND

Area 3,618,770 sq mi (9,368,900 sq km)
Highest point Mount McKinley, 20,323 ft (6,194 m)
Lowest point Death Valley, –282 ft (–86 m)
Major features Rocky Mountains, Great Plains and Central Lowlands, Appalachian Mountains

WATER

Longest river Mississippi–Missouri, 3,740 mi (6,020 km)
Largest basin Mississippi–Missouri, 1,224,000 sq mi (3,222,000 sq km)
Highest average flow Mississippi, 620,000 cu ft/sec (17,500 cu m/sec)
Largest lake Superior, 32,150 sq mi (83,270 sq km)

NOTABLE THREATENED SPECIES

Mammals Black-footed ferret (*Mustela nigripes*), Gray bat (*Myotis grisescens*), Stephens' kangaroo rat (*Dipodomys stephensi*), Red wolf (*Canis rufus*), Hawaiian monk seal (*Monachus schauinslandi*), Florida cougar (*Puma concolor coryi*)
Birds California condor (*Gymnogyps califonianus*, nene (*Branta sandvicensis*), kamao (*Myadestes myadestinus*), Oahu creeper (*Paroreomyza maculata*), Hawaiian crow (*Corvus hawaiiensis*)
Others San Joaquin leopard lizard (*Gambelia silus*), Pallid sturgeon (*Scaphirhynchus albus*), Leon Springs pupfish (*Cyprindon bovinus*), Acorn pearly mussel (*Epioblasma haysiana*), Little agate shells (*Achatinella spp.*), No-eyed and big-eyed wolf spider (*Adelocosa anops*), San Francisco forktail damselfly (*Ischnura gemina*)
Plants *Agave arizonica*; *Asimina rugelii*; American yellowwood (*Cladrastis lutea*); Cumberland rosemary (*Conradina verticillata*); white fritillary (*Fritillaria liliacea*); mountain golden heather (*Hudsonia montana*); San Clemente Island bush-mallow (*Malacothamnus clementinus*); Knowlton cactus (*Pediocactus knowltonii*); Graves's beach plum (*Prunus gravesii*); needle palm (*Rhapidophyllum hystrix*)

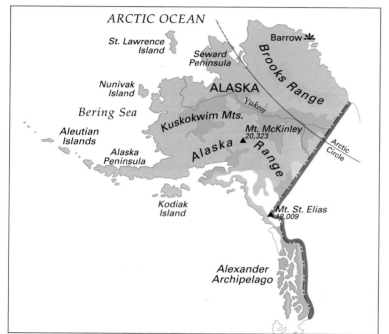

HABITATS

Physical zones

- ice and snow
- tundra
- mountains/barren land
- forest
- grassland
- semidesert
- desert

▲ mountain peak (ft)
▼ depression (ft)
🌤 climate station

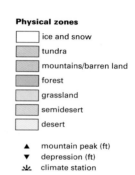

The habitats of the United States range from ice and tundra in Alaska in the far northwest, to forested mountains, flat prairies, hot deserts, and subtropical swamps in the southeast. The Cascade Range contains active volcanoes, such as Mount St. Helens, which erupted in 1980. This range, together with the volcanoes in southern Alaska, form part of a huge zone known as the Pacific "ring of fire."

CLIMATE

The northeastern and midwestern states have hot summers and cold, snowy winters, while the subtropical southeast has mild winters. The eastern coast is sometimes hit by hurricanes, while tornadoes occur in the states north of the Gulf of Mexico.

The Pacific coast as far south as San Francisco has a rainy climate, but winters are mild with temperatures mostly above freezing. This area and the southeastern states both receive over 40 in (1,000 mm) of rain every year. The mountains are cooler and wetter than the dry prairies to the east and desert basins, such as Death Valley, in the Southwest. California has a Mediterranean climate. The Northwest is cooler and wetter. Alaska has polar and subarctic climates, while the tropical climate of Hawaii is moderated by cool trade winds.

CLIMATE

| | Temperature °F (°C) | | Altitude | |
	January	July	ft (m)	
Barrow (Alaska)	–17 (–27)	39 (4)	13	(4)
Portland	39 (4)	68 (20)	39	(12)
San Francisco	48 (9)	63 (17)	16	(5)
New Orleans	54 (12)	81 (27)	30	(9)
Chicago	27 (–3)	75 (24)	623	(190)

| | Precipitation in. (mm) | | | |
	January	July	Year	
Barrow (Alaska)	0.2 (5)	0.8 (20)	4.3	(110)
Portland	5.4 (136)	0.4 (10)	37.2	(944)
San Francisco	4.0 (102)	0 (0)	18.7	(475)
New Orleans	3.9 (98)	6.7 (171)	53.9	(1,369)
Chicago	1.9 (47)	3.4 (86)	33.2	(843)

Greatest snowfall in 24 hours: 75.8 in. (1,925 mm), Silver Lake, Colorado (1921)

NATURAL HAZARDS

Tornadoes in south and Midwest, hurricanes in east, earthquakes and volcanic eruptions in west, drought and blizzards in Midwest

CLIMATE

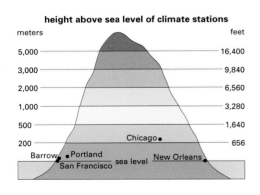

height above sea level of climate stations

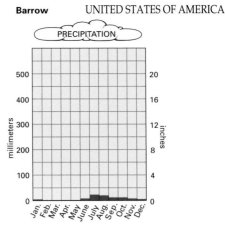
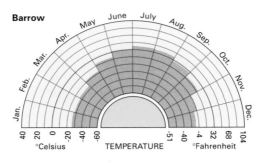

Barrow

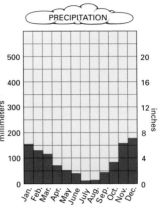
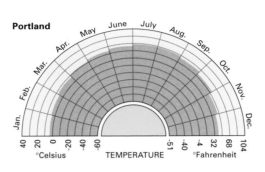

Portland

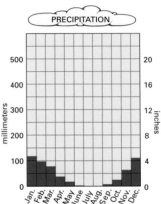
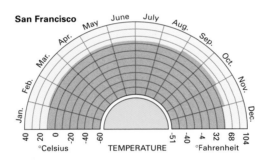

San Francisco

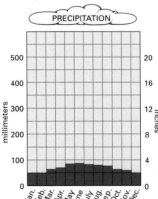
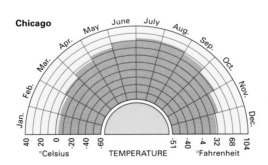

Chicago

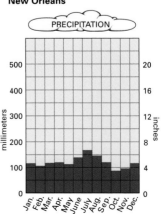
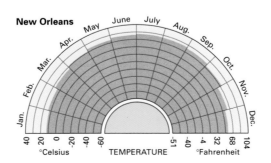

New Orleans

ENVIRONMENTAL ISSUES

Deforestation, large-scale farming, rapid population growth, and the development of industrial cities have all contributed to massive environmental changes in the United States in the last 200 years.

One problem was identified in the 1930s, when farming in the dry prairies turned parts of the midwest into a "dust bowl." New farming methods slowed down desertification and some damaged areas were reclaimed, but soil erosion continues.

Other problems, related to urban growth and rising standards of living, include air pollution, caused by power plants, factories, and car emissions, and water pollution, caused by industrial and domestic waste disposal. In the 1960s, people became more and more aware of the problems. Policies to protect the environment are now vigorously pursued.

POPULATION AND WEALTH

Population	275.5 million
Population increase (annual growth rate, 1995–2000)	1.0%
Energy use (lbs/year per person of oil equivalent)	17,540
Purchasing power parity (Int$ per year)	28,573

ENVIRONMENTAL INDICATORS

CO$_2$ emissions ('000 tons/year)	5,468,564
Car ownership (% of population)	73%
Proportion of territory protected, including marine areas	21.2%
Forests as a percentage of original forest	60%
Artificial fertilizer use (lbs/acre/year)	125
Access to safe drinking water (% population; rural/urban)	100/100%

MAJOR ENVIRONMENTAL ISSUES AND SOURCES

Air pollution: locally high, in particular urban; acid rain prevalent; high greenhouse gas emissions
River/lake pollution: medium/high; *sources:* industrial, agricultural, sewage, acid deposition
Marine/coastal pollution: local; *sources:* industrial, agricultural, sewage, oil
Land pollution: locally high; *sources:* industrial, urban/household, nuclear
Land degradation: *types:* desertification, soil erosion, salinization; *causes:* agriculture, industry
Waste disposal problems: domestic; industrial; nuclear; agricultural
Resource issues: land use competition, water supply
Major events: Love Canal (1978) and Times Beach (1986), evacuated due to chemical pollution; Three Mile Island (1979), nuclear power station accident; *Exxon Valdez* (1989), major oil spill from tanker in sea off Alaska; Dunsmuir (1991), pesticide spill during transportation; Gulf of Mexico "dead" zone (1990s); forest fires (2000)

ENVIRONMENTAL ISSUES

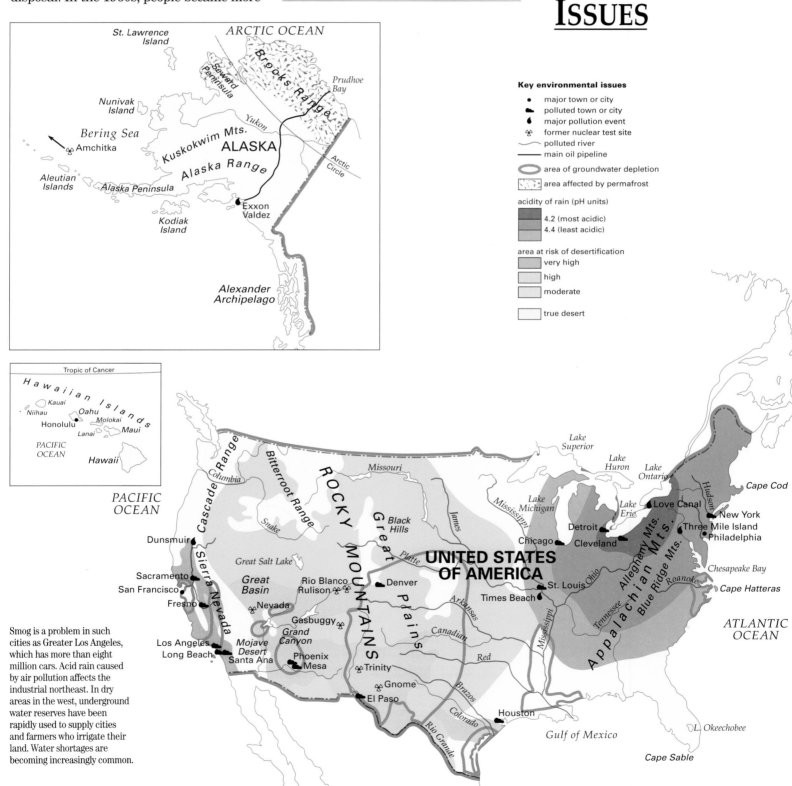

Key environmental issues

- • major town or city
- 🏭 polluted town or city
- 🛢 major pollution event
- ☢ former nuclear test site
- 〰 polluted river
- — main oil pipeline
- ⬭ area of groundwater depletion
- ▦ area affected by permafrost

acidity of rain (pH units)

- 4.2 (most acidic)
- 4.4 (least acidic)

area at risk of desertification

- very high
- high
- moderate
- true desert

Smog is a problem in such cities as Greater Los Angeles, which has more than eight million cars. Acid rain caused by air pollution affects the industrial northeast. In dry areas in the west, underground water reserves have been rapidly used to supply cities and farmers who irrigate their land. Water shortages are becoming increasingly common.

POPULATION

Between 1890 and 1940, the population of the United States more than doubled from 63 million to 131 million. By 1995, the population had doubled again, reaching more than 261 million. This population explosion was caused partly by natural growth, and partly by massive immigration of people from most parts of the world.

The twentieth century also saw another change, from a mainly rural society to an urban one. In 1900, more than 40 percent of the people lived on farms. By 1991, the percentage had fallen to 1.9. Another trend has been the growth of huge city suburbs, occupied by middle-class people who moved out of the decaying city centers, which were often occupied by poorer ethnic minorities. Some inner cities are being restored, and young people, especially, are moving in.

POPULATION

Total population of region (millions) (yr 2000)	275.5
Population density (persons per sq mi)	76
Population change (average annual percent 1995–2000)	
Urban	+1.11%
Rural	+0.08%

URBAN POPULATION

As percentage of total population	
1960	70.0%
1995–2000	77.0%

TEN LARGEST CITIES

	Population
New York	8,056,200
Los Angeles	3,749,900
Chicago	2,915,500
Houston	1,990,800
Philadelphia	1,520,300
Phoenix	1,358,000
San Diego	1,241,600
Dallas	1,211,200
San Antonio	1,166,400
Detroit	955,800

City population figures are for the city proper.

POPULATION

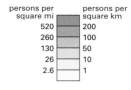

Population density

urban agglomeration
(National capital is underlined)
- ■ over 10,000,000
- ◆ 5,000,000–10,000,000
- ■ 1,000,000–4,999,999

persons per square mi	persons per square km
520	200
260	100
130	50
26	10
2.6	1

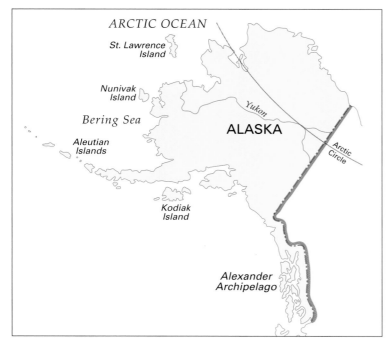

Around 1900, the greatest densities of population were in the Northeast and around the Great Lakes from Lake Michigan to Lake Ontario. In the last 90 years, the populations of the West and South have expanded greatly. The most recent trend has been a movement from the North to the "sunbelt" states of Florida, Texas, Arizona, Nevada, and California.

INDUSTRY

The United States is the world's leading industrial nation. It has huge energy resources, including coal, oil, and natural gas. Its mineral resources include most of the materials needed by modern industry. The United States also has rich human resources: a skilled and mobile workforce.

In the early twentieth century, the country developed heavy industries, such as iron and steel plants. They supplied the materials for car and machinery manufacturers. In the late twentieth century, the emphasis shifted to light and service industries.

Despite increasing competition from Japan and other Pacific nations, the United States remains a leader in high technology, including microelectronics industries. With its highly developed economy, it is also the world's leading trading nation.

INDUSTRIAL OUTPUT 1997 (US $ billion)

Total	Mining	Manufacturing	Average annual change since 1960
1,980	86.4	1,032.9	+2.1%
Industrial production growth rate (1999 est.)			−2.4%

INDUSTRIAL WORKERS (millions)
(figures in parentheses are percentages of total labor force)

Total	Mining	Manufacturing	Construction
28.97	0.57 (0.4%)	20.5 (15.3%)	7.9 (5.9%)

MAJOR PRODUCTS

Energy and minerals	1970	1995
Bituminous coal (mil m.t.)	550	561
Lignite/brown coal (mil m.t.)	5.4	376
Oil (mil m.t.)	480	383
Natural gas ('000 terajoules)	22,860	20,611
Copper ('000 m.t.)	2,035	3,738
Copper ore ('000 m.t.)	1,560	1,850
Lead ore ('000 m.t.)	519	384
Lead ('000 m.t.)	748	1,320
Cement ('000 m.t.)	67,682	75,324
Aluminum ('000 m.t.)	4,544	6,523
Gold (m.t.)	56	330
Petroleum products (mil m.t.)	496	713
Steel ('000 m.t.)	119,309	93,588
Nuclear electricity in gigawatt hrs (1996)		715,212

Manufactures		
Automobiles ('000)	8,505	6,310
Rubber – synthetic ('000 m.t.)	2,436	2,510
Fertilizers (nitogenous, '000 m.t.)	8,433	14,017
Fertilizers (phosphate, '000 m.t.)	5,795	11,055

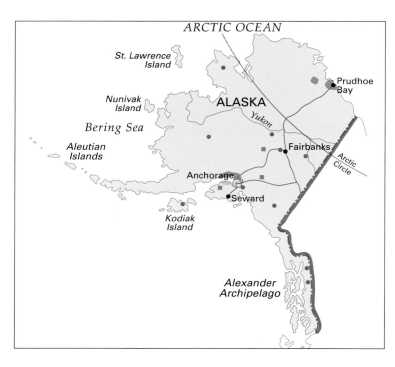

INDUSTRY

Resources and industry

- ◆ industrial center
- ○ port
- ● other town
- —— major road
- —— major railroad

mineral resources and fossil fuels

- • iron and other ferroalloy metal ores
- • other metal ores
- ▪ nonmetallic minerals
- ▨ coal
- ▨ copper
- ▨ iron ore
- ▨ lignite (brown coal)
- ▨ natural gas
- ▨ oil

Natural resources occur in most parts of the country. For example, major oil-producing states include Texas, Alaska in the North, and Louisiana. California in the West is a major manufacturing state, with high-technology industries in "Silicon Valley," near San Jose. New York, Illinois, Texas, Michigan, Pennsylvania, and New Jersey are other leading manufacturing states.

AGRICULTURE

Although farming accounts for only about 2 percent of the country's gross national product (the value of all goods and services produced), the United States is the world's leading agricultural producer. It not only supplies all its own needs, but it is also the world's leading exporter of agricultural products. For example, it dominates the world's grain markets, especially in wheat.

Farming is highly mechanized, with most farmers using scientific breeding, fertilizers, and pest-control techniques. Yields are generally high. The great variety of land and climatic types means that the country produces a wide range of products. The United States is a world leader in beef, raised largely on western ranches, citrus fruits, corn, and soybeans. It is also a major producer of cotton, dairy and poultry products, pork, tobacco, and vegetables.

LAND
Total area 3,618,770 sq mi (9,368,900 sq km)

Cropland	Pasture	Forest/Woodland
19%	25%	30%

FARMERS

Agriculture as % of GDP	2%
% of workforce	2.6%

MAJOR CROPS
Agricultural products: wheat and grains; fruits; vegetables; cotton; beef; pork; poultry; dairy products; forest products; fish

Total cropland ('000 acres)	442,309
Cropland (acres) per 1,000 people	1,628.39
Irrigated land as percentage of cropland	12%
Annual fertilizer use (lbs per acre of cropland)	125
Number of tractors	4,800,000
Change since 1987	0%
Average cereal crop yields (lbs per acre)	4,427
Average production of cereals ('000 tons)	340,985
Change since 1986–88	28%

LIVESTOCK AND FISHERIES

Average meat production ('000 tons)	35,085
Change since 1986–88	46%
Marine fish catch ('000 tons)	3,984
Change since 1986–88	5%
Aquaculture production ('000 tons)	415

FOOD SECURITY

Food aid as percentage of total imports	0
Average daily per capita calories (kilocalories)	3,699

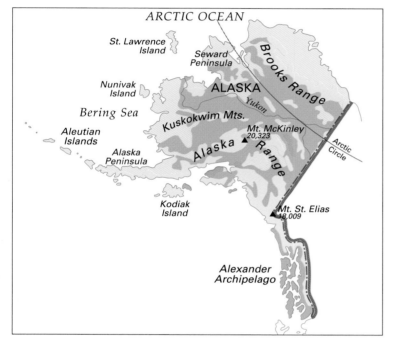

AGRICULTURE

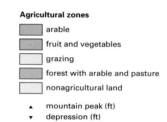

Agricultural zones

- arable
- fruit and vegetables
- grazing
- forest with arable and pasture
- nonagricultural land

▲ mountain peak (ft)
▼ depression (ft)

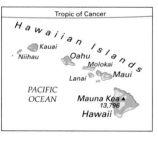

The most extensive arable farming regions are in the interior plains. The main crops are grain, especially corn and wheat. To the west, the plains are drier, and they are used for grazing on ranches. Fruit and vegetable-growing regions are in the Southwest, the Southeast (especially Florida), and small areas in the Northeast.

MEXICO, CENTRAL AMERICA, AND THE CARIBBEAN

Mexico and Central America together form a land bridge that extends to the northwest tip of South America. The region also includes 13 independent island nations in the Caribbean, two U.S. territories, and a number of European dependencies. Rugged scenery, active volcanoes, and subtropical and tropical climates are the main characteristics of the region.

The first inhabitants of the region were the Native Americans, who founded such cultures as the Mayan and Aztec empires. Spain conquered the region in the sixteenth century, and Spanish culture dominates to this day. Other people in this complex cultural mix are Africans, other Europeans, and some Asians, who were introduced as laborers.

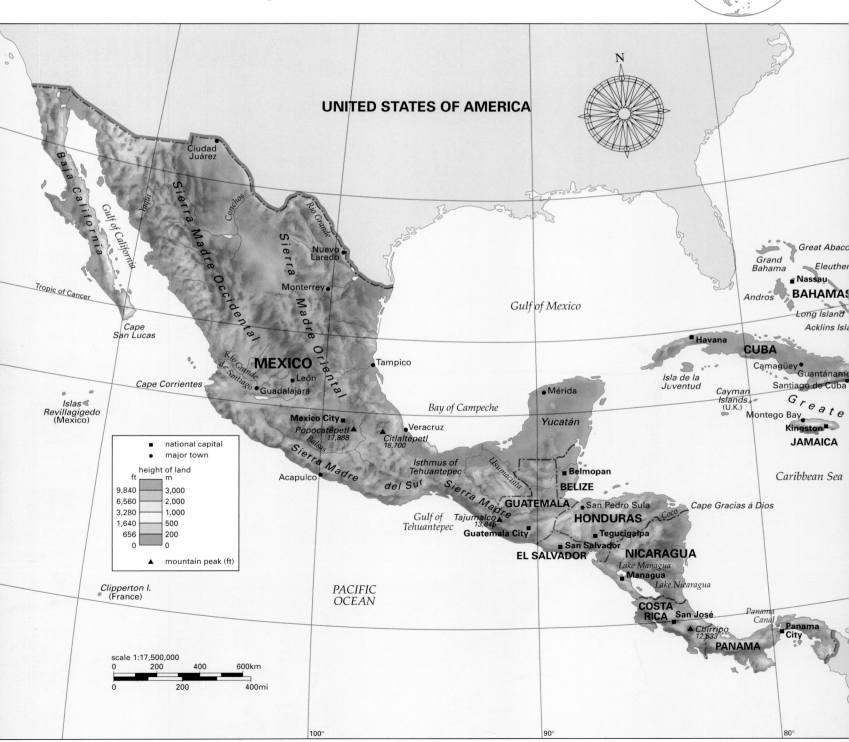

national capital ■
major town ●

height of land

ft	m
9,840	3,000
6,560	2,000
3,280	1,000
1,640	500
656	200
0	0

▲ mountain peak (ft)

scale 1:17,500,000

0   200   400   600km
0   200   400mi

THE POLITICAL AND CULTURAL WORLD

Although geographically part of North America, most of the region belongs culturally to Latin America. Spanish is the chief language, and Roman Catholicism the main religion, though some Native Americans and Africans combine the Christian faith with some of their own traditional beliefs.

In the past the region has suffered much instability. Civilian governments have been overthrown by military groups, while brutal dictatorships and civil war have hampered the region's progress. Cuba is the only communist regime. Its policies were unaffected by the changes in its former ally, the Soviet Union.

COUNTRIES IN THE REGION

Antigua and Barbuda, Bahamas, Barbados, Belize, Costa Rica, Cuba, Dominica, Dominican Republic, El Salvador, Grenada, Guatemala, Haiti, Honduras, Jamaica, Mexico, Nicaragua, Panama, St. Kitts-Nevis, St. Lucia, St. Vincent and the Grenadines, Trinidad and Tobago

Dependencies of other states Anguilla, Bermuda, British Virgin Islands, Cayman Islands, Montserrat, Turks and Caicos Islands (UK); Aruba, Netherlands Antilles (Netherlands); Guadeloupe, Martinique (France); Puerto Rico, US Virgin Islands (USA)

LANGUAGE

Countries with one official language
(English) Antigua and Barbuda, Bahamas, Barbados, Belize, Dominica, Grenada, Jamaica, St. Kitts-Nevis, St. Lucia, St. Vincent and the Grenadines, Trinidad and Tobago; (Spanish) Costa Rica, Cuba, Dominican Republic, El Salvador, Guatemala, Honduras, Mexico, Nicaragua, Panama
Country with two official languages
(Creole, French) Haiti

Other languages spoken in the region include Carib, Nahua and other indigenous languages; Creoles and French patois; and Hindi (Trinidad and Tobago).

RELIGION

Countries with one major religion (P) Antigua and Barbuda; (RC) Costa Rica, Cuba, Dominica, Dominican Republic, El Salvador, Honduras, Mexico, Nicaragua
Countries with more than one major religion (P, RC) Bahamas, Barbados, Belize, Grenada, Jamaica, St. Kitts-Nevis, St. Lucia, St. Vincent and the Grenadines; (P, RC, V) Haiti; (H, M, P, RC) Trinidad and Tobago
Key: H–Hindu, M–Muslim, P–Protestant, RC–Roman Catholic, V–Voodoo

STYLES OF GOVERNMENT

Republics Costa Rica, Cuba, Dominica, Dominican Republic, El Salvador, Guatemala, Haiti, Honduras, Mexico, Nicaragua, Panama, Trinidad and Tobago
Monarchies All other countries in the region
Multiparty states All countries except Cuba, Haiti
One-party states Cuba, Haiti
Military influence Guatemala, Haiti, Honduras

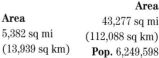

Area 171 sq mi (442 sq km) Pop. 66,422
Antigua and Barbuda

Area 10,579 sq mi (27,400 sq km) Pop. 6,867,995 **Haiti**

Area 5,382 sq mi (13,939 sq km) Pop. 294,982
Bahamas

Area 43,277 sq mi (112,088 sq km) Pop. 6,249,598 **Honduras**

Area 166 sq mi (430 sq km) Pop. 274,540
Barbados

Area 4,244 sq mi (10,991 sq km) Pop. 2,652,689 **Jamaica**

Area 8,867 sq mi (22,965 sq km) Pop. 249,183
Belize

Area 756,066 sq mi (1,958,201 sq km) Pop. 100,349,766 **Mexico**

Area 19,730 sq mi (51,100 sq km) Pop. 3,710,558
Costa Rica

Area 46,467 sq mi (120,349 sq km) Pop. 4,812,569 **Nicaragua**

Area 42,804 sq mi (110,861 sq km) Pop. 11,141,997
Cuba

Area 29,762 sq mi (77,082 sq km) Pop. 2,808,268 **Panama**

Area 290 sq mi (750 sq km) Pop. 71,540
Dominica

Area 104 sq mi (269 sq km) Pop. 38,819 **St. Kitts-Nevis**

Area 18,704 sq mi (48,443 sq km) Pop. 8,442,533
Dominican Republic

Area 238 sq mi (617 sq km) Pop. 156,260 **St. Lucia**

Area 8,124 sq mi (21,041 sq km) Pop. 6,122,515
El Salvador

Area 150 sq mi (389 sq km) Pop. 115,461 **St. Vincent and the Grenadines**

Area 133 sq mi (345 sq km) Pop. 89,018
Grenada

Area 1,980 sq mi (5,128 sq km) Pop. 1,175,523 **Trinidad and Tobago**

Area 42,042 sq mi (108,889 sq km) Pop. 12,639,939
Guatemala

HABITATS

The mainland contains a chain of volcanic highlands that form part of the Pacific "ring of fire." Volcanic eruptions and earthquakes are common. Tropical rain forest and heavy rains occur in the northeast and in the islands, while the northwest is desert or semidesert.

LAND

Area 1,056,183 sq mi (2,735,515 sq km)
Highest point Citaltépetl, 18,700 ft (5,699 m)
Lowest point Lake Enriquillo, Dominican Republic, –144 ft (–44 m)
Major features volcanic mountain chain and Mexican plateau on isthmus, island chain of the West Indies

WATER

Longest river Conchos–Grande, 1,300 mi (2,100 km)
Largest basin Grande (part), 172,000 sq mi (445,000 sq km)
Highest average flow Colorado, 3,700 cu ft/sec (104 cu m/sec) at head of Gulf of California
Largest lake Nicaragua, 3,100 sq mi (8,029 sq km)

NOTABLE THREATENED SPECIES

Mammals Haitian solenodon (*Solenodon paradoxus*), Central American squirrel monkey (*Saimiri oerstedi*), Volcano rabbit (*Romerolagus diazi*), Jamaican hutia (*Geocapromys brownii*), Gulf of California porpoise (*Phocoena sinus*)
Birds St. Vincent amazon (*Amazona guildingii*), Highland guan (*Penelopina nigra*), Resplendent quetzal (*Pharomachrus mocinno*), Ocellated turkey (*Agriocharis ocellata*), Cahow (*Procellaria cahow*)
Others Kemp's ridley turtle (*Lepidochelys kempii*), Jamaican ground iguana (*Cyclura collei*), Golden toad (*Bufo periglenes*)

CLIMATE

The climates of Mexico and Central America vary from hot, humid coastlands to cool, temperate plateaus, to cold mountain areas. Northern Mexico has deserts, but the rainfall increases in the south. The tropical Caribbean islands are warm throughout the year.

CLIMATE

	Temperature °F (°C)		Altitude	
	January	July	ft	(m)
Guayamas	64 (18)	88 (31)	13	(4)
Zacatecas	50 (10)	57 (14)	8,567	(2,612)
Mexico City	54 (12)	61 (16)	7,564	(2,306)
Havana	70 (21)	81 (27)	161	(49)
Bluefields	77 (25)	79 (26)	39	(12)
Seawell	77 (25)	81 (27)	184	(56)

	Precipitation in. (mm)		
	January	July	Year
Guayamas	0.31 (8)	1.9 (47)	9.9 (252)
Zacatecas	0.27 (7)	2.7 (69)	12.3 (313)
Mexico City	0.31 (8)	6.3 (160)	28.6 (726)
Havana	2.0 (51)	3.7 (93)	45.9 (1,167)
Bluefields	10.4 (264)	29.4 (746)	172.0 (4,370)
Seawell	2.7 (68)	5.6 (141)	59.1 (1,273)

Greatest recorded rainfall in 5 minutes, 12 in. (305 mm) at Portobello, northern Panama

NATURAL HAZARDS

Earthquakes, landslides, volcanic eruptions, hurricanes

Physical zones

- mountains/barren land
- forest
- grassland
- semidesert
- desert

- ▲ mountain peak (ft)
- ☀ climate station

THE POLITICAL WORLD

The region contains 21 independent nations and 11 dependencies. They include some of the world's oldest European colonies. Spanish settlement began on Hispaniola as early as 1493. Later colonizers included the British, Dutch, and French. Generally the passage from colonialism to independence has been peaceful.

- ■ national capital
- • other town

HABITATS

Northern Mexico is arid. In central Mexico, two ranges enclose a central, well-watered plateau. Central America has high central ranges, bordered in the east by broad coastal plains.

Great Abaco

Grand Bahama

Eleuthera

Andros

BAHAMAS

Gulf of Mexico

Long Island

Turks and Caicos Islands (U.K.)

ATLANTIC OCEAN

Havana

CUBA

Great Inagua

Isla de la Juventud

Acklins Island

Cayman Islands (U.K.)

Bay of Campeche

exico City

Yucatán

▲ Popocatépetl 17,888

Citlaltépetl 18,700

Isthmus of Tehuantepec

Usumacinta

BELIZE

a Madre del Sur

Sierra Madre

GUATEMALA

Tajumulco 13,845

Gulf of Tehuantepec

HONDURAS

Coco

Cape Gracias á Dios

EL SALVADOR

NICARAGUA

Lake Managua

Lake Nicaragua

COSTA RICA

▲ Chirripó 12,533

Panama Canal

PANAMA

Hispaniola

HAITI

DOMINICAN REPUBLIC

Puerto Rico (U.S.A.)

Greater Antilles

Bluefields

JAMAICA

Caribbean Sea

Virgin Islands (U.S.A.)

Virgin Islands (U.K.)

Barbuda

ANTIGUA AND BARBUDA

Antigua

ST. KITTS-NEVIS

Montserrat (U.K.)

Guadeloupe (France)

DOMINICA

Martinique (France)

ST. LUCIA

Seawell

BARBADOS

ST. VINCENT AND THE GRENADINES

GRENADA

Lesser Antilles

Netherlands Antilles (Neth.)

Aruba (Neth.)

Bonaire

Curaçao

Tobago

TRINIDAD AND TOBAGO

Trinidad

CLIMATE

height above sea level of climate stations

meters — feet

5,000 — 16,400

3,000 — 9,840

• Mexico City

2,000 — 6,560

1,000 — 3,280

500 — 1,640

200 — 656

• Guayamas — sea level — Havana •

Guayamas

May June July

Apr. Aug.

Mar. Sep.

Feb. Oct.

Jan. Nov.

Dec.

40 20 0 -20 -40 -60 | -51 -40 -4 32 68 104

°Celsius — TEMPERATURE — °Fahrenheit

Mexico City

May June July

Apr. Aug.

Mar. Sep.

Feb. Oct.

Jan. Nov.

Dec.

40 20 0 -20 -40 -60 | -51 -40 -4 32 68 104

°Celsius — TEMPERATURE — °Fahrenheit

Havana

May June July

Apr. Aug.

Mar. Sep.

Feb. Oct.

Jan. Nov.

Dec.

40 20 0 -20 -40 -60 | -51 -40 -4 32 68 104

°Celsius — TEMPERATURE — °Fahrenheit

Guayamas

PRECIPITATION

millimeters — inches

500 — 20

400 — 16

300 — 12

200 — 8

100 — 4

0 — 0

Jan. Feb. Mar. Apr. May June July Aug. Sep. Oct. Nov. Dec.

Mexico City

PRECIPITATION

millimeters — inches

500 — 20

400 — 16

300 — 12

200 — 8

100 — 4

0 — 0

Jan. Feb. Mar. Apr. May June July Aug. Sep. Oct. Nov. Dec.

Havana

PRECIPITATION

millimeters — inches

500 — 20

400 — 16

300 — 12

200 — 8

100 — 4

0 — 0

Jan. Feb. Mar. Apr. May June July Aug. Sep. Oct. Nov. Dec.

Anguilla (U.K.)

St. Martin (France/Neth.)

St. Barthélemy (France)

Virgin Islands (U.K.)

Virgin Islands (U.S.A.)

MINICAN EPUBLIC

San Juan

ANTIGUA & BARBUDA

Basseterre

St. John's

ST. KITTS-NEVIS

Montserrat (U.K.)

Guadeloupe (France)

Roseau

DOMINICA

Martinique (France)

Puerto Rico (U.S.A.)

nto mingo

Castries

ST. LUCIA

BARBADOS

Bridgetown

Kingstown

ST. VINCENT & THE GRENADINES

St. George's

GRENADA

Lesser Antilles

Netherlands Antilles (Neth.)

Aruba (Neth.)

Bonaire

Curaçao

Port-of-Spain

Tobago

TRINIDAD AND TOBAGO

Trinidad

33

ENVIRONMENTAL ISSUES

Two key concerns are widespread soil degradation and deforestation in the mountains of mainland Central America and some of the high islands.

Deforestation has in turn caused flooding and the silting of rivers. Other problems include severe air pollution in urban areas, the heavy impact of tourism on coastlines and coral reefs, oil contamination in the Caribbean Sea, and disturbance to the ecology of the seas through overfishing. The main causes are rapid population growth and the poverty of the people, which put excess pressure on resources.

Forests in the region continue to be under extreme pressure, with 87 percent of virgin forests under threat. Where forests have been cleared, erosion and desertification are serious problems.

Rapidly growing urban populations put enormous pressure on the environment, both locally and regionally. Mexico City alone has over 16 million inhabitants. As rural migrants flock to the cities, more and more food is demanded from already overused farmland, while pollution problems are becoming worse.

POPULATION

Central America and the Caribbean islands were home to people of a wide range of cultures who lived there for at least 12,000 years before Europeans discovered what they called the New World in the late fifteenth century. After this, waves of Europeans invaded the lands, with dreadful results for the native people. The Spanish seized control of Mexico and the Central American neck of land, and their language, religion, and customs prevail there today.

The scattered islands of the Caribbean were colonized by a number of European nations, but the main culture is African, deriving from the millions of slaves shipped there to work in the sugar plantations. People from Asia and Europe also were taken as laborers, making for a great cultural mix.

Until recently the population was mainly rural, but the decline in traditional farming (and the plantation system) has been the cause of massive movement to the cities. The growth of cities has been rapid and unplanned, leaving millions of people without homes or jobs.

POPULATION AND WEALTH

	Highest	Middle	Lowest
Population (millions)	100.349 (Mexico)	6.249 (Honduras)	0.038 (St. Kitts-Nevis)
Population increase (annual growth rate, 1990–95)	2.7% (Honduras)	1.6% (Panama)	0.4% (Cuba)
Energy use (lbs per year per person of oil equivalent)	14,151 (Trin. & Tob.)	2,859 (Cuba)	500 (Haiti)
Purchasing power parity (Int$/per year)	6,999 (Trin. & Tob.)	4,396 (Belize)	1,213 (Haiti)

ENVIRONMENTAL INDICATORS

	Highest	Middle	Lowest
CO2 emissions ('000 tons per year)	357,834 (Mexico)	29,067 (Cuba)	414 (Belize)
Car ownership (% of population)	30% (Bahamas)	8% (Panama)	1% (Haiti)
Forests as a % of original forest	96% (Belize)	46% (Guatemala)	1% (Haiti)
Artificial fertilizer use (lbs/acre/per year)	266 (Costa Rica)	88 (El Salvador)	7 (Haiti)
Access to safe drinking water (% population; rural/urban)	73/99% (Panama)	66/90% (Mexico)	28/50% (Haiti)

MAJOR ENVIRONMENTAL PROBLEMS AND SOURCES

Air pollution: high in urban areas
Land degradation: *types:* soil erosion, deforestation; *causes:* agriculture, population pressure, tourism
Resource issues: inadequate drinking water and sanitation; coastal flooding; coral bleaching and loss
Population problems: population explosion; inadequate health facilities; tourism
Major events: Ixtoc 1 (1979), oil rig fire and leak; Guadalajara (1992), series of gas explosions, frequent hurricanes

POPULATION

Total population of region (millions)			168.3

	Mexico	Jamaica	Honduras
Population density (persons per sq mi)	132.6	630	135.7
Population change (average annual percent 1995–2000)			
Urban	+1.89%	+1.73%	+4.84%
Rural	+0.90%	−0.19%	+0.64%

URBAN POPULATION

As percentage of total population 1995	73%	54%	48%

TEN LARGEST CITIES

	Country	Population
Mexico City †	Mexico	8,591,309
Havana †	Cuba	2,143,406
Guadalajara	Mexico	1,647,000
Ecatepec*	Mexico	1,619,000
Santo Domingo †	Dominican Republic	1,609,699
Puebla	Mexico	1,270,989
Netzahualcóyotl*	Mexico	1,224,500
Ciudad Juárez	Mexico	1,119,000
Tijuana	Mexico	1,115,000
Monterrey	Mexico	1,108,400

† denotes capital city

* included in Mexico City urban agglomeration

City population figures are for the city proper.

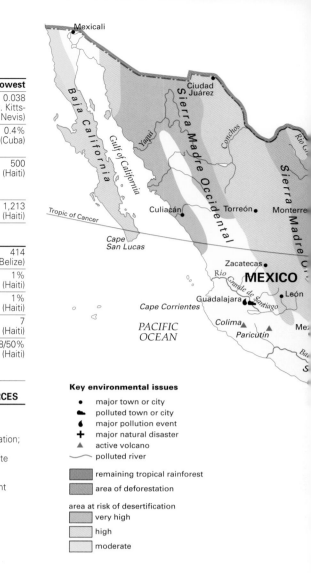

Key environmental issues

- major town or city
- polluted town or city
- major pollution event
- major natural disaster
- active volcano
- polluted river

remaining tropical rainforest

area of deforestation

area at risk of desertification
- very high
- high
- moderate

Population density

urban agglomeration
(National capital is underlined)
- over 10,000,000
- 5,000,000–10,000,000
- 1,000,000–4,999,999
- 500,000–999,999
- 250,000–499,999
- × national capital less than 250,000

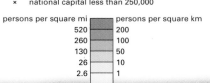

persons per square mi	persons per square km
520	200
260	100
130	50
26	10
2.6	1

ENVIRONMENTAL ISSUES

Earthquakes, such as the one that struck Mexico City in 1985, volcanic eruptions, and hurricanes on the islands and mainland coasts are natural hazards in the region.

Gulf of Mexico

Great Abaco

Grand Bahama

Eleuthera

Andros

BAHAMAS

Long Island

Turks and Caicos Islands (U.K.)

ATLANTIC OCEAN

• Havana

CUBA

Acklins Island

Great Inagua

Hispaniola

Virgin Islands (U.S.A.)

Virgin Islands (U.K.)

ANTIGUA AND BARBUDA

San Juan •

DOMINICAN REPUBLIC

Soufrière Hills

Guadeloupe (France)

• Mérida

Yucatán

Isla de la Juventud

Cayman Islands (U.K.)

HAITI

Port-au-Prince •

Santo Domingo •

Puerto Rico (U.S.A.)

ST. KITTS-NEVIS

Montserrat (U.K.)

DOMINICA

Pelée

Martinique (France)

Bay of Campeche

ocatepetl ▲

▲ Citlaltépetl

■ Ixtoc 1

G r e a t e r   A n t i l l e s

Kingston •

ST. LUCIA

BARBADOS

ST. VINCENT AND THE GRENADINES

Soufrière

dre del Sur

El Chichón ▲

Usumacinta

BELIZE

JAMAICA

Caribbean Sea

Netherlands Antilles (Neth.)

GRENADA

Tobago

Sierra Madre

GUATEMALA

HONDURAS

Cape Gracias á Dios

Aruba (Neth.)

Bonaire

Curaçao

TRINIDAD AND TOBAGO

Trinidad

Gulf of Tehuantepec Tacaná ▲

Tajumulco ▲

Atitlán ▲

Agua ▲

Coco

• Guatemala City

• Tegucigalpa

San Salvador •

Cosigüina ▲

NICARAGUA

EL SALVADOR

Momotombo ▲

• Managua

Lake Managua

Lake Nicaragua

Cuilapa   Miravalles ▲

Irazú ▲   Turrialba ▲

Panama Canal

COSTA RICA

Barú ▲

• Panama City

PANAMA

POPULATION

The population of the region used to be mainly rural. But recently enormous numbers of people have moved into the cities. Many new arrivals are poor and have no jobs.

ynosa

Matamoros

Gulf of Mexico

Great Abaco

Grand Bahama

Eleuthera

✕ Nassau

Andros

BAHAMAS

Long Island

Turks and Caicos Islands (U.K.)

ATLANTIC OCEAN

ampico

■ Havana

CUBA

Acklins Island

Great Inagua

Hispaniola

Virgin Islands (U.S.A.)

Virgin Islands (U.K.)

ANTIGUA AND BARBUDA

Camagüey ⊙

San Juan •

Santiago ⊙

DOMINICAN REPUBLIC

Basseterre ✕ St. John's

• Cancún

Isla de la Juventud

Cayman Islands (U.K.)

Santiago de Cuba ⊙

HAITI

Ponce ■

ST. KITTS-NEVIS

Guadeloupe (France)

• Mérida

Port-au-Prince ■

Santo Domingo

Puerto Rico (U.S.A.)

Montserrat (U.K.)

DOMINICA

Roseau

Martinique (France)

Bay of Campeche

⊙ Xalapa

ebla • Veracruz

HAITI

G r e a t e r   A n t i l l e s

Kingston

Castries

ST. LUCIA

BARBADOS

Bridgetown

Orizaba

⊙ Oaxaca

Coatzacoalcos

• Villahermosa

Usumacinta

✕ Belmopan

BELIZE

JAMAICA

Caribbean Sea

Netherlands Antilles (Neth.)

ST. VINCENT AND THE GRENADINES

Kingstown

GRENADA St. George's

Tobago

Gulf of Tehuantepec

Puerto Barrios ⊙   ⊙ San Pedro Sula

GUATEMALA

HONDURAS

Coco

Aruba (Neth.)

Bonaire

Curaçao

Port-of-Spain

TRINIDAD AND TOBAGO

Trinidad

Guatemala City ■

• Tegucigalpa

San Salvador ■

NICARAGUA

EL SALVADOR

Lake Managua

• Managua

Lake Nicaragua

COSTA RICA

San José ■

Panama Canal

■ Panama City

PANAMA

INDUSTRY

The region consists of developing countries that have plenty of resources but lack the money and skilled workers to create truly industrialized economies. Mexico has resources of silver, gold, copper, and oil, and exports crude oil in large quantities. Nicaragua, Guatemala, and Honduras have fewer mineral resources, though Cuba has large nickel reserves and also deposits of limestone, chromium, copper, and iron.

Trinidad and Tobago exports oil and processes chemicals, fertilizers, and machinery. As in many other countries in the Caribbean, a major industry is tourism. On islands where tourism has not developed widely, agriculture is the main industry. Belize and El Salvador, on the mainland, have small-scale industries that produce goods for the local market. Costa Rica's industries are growing, with such products as cement, clothes, cosmetics, fertilizers, foods, textiles, and medicines. Panama, in the far south, has untapped copper reserves and small local industries, but the Panama Canal provides income for the country.

INDUSTRIAL OUTPUT (U.S. $ billion)

Total	Mining	Manufacturing	Average annual change since 1960
105	n/a	80	n/a

INDUSTRIAL WORKERS (Mexico)
(figures in parentheses are percentages of total labor force)

Total	Mining	Manufacturing	Construction
n/a	n/a	6.03m (16.1%)	1.95m (5.2%)

MAJOR PRODUCTS (figures in parentheses are percentages of total world production)

Energy and minerals	Mexico (1996)
Oil* (mil barrels)	2.9 (4.9%)
Antimony ('000 tons)	1.8 (1.5%)
Silver ('000 tons)	2,536.1
Sulfur	921.3
Gypsum	3,758.9
Lead ('000 tons)	167.1
Copper ('000 tons)	328
Zinc	348.3

* figs for crude petroleum

Manufactures	
Gasoline ('000 tons)	16,795
Cement (tons)	28,168
Steel	5,867
Passenger cars	782,743

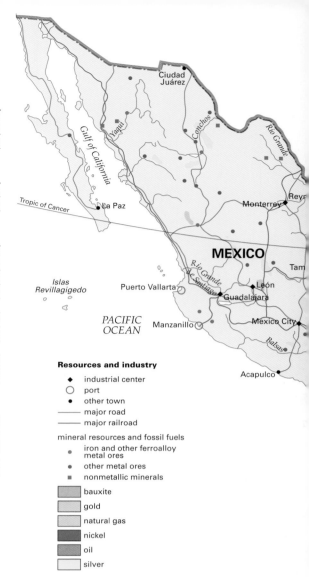

Resources and industry

- ◆ industrial center
- ○ port
- • other town
- —— major road
- —— major railroad

mineral resources and fossil fuels
- • iron and other ferroalloy metal ores
- • other metal ores
- • nonmetallic minerals
- ▢ bauxite
- ▢ gold
- ▢ natural gas
- ▣ nickel
- ▣ oil
- ▢ silver

AGRICULTURE

Agriculture plays an important part in the region's economy. Root crops were grown in the region 6,000 years ago. Large-scale commercial farming of crops on plantations and livestock on huge ranches was introduced by the Europeans. There is production of cash crops such as sugar, bananas, and coffee, while the cattle raised on ranches provide meat for consumers in the United States.

Fishing in the Caribbean islands has seen a growth in demand since tourism became a major industry. The wet, warm climate of the region allows a range of tropical crops to be cultivated. Rough pastures in drier areas support cattle ranching. Some groups of people still carry out traditional subsistence farming. Using hand tools, they cultivate corn, beans, and squash as their staple crops and also raise pigs and poultry as livestock. Subsistence farmers may also grow sorghum (a grain), potatoes or other root crops, and tropical fruits. In some parts of Cuba, Mexico, and Panama where there is high rainfall or irrigation, rice is the staple grain.

LAND
Total area 1,056,183 sq mi (2,735,515 sq km)

Cropland	Pasture	Forest/Woodland
14%	36%	28%

FARMERS	Highest	Middle	Lowest
Agriculture as % of GDP	34% (Panama)	17% (Costa Rica)	2% (Trin. & Tob.)
% of workforce	66% (Honduras)	30% (El Salvador)	1.8% (Panama)

MAJOR CROPS: Agricultural products Fruits and vegetables; livestock; sugarcane; cotton; tobacco; fish; shrimp; rice; corn; sorghum; spices

Total cropland ('000 acres)	67,458 (Mexico)	6,785 (Nicaragua)	220 (Belize)
Cropland (acres) per 1,000 people	1,450 (Nicaragua)	596 (Panama)	237 (Trin. & Tob.)
Irrigated land as % of cropland	25% (Costa Rica)	12% (Jamaica)	3% (Bel./Nicar.)
Number of tractors	172,000 (Mexico)	78,000 (Cuba)	136 (Haiti)
Average cereal crop yields (lbs/acre)	3,185 (Dom Rep)	1,790 (Panama)	801 (Haiti)
Cereal production ('000 tons)	28,839 (Mexico)	1,152 (Guatemala)	3 (Jamaica)
Change since 1986/88	27%	–17%	–39%

LIVESTOCK & FISHERIES

Meat production ('000 tons)	3,911 (Mexico)	1,152 (Guatemala)	10 (Belize)
Change since 1986/88	44%	105%	79%
Marine fish catch ('000 tons)	1,037 (Mexico)	145 (Panama)	0.1 (Belize)
Change since 1986/88	2%	–15%	–73%

FOOD SECURITY

Food aid as % of total imports	15% (Nicaragua)	5% (Guatemala)	0% (Bel., CR, Mex.)
Daily kcal/person	3,097	2,480	1,869

Agricultural zones

- ▢ arable
- ▢ fruit and vegetables
- ▢ rough grazing
- ▣ woods and forest
- ▢ nonagricultural land

- ▲ mountain peak (fts)

INDUSTRY

Mexico is a major oil producer and the world's leading silver producer. It also has many other valuable deposits. Several island nations have bauxite deposits.

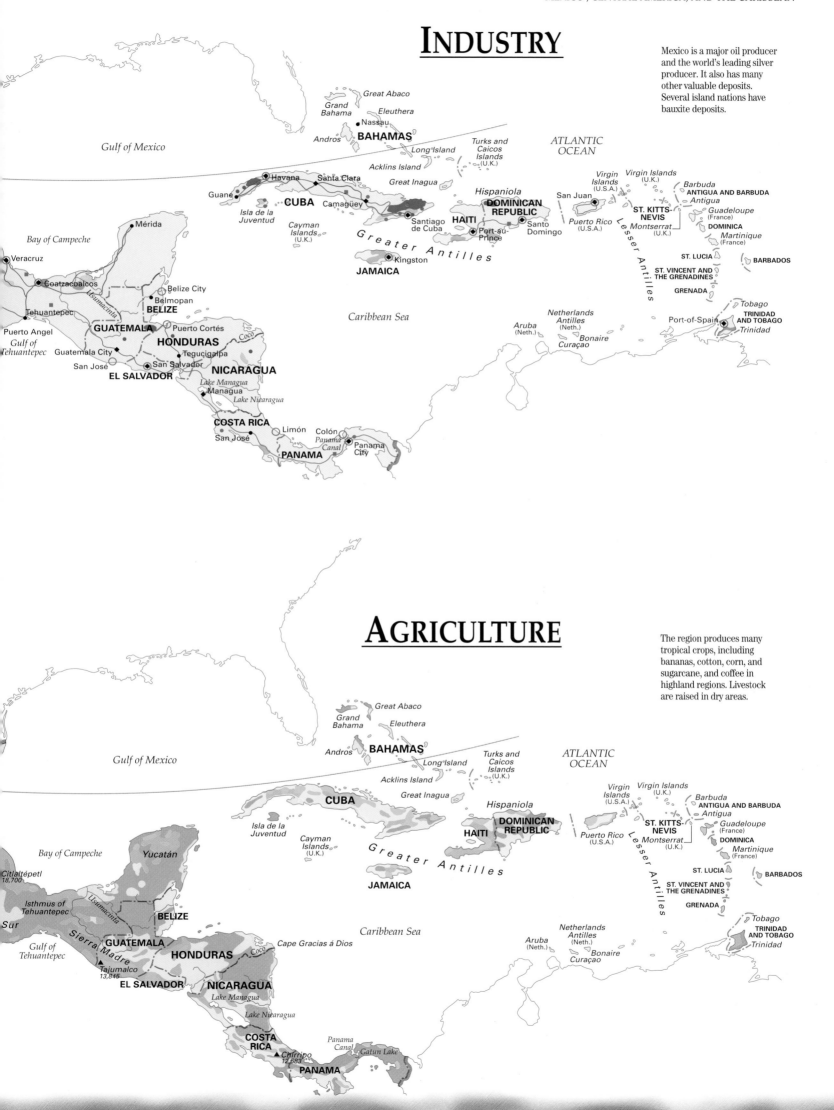

Gulf of Mexico

Great Abaco

Grand Bahama

Eleuthera

● Nassau

Andros

BAHAMAS

Long Island

Turks and Caicos Islands (U.K.)

ATLANTIC OCEAN

Acklins Island

◆ Havana

Santa Clara

Great Inagua

Hispaniola

Virgin Islands (U.S.A.)

Virgin Islands (U.K.)

Barbuda

ANTIGUA AND BARBUDA

Guane ●

CUBA

Camagüey ◆

San Juan ●

Puerto Rico (U.S.A.)

DOMINICAN REPUBLIC

ST. KITTS-NEVIS

Antigua

Guadeloupe (France)

Isla de la Juventud

Cayman Islands (U.K.)

Santiago de Cuba

HAITI

Port-au-Prince ◆

Santo Domingo ●

Montserrat (U.K.)

DOMINICA

Martinique (France)

Bay of Campeche

Mérida ●

G r e a t e r   A n t i l l e s

ST. LUCIA

BARBADOS

Veracruz ●

◆ Kingston

JAMAICA

ST. VINCENT AND THE GRENADINES

Coatzacoalcos ●

Usumacinta

Caribbean Sea

GRENADA

Tobago

Tehuantepec ●

Belize City ●

Belmopan ●

Lesser Antilles

Netherlands Antilles (Neth.)

Port-of-Spain ●

TRINIDAD AND TOBAGO

Puerto Ángel ●

BELIZE

Aruba (Neth.)

Bonaire

Trinidad

Gulf of Tehuantepec

GUATEMALA

Puerto Cortés ●

Coco

Curaçao

Guatemala City ●

HONDURAS

Tegucigalpa ●

San José ●

San Salvador ◆

EL SALVADOR

NICARAGUA

Lake Managua

Managua ◆

Lake Nicaragua

COSTA RICA

Limón ●

Colón ●

Panama Canal

San José ●

Panama City ◆

PANAMA

AGRICULTURE

The region produces many tropical crops, including bananas, cotton, corn, and sugarcane, and coffee in highland regions. Livestock are raised in dry areas.

Gulf of Mexico

Great Abaco

Grand Bahama

Eleuthera

Andros

BAHAMAS

Long Island

Turks and Caicos Islands (U.K.)

ATLANTIC OCEAN

Acklins Island

Great Inagua

CUBA

Hispaniola

Virgin Islands (U.S.A.)

Virgin Islands (U.K.)

Barbuda

ANTIGUA AND BARBUDA

Isla de la Juventud

Cayman Islands (U.K.)

DOMINICAN REPUBLIC

Puerto Rico (U.S.A.)

ST. KITTS-NEVIS

Antigua

Guadeloupe (France)

HAITI

Montserrat (U.K.)

DOMINICA

Martinique (France)

Bay of Campeche

Yucatán

G r e a t e r   A n t i l l e s

ST. LUCIA

Citlaltépetl 18,700

JAMAICA

ST. VINCENT AND THE GRENADINES

Isthmus of Tehuantepec

Usumacinta

BELIZE

Caribbean Sea

Lesser Antilles

Netherlands Antilles (Neth.)

BARBADOS

Sur

Sierra Madre

GUATEMALA

Cape Gracias á Dios

GRENADA

Aruba (Neth.)

Tobago

Gulf of Tehuantepec

▲ Tajumalco 13,846

HONDURAS

Coco

TRINIDAD AND TOBAGO

EL SALVADOR

NICARAGUA

Lake Managua

Bonaire

Trinidad

Curaçao

Lake Nicaragua

COSTA RICA

Panama Canal

▲ Chirripó 12,683

Gatun Lake

PANAMA

SOUTH AMERICA

South America, the fourth largest continent, contains the Andes, the world's longest unbroken mountain range, and the mighty Amazon River, which discharges one-fifth of the world's flow of fresh water into the sea.

Extending from the equatorial lands in the north to Cape Horn, which is just 500 miles (800 km) from Antarctica, the continent has a wide range of climates and habitats.

Native Americans migrating from North America reached the southern tip of South America about 8,000 years ago. One group, the Incas, founded a major civilization in the Andes, but it was crushed by Spanish soldiers in the 1530s. The predominant culture in South America today is Latin American. Roman Catholicism is the main religion, and Spanish and Portuguese are the chief languages.

South America was once joined to Africa, forming part of the supercontinent of Gondwanaland. When the two continents began to move apart about 150 million years ago, the South Atlantic Ocean opened up between them. Plate movements are still going on, further widening the Atlantic.

national capital
major town

height of land
ft   m
16,400   5,000
9,840   3,000
6,560   2,000
3,280   1,000
1,640   500
656   200
0   0

▲ mountain peak (ft)

scale 1:39,000,000
0   400   800   1200km
0   400   800mi

THE POLITICAL AND CULTURAL WORLD

Latin American culture is a complex blend of Native American, European, and African influences. The carnivals held in Rio de Janeiro combine Christian and African traditions, while many Native American Roman Catholics combine Christian dogma with some of the beliefs of their ancestors.

Deep divisions exist between rural people, who are often Native Americans, and urban societies, which are often dominated by people of European or of mixed European and Native American descent. In Peru, for example, such differences have led to civil war. Political instability and the suppression of human rights are occasionally still happening in South America.

COUNTRIES IN THE REGION

Argentina, Bolivia, Brazil, Chile, Colombia, Ecuador, Guyana, Paraguay, Peru, Suriname, Uruguay, Venezuela

Island territories Easter Island, Juan Fernández (Chile); Galápagos (Ecuador); Tierra del Fuego (Argentina/Chile)
Disputed borders Guyana/Venezuela; Peru/Ecuador
Dependencies of other states Falkland Islands, South Georgia, South Sandwich Islands (U.K.); French Guiana (France)

LANGUAGE

Countries with one official language (Dutch) Suriname; (English) Guyana; (Portuguese) Brazil; (Spanish) Argentina, Chile, Colombia, Ecuador, Paraguay, Uruguay, Venezuela
Country with two official languages (Quechua, Spanish) Peru
Country with three official languages (Aymara, Quechua, Spanish) Bolivia

Other languages spoken in the region include Arawak, Carib, Jivaro, Lengua, Mapuche, Sranang Tongo, Toba, and numerous other indigenous languages.

RELIGION

Countries with one major religion (RC) Argentina, Bolivia, Brazil, Chile, Colombia, Ecuador, Paraguay, Peru, Venezuela
Countries with more than one major religion (A, N, P, RC) Uruguay; (H, I, M, P, RC) Guyana, Suriname

Key: A–Atheist, H–Hindu, I–Indigenous religions, M–Muslim, N–Nonreligious, P–Protestant, RC–Roman Catholic

STYLES OF GOVERNMENT

Republics All countries of the region
Federal states Argentina, Brazil, Venezuela
Multiparty states All countries of the region

ECONOMIC INDICATORS

	Brazil	Colombia	Bolivia
GDP (US$ billions)	786.4	96.4	8.1
GNP per capita (US$)	6,240	6,720	3,280
Annual rate of growth of GDP, 1990-97	3.4%	4.4%	4.0%
Manufacturing as % of GDP	19.7%	9.6%	16.4%
Central government spending as % of GNP	39.6%	17.2%	19.6%
Merchandise exports (US$ billions)	47.7	10.6	1.1
Merchandise imports (US$ billions)	53.2	12.8	1.4
Aid received as % of GNP	0.1%	0.3%	13.3%
Total external debt as % of GDP	24.1%	34.9%	64.7%

WELFARE INDICATORS

	Brazil	Colombia	Bolivia
Infant mortality rate (per 1,000 live births)			
1965	104	86	160
2000	38.04	24.7	60.44
Malnutrition in children under 5	10.5%	15%	29.1%
Population per physician (1993)	844	1,105	2,348
Teacher-pupil ratio (primary school, 1998)	1 : 25	1 : 25	1 : 25

- ■ national capital
- ● other town

Like many former European colonies, the countries of South America have made slow progress toward democracy and have seen much political upheaval in recent times. There have been periods of military rule in most countries in the region, with resulting human rights abuses. Chile and Paraguay have recently ended rule by the military.

Area 292,135 sq mi (756,626 sq km)
Population 14,973,843 **Chile**

Area 440,831 sq mi (1,141,748 sq km)
Population 39,309,422 **Colombia**

Area 103,930 sq mi (269,178 sq km)
Population 12,562,496 **Ecuador**

Area 83,044 sq mi (215,083 sq km)
Population 705,156 **Guyana**

Area 157,048 sq mi (406,752 sq km)
Population 5,434,095 **Paraguay**

Area 496,225 sq mi (1,285,216 sq km)
Population 26,624,582 **Peru**

Area 63,251 sq mi (163,820 sq km)
Population 431,156 **Suriname**

Area 67,574 sq mi (175,016 sq km)
Population 3,308,523 **Uruguay**

Area 352,144 sq mi (912,050 sq km)
Population 23,203,466 **Venezuela**

Area 1,073,399 sq mi (2,780,092 sq km)
Population 36,737,664 **Argentina**

Area 424,164 sq mi (1,098,581 sq km)
Population 7,982,850 **Bolivia**

Area 3,265,076 sq mi (8,456,508 sq km)
Population 171,853,126 **Brazil**

HABITATS

South America covers almost one-seventh of the world's land surface and contains a wide range of habitats. It stretches from north of the equator almost to Antarctica. The great Amazon River dominates much of the north of the region.

Tropical grasslands, called llanos, are in the north; rain forests, called selvas, cover large areas around the equator; temperate grasslands, or pampas, are in the south; hot deserts border the coasts of Peru and Chile; and arid grasslands cover the cold Patagonian region in the south. The western edge of the continent is divided from the east by the great mountain range of the Andes. Extensive mountain habitats, including snowy peaks and high, wind-swept plateaus, or altiplanos, are found in the Andes ranges.

LAND

Area 6,874,600 sq mi (17,084,526 sq km)
Highest point Aconcagua, 22,836 ft (6,960 m)
Lowest point Salinas Grandes, Argentina, −131 ft (−40 m)
Major features Andes, world's longest mountain chain, Guiana Highlands and Plateau of Brazil, Amazon basin

WATER

Longest river Amazon, 4,080 mi (6,570 km)
Largest basin Amazon, 2,375,000 sq mi (6,150,000 sq km)
Highest average flow Amazon, 6,350,000 cu ft/sec (180,000 cu m/sec)
Largest lake Titicaca, 3,220 sq mi (8,340 sq km)
Amazon has world's largest drainage basin and greatest flow
Angel Falls, Venezuela, 3,212 ft (979 m) are world's highest
Iguaçu Falls, Brazil–Argentina, one of the widest, 2.5 mi (4 km)

NOTABLE THREATENED SPECIES

Mammals Golden lion tamarin (*Leontopithecus rosalia*), Emperor tamarin (*Saguinus imperator*), Woolly spider monkey (*Brachyteles arachnoides*), Giant armadillo (*Priodontes maximus*), Maned wolf (*Chrysocyon brachyurus*), Giant river otter (*Pteronura brasiliensis*), Mountain tapir (*Tapirus pinchaquel*), Marsh deer (*Blastocerus dichotomus*)
Birds Junin grebe (*Podiceps taczanowskii*), White-winged guan (*Penelope albipennis*), Little blue macaw (*Cyanopsitta spixii*), Esmereldas woodstar (*Acestrura beriepschi*), Torrent duck (*Merganetta armata*)
Others South American river turtle (*Podocnemis expansa*), Black caiman (*Melanosuchus niger*), Ginger pearlfish (*Cynolebias marmoratus*), Galapagos land snails (*Bulimulus*), Orinoco crocodile (*Crocodylus intermedius*)
Plants *Aechmea dichlamydea*; *Amaryllis traubii*; *Dalbergia nigra*; *Dicliptera dodsonii*; *Glomeropitcairnia erectiflora*; *Legrandia concinna*; snow mimosa (*Mimosa lanuginosa*); *Mutisia retrorsa*; Rio Palenue mahogany (*Persea theobromifolia*); *Spergularia congestifolia*

HABITATS

The Andes Mountains dominate western South America. The world's largest rain forest covers much of the Amazon basin, while tropical grasslands dominate large parts of the countries in the east. The western coast of Peru is desert.

Physical zones

- mountains/barren land
- forest
- grassland
- semidesert
- desert

▲ mountain peak (ft)
☆ climate station

CLIMATE

The climates of South America vary greatly. The northern regions straddle the equator and are hot and rainy. The south has a more temperate climate. The Andes range contains many climatic zones based on altitude.

Rainfall on the eastern slopes facing the Amazon basin may reach 200 inches (500 cm) a year. The interior basins and gorges have one-tenth of that heavy rainfall. The western coasts of Peru and northern Chile, though often blanketed in low clouds, have almost no rainfall at all. West of the Andes are some of the world's driest deserts. Central Chile has a Mediterranean climate, with hot, dry summers and warm, moist winters, but the south is rainy with cool summers.

CLIMATE

	Temperature °F (°C)		Altitude
	January	July	ft (m)
Maracaibo	79 (26)	84 (29)	157 (48)
Manaus	79 (26)	81 (27)	272 (83)
La Paz	48 (9)	46 (8)	13.461 (4,103)
Buenos Aires	75 (24)	52 (11)	82 (25)
Ushuaia	48 (9)	36 (2)	20 (6)

	Precipitation in. (mm)		Year
	January	July	
Maracaibo	0.1 (3)	1.1 (28)	15.2 (387)
Manaus	10.9 (276)	2.4 (61)	82.7 (2,102)
La Paz	5.5 (139)	0.2 (4)	21.9 (555)
Buenos Aires	4.1 (104)	2.4 (61)	40.4 (1,027)
Ushuaia	2.3 (58)	1.9 (47)	22.6 (574)

Atacama Desert has rainfall of less than 1 in. (25.4 mm) every 100 years

NATURAL HAZARDS

Volcanic eruptions, earthquakes, landslides and mudslides

CLIMATE

height above sea level of climate stations

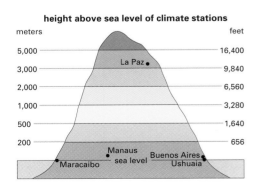

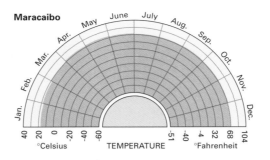

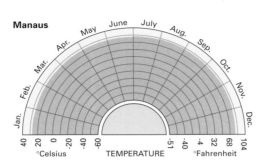

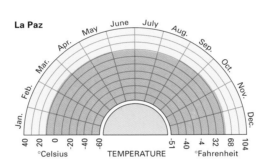

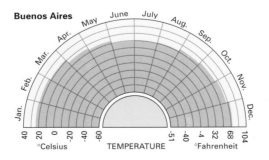

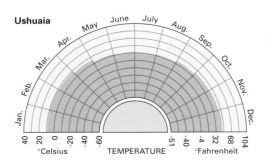

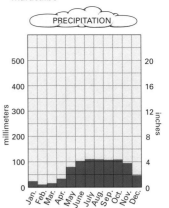

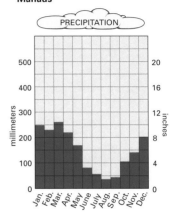

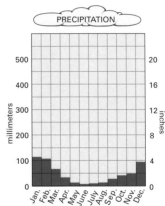

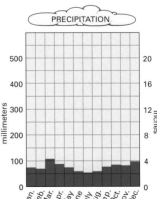

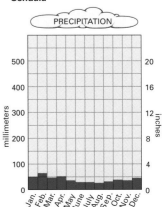

ENVIRONMENTAL ISSUES

The cutting down of the world's largest rain forest in the Amazon basin, together with the disappearance of the world's richest plant and animal life, has become a symbol of human misuse of the planet. Brazil lost 37 million acres of forest between 1988 and 1997. Deforestation also threatens the Amerindians who live there. Nearly 100 groups of Amerindians have been wiped out in the last 90 years.

Soil erosion is severe in many areas, especially the Andes, while heavy industrial and urban pollution and poor conditions of sanitation exist in and around the biggest cities. Economic development and improvements in living conditions have been made a high priority, but the impact on the environment has been great.

POPULATION AND WEALTH

	Highest	Middle	Lowest
Population	171,853,126 (Brazil)	14,973,843 (Chile)	431,156 (Suriname)
Population increase (annual growth rate, 1990–95)	2.6% (Paraguay)	1.4% (Chile)	0.7% (Uruguay)
Energy use (oil equivalent in lbs/year per person)	5,569 (Venezuela)	2,317 (Brazil)	1,206 (Bolivia)
Purchasing power parity (Int$/per person)	$12,273 (Chile)	$6,475 (Brazil)	$2,881 (Bolivia)

ENVIRONMENTAL INDICATORS

	Highest	Middle	Lowest
CO_2 emissions ('000 tons/ year)	249,196 (Brazil)	67,524 (Colombia)	934 (Ecuador)
Car ownership (% of population)	19% (Argentina)	8% (Paraguay)	4% (Bolivia)
Protected territory including marine areas	61% (Venezuela)	19% (Chile)	0.3% (Guyana)
Forests as a % of original forest	97% (Guyana)	66% (Ecuador)	41% (Chile)
Artificial fertilizer use (lbs/acre/year)	174 (Chile)	103 (Colombia)	4.1 (Bolivia)
Access to safe drinking water (% population; rural/urban)	85/96% (Guyana)	49/80% (Ecuador)	6/70% (Paraguay)

MAJOR ENVIRONMENTAL ISSUES AND SOURCES

Air pollution: high (urban); greenhouse gas emissions
River pollution: medium; *sources*: agriculture, sewage
Land degradation: *types*: soil erosion, deforestation, habitat destruction; *causes*: agriculture, industry, population pressure
Resource issues: fuelwood shortage; inadequate drinking water and sanitation; contamination of drinking water; land use competition
Population issues: population explosion; urban overcrowding; inadequate health facilities
Major events: Cubatão, Brazil (1984), accident in petroleum refining facility; ruptured pipeline, Iguaçu River, Brazil (2000); oil tanker spill threatens Galápagos Islands (2001)

ENVIRONMENTAL ISSUES

Besides deforestation, South America also suffers soil erosion in upland areas, desertification, urban and industrial pollution, and land degradation caused by mining and the building of dams.

Key environmental issues

- • major town or city
- ◕ polluted town or city
- ◖ major pollution event
- polluted river
- remaining tropical rainforest
- area of deforestation

area at risk of desertification
- very high
- high
- moderate

POPULATION

South America's population of 76 million in 1930 had risen to 110 million by 1950, and by 2000 had grown to 350 million, more than a fourfold increase. The population explosion is still continuing at about 2 percent a year, making South America's population one of the fastest growing in the world.

City populations have increased rapidly as people have moved away from the countryside. Many cities have elegant districts for the rich elite, and vast shanty towns where the poor live.

For vast numbers of urban dwellers, life is hard. Incomes and standards of living declined throughout the 1980s. The majority now live in overcrowded housing with poor access to services such as water, sanitation, and power. In Venezuela, new city dwellers have built on land they have occupied illegally.

POPULATION

Total population of region		343.1 million	
	Brazil	**Colombia**	**Bolivia**
Population density (persons per sq mi)	46.6	104.1	18.6
Population change (average annual percent 1990–95)			
Urban	+2.04	+2.46	+3.32
Rural	−1.58	+0.30	+0.78
Population growth (1995–2000)	1.2%	1.7%	2.3%

URBAN POPULATION

As percentage of total population (1990)	78%	72%	60%

TEN LARGEST CITIES

	Country	Population
Buenos Aires †	Argentina	11,624,000
São Paulo	Brazil	9,921,200
Lima †	Peru	7,451,900
Bogotá †	Colombia	6,540,400
Rio de Janeiro	Brazil	5,939,500
Santiago †	Chile	4,939,000
Salvador	Brazil	2,489,300
Belo Horizonte	Brazil	2,268,500
Fortaleza	Brazil	2,184,100
Cali	Colombia	2,161,000

† denotes capital city
City population figures are for the city proper.

POPULATION

The distribution of South America's population is very uneven. Large areas of forest, mountains, and desert are thinly populated, while some coastal areas are overcrowded.

Population density

urban agglomeration
(National capital is underlined)

- ■ over 10,000,000
- ◆ 5,000,000–10,000,000
- ■ 1,000,000–4,999,999
- ● 500,000–999,999
- × national capital less than 500,000

persons per square mi	persons per square km
520	200
260	100
130	50
26	10
2.6	1

INDUSTRY

Apart from Guyana, the least developed country on the continent, economists classify South American countries as middle-income developing nations. But Argentina and Brazil both have massive industries and are likely to become high-income economies in the twenty-first century. Argentina's factories process food (especially meat), refine oil, produce chemicals, and make electrical equipment and vehicles. Brazil also produces vehicles, as well as aircraft, cement, chemicals, machinery, textiles, foods, and pharmaceuticals. In most other countries, industry is dominated by mining. Chile is the world's leading copper producer. Other minerals include gold and nitrates. Many minerals are exported as raw materials.

INDUSTRIAL OUTPUT (US$ billion)

	Brazil	Colombia	Bolivia
	247	19	n/a

INDUSTRIAL GROWTH RATE

	4.5%	−1.2%	4%

INDUSTRIAL WORKERS (% of total labor force)

Mining	(1993) n/a	(1980) 0.6%	(1992) 2.1%
Manufacturing	13.4%	13.4%	8.8%
Construction	6.0%	2.9%	5.1%

MAJOR PRODUCTS (figures in parentheses are percentages of total world production)

BRAZIL	Output 1970	1996	Change %
Oil (mil barrels)	8	40	400%
Iron ore (mil m.t.)	20	121 (11.9)	505%
Bauxite (mil m.t.)	40	1,021 (9.1)	2,452.5%
Copper ('000 m.t.)	19	219	1,052.63%
Tin ('000 m.t.)	3.5	15 (7.5)	328.57%
Silver (m.t.)	11	170	1,445.45%
Gold (m.t.)	11	67	1,906.43%

Manufactures

Cement ('000 m.t.)	9,002	28,224	213.53%
Steel ('000 m.t.)	5,390	25,932 (9)	364.42%
Commercial vehicles ('000)	236	960 (8.9)	306.78%
Tires ('000)	7,847	30,720 (3.4)	291.48%
Rubber (synthetic – '000 m.t.)	96	295 (3.6)	207%

INDUSTRY

South America's many rich resources include bauxite in Suriname, copper in Chile, tin in Bolivia, and oil in Venezuela. Argentina was the first country in the region to set up large manufacturing industries.

Resources and industry

- ◆ industrial center
- ○ port
- ● other town
- —— major road
- —— major railroad

mineral resources and fossil fuels
- ▪ iron and other ferroalloy metal ores
- ● other metal ores
- ■ nonmetallic minerals

- bauxite
- coal
- copper
- gold
- iron ore
- oil
- silver
- tin

AGRICULTURE

Agriculture employs about one-fourth of
the workforce, and the region produces
a wide range of farm products.
Argentina's Pampas is one of the
world's major cereal-growing zones. The
largest cereal crop is that of corn, the
only cereal native to the region. It is the
staple crop, and contains up to 15
percent protein. Tropical crops, such as
bananas and sugarcane, grow in the
north, though in some areas farmers
find it more profitable to grow plants for
the illegal drug trade. Brazil and
Colombia are two of the principal
producers of coffee beans. Raising cattle
is the major activity in Brazil and
Argentina, while llamas are raised in
the high altitudes of the Peruvian
Andes. Fishing and forestry are other
major industries.

LAND

Total area 6,874,600 sq mi (17,084,526 sq km)

Cropland	Pasture	Forest/Woodland
6%	28%	48%
(417,650 sq mi)	(1,959,911 sq mi)	(3,341,716 sq mi)

FARMERS	Highest	Middle	Lowest
Agriculture as % of GDP	36% (Guyana)	12% (Ecuador)	4% (Venezuela)
% of workforce	45% (Paraguay)	30% (Col., Ecuador)	13% (Uruguay)

MAJOR CROPS: Agricultural products Fruit: lemons, grapes, bananas; potatoes; soya; sugarcane; corn, wheat, rice; peanuts; beef, pork, poultry; dairy products; tea, coffee; cotton; tobacco; sorghum; manioc; timber and forest products

Total cropland ('000 acres)	161,356 (Brazil)	10,947 (Colombia)	166 (Suriname)
Cropland (acre) per 1000 people	1,885 (Argentina)	986 (Brazil)	274 (Colombia)
Irrigated land as % of cropland	90% (Suriname)	24% (Colombia)	3% (Paraguay)
Number of tractors	805,000 (Brazil)	280,000 (Argentina)	1,330 (Suriname)
Average cereal crop (lbs/acre)	3,294 (Guyana)	2,033 (Brazil)	1,317 (Bolivia)
Cereal production ('000 tons)	44,725 (Brazil)	3,378 (Colombia)	221 (Suriname)
Change since 1986/88	8%	−1%	−21%

LIVESTOCK & FISHERIES

Meat production ('000 tons)	12,184 (Brazil)	1,325 (Colombia)	6 (Suriname)
Change since 1986/88	124%	59%	−66%
Marine fish catch ('000 tons)	8,676 (Peru)	115 (Uruguay)	365 (Guyana)
Change since 1986/88	85%	−15%	9%

FOOD SECURITY

Food aid as % of total imports	40% (Guyana)	26% (Suriname)	n/a
Daily kcal/person	3,093 (Argentina)	2,597 (Colombia)	2,174 (Bolivia)

AGRICULTURE

Only about one-third of South
America is used for
agriculture, including simple
subsistence farming and high-
technology plantations. Large
areas are used for grazing.

Agricultural zones

- arable
- fruit and vegetables
- pasture
- rough grazing
- woods and forest
- nonagricultural land
- ▲ mountain peak (ft)

NORDIC COUNTRIES

The Nordic countries include Norway, Sweden, Denmark, Finland, and Iceland. Glacial erosion has shaped the land, sculpting rugged mountain scenery, deep fjords, and many ice-scoured basins that now contain lakes.

Iceland has icecaps and volcanoes. Because it straddles the Atlantic ridge, new crustal rock is being formed in Iceland as the plates on either side of the ridge slowly move apart.

Except for Finnish and Lapp, the Nordic peoples speak closely related languages. Their historic Viking traditions have given them a distinctive personality and sense of adventure.

Natural resources, including North Sea oil and hydroelectric power supplies in Norway, iron ore in Sweden, and fisheries and forests, support the economies of the Nordic countries. Farming is important in the south.

The Nordic countries occupy the northwestern corner of Europe. They include various islands. The Faeroe Islands and Greenland are Danish, the Jan Mayen Islands, Bear Island, and Svalbard are Norwegian, and the Åland Islands in the Baltic are Finnish.

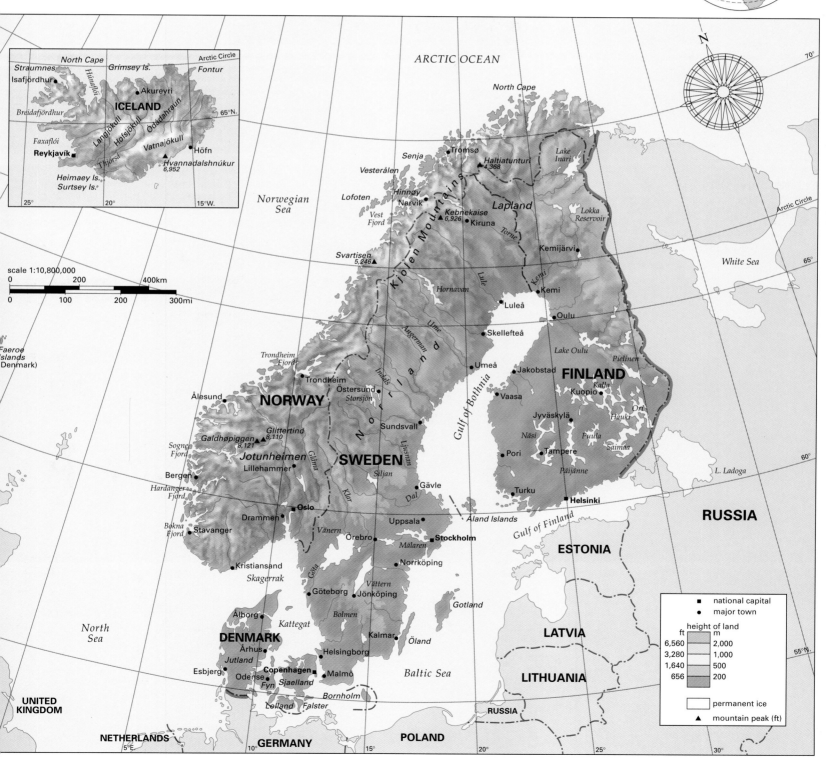

THE POLITICAL AND CULTURAL WORLD

The modern Nordic states began to evolve in the early nineteenth century. Norway became an independent country in 1905, when it broke away from its union with Sweden. In 1944 Iceland broke away from Denmark, which had lost Schleswig and Holstein in a war with Prussia in 1864. Finland declared its independence from Russia in 1917, though it lost land to the Soviet Union in 1944.

Because of their cultural affinity, the Nordic countries collaborate through the Nordic Council of Ministers. Established in 1971, it provides funds for joint institutions. The related Nordic Council is an advisory body.

COUNTRIES IN THE REGION

Denmark, Finland, Iceland, Norway, Sweden

Island territories Åland Islands (Finland); Faeroe Islands (Denmark); Jan Mayen, Svalbard Islands (Norway)
Territories outside region Greenland (Denmark)

Norway has a territorial claim in Antarctica.

LANGUAGE

Countries with one official language (Danish) Denmark; (Icelandic) Iceland; (Norwegian) Norway; (Swedish) Sweden
Country with two official languages (Finnish, Swedish) Finland

Faeroese is recognized with Danish as an official language in the Faeroe Islands.

RELIGION

Denmark Protestant (95%), nonreligious and atheist (3%)
Finland Protestant (92%), nonreligious and atheist (5%), Eastern Orthodox (1%)
Iceland Protestant (96%), nonreligious and atheist (2%), Roman Catholic (1%)
Norway Protestant (98%), nonreligious and atheist (1%)
Sweden Protestant (68%), nonreligious and atheist (28%), Eastern Orthodox (1%)

STYLES OF GOVERNMENT

Republics Finland, Iceland
Monarchies Denmark, Norway, Sweden
Multiparty states Denmark, Finland, Iceland, Norway, Sweden
One-chamber assembly Denmark, Finland, Norway, Sweden
Two-chamber assembly Iceland

MEMBERSHIP OF INTERNATIONAL ORGANIZATIONS

Council of Europe Denmark, Iceland, Norway, Sweden
European Union (EU) Denmark, Finland, Sweden
European Free Trade Association (EFTA) Iceland, Norway
North Atlantic Treaty Organization (NATO) Denmark, Iceland, Norway
Nordic Council Denmark, Finland, Iceland, Norway, Sweden
Organization for Economic Cooperation and Development (OECD) Denmark, Finland, Iceland, Norway, Sweden

Iceland has no military forces and is not a member of NATO Military Command.

ECONOMIC INDICATORS

	Denmark	Norway	Sweden
GDP (US$ billions)	163	153.4	227.8
GNP per capita (US$)	22,740	23,940	19,030
Annual rate of growth of GDP, 1990–1997	2.5%	4.0%	0.9%
Manufacturing as % of GDP	20.2%	12.6%	24.3%
Central government spending as % of GNP	59.6%	45.8%	63.8%
Merchandise exports (US$ billions)	48.5	48.8	83.1
Merchandise imports (US$ billions)	43.0	37.7	65.2
Aid given as % of GNP	1.04%	0.85%	0.84%

WELFARE INDICATORS

	Denmark	Norway	Sweden
Infant mortality rate (per 1,000 live births)			
1965	19	17	13
2000	7	5	5
Daily food supply available (calories per capita)	3,704	3,274	2,117
Population per physician (1996)	345	357	323
Teacher-pupil ratio (primary school, 1995)	1 : 11	1 : 12	1 : 13

Iceland
Area 39,769 sq mi (103,000 sq km)
Population 276,365
Currency 1 Icelandic króna (IsK) = 100 aurar

■ national capital
● other town

Norway
Area 125,182 sq mi (324,220 sq km)
Population 4,481,162
Currency 1 Norwegian krone (NKr) = 100 øre

Sweden
Area 173,732 sq mi (449,964 sq km)
Population 8,873,052
Currency 1 Swedish krona (SKr) = 100 öre

Finland
Area 130,128 sq mi (337,030 sq km)
Population 5,167,486
Currency 1 markka (Fmk) = 100 pennia
Euro (€) also in use
€ = 100 cents

Denmark
Area 16,639 sq mi (43,094 sq km)
Population 5,336,394
Currency 1 Danish krone (DKr) = 100 øre

Denmark, Norway, and Sweden are constitutional monarchies, whose governments are led by elected prime ministers and cabinets. The monarchs have little real power. Finland and Iceland are democratic republics. Finland's president is the country's chief executive. In Iceland, the president's power is limited.

HABITATS

The glaciated mountain core of Norway and Sweden lies between the indented west coast and the hilly Norrland region. There is tundra in Lapland. Fertile lowland plains are situated in southern Finland, Sweden, and Denmark. Iceland is mostly barren.

LAND

Area   485,450 sq mi (1,257,308 sq km)
Highest point   Galdhøpiggen, 8,121 ft (2,475 m)
Lowest point   sea level
Major features   islands, fjords, mountains and high plateau in west, lakelands east and west of Gulf of Bothnia, lowlands in south

WATER

Longest river   Göta–Klar, 477 mi (720 km)
Largest basin   Kemi, 20,000 sq mi (51,000 sq km)
Highest average flow   Kemi, 19,000 cu ft/sec (534 cu m/sec)
Largest lake   Vänern, 2,080 sq mi (5,390 sq km)

NOTABLE THREATENED SPECIES

Mammals   Gray wolf (Canis lupus), Wolverine (Gulo gulo), Polar bear (Ursus maritimus), Harbor propoise (Phocoena phocoena), Northern bottlenose whale (Hyperoodon ampullatus), Fin whale (Balaenoptera physalus), Blue whale (Balaenoptera musculus), Bowhead whale (Balaeno mysticetus), Humpback whale (Megaptera novangliae), narwhal (Monodon monoceros)
Birds   Lesser white-fronted goose (Anser erythropus), Red kite (Milvus migrans), White-tailed sea eagle (Haliaeetus albicilla), Corncrake (Crex crex)
Others   Hermit beetle (Osmoderma eremita), Tree snail (Balea perversa), Large blue butterfly (Maculinea arion), Noble crayfish (Astacus astacus)
Plants   Braya linearis; Cephalanthera rubra; Gentianella uliginosa; Liparis loeselii; Najas flexilis; Oxytropis deflexa norvegica; Papaver lapponicum; Platanthera obtusata oligantha; Polemonium boreale; Potamogeton rutilus

CLIMATE

The climate of the coasts of Iceland and western Norway are moderated by the North Atlantic Current. The interior of Iceland has icecaps, while northern Sweden and Finland have subarctic climates. Southern Sweden has mild winters, and Norway, the greatest rainfall.

CLIMATE

	Temperature °F (°C)		Altitude
	January	July	ft (m)
Bergen	36 (2)	59 (15)	144 (44)
Oslo	23 (–5)	63 (17)	315 (96)
Stockholm	27 (–3)	64 (18)	36 (11)
Helsinki	19 (–7)	63 (17)	190 (58)
Reykjavik	32 (0)	52 (11)	413 (126)

	Precipitation in. (mm)		
	January	July	Year
Bergen	7.1 (179)	5.6 (141)	77.1 (1,958)
Oslo	1.9 (49)	3.3 (84)	29.1 (740)
Stockholm	1.7 (43)	2.4 (61)	21.9 (555)
Helsinki	1.9 (49)	2.7 (68)	25.2 (641)
Reykjavik	3.5 (90)	1.9 (48)	31.7 (805)

NATURAL HAZARDS

Cold, snow, glacier surges, volcanic eruptions in Iceland

ENVIRONMENTAL ISSUES

The main environmental issues in the Nordic countries are pollution of the Baltic Sea and acid rain. Clouds containing acid raindrops drift over from Germany, Poland, and the former Soviet Union. Acid rain has poisoned many lakes, rivers, and forests.

ENVIRONMENTAL INDICATORS

	Highest	Middle	Lowest
CO₂ emissions ('000 tons/year)	72,452 (Norway)	44,591 (Sweden)	1,803 (Iceland)
Car ownership (% of population)	49% (Iceland)	42% (Finland)	37% (Denmark)
Protected territory, including marine areas	32% (Denmark)	10% (Iceland)	6% (Norway)
Forests as a % of original forest	90% (Norway)	86% (Sweden)	1% (Denmark)
Artificial fertilizer use (lbs/acre/year)	2,836 (Iceland)	180 (Norway)	93 (Sweden)
Access to safe drinking water (% population; rural/urban)	100/100% (Sweden)	100/100% (Iceland)	100/100% (Finland)

MAJOR ENVIRONMENTAL PROBLEMS AND SOURCES

Air pollution: acid rain prevalent
River/lake pollution: high; sources: acid deposition
Marine/coastal pollution: medium; sources: industry, agriculture; fish farming
Land pollution: local; sources: industrial; acid deposition
Waste disposal problems: domestic; industrial
Major events: Aker River, Oslo (1980), acid leak from factory; Ålesund (1992), oil spill from tanker Arisan

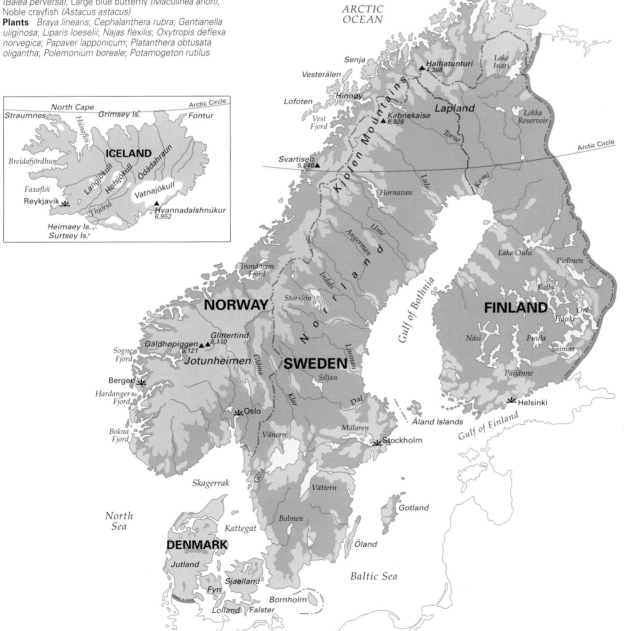

HABITATS

Physical zones

- ice and snow
- mountains/barren land
- forest
- grassland

▲ mountain peak (ft)
☼ climate station

During the last ice age, which ended only about 10,000 years ago, ice sheets advanced and retreated over the region. They left their mark in the many glacial features found in the highlands and lowlands.

ENVIRONMENTAL ISSUES

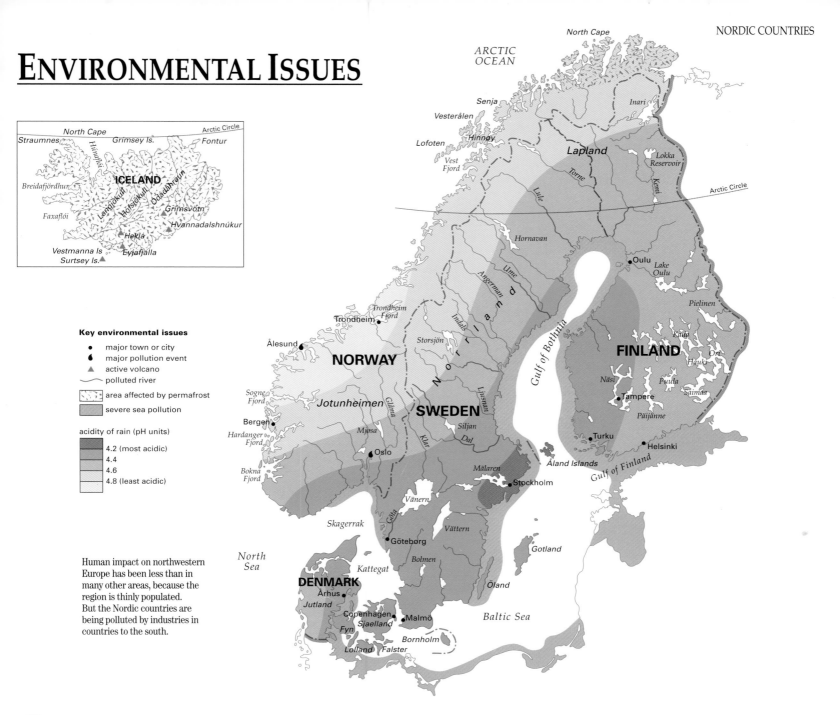

North Cape

ARCTIC OCEAN

ICELAND

North Cape · *Grimsey Is.* · *Fontur*
Straumnes · *Hunaflói*
Arctic Circle
Breidafjördhun
Langjökull · *Hofsjökull* · *Odádahraun*
Faxaflói
Grimsvötn
Hvannadalshnúkur
Hekla
Vestmanna Is · *Eyjafjalla*
Surtsey Is.

Senja
Vesterålen
Lofoten · *Hinnøy*
Vest Fjord
Lapland
Inari
Lokka Reservoir
Torne
Lule
Arctic Circle
Kemi

Key environmental issues

- • major town or city
- ◖ major pollution event
- ▲ active volcano
- ⌇ polluted river
- ⬚ area affected by permafrost
- ▨ severe sea pollution

acidity of rain (pH units)

- ▨ 4.2 (most acidic)
- ▨ 4.4
- ▨ 4.6
- ▨ 4.8 (least acidic)

Hornavan
Ume
Angerman
Oulu · *Lake Oulu*
Pielinen
FINLAND
Kalla
Ort
Hauk
Näsi · *Puula* · *Saimaa*
Tampere
Päijänne
Turku
Helsinki

Trondheim Fjord
Trondheim
Ålesund
Storsjön
NORWAY
Indals
Ljusnan
Sogne Fjord
Jotunheimen
Gloma
Bergen
Mjøsa
SWEDEN
Siljan
Hardanger Fjord
Klar
Dal
Oslo
Gulf of Bothnia
Åland Islands
Gulf of Finland
Bokna Fjord
Mälaren
Stockholm
Vänern
Vättern
Göteborg
Gotland
North Sea
Skagerrak
Bolmen
Öland
Kattegat
DENMARK
Århus
Jutland
Baltic Sea
Copenhagen
Sjaelland · *Malmö*
Fyn
Bornholm
Lolland *Falster*

Human impact on northwestern Europe has been less than in many other areas, because the region is thinly populated. But the Nordic countries are being polluted by industries in countries to the south.

CLIMATE

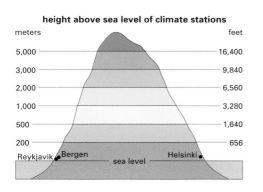

height above sea level of climate stations

meters		feet
5,000		16,400
3,000		9,840
2,000		6,560
1,000		3,280
500		1,640
200		656

Reykjavik · Bergen · Helsinki
sea level

Reykjavik
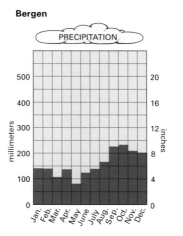
PRECIPITATION

Bergen
PRECIPITATION

Helsinki
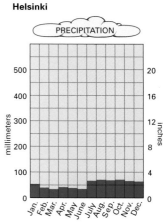
PRECIPITATION

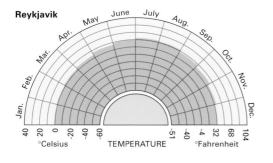

Reykjavik · May June July Aug. · TEMPERATURE · °Celsius °Fahrenheit

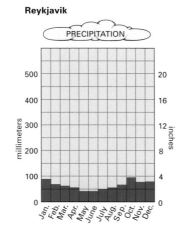

Bergen · May June July Aug. · TEMPERATURE · °Celsius °Fahrenheit

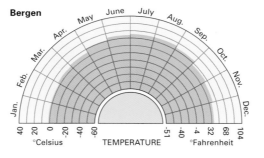

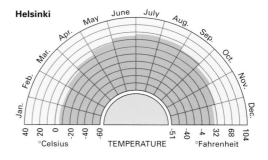

Helsinki · May June July Aug. · TEMPERATURE · °Celsius °Fahrenheit

POPULATION

The rugged, mostly forested terrain, combined with the hostile climate, has restricted the population of most Nordic countries to coastal areas except in the far south. Only in Denmark is the population spread evenly, based on a network of farming villages.

POPULATION

Total population of region (millions)			24.1
	Denmark	**Norway**	**Sweden**
Population density (persons per sq mi)	326.1	37.3	55.9
Population change (1995–2000)			
Urban	+0.32%	+0.99%	+0.30%
Rural	−0.07%	−0.86%	−0.02%

URBAN POPULATION

As percentage of total population			
1995	85%	74%	83%

TEN LARGEST CITIES

	Country	Population
Stockholm †	Sweden	1,226,200
Copenhagen †	Denmark	1,086,000
Oslo †	Norway	778,200
Helsinki †	Finland	566,800
Göteborg	Sweden	500,800
Malmö	Sweden	242,700
Espoo	Finland	219,400
Århus	Denmark	218,100
Bergen	Norway	200,200
Tampere	Finland	197,200

† denotes capital city

City population figures are for the city proper.

POPULATION

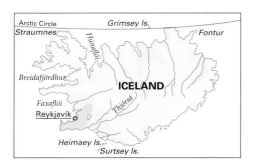

Population density

urban agglomeration
(National capital is underlined)

- ■ 1,000,000–5,000,000
- ● 500,000–999,999
- ◉ 250,000–499,999
- ○ 100,000–249 999

persons per square mi	persons per square km
260	100
130	50
26	10
2.6	1

Most people live in well-planned cities and towns. With green parks, woodlands, and often lakes and waterways, the towns and cities are pleasant places to live.

INDUSTRY

The region's natural resources include offshore oil and gas fields belonging to Denmark and Norway, together with metal ores in Norway and Sweden. Sweden has some of the world's richest iron ore deposits in Lapland. The region's leading industry is papermaking.

TOTAL INDUSTRIAL OUTPUT (US$ billion)

Denmark	Norway	Sweden
42 (1995)	n/a	73 (1995)

INDUSTRIAL WORKERS (millions)
(figures in parentheses are percentages of total labor force)

	Mining	Manufacturing	Construction
Denmark	0.004 (0.1%)	0.52 (18.6%)	0.16 (5.9%)
Norway	0.023 (1.1%)	0.30 (14.1%)	0.13 (5.8%)
Sweden	0.008 (0.2%)	0.76 (17.6%)	0.033 (0.8%)

MAJOR PRODUCTS – Norway

Energy and minerals	Output	
	1970	1995
Petroleum products (mil m.t.)	5.5	12
Oil (crude, mil m.t.)	26	156
Natural gas ('000 terajoules)	0	1,541
Iron ore (mil m.t.)	2.6	1
Copper (mil m.t.)	26	35
Zinc ('000 m.t.)	62	146
Aluminum ('000 m.t.)	527	913
Steel ('000 m.t.)	869	504

AGRICULTURE

Most of the productive arable land is in Denmark and southern Sweden. Mixed farming is important, especially dairy farming, though livestock are found extensively in the south. To the north, farming is combined with the industries of forestry and fishing.

LAND
Total area 485,450 sq mi (1,257,308 sq km)

Cropland	Pasture	Forest/Woodland
7% (36,059 sq mi)	7% (35,426 sq mi)	52% (250,494 sq mi)

MAJOR CROPS: Agricultural products Grain; potatoes; turnips; rapeseed; beets; beef; sheep; dairy products; fish

Total cropland ('000 acres)	6,916 (Sweden)	5,261 (Finland)	14.8 (Iceland)
Cropland (acres) per 1,000 people	1,114 (Denmark)	781 (Sweden)	54 (Iceland)
Irrigated land as % of cropland	20% (Denmark)	4% (Sweden)	0% (Iceland)
Number of tractors	194,750 (Finland)	165,000 (Sweden)	10,519 (Iceland)
Average cereal crop (lbs/acre)	5,070 (Denmark)	3,893 (Sweden)	2,797 (Finland)
Cereal production ('000 tons)	9,351 (Denmark)	5,893 (Sweden)	1,346 (Norway)
Change since 1986/88	21%	12%	17%

INDUSTRY

The exploitation of their forests and mineral resources has enabled the Nordic countries to become a major trading region. It accounts for more than 4.5 percent of world exports.

Resources and industry

- ◆ industrial center
- ○ port
- • other town
- — major road
- — major railroad

mineral resources and fossil fuels

- ◆ iron and other ferroalloy metal ores
- • other metal ores
- ■ nonmetallic minerals

coal
copper
iron ore
nickel

Map labels (Industry main map):

North Cape, ARCTIC OCEAN, Kirkenes, Lake Inari, Senja, Vesterålen, Lofoten, Hinnøy, Narvik, Vest Fjord, Kiruna, Torne, Lokka Reservoir, Kemi, Arctic Circle, Gällivare, Törnio, Kemi, Luleå, Lake Oulu, Hornavan, Angerman, Ume, Pielinen, Umeå, Kokkola, Kati, Ort, Hauki, Trondheim Fjord, Trondheim, Storsjön, Vaasa, FINLAND, Ålesund, NORWAY, SWEDEN, Näsi, Puula, Saimaa, Sogne Fjord, Indals, Pori, Tampere, Päijänne, Bergen, Mjøsa, Siljan, Dal, Gävle, Turku, Helsinki, Hardanger Fjord, Klar, Mälaren, Åland Islands, Gulf of Finland, ugesund, Bokna Fjord, Oslo, Vänern, Stockholm, Stavanger, Ljusnan, Norrköping, Kristiansand, Vättern, Gotland, Skagerrak, Trollhättan, Skagen, Göteborg, Bolmen, Öland, North Sea, DENMARK, Kattegat, Århus, Jutland, Helsingborg, Esbjerg, Copenhagen, Fyn, Sjaelland, Malmö, Baltic Sea, Bornholm, Lolland, Falster, Gulf of Bothnia

Iceland inset (Industry):

Grímsey Is., Arctic Circle, Straumnes, Siglufjördhur, Fontur, Hólmavík, Akureyri, Húsavík, Breidafjördhur, Seydisfjördhur, ICELAND, Ólafsvík, Faxaflói, Djúpivogur, Thjórsá, Reykjavík, Keflavík, Hafnarfjördhur, Heimaey Is., Surtsey Is., Vestmannaeyjar

AGRICULTURE

Iceland inset (Agriculture):

North Cape, Grímsey Is., Arctic Circle, Straumnes, Fontur, Húnaflói, Breidafjördhur, Langjökull, ICELAND, Hofsjökull, Ödádahraun, Faxaflói, Vatnajökull, Thjórsá, Hvannadalshnúkur 6,952, Heimaey Is., Surtsey Is.

Agricultural zones

- arable
- fruit and vegetables
- rough grazing
- woods and forest with some arable
- woods and forest with some grazing
- nonagricultural land
- ▲ mountain peak (ft)

To counter the largely unfavorable conditions, Nordic farmers have developed intensive agricultural methods. Denmark has better conditions and is one of the world's most successful farming countries.

Map labels (Agriculture main map):

North Cape, ARCTIC OCEAN, Senja, Vesterålen, Hinnøy, Lofoten, Vest Fjord, Haltiatunturi 4,368, Inari, Lapland, Kebnekaise 6,926, Lokka Reservoir, Kjølen Mountains, Torne, Arctic Circle, Svartisen 5,246, Lule, Kemi, Hornavan, Ume, Angerman, Lake Oulu, Pielinen, Trondheim Fjord, Storsjön, NORWAY, Indals, FINLAND, Galdhøpiggen 8,121, Glittertind 8,110, Jotunheimen, SWEDEN, Kati, Sogne Fjord, Siljan, Hauki, Hardanger Fjord, Mjøsa, Glama, Näsi, Puula, Saimaa, Bokna Fjord, Klar, Dal, Påijänne, Vänern, Mälaren, Åland, Gulf of Finland, Skagerrak, Göta, Vättern, Gotland, North Sea, Kattegat, Öland, DENMARK, Jutland, Bolmen, Fyn, Sjaelland, Bornholm, Lolland, Falster, Baltic Sea, Gulf of Bothnia, Ljusnan, Norrland

BRITISH ISLES

The British Isles contain a great variety of geology and a wide range of highland and lowland scenery that is unusual in such a small area. The climate is mild, mainly because of the influence of the North Atlantic Current, the northern extension of the warm Gulf Stream. The weather is also distinguished by its variability, caused by the depressions that regularly cross the islands from west to east.

Celts settled in the region about 450 B.C. But the population also owes its ancestry to invaders, such as the Romans, Vikings, and Normans. There has recently been further diversification with the arrival of immigrants from Africa, Asia, and the West Indies.

The United Kingdom once ruled the largest empire in history. Though the imperial era has ended, the country remains a world power.

The British Isles consists of two large islands and more than 5,000 smaller ones, rising from the continental shelf off the coast of northwest Europe. It was cut off from the mainland about 7,500 years ago when melting ice sheets filled the North Sea and English Channel.

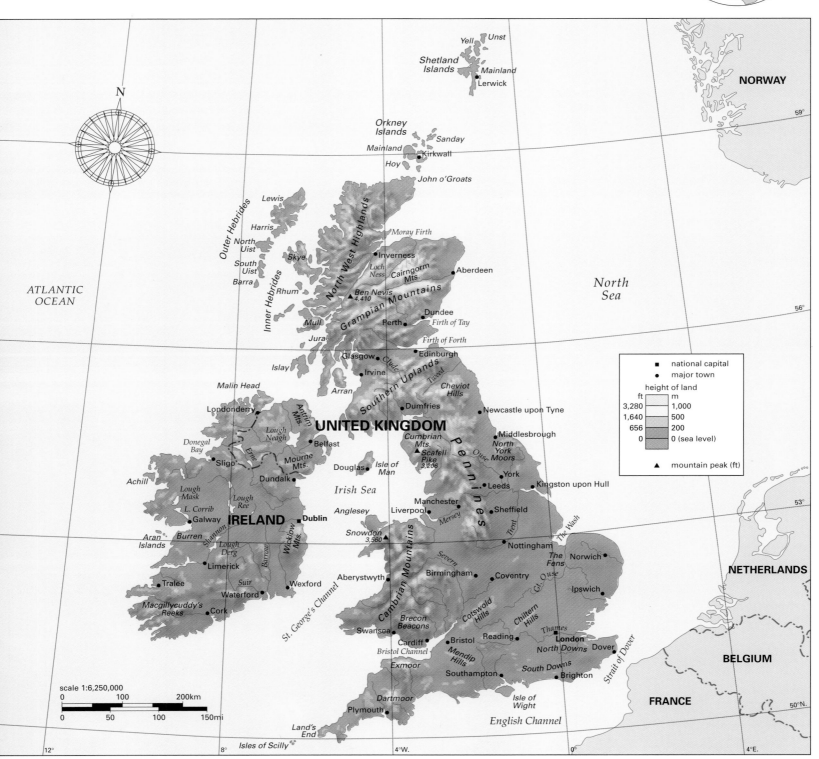

scale 1:6,250,000

| | national capital |
| | major town |

height of land

ft	m
3,280	1,000
1,640	500
656	200
0	0 (sea level)

▲ mountain peak (ft)

THE POLITICAL AND CULTURAL WORLD

The United Kingdom of Great Britain and Northern Ireland is often called Britain. Great Britain consists of England; Wales, which was absorbed by England in 1277; and Scotland, which was formally united with England under the Act of Union of 1707.

Ireland was united with Great Britain in 1801, but it became independent in 1921, with the exception of the six counties of Northern Ireland, which stayed in the United Kingdom.

The rest of Ireland is now a republic, while Britain is a constitutional monarchy. The Channel Islands and the Isle of Man are self-governing territories under the British Crown.

COUNTRIES IN THE REGION

Ireland, United Kingdom

Island territories Channel Islands, Isle of Man (U.K.)
Territories outside the region Anguilla, Ascension, Bermuda, British Indian Ocean Territory, British Virgin Islands, Cayman Islands, Falkland Islands, Gibraltar, Montserrat, Pitcairn Island, St. Helena, South Georgia, South Sandwich Islands, Tristan de Cunha, Turks and Caicos Islands (U.K.)

RELIGION

Ireland Roman Catholic (93.1%), Anglican (2.8%), Protestant (0.4%), others (3.7%)
United Kingdom Anglican (56.8%), Roman Catholic (13.1%), Protestant (12.7%), nonreligious (8.8%), Muslim (1.4%), Jewish (0.8%), Hindu (0.7%), Sikh (0.4%)

LANGUAGE

Country with one official language (English) U.K.
Country with two official languages (English, Irish) Ireland

Local minority languages are Gaelic, Irish, and Welsh. Significant immigrant languages include Bengali, Chinese, Greek, Gujarati, Italian, Polish, and Punjabi.

STYLES OF GOVERNMENT

Republic Ireland
Monarchy United Kingdom
Multiparty states Ireland, U.K.
Two-chamber assembly Ireland, U.K.

MEMBERSHIP OF INTERNATIONAL ORGANIZATIONS

Council of Europe Ireland, U.K.
Colombo Plan U.K.
European Union (EU) Ireland, U.K.
North Atlantic Treaty Organization (NATO) U.K.
Organization for Economic Cooperation and Development (OECD) Ireland, U.K.

ECONOMIC INDICATORS

	Ireland	United Kingdom
GDP (US$ billions)	72.7	1,278.4
GNP per capita (US$)	16,740	20,520
Annual rate of growth of GDP, 1988–1998	7.3%	1.7%
Manufacturing as % of GDP	n/a	19.9%
Central government spending as % of GNP	36.3%	41.4%
Merchandise exports (US$ billions)	45.5	259.0
Merchandise imports (US$ billions)	35.7	283.7
Aid given as % of GDP	0.3%	0.27%

WELFARE INDICATORS

	Ireland	United Kingdom
Infant mortality rate (per 1,000 live births)		
1965	25	20
1998	7	7
Daily food supply available (calories per capita, 1996)	3,636	3,237
Teacher–pupil ratio (primary school, 1995)	1 : 23.5	1 : 21.2

- ■ national capital
- ■ regional capital
- ● other town

Ireland
Area 27,135 sq mi (70,280 sq km)
Population 3,797,257
Capital Dublin
Currency 1 Irish pound (Ir$) = 100 new pence
Euro (€) also in use
€ = 100 cents

United Kingdom
Area 94,526 sq mi (244,820 sq km)
Population 59,511,464
Capital London
Currency 1 pound sterling (£) = 100 new pence

Regional loyalties are strong throughout the British Isles. Both Scotland and Wales have nationalist movements that have demanded a greater degree of home rule and local parliaments.

HABITATS

The scenery of the British Isles is varied. There are areas of rocky and barren uplands; low, fertile plains, mostly on coasts; and soft, rolling hills resulting from glaciation, with some forests, moors, and downland kept free from agricultural use.

LAND

Area   121,661 sq mi (315,100 sq km)
Highest point   Ben Nevis   4,410 ft (1,344 m)
Lowest point   Holme Fen, Great Ouse   –9 ft (–3 m)
Major features   mountains chiefly in northern and western areas, with lower-lying areas in east and south

WATER

Longest river   Shannon, 230 mi (370 km)
Largest basin   Severn, 8,000 sq mi (21,000 sq km)
Highest average flow   Shannon, 7,600 cu ft/sec (198 cu m/sec)
Largest lake   Lough Neagh, 150 sq mi (400 sq km)

NOTABLE THREATENED SPECIES

Mammals   Harbor porpoise (*Phocoena phocoena*)
Birds   Red kite (*Milvus migrans*), White-tailed sea eagle (*Haliaeetus albicilla* – reintroduced), Corncrake (*Crex crex*)
Others   Kerry slug (*Geomalachus maculosus*), Chequered skipper butterfly (*Carterocephalus palaemon*), Freshwater pearl mussel (*Margaritifera margaritifera*), Ladybird spider (*Eresus niger*)

BOTANIC GARDENS

National Botanic Gardens, Dublin (25,000 species); Oxford (10,000 species); Royal Botanic Gardens, Edinburgh (12,200 species); Royal Botanic Gardens, Kew (30,000 species)

CLIMATE

The British Isles has a mild, moist climate that is ever-changing because low pressure areas continually arrive from the Atlantic. It is windier in the west. More stable conditions occur when the British Isles comes under the influence of high pressure areas.

CLIMATE

	Temperature °F (°C)		Altitude
	January	July	ft (m)
Aberdeen	36 (2)	57 (14)	194 (59)
Dublin	41 (5)	59 (15)	266 (81)
Valentia	45 (7)	59 (15)	46 (14)
Kew	39 (4)	64 (18)	16 (5)
Plymouth	43 (6)	61 (16)	89 (27)

	Precipitation in. (mm)		
	January	July	Year
Aberdeen	3.0 (77)	3.6 (92)	33.0 (837)
Dublin	2.7 (67)	2.8 (70)	30 (762)
Valentia	6.5 (164)	4.2 (107)	55.0 (1,398)
Kew	2.1 (53)	2.2 (56)	23.4 (594)
Plymouth	4.1 (105)	2.8 (71)	39 (990)

NATURAL HAZARDS

Storms, floods

ENVIRONMENTAL ISSUES

Britain was the first nation to industrialize, and the rapid growth of mining, together with industries burning coal and oil, has caused much environmental damage. New development is currently threatening many habitats even in protected areas.

POPULATION AND WEALTH

	Ireland	U.K.
Population (millions)	3.797	59.511
Population increase (annual growth rate, 1990–95)	0.7%	0.2%
Energy use (oil equivalent in lbs/year per person)	7,529	8,585
Purchasing power parity (Int$/annum)	20,725	20,900

ENVIRONMENTAL INDICATORS

CO$_2$ emissions ('000 tons/year)	32,236	542,140
Car ownership (% of population)	29%	42%
Protected territory including marine areas	1%	20%
Forests as % of original forest	4%	6%
Artificial fertilizer use (lbs/acre/annum)	441	284
Access to safe drinking water (% of population, rural/urban)	100/100%	100/100%

MAJOR ENVIRONMENTAL PROBLEMS AND SOURCES

Air pollution: locally high, in particular urban; acid rain prevalent; high greenhouse gas emissions
River/lake pollution: local; *sources*: agriculture, sewage, acid deposition, industry
Marine/coastal pollution: medium; *sources*: industry, agriculture, sewage, oil, fish farming
Land pollution: local; *sources*: industrial, agricultural, urban/household
Waste disposal issues: domestic; industrial; nuclear
Major events: *Torrey Canyon* (1967), *Braer* (1993), *Sea Empress* (1996) oil tanker accidents; Camelford (1989), chemical accident; Mersey River (1989), oil spill
Resource issues: overfishing; loss of habitat

HABITATS

Generally the older highland regions are in the north and west. Younger, lower rocks, which produce more gentle landscapes of limestone and chalk ridges and clay vales, are found in the south and east.

Physical zones
- mountains/barren land
- forest
- grassland

▲ mountain peak (ft)
⚘ climate station

ENVIRONMENTAL ISSUES

Problems include river and sea pollution, nuclear waste dumping, air pollution in cities caused by the increasing numbers of vehicles, and acid rain caused by industry and power plants.

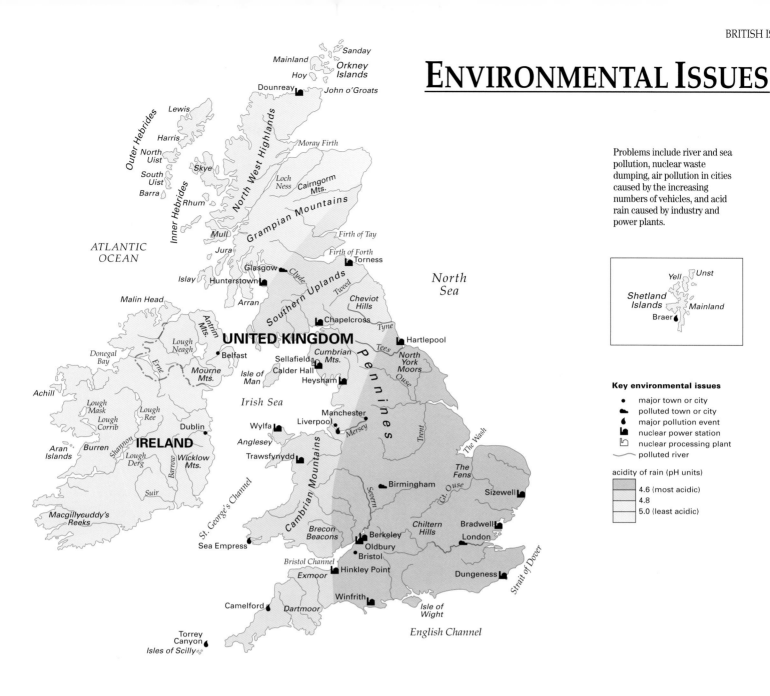

Key environmental issues

- • major town or city
- 🏭 polluted town or city
- 💧 major pollution event
- 🏭 nuclear power station
- 🏭 nuclear processing plant
- ∿ polluted river

acidity of rain (pH units)

▨	4.6 (most acidic)
▨	4.8
▨	5.0 (least acidic)

CLIMATE

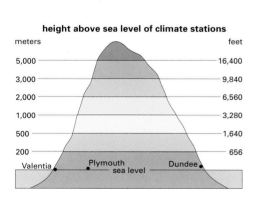

height above sea level of climate stations

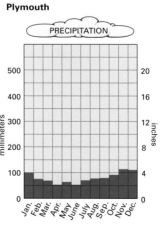

Valentia

PRECIPITATION

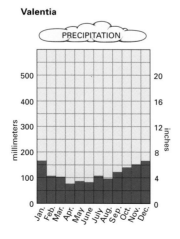

Plymouth

PRECIPITATION

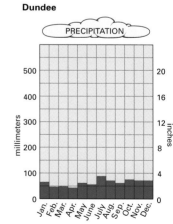

Dundee

PRECIPITATION

Valentia

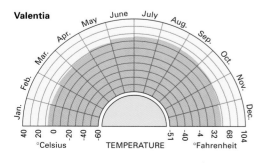

TEMPERATURE

Plymouth

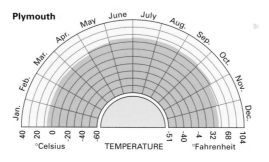

TEMPERATURE

Dundee

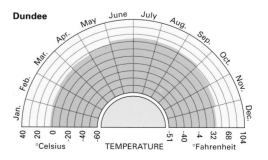

TEMPERATURE

POPULATION

Britain's population density is more than four times greater than the population density in Ireland. The chief centers of population are in England, central Scotland, and south Wales, mainly in the older industrial cities. Fewer people live in rural areas.

POPULATION

Total population of region (millions)		63.3
	U.K.	**Ireland**
	59,511,464	3,797,257
Population density (persons per sq mi)	632	135
Population change (average annual percent 1995–2000)		
Urban	+0.23%	+1.03%
Rural	−0.30%	+0.14%
Population growth rate	0.24%	0.38%

URBAN POPULATION

As percentage of total population (1995)	58%	89%

TEN LARGEST CITIES

	Country	Population
London †	United Kingdom	7,341,500
Birmingham	United Kingdom	988,200
Dublin †	Ireland	986,600
Glasgow	United Kingdom	610,700
Liverpool	United Kingdom	468,300
Sheffield	United Kingdom	422,900
Leeds	United Kingdom	420,900
Bristol	United Kingdom	409,400
Manchester	United Kingdom	395,300
Edinburgh	United Kingdom	382,600

† denotes capital city

City population figures are for the city proper.

INDUSTRY

Since the 1960s, the extraction of North Sea natural gas and oil have made Britain the world's fifth largest energy producer. Until recently, Ireland's main source of energy was peat, but offshore gas deposits are now being exploited. Britain has large coal deposits.

MAJOR PRODUCTS (figures in parentheses are percentages of total world production)

Energy and minerals	Output 1970	1995	Change since 1970
Coal (mil m.t.)	145	53	−63.4%
Oil (mil m.t.) (1996)	0.1	130	129,900.0%
Natural gas (1996)	434	3,187 (3.8%)	734.3%
Cement ('000 m.t.)	17,171	11,808	−31.2%
Zinc ('000 m.t.)	239	160	−33.1%

Manufactures			
Automobiles ('000)	1,641	1,532 (4.3%)	−6.6%
Commercial Vehicles ('000)	0	236	236%
Steel ('000 m.t.)	28,316	17,208	−39.2%
Synthetic rubber ('000 m.t.)	345	320 (3.2%)	−7.2%
Raw wool ('000 m.t.)	47	67 (2.6%)	143%

AGRICULTURE

Farming in both Britain and Ireland has become increasingly specialized since the countries joined the European Union. Arable farming is now concentrated in the drier eastern lowlands, with livestock farming in the wetter uplands.

LAND
Total area 121,661 sq mi (315,100 sq km)

Cropland	Pasture	Forest/Woodland
22%	51%	9%
(27,095 sq mi)	(61,581 sq mi)	(10,785 sq mi)

FARMERS

	U.K.	Ireland
Agriculture as % of GDP	2%	6%
% of workforce	1.1%	9%

MAJOR CROPS
Agricultural products: cereals; oilseed; potatoes and other vegetables; beef; sheep; poultry; dairy products; sugar beet; fish

Total cropland ('000 acres)	15,876	3,326
Cropland (acres) per 1,000 people	272	909
Irrigated land as percentage of cropland	2%	0%
Annual fertilizer use (lbs per acre of cropland)	284	441
Number of tractors	500,000	167,500
Percentage change since 1987	−4%	3%
Average cereal crop yields (lbs per acre)	5,691	5,559
Average production of cereals ('000 tons)	23,585	1,984
Percentage change since 1986–88	5%	−3%

LIVESTOCK AND FISHERIES

Average meat production ('000 tons)	3,658	981
Percentage change since 1986–88	14%	46%
Marine fish catch ('000 tons)	751.2	306.6
Percentage change since 1986–88	−4%	46%
Aquaculture production ('000 tons)	111.2	33

FOOD SECURITY

Average daily per capita calories (kilocalories)	3,276	3,565

POPULATION

About 200 years ago, most people in the region lived in small rural communities. Today, the United Kingdom is a highly urbanized country, though much of Wales, Scotland, and Northern Ireland remains very rural.

Population density

urban agglomeration
(National capital is underlined)

■	over 10,000,000
◆	5,000,000–10,000,000
■	1,000,000–4,999,999
●	500,000–999,999
◉	250,000–499,999

persons per square mi	persons per square km
520	200
260	100
130	50
26	10

INDUSTRY

Yell Unst
Shetland
Islands Mainland
Lerwick

Britain has a wide range of
mineral resources, though many
are expensive to extract. As a
result, many raw materials used
in industry are imported.

Resources and industry

- ◆ industrial center
- ○ port
- ● other town
- — major road
- — major railroad

mineral resources and fossil fuels
- ◆ iron and other ferroalloy metal ores
- ● other metal ores
- ● nonmetallic minerals
- coal
- iron ore

Orkney Islands
Mainland Sanday
Kirkwall
Hoy

Lewis
Outer Hebrides
Harris
North Uist
South Uist
Barra
Skye
Inner Hebrides
Rhum
Mull
Jura
Islay
Arran

Moray Firth
Inverness
Loch Ness
Peterhead
Aberdeen
Dundee
Firth of Tay
Firth of Forth
Grangemouth
Greenock
Glasgow
Edinburgh
Irvine
Clyde
Tweed

ATLANTIC OCEAN

North Sea

Malin Head
Londonderry
Lough Neagh
Belfast
Carlisle
Newcastle upon Tyne
Middlesbrough
Darlington

Donegal Bay
Sligo
Erne
Dundalk

Achill
Lough Mask
L. Corrib
Lough Ree
Galway
IRELAND
Dublin
Shannon
Lough Derg
Aran Islands
Limerick
Suir
Barrow
Wexford
Waterford
Cork

Isle of Man
Irish Sea
Anglesey
Holyhead
Blackpool
Liverpool
Manchester
Stoke on Trent
Shrewsbury
Aberystwyth

UNITED KINGDOM

Ouse
Bradford Leeds Kingston upon Hull
Immingham
Grimsby
Sheffield
The Wash
Nottingham
Trent
Leicester
Norwich
Birmingham
Coventry
Cambridge
Felixstowe
Severn
Oxford
Thames
London
Gillingham
Dover
Strait of Dover
Swansea
Milford Haven
Cardiff
Bristol
Reading
Bristol Channel
Southampton
Brighton
Hastings
Portsmouth
Isle of Wight
Exeter
Bournemouth
English Channel
Plymouth
Penzance
Isles of Scilly

St. George's Channel

Orkney Islands
Sanday
Hoy Mainland
John o'Groats

Lewis
Outer Hebrides
Harris
North Uist
South Uist
Barra
Skye
Inner Hebrides
Rhum
Mull
Jura
Islay
Arran

North West Highlands
Moray Firth
Loch Ness
Cairngorm Mts.
Ben Nevis 4,410
Grampian Mountains
Firth of Tay
Firth of Forth
Southern Uplands
Clyde
Tweed
Cheviot Hills

ATLANTIC OCEAN

Malin Head
Antrim Mts.
Lough Neagh
Mourne Mts.
Donegal Bay
Erne
Shannon

Achill
Lough Mask
L. Corrib
Lough Ree
IRELAND
Burren
Aran Islands
Shannon
Lough Derg
Barrow
Wicklow Mts.
Suir
Macgillycuddy's Reeks

St. George's Channel

Isle of Man
Irish Sea
Cumbrian Mts.
Scafell Pike 3,206
North York Moors
Ouse
Pennines
The Wash
Anglesey
Mersey
Trent
Snowdon 3,560
Cambrian Mountains
Severn
The Fens
Gt. Ouse
Brecon Beacons
Cotswold Hills
Thames
Chiltern Hills
North Downs
Strait of Dover
Mendip Hills
South Downs
Bristol Channel
Exmoor
Isle of Wight
Dartmoor
English Channel
Land's End
Isles of Scilly

North Sea

AGRICULTURE

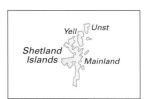

Yell Unst
Shetland
Islands Mainland

Agricultural zones

- arable
- fruit and vegetables
- pasture and arable
- rough grazing
- woods and forest
- nonagricultural land
- ▲ mountain peak (ft)

Most modern farms, especially in
eastern England, concentrate on
monoculture, such as wheat
production. Smaller mixed farms
are found in the west, with sheep
farms in upland areas.

FRANCE

France is the largest country in Western Europe. Its varied landscapes include rolling plains, hills, beautiful river valleys, the remains of ancient volcanoes, and dramatic mountain scenery in the Alps and Pyrenees.

The north has a cool temperate climate, while the south has the typical hot summers and mild, moist winters of Mediterranean lands. Other variations occur from west to east. While the west comes under the moderating influence of the Atlantic, to the east the climate becomes increasingly continental. Summers are hotter and winters are much colder.

The French have a strong sense of identity, a pride in their culture, and a firm belief in the preeminence of their capital, Paris, as a world center of art and learning. Yet the French owe their origins to many diverse groups, including Celts, Romans, Franks, and Vikings. Recent immigration has been from North Africa, Southeast Asia, and other parts of Europe.

France is a major industrial power, with an increasingly urbanized population. It is also the largest producer of farm products in Western Europe. It is especially famous for its fine wines and wide range of cheeses.

Northern France lies at the western end of the North European Plain – an ancient pathway of human migrations – that extends from the Ural Mountains of Russia to southeastern England. The south and southeast lie in a zone where the African and Eurasian plates have collided, thrusting up young ranges, including the snow-capped Pyrenees and Alps.

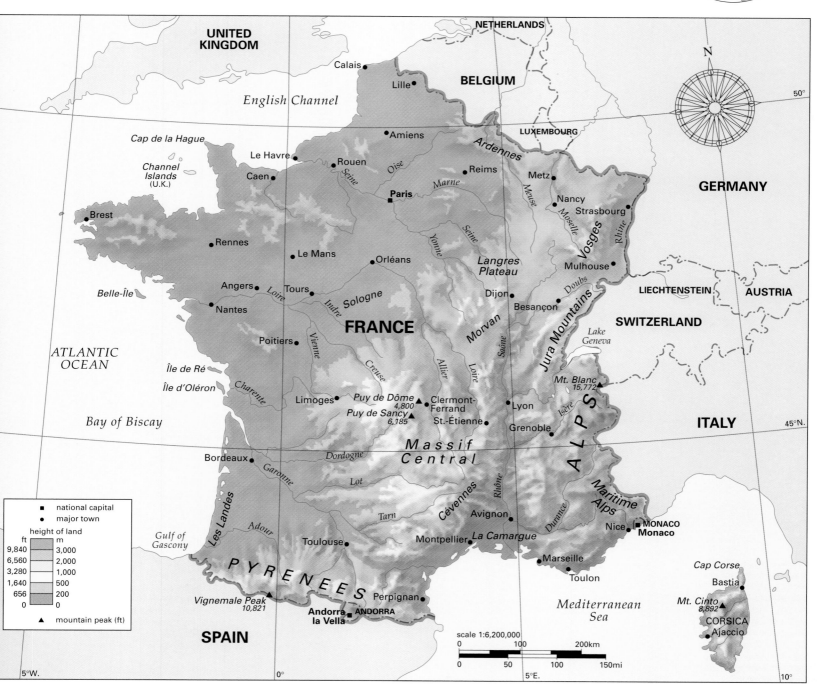

THE POLITICAL AND CULTURAL WORLD

Modern France owes its origins to the French Revolution of 1789 and its principles of liberty, equality, and fraternity, which have been incorporated into the constitutions of many other countries. Today France is a parliamentary democracy, whose executive branch is headed by the president and the prime minister.

France has two of Europe's ministates as neighbors. Nestling in the Pyrenees is the tiny state of Andorra, a principality whose heads of state are the president of France and the bishop of Urgel in Spain. The other ministate is Monaco, a principality ruled by the House of Grimaldi since 1308.

COUNTRIES IN THE REGION

Andorra, France, Monaco

Island provinces Corsica (France)
Territories outside the region French Guiana, French Polynesia, Guadeloupe, Martinique, Mayotte, New Caledonia, Réunion, St. Pierre and Miquelon, Wallis and Futuna (France)

France has a territorial claim in Antarctica.

LANGUAGE

Countries with one official language (Catalan) Andorra; (French) France, Monaco

Local minority languages in France are Basque, Breton, Catalan, Corsican, Flemish, German (Alsatian), and Provençal. Significant immigrant languages include Arabic, Italian, Polish, Portuguese, Spanish, and Turkish. English, Italian, and Monégasque are spoken in Monaco; Spanish in Andorra.

RELIGION

Andorra Roman Catholic (94.2%)
France Roman Catholic (76%), Muslim (3%), non-religious and atheist (3%) Protestant (2%), Jewish (1%)
Monaco Roman Catholic (91%), Anglican (1%), Protestant (1%), Eastern Orthodox (1%)

STYLES OF GOVERNMENT

Republic France
Principalities Andorra, Monaco
Multiparty state France
States without parties Andorra, Monaco
One-chamber assembly Andorra
Two-chamber assembly France, Monaco

MEMBERSHIP OF INTERNATIONAL ORGANIZATIONS

Council of Europe France
European Union (EU) France
North Atlantic Treaty Organization (NATO) France
Organization for Economic Cooperation and Development (OECD) France

ECONOMIC INDICATORS

	France
GDP (US$ trillions)	1.394
GNP per capita (US$)	21,860
Annual rate of growth of GDP, 1990–1997	1.3%
Manufacturing as % of GDP	21.8%
Central government spending as % of GDP	51.6%
Merchandise exports (US$ billions)	284.2
Merchandise imports (US$ billions)	256.1
Aid given as % of GNP (France)	0.46%

WELFARE INDICATORS

	France
Infant mortality rate (per 1,000 live births)	
1965	22
1997	6
Daily food supply available (calories per capita, 1995)	3,588
Population per physician (1996)	345
Internet users (million, 1998)	2.5

France
Area 211,210 sq mi (547,030 sq km)
Population 59,329,691
Currency 1 franc (f) = 100 centimes
Euro (€) also in use
€ = 100 cents

Andorra
Area 181 sq mi (468 sq km)
Population 66,824
Currency 1 French franc (f) = 100 centimes
1 Spanish peseta (Pts) = 100 céntimos

Monaco
Area 0.75 sq mi (1.95 sq km)
Population 31,693
Currency 1 French franc (f) = 100 centimes

France is divided into 22 metropolitan regions, each governed by an elected council and its own president. The regions are responsible for their own economic planning. The regions are divided into 96 metropolitan departments, each with its own elected council. These councils are responsible for local social services.

- ▣ national capital
- ▪ regional capital
- ● other town

Calais
Boulogne
Lille
NORD-PAS-DE-CALAIS
Lens
Valenciennes
Dieppe
Amiens
Cherbourg
Le Havre
UPPER NORMANDY
PICARDY
Thionville
Rouen
Reims
Metz
Caen
Châlons-sur-Marne
LORRAINE
Paris
Nancy
Strasbourg
St. Malo
LOWER NORMANDY
ÎLE-DE-FRANCE
ALSACE
Brest
Chartres
CHAMPAGNE-ARDENNE
BRITTANY
Troyes
Quimper
Rennes
Le Mans
Mulhouse
Lorient
PAYS DE LA LOIRE
Orléans
Auxerre
FRANCHE-COMTÉ
St.-Nazaire
Angers
CENTRE
Tours
Dijon
Besançon
Nantes
Bourges
BURGUNDY
Chalon
Poitiers
FRANCE
La Rochelle
POITOU-CHARENTES
Limoges
RHÔNE-ALPES
Annecy
Saintes
Clermont-Ferrand
Lyon
LIMOUSIN
St.-Étienne
Périgueux
AUVERGNE
Grenoble
Bordeaux
Valence
AQUITAINE
MIDI-PYRÉNÉES
Avignon
PROVENCE-ALPES-CÔTE-D'AZUR
Nîmes
Nice
Monaco MONACO
Bayonne
Toulouse
Montpellier
Aix-en-Provence
Cannes
Pau
Lourdes
LANGUEDOC-ROUSSILLON
Marseille
Toulon
Perpignan
Andorra la Vella ANDORRA

Bastia
CORSICA
Ajaccio

HABITATS

Much of northern and western France consists of flat, fertile grassy plains or low, rolling hills. Much of this land is farmed. Wooded mountains rise in the east and south. The southern Massif Central with its spectacular river gorges contains largely poor soils.

LAND

Area 211,391 sq mi (547,500 sq km)
Highest point Mont Blanc, 15,772 ft (4,807 m)
Lowest point sea level
Major features Pyrenees, Alps, and Jura Mountains, Massif Central, Paris basin and basins of Garonne and Rhône rivers

WATER

Longest river Loire, 630 mi (1,020 km)
Largest basin Loire, 44,377 sq mi (115,000 sq km)
Highest average flow Rhône, 53,000 cu ft/sec (1,500 cu m/sec)
Largest lake Geneva, 224 sq mi (580 sq km)

NOTABLE THREATENED SPECIES

Mammals Long-fingered bat (Myotis capaccinii), Pond bat (Myotis dasycneme), Mouse-eared bat (Myotis myotis), Pyrenean desman (Galemys pyrenaicus), European mink (Mustela lutreola), Harbor porpoise (Phocoena phocoena), Fin whale (Balaenoptera physalus)
Birds Red kite (Mylvus migrans), White-tailed sea eagle (Haliaeetus albicilla), Corncrake (Crex crex), Little bustard (Tetrax tetrax), Audouin's gull (Larus audouinii)
Others Corsican swallowtail butterfly (Papilio hospiton), Quimper snail (Elona quimperiana), Shining macromia dragonfly (Macromia splendens), Longhorn beetle (Cerambyx cerdo)
Plants Aldrovanda vesiculosa; Atlantic angelica (Angelica heterocarpa); Caldensia parnassifolia; bog orchid (Hammarbya paludosa); Pyrenean alyssum (Hormathophyllum pyrenaica); Leucojum nicaeense; Lythrum thesioides; Primula allionii; Saxifraga florulenta; raven violet (Viola hispida)

CLIMATE

Western France is rainy, with cool summers and mild winters. The east is drier, with hotter summers and colder winters. The eastern mountains are snowy. The south has a Mediterranean climate, with hot, dry summers and mild, moist winters.

CLIMATE

| | Temperature °F (°C) | | Altitude |
	January	July	ft (m)
Brest	43 (6)	61 (16)	338 (103)
Paris	37 (3)	66 (19)	174 (53)
Strasbourg	32 (0)	66 (19)	505 (154)
Bordeaux	41 (5)	68 (20)	167 (51)
Marseille	43 (6)	73 (23)	26 (8)

| | Precipitation in. (mm) | | |
	January	July	Year
Brest	5.2 (135)	2.4 (62)	44.3 (1,126)
Paris	2.1 (54)	2.2 (55)	23.0 (585)
Strasbourg	1.5 (39)	3.0 (77)	23.9 (607)
Bordeaux	3.5 (90)	2.2 (56)	35.4 (900)
Marseille	1.7 (43)	0.4 (11)	21.5 (546)

NATURAL HAZARDS

Storms and floods, landslides, avalanches

ENVIRONMENTAL ISSUES

By 1994, about 80 percent of France's electricity was produced by the country's 56 nuclear power stations. Hence France is much less affected than most other parts of Europe by the air pollution and acid rain caused by burning fossil fuels.

POPULATION AND WEALTH *Andorra, France, *Monaco

Population (millions)	59.428
Population increase (annual growth rate, % 1990–95)	0.4%
Energy use (lbs per year per person of oil equivalent)	9,332
Purchasing power parity (Int$ per year)	22,077

ENVIRONMENTAL INDICATORS

CO$_2$ emissions ('000 tons/year)	340,085
Car ownership (% of population)	49%
Proportion of territory protected, including marine areas (%)	10%
Forests as a % of original forest	16%
Artificial fertilizer use (lbs/acre/year)	217
Access to safe drinking water (% population, rural/urban)	100%/100%

* Not included in figures

MAJOR ENVIRONMENTAL PROBLEMS AND SOURCES

Air pollution: locally high, in particular urban, acid rain
Marine/coastal pollution: medium; sources: industry, sewage, oil, agriculture
Land pollution: medium; sources: industry, nuclear, agriculture
Waste disposal issues: domestic; industrial; nuclear
Population issues: tourism
Major events: Val d'Isère (1970), major avalanche; Amoco Cadiz (1978), oil tanker accident; Les Arcs (1981), landslide; le Grand Bornand (1987), major flood; Nîmes (1988), major flood; Protex plant, Tours (1988), fire at chemical plant; major forest damage from windstorm (1999); marine pollution from tanker Erika (2000) off southern Brittany

HABITATS

Physical zones

- mountains/barren land
- forest
- grassland

▲ mountain peak (ft)
☀ climate station

Northern and southwestern France are made up of plains and low hills. The uplands or massifs in the center are divided from those in the east by the valley of the Rhône and Saône running north to south.

ENVIRONMENTAL ISSUES

Tourism and industry have
polluted coastal areas, while
forest fires, avalanches, and
soil erosion are common hazards
in the south. In recent years,
the government has introduced
many policies aimed at
protecting the environment.

English Channel

Gravelines
Dunkirk
Lille
Penly
Chooz
Ardennes
Cap de la Hague
La Hague
Paluel
Flamanville
Le Havre
Cattenom
Rouen
Seine
Oise
Marne
Caen
Meuse
Paris
Strasbourg
Amoco Cadiz
Nogent-sur-Seine
Soulaines
Moselle
Rhine
Fessenheim
Erika
Langres
Plateau
St. Laurent
Dampierre
Tours
Sologne
Belleville
Yonne
Seine
Belle-Île
Loire
Chinon
FRANCE
Morvan
Saône
Doubs
Jura Mountains
Lake
Geneva
Vienne
Indre
Creuse
le Grand Bornand
Île de Ré
Civaux
Allier
Loire
Bugey
ALPS
Île d'Oléron
Charente
Superphénix
Val d'Isère
Bay of Biscay
St. Alban
Isère
Le Blayais
Massif
Central
Bordeaux
Dordogne
Cruas
Garonne
Maritime
Alps
Lot
Tricastin
Marcoule
Golfech
Tarn
Nîmes
Durance
Rhône
Nice
MONACO
Les Landes
Adour
Gulf of
Gascony
Toulouse
La Camargue
Les Arcs
Marseille
PYRENEES
Toulon
ANDORRA
Mediterranean
Sea

Cap
Corse
CORSICA

Key environmental issues

- • major town or city
- ♦ major pollution event
- + major natural disaster
- 🏭 nuclear power station
- 🗎 nuclear processing plant
- ～ river with polluted stretches
- ▬ main area of coastal tourism
- ◎ main skiing area
- ◯ area at risk of fire

remaining forest
- coniferous
- mixed
- broadleaf
- scrub

CLIMATE

height above sea level of climate stations

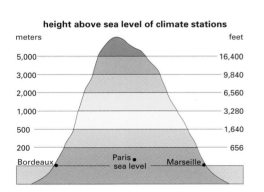

meters		feet
5,000		16,400
3,000		9,840
2,000		6,560
1,000		3,280
500		1,640
200		656

Bordeaux   Paris   Marseille
sea level

Bordeaux

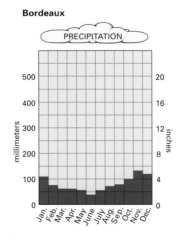

PRECIPITATION

Paris

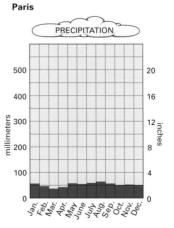

PRECIPITATION

Marseille

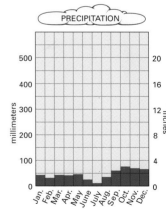

PRECIPITATION

Bordeaux

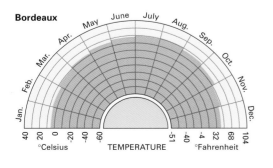

°Celsius   TEMPERATURE   °Fahrenheit

Paris

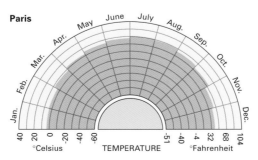

°Celsius   TEMPERATURE   °Fahrenheit

Marseille

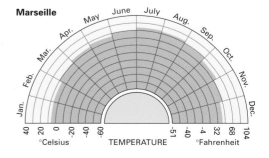

°Celsius   TEMPERATURE   °Fahrenheit

POPULATION

Before 1945, the movement of people from the countryside to urban areas was slower in France than in most parts of Europe. But urban areas now house about 75 percent of the people, largely in apartment buildings. Greater Paris is one of the world's largest metropolitian areas.

POPULATION

Total population of region (millions)	59.42
Population density (persons per sq mi) (France)	277
Population change (average annual percent 1995–2000)	
Urban	+0.6%
Rural	–0.36%

URBAN POPULATION

As percentage of total population	
1960	62.4%
1990	75%

TEN LARGEST CITIES

	Population
Paris †	2,115,400
Marseille	809,400
Lyon	444,300
Toulouse	400,600
Nice	336,300
Nantes	275,400
Strasbourg	268,300
Montpellier	228,100
Bordeaux	216,100
Rennes	209,400

† *denotes capital city*

City population figures are for the city proper.

INDUSTRY

France is a major manufacturing nation. Its traditional industries were originally built on local energy and mineral resources, mainly coal and iron. But it now has many dynamic high-tech industries, including aerospace and telecommunications.

INDUSTRIAL OUTPUT (US $ billion, France, 1995)

Total	Mining and Manufacturing	Average annual change since 1960
399	n/a	n/a

INDUSTRIAL WORKERS (millions)
(figures in parentheses are percentages of total labor force)

Total	Mining	Manufacturing	Construction
5.6	0.1 (0.5%)	3.9 (15.8%)	1.4 (5.8%)

MAJOR PRODUCTS (figures in parentheses are percentages of total world production)

Energy and minerals	Output % 1970	1995	Change since 1970
Coal (mil m.t.)	39.8	8.4	–78.9%
Crude oil (mil m.t.)	2.3	1.8	–21.7%
Natural Gas ('000 terjoules)	271	139	–48.7%
Nuclear electricity (1996) (gigawatt hours)	n/a	397,340	
Potash ('000 m.t.)	1,904	850	–55.4%
(France produces 3.5% of world potash (ranked 9th))			
Bauxite ('000 m.t.)	2,992	131	–95.6%

Manufactures				
Lead ('000 m.t.)	170	297	74.7%	(5.5%)
Cement ('000 m.t.)	29,009	19,896		–31.4%
Steel ('000 m.t.)	23,773	18,132		–23.7%
Commercial vehicles ('000)	292	442	51.4%	(2.8%)
Automobiles ('000)	2,498	3,042	23.8%	(28.5%)
Fertilizer ('000 tons)				
Potash	1,664	869	–47.8%	(3%)
Phosphate	1,611	497	–69.1%	(1.5%)
Nitrogenous	1,476	1,396	–5.4%	(1.7%)
Televisions ('000)	1,511	2,796	85.0%	(2.1%)
Tires ('000)	39,415	59,268	50.4%	(6.6%)
Radios ('000)	2,921	2,804	–4.0%	(2.1%)

AGRICULTURE

France is a major producer of farm products. It is the second largest producer of wine and ranks among the world's top ten producers of milk, butter, meat, eggs, wheat, and barley. Only the United States exports more agricultural produce.

LAND
Total area 211,391 sq mi (547,500 sq km)

Cropland	Pasture	Forest/Woodland
35%	20%	27%
(73,516 sq mi)	(42,086 sq mi)	(56,770 sq mi)

FARMERS

	France
Agriculture as % of GDP	2%
% of workforce	5%

MAJOR CROPS
Agricultural products: wheat; cereals; sugar beet; potatoes; wine grapes; beef; dairy products; fish

Total cropland ('000 acres)	48,105
Cropland (acres) per 1,000 people	823
Irrigated land as percentage of cropland	9
Annual fertilizer use (lbs per acre of cropland)	217
Number of tractors	1,312,000
Percentage change since 1987	–11%
Average cereal crop yields (lbs per acre)	5880
Average production of cereals ('000 tons)	64,578
Percentage change since 1986–88	22%

LIVESTOCK AND FISHERIES

Average meat production ('000 tons)	6,533
Percentage change since 1986–88	27%
Marine fish catch ('000 tons)	491
Percentage change since 1986–88	–11%
Aquaculture production ('000 tons)	284.7

FOOD SECURITY

Average daily per capita calories (kilocalories)	3,518

POPULATION

Population density

urban agglomeration
(National capital is underlined)

◆ 5,000,000–10,000,000
■ 1,000,000–4,999,999
● 500,000–999,999
⊙ 250,000–499,999
× national capital less than 250,000

persons per square mi	persons per square km
520	200
260	100
130	50
65	25

Areas of high population density occur around Paris and in the northern industrial areas. Migration to the south has created some high density areas in the Rhône valley and on the southeast coast.

INDUSTRY

The earliest industrial regions grew up in the northern mining districts. The recent decline in mining has led to the spread of industry to other areas.

Resources and industry

- ◆ industrial center
- ○ port
- • other town
- —— major road
- —— major railroad

mineral resources and fossil fuels

- • iron and other ferroalloy metal ores
- • other metal ores
- • nonmetallic minerals
- ▨ bauxite
- ▨ coal
- ▨ iron ore
- ▨ lignite (brown coal)
- ▨ potash

AGRICULTURE

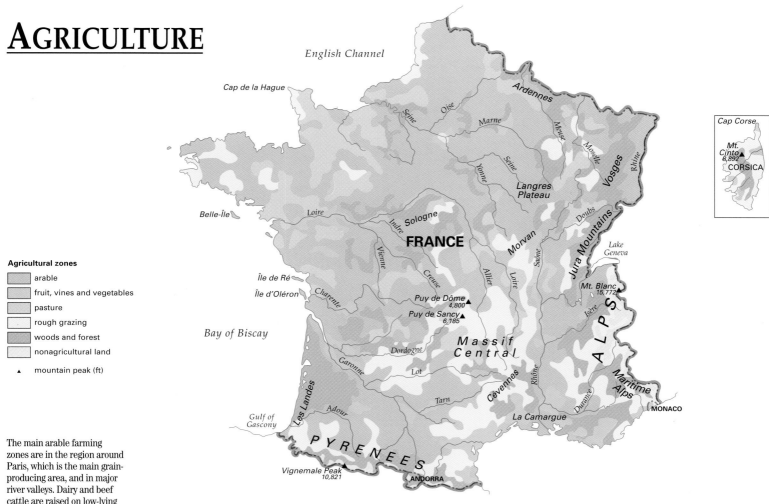

Agricultural zones

- ▨ arable
- ▨ fruit, vines and vegetables
- ▨ pasture
- ▨ rough grazing
- ▨ woods and forest
- ▨ nonagricultural land
- ▲ mountain peak (ft)

The main arable farming zones are in the region around Paris, which is the main grain-producing area, and in major river valleys. Dairy and beef cattle are raised on low-lying pasture, while sheep farms are found in upland areas.

SPAIN AND PORTUGAL

The Iberian Peninsula occupies the south-western corner of Europe. Separated from North Africa by the Strait of Gibraltar, Iberia often seems to visitors to be almost as much African as European. Spain also includes the Balearic Islands in the Mediterranean and the Canary Islands in the Atlantic. Portugal has two autonomous regions, the Azores in the North Atlantic and the Madeira Islands off the northwest coast of Africa.

Spain, Portugal, and the tiny British dependency of Gibraltar, which occupies a strategic position near the Strait of Gibraltar, form the Iberian Peninsula, isolated from the rest of Europe by the Pyrenees Mountains.

Much of the peninsula is a high plateau, called the Meseta. The Meseta is bordered not only by the Pyrenees, but also by the Cantabrian Mountains in the northwest and the Sierra Nevada in the southeast. Because of its altitude, the Meseta has a severe climate, with hot summers and bitterly cold winters. The Meseta is arid, and parts of the southeast are semidesert. Lowland Portugal's climate is moderated by moist Atlantic winds. Other lowlands include the Ebro and Guadalquivir river valleys in Spain.

From early times, Iberia was invaded by waves of colonizers, including Celts, Phoenicians, Greeks, Carthaginians, Romans, and Visigoths, each of whom left their imprint on Iberian culture. The last invaders were the Moors (Muslim Arabs), who entered the peninsula in the year 711. Their last bastion, the Alhambra palace in Granada, did not fall until 1492, the year Columbus sailed from Spain.

Although Spain and Portugal were both leaders in terms of world exploration, both countries were, by the early twentieth century, among Europe's poorest. Today, as members of the European Union, their economies have been expanding quickly, and Spain is growing especially rapidly. Tourism plays a major part in the economies of both countries.

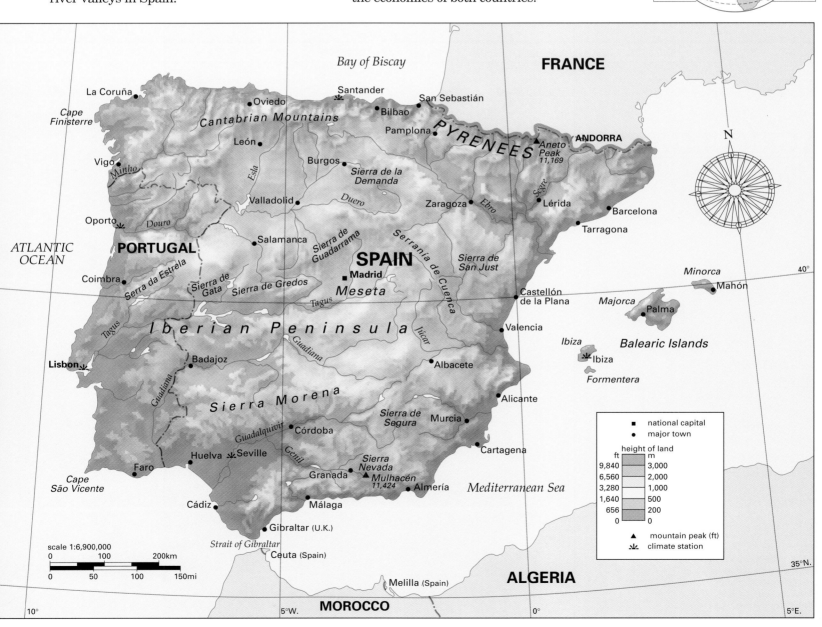

THE POLITICAL AND CULTURAL WORLD

After the Spanish civil war (1936–1939), Spain became a dictatorship under General Franco. When he died in 1975, the monarchy was restored, and Spain became a parliamentary democracy. Between 1928 and 1974, Portugal was also a dictatorship. But after the overthrow of its military leaders, it became a democratic republic.

Spain claims Gibraltar, the world's smallest colony, but Britain justifies its control over the territory by arguing that the majority of Gibraltarians want to remain British. Despite the lack of agreement over sovereignty, cooperation over such matters as the shared use of Gibraltar's airport has increased.

Portugal

Area 35,672 sq mi
(92,389 sq km)
Population 10,048,000
Capital Lisbon
Currency 1 escudo
(Esc) = 100 centavos
Euro (€) also in use
€ = 100 cents

COUNTRIES IN THE REGION

Portugal, Spain

Territories outside the region Azores, Madeira (Portugal); Balearic Islands, Canary Islands, Ceuta, Melilla (Spain)

LAND

Highest point on mainland, Mulhacén, 11,424 ft (3,482 m); Pico de Teide on Tenerife in the Canary Islands, 12,195 ft (3,718 m)
Lowest point sea level
Major features Meseta plateau in center, Cantabrian Mountains and Pyrenees in north, Sierra Nevada in south

WATER

Longest river Tagus, 630 mi (1,010 km)
Largest basin Duero, 38,000 sq mi (98,000 sq km)
Highest average flow Duero, 11,000 cu ft/sec (312 cu m/sec)

CLIMATE

| | Temperature °F (°C) | | Altitude |
	January	July	ft (m)
Oporto	48 (9)	68 (20)	239 (73)
Lisbon	52 (11)	72 (22)	361 (110)
Santander	48 (9)	66 (19)	210 (64)
Seville	50 (10)	79 (26)	43 (13)
Ibiza	52 (11)	75 (24)	23 (7)
	Precipitation in. (mm)		
	January	July	Year
Oporto	6.3 (159)	0.8 (20)	45.3 (1,150)
Lisbon	4.4 (111)	0.1 (3)	27.9 (708)
Santander	4.9 (124)	2.5 (64)	47.6 (1,208)
Seville	2.9 (73)	0.4 (1)	22.0 (559)
Ibiza	1.7 (42)	0.2 (5)	17.5 (444)

LANGUAGE

Countries with one official language
(Portuguese) Portugal; (Spanish) Spain

Local minority languages spoken in Spain are Basque, Catalan, and Galician.

RELIGION

Portugal Roman Catholic (94%), nonreligious and atheist (3.8%)
Spain Roman Catholic (97%), nonreligious and atheist (2.6%), Protestant (0.4%)

STYLES OF GOVERNMENT

Republic Portugal
Monarchy Spain
Multiparty states Portugal, Spain
One-chamber assembly Portugal
Two-chamber assembly Spain

ECONOMIC INDICATORS

	Spain	Portugal
GDP (US$ billions)	531.3	97.5
GNP per capita (US$)	15,720	13,840
Annual rate of growth of GDP, 1990–1997	1.6%	2.1%
Manufacturing as % of GDP	23.7%*	25.8%
Central government spending as % of GDP	38.2%	44.2%
Merchandise exports (US$ billions)	104.5	24.7
Merchandise imports (US$ billions)	117.8	34.3
Aid given as % of GNP	0.22%	0.21%

* Includes mining and public utilities.

WELFARE INDICATORS

	Spain	Portugal
Infant mortality rate (per 1,000 live births)		
1965	38	65
2000	4.99	6.05
Daily food supply available (calories per capita, 1995)	3,338	3,639
Population per physician (1996)	238	333
Teacher-pupil ratio (primary school, 1995)	1 : 17.8	1 : 12.4

■ national capital
● other town

Both Spain and Portugal are now democracies; Spain was governed by General Franco until 1975 and Portugal by the dictator Salazar until 1968. Spain's head of state is King Juan Carlos, who came to the throne in 1975.

Area 194,885 sq mi
(504,750 sq km)
Population 39,996,671
Capital Madrid
Currency 1 peseta
(Pta) = 100 centimos
Euro (€) also in use
€ = 100 cents

Spain

ENVIRONMENTAL ISSUES

The Iberian Peninsula is one of the fastest changing parts of Europe, with new investments paying for rapid development. Tourism has led to the destruction of many coastal wildlife habitats, while the growth of cities has led to serious air and water pollution.

POPULATION AND WEALTH

	Portugal	Spain
Population (millions)	10.048	39.996
Population increase (1990–95)	0.0%	0.0%
Energy use (lbs/year per person oil equivalent)	4,559	5,972
Purchasing power parity (Int$/year)	14,386	15,812

ENVIRONMENTAL INDICATORS

	Portugal	Spain
CO$_2$ emissions ('000 tons/year)	51,926	231,605
Car ownership (% of population)	44%	41%
Protected territory including marine areas (%)	7%	8%
Forests as % of original forest	9%	15%
Artificial fertilizer use (lbs/acre/year)	69	102
Access to safe drinking water (% of population, rural/urban)	100/100%	100/100%

MAJOR ENVIRONMENTAL PROBLEMS AND SOURCES

Air pollution: urban high
Marine/coastal pollution: medium; *sources*: industry, agriculture, sewage, oil
Land degradation: soil erosion; salinization; habitat destruction; *causes*: agriculture, industry, population pressure
Population issues: tourism
Major events: San Carlos de la Ràpita (1978), transportation accident; Greek tanker *Aegean Sea* crude oil spill off northwestern Spain (1992); Coto Doñana (1998) toxic waste water entered river

POPULATION

Industrialization occurred later in the Iberian Peninsula than in other parts of Europe. But the industrial cities have grown steadily in the twentieth century. Tourism has led to the development of an urban ring along the coasts, while the interior is thinly populated.

POPULATION

Total population of region (millions)		50.04

	Portugal	Spain
Population density (persons/sq mi)	280.5	203
Population change (1995–2000)		
Urban	+2.7%	+.33%
Rural	–4.0%	–.99%

URBAN POPULATION

As percentage of total population (1995) 56%		77%

TEN LARGEST CITIES

	Country	Population
Madrid †	Spain	2,940,200
Barcelona	Spain	1,523,700
Valencia	Spain	739,200
Seville	Spain	708,200
Lisbon †	Portugal	653,700
Zaragoza	Spain	603,400
Málaga	Spain	534,700
Las Palmas (Canary Islands)	Spain	362,500
Bilbao	Spain	357,600
Oporto	Portugal	314,800

† denotes capital city

City population figures are for the city proper.

AGRICULTURE

Despite the growing importance of manufacturing, agriculture remains important in both Spain and Portugal. The main agricultural activities are the cultivation of citrus fruits, olives, grapes, and wheat, and the raising of sheep, pigs, and cattle in the less fertile areas.

LAND
Total area 230,557 sq mi (597,139 sq km)

Cropland	Pasture	Forest/Woodland
38%	19%	33%
(88,510 sq mi)	(44,147 sq mi)	(75,221 sq mi)

FARMERS

	Portugal	Spain
Agriculture as % of GDP	4%	3%
% of workforce	10%	8%

MAJOR CROPS
Agricultural products: fruit and vegetables: citrus, grapes, potatoes etc; sugar beet; grain; cattle, sheep, goats, poultry; dairy products; fish

	Portugal	Spain
Total cropland ('000 acres)	7,166	47,354
Cropland (acres) per 1,000 people	726	1,196
Irrigated land as percentage of cropland	22%	19%
Annual fertilizer use (lbs per acre of cropland)	69	102
Number of tractors	150,000	841,932
Change since 1987	23%	24%
Average cereal crop yields (lbs per acre)	5,287	6,958
Average production of cereals ('000 tons)	1,476	21,281
Change since 1986–88	–9%	5%

LIVESTOCK AND FISHERIES

	Portugal	Spain
Average meat production ('000 tons)	689	4,355
Change since 1986–88	73%	63%
Marine fish catch ('000 tons)	224	978
Change since 1986–88	–35%	–9%
Aquaculture production ('000 tons)	5.8	231.6

FOOD SECURITY

	Portugal	Spain
Food aid as percentage of total imports	0	0
Average daily per capita calories (kilocalories)	3,667	3,310

ENVIRONMENTAL ISSUES

Key environmental issues

- • major town or city
- ◣ polluted town or city
- ◊ major pollution event
- ⌒ polluted river
- main area of coastal tourism

soil degradation
- severe
- high
- moderate
- low

Soil erosion caused by farming, combined with drought and deforestation, has affected much of the Iberian Peninsula. Public debate about green issues and conservation is increasing.

POPULATION

Population density

urban agglomeration
(National Capital is underlined)

◆ 5,000,000–10,000,000
■ 1,000,000–5,000,000
● 500,000–999,999
◉ 250,000–499,999

persons per square mi	persons per square km
520	200
260	100
130	50
65	25

The areas of high population density in the Iberian Peninsula are mainly situated along the coasts, especially around such industrial cities as Barcelona, Bilbao, Lisbon, Málaga, and Valencia.

AGRICULTURE

Agricultural zones

- arable
- fruit, vines and vegetables
- rough grazing
- woods and forest
- nonagricultural land

▲ mountain peak (ft)

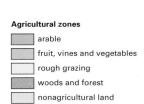

Fruits and vegetables are grown on the coasts, while dry parts of the Meseta are used to graze sheep. Many river valleys in the interior are cultivated.

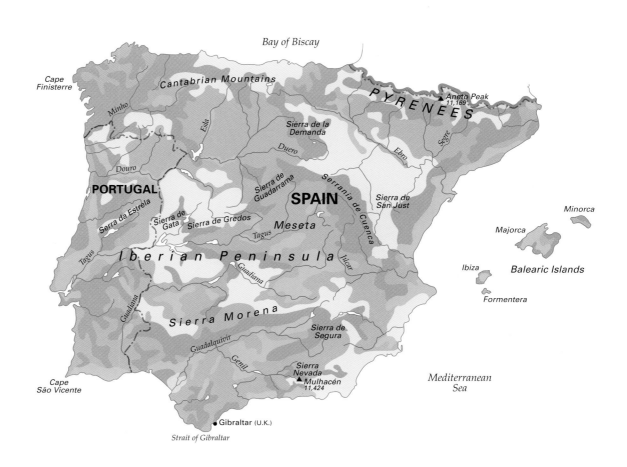

ITALY AND GREECE

I taly and Greece occupy a region where the earth's crust is unstable; there are frequent earthquakes and spectacular volcanic eruptions, especially in southern Italy. The snow-capped Alps in northern Italy were raised up as the result of a collision between the northward-moving African plate and the Eurasian plate.

About 40 percent of the land is mountainous, the Po valley being the most extensive lowland.

The coastlands, with their hot, dry summers and mild, wet winters, are tourist magnets for north Europeans. But the mountains of southern Italy and Greece can be bitterly cold and snowy in the winter months.

The ancient ruins of Greece and Italy are testimony to two major civilizations, whose art, philosophy, and politics lie at the heart of European culture.

Italy and Greece are on two peninsulas that jut into the Mediterranean Sea. Both countries include many islands. Around 440 islands make up about one-fifth of Greece's area.

Malta is an island republic south of Sicily. Cyprus is another island republic in the east.

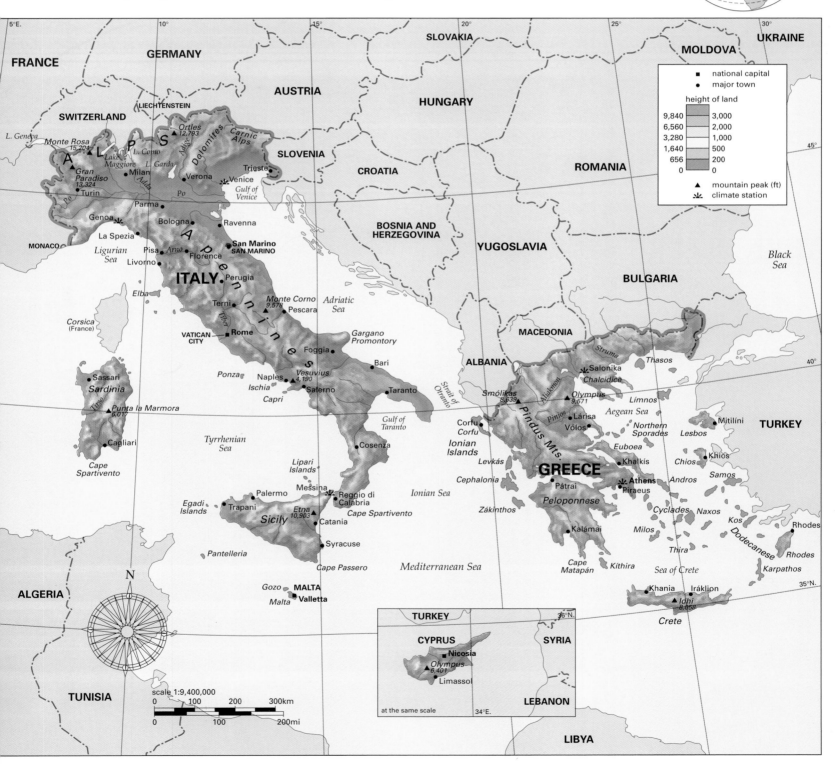

THE POLITICAL AND CULTURAL WORLD

Italy and Greece both underwent periods of instability and dictatorship in the twentieth century, though today they are democratic republics.

Greece has a long-standing dispute with Turkey over Cyprus, an island with a Greek majority and a Turkish minority. In 1974 Greece's military regime was implicated in moves to unite Cyprus with Greece. (Cyprus had been independent since 1960.) Turkey invaded northern Cyprus and set up the Turkish Republic of Northern Cyprus, a state that is recognized only by Turkey.

Cyprus **Area** 3,572 sq mi
(9,251 sq km)
Population 758,363
Capital Nicosia
Currency 1 Cyprus pound
(C£) = 100 cents
[1 Turkish lira (TL) = 100 kurus]

Greece **Area** 50,949 sq mi
(131,957 sq km)
Population 10,601,527
Capital Athens
Currency 1 drachma
(Dr) = 100 lepta
Euro (€) also in use
€ = 100 cents

COUNTRIES IN THE REGION

Cyprus, Greece, Italy, Malta, San Marino, Vatican City

Island areas Aegean Islands, Crete, Ionian Islands, (Greece); Egadi Islands, Elba, Capri, Ischia, Lipari Islands, Pantelleria, Ponza, Sardinia, Sicily (Italy)

LAND

Highest point Monte Rosa, 15,204 ft (4,634 m)
Lowest point sea level
Major features Alps, Apennines, Pindus Mountains, Po valley, islands including Sardinia, Crete, Greek archipelago, and Cyprus

WATER

Longest river Po, 380 mi (620 km)
Largest basin Po, 29,000 sq mi (75,000 sq km)
Highest average flow Po, 54,000 cu ft/sec (1,540 cu m/sec)
Largest lake Garda, 140 sq mi (370 sq km)

CLIMATE

	Temperature °F (°C)		Altitude
	January	July	ft (m)
Genoa	46 (8)	75 (24)	69 (21)
Venice	36 (2)	73 (23)	7 (2)
Messina	52 (11)	79 (26)	177 (54)
Salonika	42 (6)	82 (28)	226 (69)
Athens	48 (9)	82 (28)	351 (107)

	Precipitation in. (mm)		
	January	July	Year
Genoa	3.1 (79)	1.6 (40)	50 (1,270)
Venice	2.0 (50)	2.6 (67)	33.6 (854)
Messina	5.7 (146)	0.7 (19)	38.3 (974)
Salonika	1.7 (45)	0.9 (23)	18.3 (465)
Athens	2.4 (62)	0.4 (1)	13.3 (339)

LANGUAGE

Countries with one official language : Greece (Greek); Italy, San Marino (Italian)
Countries with two official languages Malta (English, Maltese); Cyprus (Greek, Turkish); Vatican City (Italian, Latin)

Other languages spoken in the region include Albanian, Macedonian, and Turkish (Greece); Albanian, Catalan, French, German, Greek, Ladin, Sardinian, and Slovenian (Italy).

RELIGION

Cyprus Greek Orthodox (80%), Muslim (19%)
Greece Greek Orthodox (97.6%), Muslim (1.5%), other Christian (0.5%)
Italy Roman Catholic (81.7%), nonreligious and atheist (13.6%), Muslim (1.2%), others (3.5%)
Malta Roman Catholic (97.3%), Anglican (1.2%), others (1.5%)
San Marino Roman Catholic (95%), nonreligious and atheist (3%)
Vatican City Roman Catholic (100%)

STYLES OF GOVERNMENT

Republics Cyprus, Greece, Italy, Malta, San Marino
City state Vatican City
Multiparty states Cyprus, Greece, Italy, Malta, San Marino
State without parties Vatican City
One-chamber assembly Cyprus, Greece, Malta, San Marino
Two-chamber assembly Italy

ECONOMIC INDICATORS

	Greece	Italy
GDP (US$ billions)	119.1	1.212 trillion
GNP per capita (US$)	13,080	20,060
Annual rate of growth of GDP, 1990–1997	1.6%	1.1%
Manufacturing as % of GDP	13.9%	16.4%
Central government spending as % of GDP	33.6%	48.6%
Merchandise exports (US$ billions)	5.6	238.2
Merchandise imports (US$ billions)	21	191.5
Aid given as % of GNP	0.16%	

WELFARE INDICATORS

	Greece	Italy
Infant mortality rate (per 1,000 live births)		
1965	34	36
2000	8	7
Daily food supply available (calories per capita, 1995)	3,825	3,216
Population per physician (1995)	256	182
Teacher-pupil ratio (primary school, 1995)	1 : 22	1 : 12

- national capital
• other town

Italy **Area** 116,324 sq mi
(301,277 sq km)
Population 57,634,327
Capital Rome
Currency 1 lira
(Lit) = 100 centesimi
Euro (€) also in use
€ = 100 cents

Malta **Area** 122 sq mi
(316 sq km)
Population 391,670
Capital Valletta
Currency 1 Maltese lira
(Lm) = 100 cents = 1,000 mils

San Marino **Area** 24 sq mi
(61 sq km)
Population 26,937
Capital San Marino
Currency 1 Italian lira
(Lit) = 100 centesimi

Vatican City **Area** 0.17 sq mi
(0.44 sq km)
Population 900
Currency 1 Vatican lira
(VL) = 1 Italian lira = 100 centesimi

Both Italy and Greece are republics that once had monarchies and abolished them. Both are highly centralized states. Malta has been a democratic republic within the British Commonwealth since 1964. San Marino claims to be the world's oldest republic.

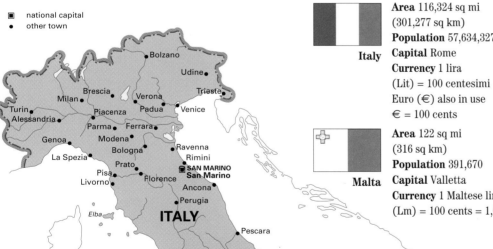

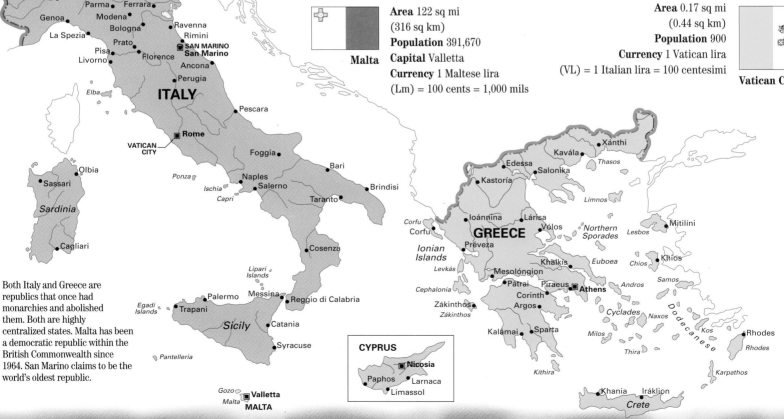

Environmental Issues

Deforestation in the past has caused extensive soil erosion and has increased the frequency of floods and avalanches. The growth of industrial areas in northern Italy and around Athens in Greece has caused large-scale air, river, and sea pollution.

POPULATION AND WEALTH

	Greece	Italy	Malta
Population (millions)	10.601	57.634	0.392
Population increase (annual growth rate, 1990–95)	0.3%	0.0%	n/a
Energy use (lbs/year per person oil equivalent)	5,331	6,274	n/a
Purchasing power parity (Int$/per year)	12,485	20,354	n/a

ENVIRONMENTAL INDICATORS

	Greece	Italy	Malta
CO₂ emissions ('000 tons/year)	76,284	409,983	n/a
Car ownership (% of population)	27%	59%	55%
Protected territory including marine areas	3%	7%	1%
Forests as a % of original forest	17%	20%	n/a
Artificial fertilizer use (lbs/acre/year)	110	188	n/a
Access to safe drinking water (% population; rural/urban)	100/100%	100/100%	100/100%

MAJOR ENVIRONMENTAL PROBLEMS AND SOURCES

Air pollution: Locally high, in particular urban; acid rain prevalent; high greenhouse gas emissions
River pollution: medium; *sources:* agriculture, sewage
Marine/coastal pollution: medium/high; *sources:* industry, agriculture, sewage, oil
Major events: Seveso (1976), poisonous chemical leakage; Rhodes (1987), major forest fire; Adda Valley (1987), major floods; *Haven* (1991) oil tanker spill

Population

During the Renaissance in the fifteenth to sixteenth centuries, Italy had many wealthy cities that were centers of art and learning. But the population remained largely rural in both Italy and Greece until recent times, when industrial cities began to develop.

POPULATION

Total population of region (millions)	69.4

	Greece	Italy
Population density (persons per sq mi)	207	495
Population change (average annual percent 1995–2000) Urban	0.58%	0.10%
Rural	–0.13%	–0.24%

URBAN POPULATION

As percentage of total population		
2000	60%	67%

TEN LARGEST CITIES

	Country	Population
Rome †	Italy	2,643,581
Milan	Italy	1,300,977
Naples	Italy	1,002,619
Turin	Italy	903,730
Athens	Greece	772,072
Palermo	Italy	683,794
Genoa	Italy	636,104
Florence	Italy	417,000
Salonika	Greece	383,967
Bologna	Italy	381,161

† denotes capital city

City population figures are for the city proper.

Agriculture

Mountainous terrain, summer droughts, and poor soils have created many problems for farmers. To overcome these difficulties and achieve high agricultural yields, the people have terraced the slopes, drained marshes, and built irrigation systems.

LAND
Total area 170,991 sq mi (442,862 sq km)

Cropland	Pasture	Forest/Woodland
36% (62,108 sq mi)	22% (38,236 sq mi)	22% (37,408 sq mi)

FARMERS

	Greece	Italy
Agriculture as % of GDP	11%	3%
% of workforce	19.8%	7%

MAJOR CROPS
Agricultural products: fruits and vegetables; grains; grapes; olives; beef, pork; dairy products; poultry; sugar beet; fish; tobacco; soybeans

	Greece	Italy
Total cropland ('000 acres)	9,674	27,001
Cropland (acres) per 1,000 people	914	469
Irrigated land as percentage of cropland	35%	25%
Annual fertilizer use (lbs per acre of cropland)	110	188
Number of tractors Change since 1987	236,100 16%	1,480,000 13%
Average cereal crop yields (lbs per acre)	2,924	4,070
Average production of cereals ('000 tons) Change since 1986–88	4,621 –15%	20,486 13%

LIVESTOCK AND FISHERIES

	Greece	Italy
Average meat production ('000 tons) Change since 1986–88	512 –1%	4,061 11%
Marine fish catch ('000 tons) Change since 1986–88	116.8 15%	236 –25%

Environmental Issues

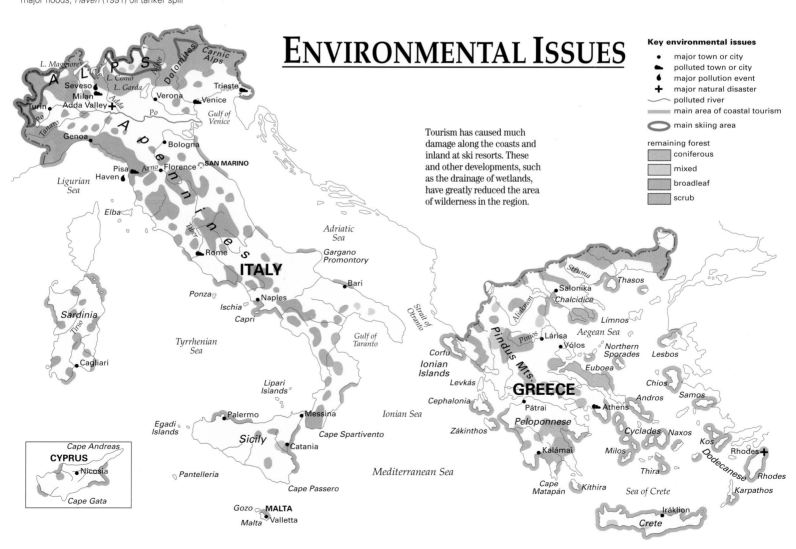

Tourism has caused much damage along the coasts and inland at ski resorts. These and other developments, such as the drainage of wetlands, have greatly reduced the area of wilderness in the region.

Key environmental issues
- • major town or city
- ● polluted town or city
- major pollution event
- ✛ major natural disaster
- polluted river
- main area of coastal tourism
- ⬭ main skiing area

remaining forest
- coniferous
- mixed
- broadleaf
- scrub

POPULATION

Greece is dominated by its capital, Athens, which with its suburbs contains about 30 percent of the country's population. Malta and Cyprus are also dominated by their capitals. Italy's population is more dispersed, with six cities having more than 500,000 people.

Population density

urban agglomeration
(National capital is underlined)

- ■ 1,000,000–5,000,000
- ● 500,000–999,999
- ◉ 250,000–499,999
- ○ 100,000–249,999
- × national capital less than 100,000

persons per square mi	persons per square km
520	200
260	100
130	50
65	25

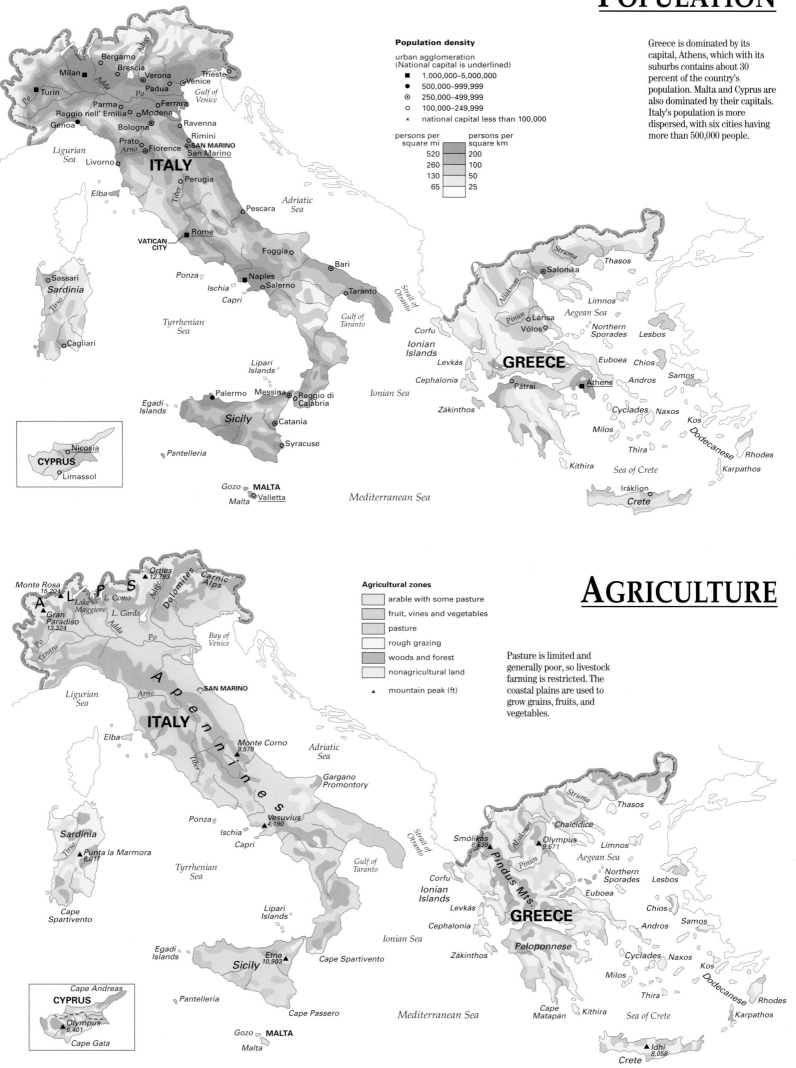

ITALY (Population map labels)

Turin, Milan, Bergamo, Brescia, Verona, Padua, Venice, Trieste, Parma, Modena, Ferrara, Reggio nell' Emilia, Genoa, Bologna, Ravenna, Prato, Rimini, Florence, SAN MARINO, San Marino, Livorno, Perugia, Pescara, VATICAN CITY, Rome, Foggia, Bari, Naples, Salerno, Taranto, Palermo, Messina, Reggio di Calabria, Catania, Syracuse, Valletta, MALTA, Gozo, Malta

Ligurian Sea, Po, Adda, Adige, Gulf of Venice, Tiber, Arno, Elba, Ponza, Ischia, Capri, Tyrrhenian Sea, Sardinia, Sassari, Cagliari, Tirso, Egadi Islands, Sicily, Lipari Islands, Pantelleria, Adriatic Sea, Strait of Otranto, Gulf of Taranto, Mediterranean Sea

CYPRUS — Nicosia, Limassol

GREECE (Population map labels)

Salonika, Thasos, Struma, Aliákmon, Límnos, Pinios, Lárisa, Vólos, Northern Sporades, Lesbos, Corfu, Ionian Islands, Levkás, GREECE, Euboea, Chios, Samos, Cephalonia, Pátrai, Athens, Andros, Cyclades, Naxos, Kos, Zákinthos, Milos, Dodecanese, Rhodes, Thira, Karpathos, Kíthira, Sea of Crete, Iráklion, Crete, Aegean Sea, Ionian Sea

AGRICULTURE

Pasture is limited and generally poor, so livestock farming is restricted. The coastal plains are used to grow grains, fruits, and vegetables.

Agricultural zones

- arable with some pasture
- fruit, vines and vegetables
- pasture
- rough grazing
- woods and forest
- nonagricultural land

- ▲ mountain peak (ft)

ITALY (Agriculture map labels)

Monte Rosa 15,204, Gran Paradiso 13,324, Ortles 12,793, Dolomites, Carnic Alps, ALPS, Lake Maggiore, L. Como, L. Garda, Adige, Po, Tanaro, Adda, Bay of Venice, Ligurian Sea, Arno, Apennines, Elba, SAN MARINO, ITALY, Monte Corno 9,578, Adriatic Sea, Gargano Promontory, Tiber, Ponza, Ischia, Capri, Vesuvius 4,190, Tyrrhenian Sea, Sardinia, Punta la Marmora 6,017, Tirso, Cape Spartivento, Egadi Islands, Sicily, Etna 10,903, Cape Spartivento, Lipari Islands, Gulf of Taranto, Pantelleria, Cape Passero, Gozo, MALTA, Malta, Mediterranean Sea, Strait of Otranto

CYPRUS — Cape Andreas, Olympus 6,401, Cape Gata

GREECE (Agriculture map labels)

Struma, Thasos, Chalcidice, Aliákmon, Smólikas 8,639, Olympus 9,571, Límnos, Pindus Mts, Pinios, Aegean Sea, Corfu, Ionian Islands, Northern Sporades, Lesbos, Levkás, Euboea, Chios, GREECE, Cephalonia, Andros, Samos, Peloponnese, Zákinthos, Cyclades, Naxos, Kos, Milos, Dodecanese, Ionian Sea, Thira, Rhodes, Cape Matapán, Kíthira, Sea of Crete, Karpathos, Idhi 8,058, Crete

CENTRAL EUROPE AND THE LOW COUNTRIES

The Low Countries—Belgium, Luxembourg, and the Netherlands—together with northern Germany are part of the North European Plain. The flat land of the north contrasts with the spectacular rugged Alpine scenery in the south, which includes Switzerland, Liechtenstein, and Austria.

Most people of the region speak Germanic languages, notably Dutch and German, though French is spoken in Belgium and Switzerland. Highly efficient farms are found throughout the region. Manufacturing is the main source of wealth, and products include chemicals, electronic goods, and vehicles.

The Low Countries and their neighbors in Central Europe form part of the world's temperate zone. In the Low Countries, large areas are below sea level—much of the Netherlands has been reclaimed from the sea. The Alps in the south contain majestic peaks and sparkling lakes.

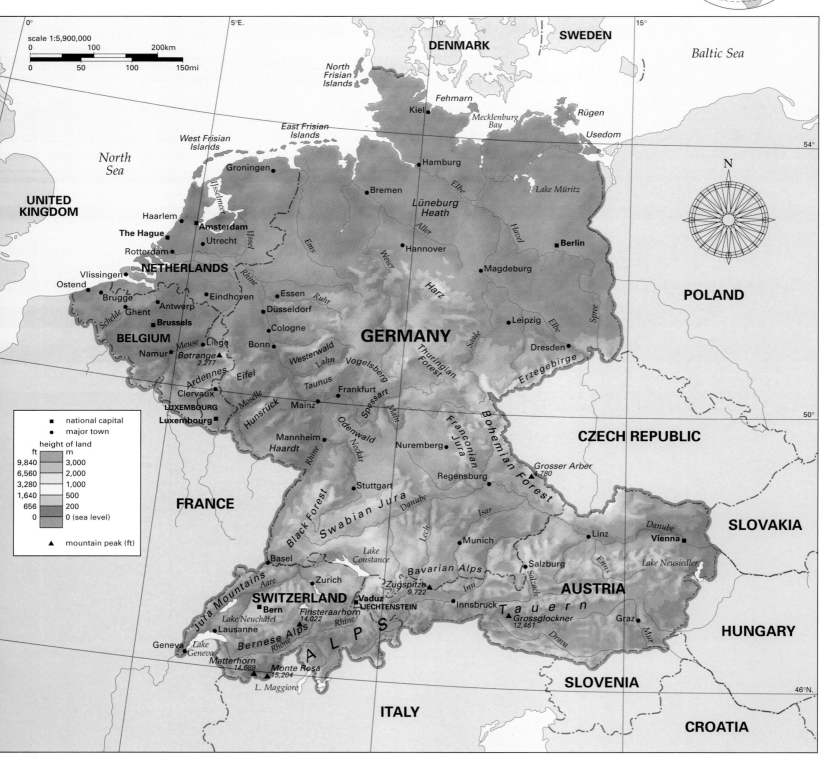

scale 1:5,900,000

| national capital |
| major town |

height of land

ft	m
9,840	3,000
6,560	2,000
3,280	1,000
1,640	500
656	200
0	0 (sea level)

▲ mountain peak (ft)

THE POLITICAL AND CULTURAL WORLD

Of the seven countries in the region, four are parliamentary democracies with monarchs as heads of state. They are the kingdoms of Belgium and the Netherlands, the Grand Duchy of Luxembourg, and the Principality of Liechtenstein. The other three countries—Austria, Germany, and Switzerland—are federal republics.

After World War II, Central Europe played an important part in the Cold War. But communism collapsed in Eastern Europe in 1990. West and East Germany, which were divided in 1945, were reunified politically. The task of economic integration, however, proved to be more costly than many Germans had expected.

Austria

Area 32,377 sq mi (83,857 sq km)
Population 8,131,111
Currency 1 Schilling (S) = 100 Groschen
Euro (€) also in use
€ = 100 cents

Belgium

Area 11,782 sq mi (30,518 sq km)
Population 10,241,506
Currency 1 Belgian franc (BF) = 100 centimes
Euro (€) also in use
€ = 100 cents

Belgium, Luxembourg, Netherlands, and former West Germany were founder members in the 1950s of what is now the European Union. Both Switzerland and Liechtenstein were politically neutral during both world wars, while Austria was allied to Germany. After its defeat in 1945, Germany was divided, and its eastern part came under Soviet influence. The two parts of the country were reunited in October 1990.

COUNTRIES IN THE REGION
Austria, Belgium, Germany, Liechtenstein, Luxembourg, Netherlands, Switzerland

Territories outside the region
Aruba, Netherlands Antilles (Netherlands)

LANGUAGE
Countries with one official language (Dutch) Netherlands; (German) Austria, Germany, Liechtenstein
Country with two official languages (French, German) Luxembourg
Countries with three official languages (Dutch, French, German) Belgium; (French, German, Italian) Switzerland

RELIGION
Austria Roman Catholic (85%), Protestant (6%), other (9%)
Belgium Roman Catholic (90%), nonreligious and atheist (7.5%), Muslim (1.1%), Protestant (0.4%)
Germany Protestant (40.8%), Roman Catholic (33.9%), nonreligious and atheist (3.6%), Muslim (2.1%), other (19.6%)
Liechtenstein Roman Catholic (87.3%), Protestant (8.3%), other (4.4%)
Luxembourg Roman Catholic (97%), Protestant (1.3%)
Netherlands Roman Catholic (32%), nonreligious and atheist (38%), Dutch Reformed (15%), Muslim (4.3%)
Switzerland Roman Catholic (47.6%), Protestant (44.3%)

■ national capital
• other town

STYLES OF GOVERNMENT
Republics Austria, Germany, Switzerland
Monarchies Belgium, Liechtenstein, Luxembourg, Netherlands
Federal states Austria, Germany, Switzerland
Multiparty states Austria, Belgium, Germany, Liechtenstein, Luxembourg, Netherlands, Switzerland
One-chamber assembly Liechtenstein
Two-chamber assembly Austria, Belgium, Germany, Netherlands, Switzerland

ECONOMIC INDICATORS
	Belguim	Netherlands
GDP (US$ billions)	242.5	360.5
GNP per capita (US$)	22,370	21,340
Annual rate of growth of GDP, 1990–1997	1.4%	2.4%
Manufacturing as % of GDP	19%	18%
Central government spending as % of GDP	49.4%	50.8%
Merchandise exports (US$ billions)	150.4	163.7
Merchandise imports (US$ billions)	142.9	146.0
Aid given as % of GNP	0.34%	0.81%

WELFARE INDICATORS
	Belguim	Netherlands
Infant mortality rate (per 1,000 live births)		
1965	24	14
2000	4.76	4.42
Daily food supply available (calories per capita, 1995)	3,530	3,230
Population per physician (1995)	267	394
Teacher-pupil ratio (primary school, 1995)	1 : 13	1 : 16

Area 137,821 sq mi (356,954 sq km)
Population 82,797,408
Currency 1 Deutsche mark (DM) = 100 Pfennig
Euro (€) also in use
€ = 100 cents

Germany

Area 62 sq mi (160 sq km)
Population 32,207
Currency 1 Swiss franc (SF) = 100 centimes

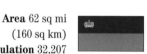

Liechtenstein

Area 998 sq mi (2,586 sq km)
Population 437,389
Currency 1 Luxembourg franc (LuxF) = 100 centimes
Euro (€) also in use
€ = 100 cents

Luxembourg

Area 16,163 sq mi (41,863 sq km)
Population 15,892,237
Currency 1 guilder (G) = 100 cents
Euro (€) also in use
€ = 100 cents

Netherlands

Area 15,943 sq mi (41,293 sq km)
Population 7,262,372
Currency 1 Swiss franc (SF) = 100 centimes

Switzerland

Map labels:

North Frisian Islands
Flensburg
Kiel
Fehmarn
East Frisian Islands
West Frisian Islands
Rostock
Lübeck
Bremerhaven
Hamburg
Schwerin
Groningen
Oldenburg
Bremen
NETHERLANDS
Zwolle
Haarlem
■ Amsterdam
The Hague ■
Utrecht
Enschede
Osnabrück
Hannover
■ Berlin
Rotterdam
Arnhem
Bielefeld
Hildesheim
Potsdam
Magdeburg
Vlissingen
Nijmegen
Münster
Ostend
Brugge
Essen
Dortmund
Göttingen
Cottbus
Ghent
Eindhoven
Duisburg
Düsseldorf
Kassel
Antwerp
■ Brussels
Maastricht
Cologne
Leipzig
BELGIUM
Liège
Aachen
Erfurt
Dresden
Mons
Namur
Bonn
GERMANY
Chemnitz
Koblenz
Wiesbaden
Frankfurt
LUXEMBOURG
Mainz
Offenbach
Arlon
■ Luxembourg
Würzburg
Mannheim
Saarbrücken
Nuremberg
Karlsruhe
Regensburg
Stuttgart
Ulm
Augsburg
Freiburg
Munich
Linz
St. Pölten
■ Vienna
Basel
Bregenz
Wels
Salzburg
Eisenstadt
St. Gall
Bad Ischl
Neuchâtel
■ Bern
Lucerne
■ Vaduz
LIECHTENSTEIN
Innsbruck
AUSTRIA
Fohnsdorf
Zurich
SWITZERLAND
Chur
Lienz
Graz
Lausanne
Geneva
Sion
Villach
Klagenfurt
Bellinzona

HABITATS

There is a sharp contrast between the Netherlands' flat, cultivated polders, or land reclaimed from the sea, and the Alps, which contain some of Europe's finest scenery. Several rivers, including the Rhine, flow through scenic valleys, with forested mountains on each side.

LAND

Area 215,149 sq mi (557,231 sq km)
Highest point Monte Rosa, 15,204 ft (4,634 m)
Lowest point in west Netherlands, –22 ft (–7 m)
Major features High Alps, Bohemian Forest, Black Forest, very low-lying areas in north Low Countries, Rhine rift valley

WATER

Longest river Rhine 820 mi (1,320 km), Rhine basin 97,000 sq mi (252,000 sq km), also the upper part of the Danube
Highest average flow Rhine 88,000 cu ft/sec (2,490 cu m/sec)
Largest lake IJsselmeer, 467 sq mi (1,210 sq km)

NOTABLE THREATENED SPECIES

Mammals Pond bat (*Myotis dasycneme*), Mouse-eared bat (*Myotis myotis*), Harbor porpoise (*Phocoena phocoena*), European mink (*Mustela lutreola*)
Birds Red kite (*Milvus milvus*), White-tailed sea eagle (*Haliaeetus albicilla*), Corncrake (*Crex crex*), Great bustard (*Otis tarda*), Aquatic warbler (*Acrocephalus paludicola*), Long-billed curlew (*Numerius tenvirostris*), Lesser kestrel (*Falco naumanni*)
Plants *Artemisia laciniata, Betula humilis*, Bog orchid (*Hammarbya paludosa*), Corncockle (*Agrostemma githago*), *Crassula aquatica, Dracocephalum austriacum, Echinodorus repens*, Elbe water dropwort (*Oenanthe conioides*), *Eriophorum gracile, Gentiana pneumonanthe, Halimione pedunculata, Jurinea cyanoides*, Lake Constance forget-me-not (*Myosotis rehsteineri*), *Luronium natans, Petroselinum segetum, Pulsatilla patens, Salvina natans, Spiranthes aestivalis*, Spiral orchid (*Spiranthes spiralis*)

CLIMATE

The western part of the region has a temperate, wet climate, with moderately warm summers and cool, mild winters. Eastern Germany has hotter summers and colder winters. Austria and Switzerland have permanently snow-capped mountains.

CLIMATE

	Temperature °F (°C)		Altitude
	January	July	ft (m)
Hamburg	32 (0)	63 (17)	46 (14)
Zurich	30 (–1)	64 (18)	1,886 (569)
Lugano	36 (2)	70 (21)	905 (276)
Munich	28 (–2)	64 (18)	1,732 (528)
Vienna	30 (–1)	68 (20)	695 (212)
Ostend	37 (3)	61 (16)	33 (10)

	Precipitation in. (mm)		
	January	July	Year
Hamburg	2.2 (57)	3.3 (84)	28.3 (720)
Zurich	2.9 (75)	5.6 (143)	44.8 (1,137)
Lugano	2.5 (63)	7.3 (185)	68.7 (1,744)
Munich	2.3 (59)	5.5 (140)	38.0 (964)
Vienna	1.6 (40)	3.3 (83)	26.0 (660)
Ostend	1.6 (41)	2.4 (62)	23.5 (598)

NATURAL HAZARDS

Avalanches and landslides in mountains, tidal surges in coastal areas, flooding in flat river valleys

ENVIRONMENTAL ISSUES

The Low Countries are among the world's most densely populated areas, and the population has had a great impact on the land. Deforestation and acid rain have damaged the entire region, and industrial pollution has greatly affected eastern Germany.

POPULATION AND WEALTH

	Belgium	Germany	Netherlands
Population (millions)	10.241	82.797	15.892
Population increase (annual growth rate, % 1990–95)	0.1%	0.1%	0.4%
Energy use (lbs per year per equivalent)	12,436	9,330	10,578
Purchasing power parity (Int$/per year)	22,892	21,265	21,104

ENVIRONMENTAL INDICATORS

CO$_2$ emissions ('000 tons/year)	103,816	835,099	135,509
Car ownership (% of population)	44%	n/a	42%
Proportion of territory protected, including marine areas (%)	3%	27%	12%
Forests as a % of original forest	21%	26%	5%
Artificial fertilizer use lbs/acre/year	1,220	207	679
Access to safe drinking water (% population; rural/urban)	100%/100%	100%/100%	100%/100%

MAJOR ENVIRONMENTAL PROBLEMS AND SOURCES

Air pollution: locally high
River/lake pollution: high; *sources*: agriculture, industry, sewage
Marine/coastal pollution: high; *sources*: industry, agriculture, sewage, oil, transport infrastructure
Land pollution: high; *sources*: industry; agriculture, urban/household
Waste disposal issues: domestic; industrial; nuclear
Resource issues: land use competition; coastal flooding; water level control and flooding
Major events: Lekkerkerk (1980), toxic waste dump discovered; Brussels (1999), dioxin in food crisis; Sandoz near Basel (1987), chemical spill; Central European floods (1997)

HABITATS

Glaciation has left its mark on the land. Northern Germany is covered by moraine left behind by the Scandinavian glaciers. Glaciers continue to shape the land in the Alps.

Physical zones
- mountains/barren land
- forest
- grassland

▲ mountain peak (ft)
�▲ climate station

ENVIRONMENTAL ISSUES

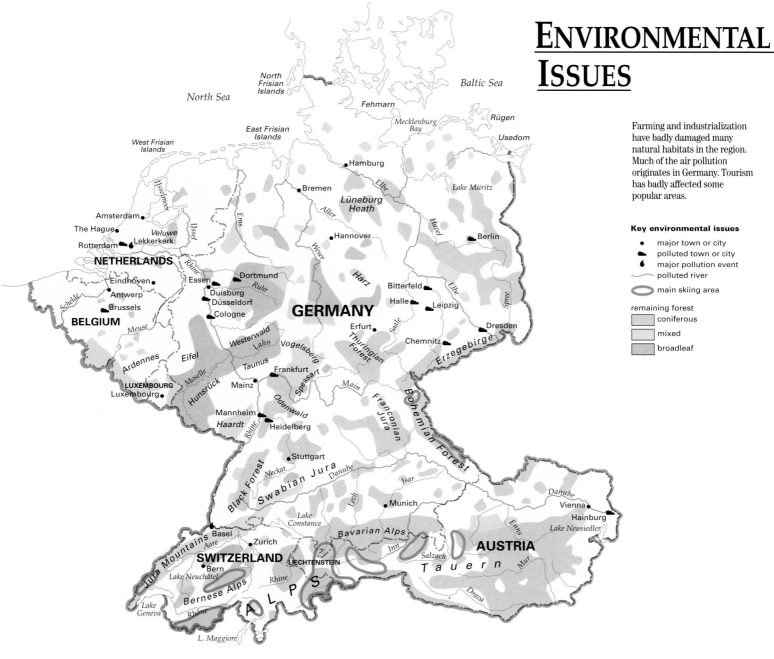

Farming and industrialization have badly damaged many natural habitats in the region. Much of the air pollution originates in Germany. Tourism has badly affected some popular areas.

Key environmental issues

- • major town or city
- 🌫 polluted town or city
- 🌡 major pollution event
- ∿ polluted river
- ⬭ main skiing area

remaining forest

	coniferous
	mixed
	broadleaf

CLIMATE

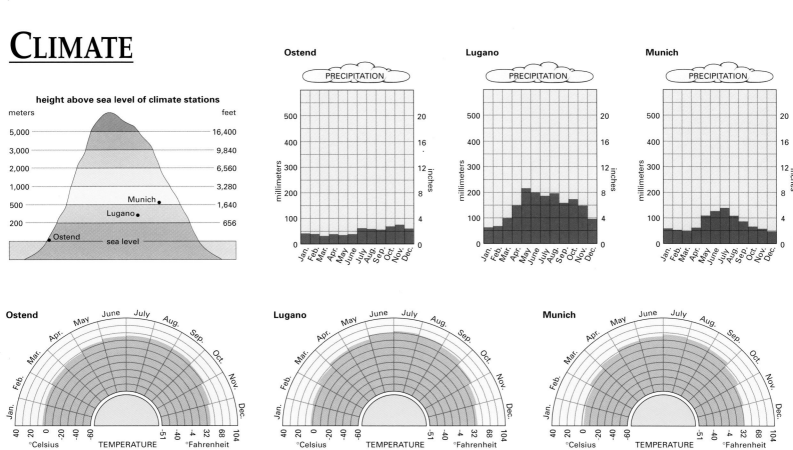

height above sea level of climate stations

meters		feet
5,000		16,400
3,000		9,840
2,000		6,560
1,000		3,280
500	Munich	1,640
200	Lugano	656
	Ostend	sea level

Ostend — PRECIPITATION

Lugano — PRECIPITATION

Munich — PRECIPITATION

Ostend — TEMPERATURE

Lugano — TEMPERATURE

Munich — TEMPERATURE

POPULATION

Industrialization led to a rapid increase in the region's population from the late 1800s. New cities grew up near coal or iron fields. Older cities, such as Berlin and Vienna, have also grown in the last 50 years. The Netherlands has towns on land reclaimed from the sea.

POPULATION

Total population of region (millions)		124.794
	Germany	Netherlands
Population density (persons per sq mi)	593	1,200
Population change (average annual percent 1995–2000)		
Urban	+0.38%	+0.50%
Rural	−1.48%	-0.27%

URBAN POPULATION

As percentage of total population		
2000	88%	89%

TEN LARGEST CITIES

	Country	Population
Berlin †	Germany	3,472,000
Hamburg	Germany	1,706,000
Vienna †	Austria	1,609,631
Brussels †	Belgium	1,331,000
Munich	Germany	1,245,000
Amsterdam †	Netherlands	1,102,000
Rotterdam	Netherlands	1,077,000
Cologne	Germany	964,000
The Hague †	Netherlands	695,000
Zurich	Switzerland	336,821

† denotes capital city

City population figures are for the city proper.

INDUSTRY

Germany is Europe's top industrial power. Its industries were based on local supplies of fuels and metals, but many raw materials are now imported. In some countries, such as Switzerland, much industry has been based on crafts, such as clock-making.

INDUSTRIAL OUTPUT (US $ billion)

Germany	Austria	Netherlands
780 (1995)	70 (1996)	107 (1995)

INDUSTRIAL WORKERS (millions)
(figures in parentheses are percentages of total labor force)

	Mining	Manufacturing	Construction
Germany	0.45 (1.1%)	8.4 (20.9%)	2.8 (7.2%)
Netherlands	0.01 (0.2%)	1.0 (14.8%)	0.4 (5.6%)

MAJOR PRODUCTS (Germany)

	Output 1970	1995	Change since 1970
Coal (mil m.t.)	369	193	−47.7%
Gas ('000 terajoules)	479	657	37.2%
Potash ('000 tons)	5,064	3,300	−34.8%
Salt ('000 tons)	23,202	12,700	−45.3%

MAJOR PRODUCTS (Netherlands)

Petroleum Products (mil m.t.)	52	63	21.2%
Oil (crude, mil m.t.)	1.8	2.3	27.8
Natural gas ('000 terajoules)	1,116	2,856	155.9 (3.4%)
Zinc ('000 tons)	46	206	347.8

AGRICULTURE

The farmers of the Low Countries produce some of the world's highest yields. Arable farming is important in northern and central Germany, but more than 50 percent of the land in Austria and 75 percent in Switzerland is too mountainous to be farmed.

LAND
Total area 215,149 sq mi (557,231 sq km)

Cropland	Pasture	Forest/Woodland
29% (62,245 sq mi)	18% (39,116 sq mi)	30% (64,416 sq mi)

FARMERS

	Austria	Germany	Netherlands
Agriculture as % of GDP	1%	1%	3%
% of workforce	3%	2.7%	4%

MAJOR CROPS
Agricultural products: grains; potatoes; sugar beet; fruit; wine; beef; pork; poultry; dairy products; wood and forest products

Total cropland ('000 acres)	3,655	29,800	2,310
Cropland (acres) per 1,000 people	452	363	148
Irrigated land as % of cropland	0%	4%	60%
Number of tractors	352,375	1,215,700	173,000
Average cereal crop yields (lbs/acre)	4,681	5,266	6,158
Cereal production ('000 tons)	4,746	44,067	1,489
Change since 1986/88	−8%	21%	24%

LIVESTOCK & FISHERIES

Meat production ('000 tons)	896	6,069	260
Change since 1986/88	15%	−27%	31%
Marine fish catch ('000 tons)	0	203	398.2
Change since 1986/88	n/a	−34%	10%

FOOD SECURITY

Food aid as % of total imports	0	0	n/a
Daily kcal/person	3,536	3,382	3,284

POPULATION

The Netherlands and Belgium, together with the Ruhr and Rhine valleys in Germany, have population densities of more than 500 per sq mi (200 per sq km). Parts of Switzerland and Austria are thinly populated.

Population density

urban agglomeration
(National capital is underlined)

◆	5,000,000–10,000,000
■	1,000,000–4,999,999
●	500,000–999,999
⊙	250,000–499,999
×	national capital less than 250,000

persons per square mi	persons per square km
520	200
260	100
130	50
65	25

INDUSTRY

Apart from Germany, most countries in the region have limited resources. They have concentrated on being highly efficient and specializing in high-cost products.

Map 1 — Industry

North Sea

North Frisian Islands

Baltic Sea

Kiel
Fehmarn
Rügen
Stralsund
Usedom
Rostock
East Frisian Islands
Lübeck
Bremerhaven
Hamburg
Emden
Bremen
Groningen
Lake Müritz
Hannover
IJsselmeer
Enschede
Haarlem
Amsterdam
The Hague
Utrecht
Aller
Berlin
Harvel
Europoort
Rotterdam
Magdeburg
NETHERLANDS
Rhine
Ems
Weser
Ostend
Essen
Dortmund
Ghent
Antwerp
Ruhr
Kassel
Saale
Elbe
Spree
Brussels
Düsseldorf
Leipzig
Schelde
Cologne
BELGIUM
Liège
Meuse
Dresden
Charleroi
Chemnitz
GERMANY
Moselle
Frankfurt
LUXEMBOURG
Lahn
Main
Luxembourg
Mainz
Esch
Mannheim
Nuremberg
Neckar
Karlsruhe
Regensburg
Rhine
Stuttgart
Danube
Isar
Linz
Danube
Vienna
Basel
Lake Constance
Lech
Munich
Lake Neusiedler
Salzburg
AUSTRIA
Aare
Zurich
Inn
Salzach
Bern
Vaduz
Innsbruck
LIECHTENSTEIN
Lake Neuchâtel
Rhine
Drava
SWITZERLAND
Graz
Mur
Lake Geneva
Rhône
L. Maggiore

Resources and industry

- ◆ industrial center
- ○ port
- ● other town
- —— major road
- —— major railroad

mineral resources and fossil fuels

- ● iron and other ferroalloy metal ores
- ● other metal ores
- ■ nonmetallic minerals
- coal
- iron ore
- lignite (brown coal)
- natural gas
- oil
- potash
- salt

AGRICULTURE

Map 2 — Agriculture

North Frisian Islands

Baltic Sea

North Sea
Fehmarn
Mecklenburg Bay
Rügen
Usedom
West Frisian Islands
East Frisian Islands
Lüneburg Heath
Elbe
Lake Müritz
Veluwe
IJsselmeer
Aller
Harvel
IJssel
Ems
Weser
NETHERLANDS
Rhine
Harz
Spree
Kempenland
Ruhr
Elbe
Saale
Schelde
BELGIUM
Meuse
Westerwald
Lahn
Thuringian Forest
Botrange 2,277
Eifel
Vogelsberg
Erzegebirge
Ardennes
Taunus
LUXEMBOURG
Moselle
Hunsrück
Spessart
Main
Franconian Jura
Bohemian Forest
Haardt
Odenwald
GERMANY
Rhine
Neckar
Grosser Arber 4,780
Black Forest
Swabian Jura
Danube
Isar
Lech
Danube
Lake Constance
Inn
Lake Neusiedler
Bavarian Alps
Salzach
Jura Mountains
Zugspitze 9,722
Drava
SWITZERLAND
Aare
Tauern
AUSTRIA
Finsteraarhorn 14,022
LIECHTENSTEIN
Grossglockner 12,461
Lake Neuchâtel
ALPS
Mur
Bernese Alps
Rhine
Lake Geneva
Matterhorn 14,689
Monte Rosa 15,204
L. Maggiore

Agricultural zones

- arable and pasture
- fruit, vines and vegetables
- pasture
- rough grazing
- woods and forest
- nonagricultural land
- ▲ mountain peak (ft)

Arable farming predominates in low-lying areas in the Low Countries, northern Germany, and sheltered valleys in the south. Forestry, livestock, and dairy farming are more important in the uplands.

EASTERN EUROPE

Eastern Europe extends from the dune-lined Baltic coast in the north, through part of the North European Plain in Poland and a series of uplands in the south, to the Adriatic Sea in the southwest, and the Black Sea, outlet of the Danube River, in the southeast. An important plain in the region is the Great Alföld in Hungary. The north is cold and dry, but the south has a subtropical climate.

The region is culturally complex. It contains several language groups, including Slavic, Germanic, Finno-Ugric, and Romance languages. Religions, mainly Roman Catholicism, Orthodox Christianity, and Islam, also characterize the people.

Agriculture was the chief activity in the past. Under communism, however, great efforts were made to industrialize the region. This has caused extensive damage to the environment.

Eastern Europe extends from the cool Baltic Sea region in the north to the Mediterranean lands in the south. Until 1989, Eastern Europe formed a buffer zone of communist states between Western Europe and the Soviet Union. By 2001 some were considering joining the European Union.

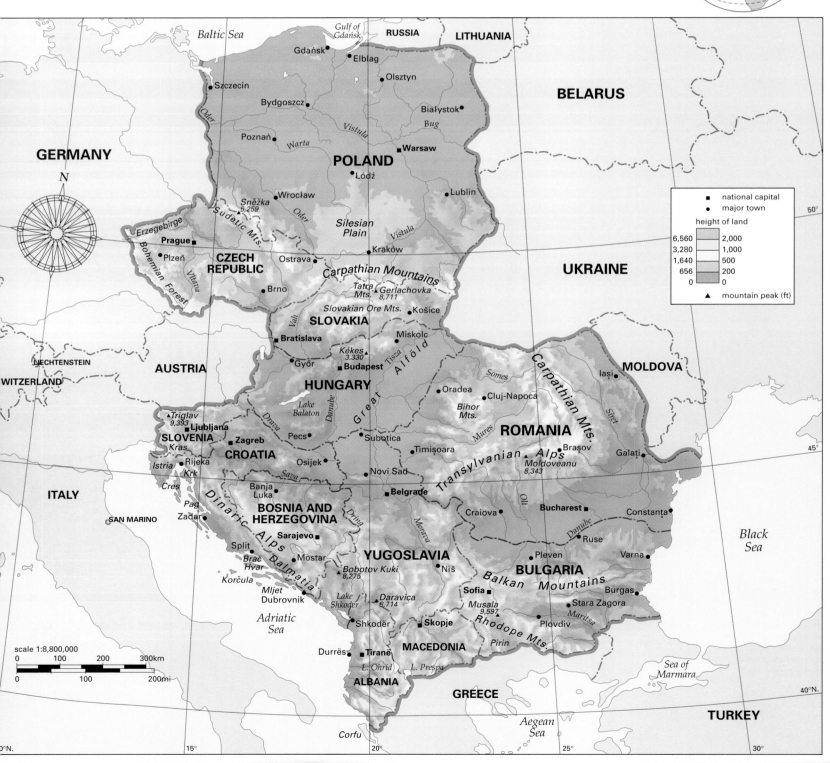

THE POLITICAL AND CULTURAL WORLD

Eastern Europe contains 12 countries. Of these, Bosnia and Herzegovina, Croatia, Macedonia, Slovenia, and Yugoslavia (now consisting only of Serbia and Montenegro) made up Yugoslavia between 1918 and 1991. The Czech Republic and Slovakia came into being on January 1, 1993, when Czechoslovakia was divided into two parts.

This group of formerly communist countries has faced many problems since the collapse of their ideology in the late 1980s and early 1990s. Rivalries between ethnic groups have resurfaced, causing civil war in Yugoslavia, most recently in Kosovo. The countries have also faced many problems as they seek to reestablish free-enterprise economies.

COUNTRIES IN THE REGION

Albania, Bosnia and Herzegovina, Bulgaria, Croatia, Czech Republic, Hungary, Macedonia, Poland, Romania, Slovakia, Slovenia, Yugoslavia (Serbia and Montenegro)

LANGUAGE

(Albanian) Albania; (Croatian, Serbian, Bosnian) Bosnia and Herzegovina; (Bulgarian) Bulgaria; (Croatian) Croatia; (Czech) Czech Republic; (Hungarian) Hungary; (Macedonian) Macedonia; (Polish) Poland; (Romanian) Romania; (Slovak) Slovakia; (Slovenian) Slovenia; (Serbo-Croat) Yugoslavia

Albanian is a minority language in Macedonia and Yugoslavia; Hungarian in Yugoslavia and Slovakia. Other languages spoken in the region include German (Czech Republic, Hungary), Greek (Albania), Romany (Bulgaria, Romania, Yuogoslavia), Tatar (Romania), Turkish (Bulgaria), and Ukrainian (Slovakia, Poland, Romania)

RELIGION

Countries with one major religion (BO) Bulgaria; (M) Albania; (RC) Czech Republic, Hungary, Poland, Slovakia, Slovenia; (RO) Romania

Countries with more than one major religion (RC, EO) Croatia; (MO, M) Macedonia; (M, RC, SO) Bosnia and Herzegovina, Yugoslavia
Key: BO–Bulgarian Orthodox, EO–Eastern Orthodox, M–Muslim, MO–Macedonian Orthodox, RC–Roman Catholic, RO–Romanian Orthodox, SO–Serbian Orthodox

STYLES OF GOVERNMENT

Republics All countries in the region
Multiparty states All countries in the region
One-chamber assembly Albania, Bulgaria, Hungary, Macedonia, Slovakia
Two-chamber assembly Bosnia and Herzegovina, Croatia, Czech Republic, Poland, Romania, Slovenia, Yugoslavia

ECONOMIC INDICATORS

	Hungary	Poland	Romania
GDP (US$ billions)	44	135.6	35.2
GNP per capita (US$)	7,000	6,380	4,290
Annual rate of growth of GDP, 1990–1997	-0.2%	4.1%	0%
Manufacturing as % of GDP	20.5%*	25.2%*	n/a
Central government spending as % of GDP	n/a	43%	32%
Merchandise exports (US$ billions)	19.6	30.7	8.4
Merchandise imports (US$ billions)	21.4	40.6	10.4
Aid received as % of GNP	0.4%	0.6%	0.6%

Figures include mining, 1995. (Polish figure is for 1993.)

WELFARE INDICATORS

	Hungary	Poland	Romania
Infant mortality rate (per 1,000 live births)			
1965	39	42	44
2000	10	15	23
Daily food supply available (calories per capita, 1995)	n/a	3,307	3,166
Population per physician (1995)	238	435	561
Teacher-pupil ratio (primary school, 1995)	1 : 11.5	1 : 15.8	1 : 15

Major changes occurred in Eastern Europe in the 1980s and 1990s. Those countries under communist rule emerged as struggling new democracies. Both Yugoslavia and Czechoslovakia refused to remain artificial unions of diverse nations, and they divided, in Yugoslavia's case with great violence and bloodshed. All the region's nations face economic hardship.

■ national capital
• other town

Albania
Area 11,100 sq mi (28,748 sq km)
Population 3,490,435

Bosnia and Herzegovina
Area 19,741 sq mi (51,129 sq km)
Population 3,835,777

Bulgaria
Area 42,855 sq mi (110,994 sq km)
Population 8,194,772

Croatia
Area 21,829 sq mi (56,538 sq km)
Population 4,282,216

Czech Republic
Area 30,450 sq mi (78,865 sq km)
Population 10,272,179

Hungary
Area 35,919 sq mi (93,031 sq km)
Population 10,138,844

Macedonia
Area 9,928 sq mi (25,713 sq km)
Population 2,041,467

Poland
Area 120,728 sq mi (312,683 sq km)
Population 38,646,023

Romania
Area 91,699 sq mi (237,500 sq km)
Population 22,411,121

Slovakia
Area 18,933 sq mi (49,035 sq km)
Population 5,407,956

Slovenia
Area 7,819 sq mi (20,251 sq km)
Population 1,927,593

Yugoslavia
Area 39,518 sq mi (102,350 sq km)
Population 10,662,087

HABITATS

The region contains large farming areas, grasslands, and wooded mountain ranges. The cool northern plains are drained by rivers that rise in the Sudetic and Carpathian mountains. The warmer southern plains are drained by the Danube River.

LAND

Area 450,519 sq mi (1,166,837 sq km)
Highest point Musala, 9,597 ft (2,925 m)
Lowest point near Gulf of Gdansk, −33 ft (−10 m)
Major features northern lowlands, Carpathian Mountains, Balkan Mountains, Dinaric Alps, Great Alföld, Danube valley

WATER

Longest river Danube, 1,770 mi (2,850 km)
Largest basin Danube, 298,000 sq mi (773,000 sq km)
Highest average flow Danube, 227,000 cu ft/sec (6,430 cu m/sec)
Largest lake Balaton, 230 sq mi (590 sq km)

NOTABLE THREATENED SPECIES

Mammals European bison (*Bison bonasus*), Gray wolf (*Canis lupus*), European mink (*Mustela lutreola*), Long-fingered bat (*Myotis capaccinii*), Mouse-eared bat (*Myotis myotis*)
Birds Dalmatian pelican (*Pelicanus crispus*), White-headed duck (*Oxyura leucocephala*), Lesser kestrel (*Falco naumanni*), Great bustard (*Otis tarda*), Aquatic warbler (*Acrocephalus paludicola*), Long-billed curlew (*Numenius tenuirostris*)
Plants *Astragalus ornacantha*; *Cochlearia polonica*; *Daphne arbuscula*; *Degenia velebitica*; *Dianthus uromoffii*; *Forsythia europaea*; *Lilium rhodopaeum*; *Onosma tornensis*; *Pulsatilla hungarica*; *Rhinanthus halophilus*
Others Olm (*Proteus anguinus*), Danube salmon (*Hucho hucho*), Scarce fritillary butterfly (*Euphydryas maturna*), Wild common carp (*Cyprinus carpio*)

HABITATS

The mountains include the young Carpathians and the old Sudetic Mountains. Some old ranges have been worn down to form plateaus. Lowlands occur in the north and center.

CLIMATE

The northern parts of Eastern Europe have a continental climate, with rain throughout the year. The southern part of the region has warmer summers. Winters are cool, and occasionally a strong, cold wind, called the bora, blows down from the north.

CLIMATE

	Temperature °F (°C) January	July	Altitude ft (m)
Gdansk	30 (−1)	64 (18)	39 (12)
Prague	27 (−3)	64 (18)	1,227 (374)
Tiranë	45 (7)	77 (25)	292 (89)
Bucharest	27 (−3)	73 (23)	269 (82)
Ljubljana	30 (−1)	70 (21)	931 (284)

	Precipitation in. (mm) January	July	Year
Gdansk	1.2 (31)	2.9 (73)	19.6 (499)
Prague	0.9 (23)	3.2 (82)	20.0 (508)
Tiranë	5.2 (132)	1.1 (28)	46.8 (1,189)
Bucharest	1.7 (43)	2.2 (55)	22.8 (578)
Ljubljana	3.5 (88)	4.5 (113)	55 (1,383)

NATURAL HAZARDS

Earthquakes, landslides, and floods

ENVIRONMENTAL ISSUES

Deforestation, intensive farming, and industrialization have caused much environmental damage in Eastern Europe in the last 40 years. Coal-burning power plants have caused air pollution and acid rain, especially in Poland and the Czech Republic.

POPULATION AND WEALTH

	Highest	Middle	Lowest
Population (millions)	38.646 (Poland)	10.138 (Hungary)	1.927 (Slovenia)
Population increase (annual growth rate, % 1990–95)	0.6% (Macedonia)	0.0% (Slovenia)	−0.7% (Bulgaria)
Energy use (lbs per year per person of oil equivalent)	8,684 (Czech Rep.)	4,314 (Romania)	739 (Albania)
Purchasing power parity (Int$/per year)	11,749 (Slovenia)	6,516 (Poland)	2,250 (Albania)

ENVIRONMENTAL INDICATORS

CO_2 emissions ('000 tons year)	338,044 (Poland)	112,049 (Czech Rep.)	1,843 (Bosnia Herz.)
Car ownership (% of population)	29% (Czech Rep.)	23% (Hungary)	19% (Bulgaria)
Proportion of territory protected, including marine areas (%)	76% (Slovakia)	9% (Poland)	0.5% (Bosnia Herz.)
Forests as a % of original forest	41% (Romania)	32% (Bulgaria)	85 (Hungary)
Artificial fertilizer use (lbs/acre/year)	213 (Slovenia)	100 (Poland)	5.8 (Albania)
Access to safe drinking water (% population, rural/urban)	100%/100% (Czech Rep.)	100%/100% (Hungary)	70%/90% (Albania)

MAJOR ENVIRONMENTAL PROBLEMS AND SOURCES

Air pollution: generally high, urban very high; acid rain prevalent; high greenhouse gas emissions, high particulate counts
River/lake pollution: high; *sources*: industry, agriculture, sewage, acid deposition, war
Land pollution: high; *sources*: industry, agriculture, urban/household, nuclear, war waste, Central European floods (1997); cyanide poisoning, Tisza River (2000)
Major events: flooding (1997 and 2000); cyanide spill at Baia Mare, Romania (2000)

Physical zones
mountains/barren land
forest
grassland
▲ mountain peak (ft)
🜨 climate station

ENVIRONMENTAL ISSUES

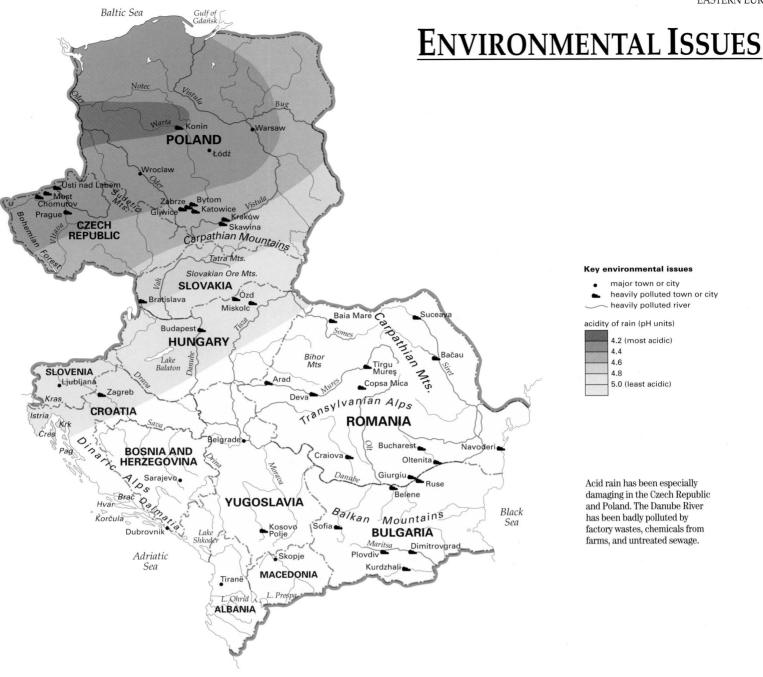

Key environmental issues

- · major town or city
- ◆ heavily polluted town or city
- ∽ heavily polluted river

acidity of rain (pH units)

- 4.2 (most acidic)
- 4.4
- 4.6
- 4.8
- 5.0 (least acidic)

Acid rain has been especially damaging in the Czech Republic and Poland. The Danube River has been badly polluted by factory wastes, chemicals from farms, and untreated sewage.

CLIMATE

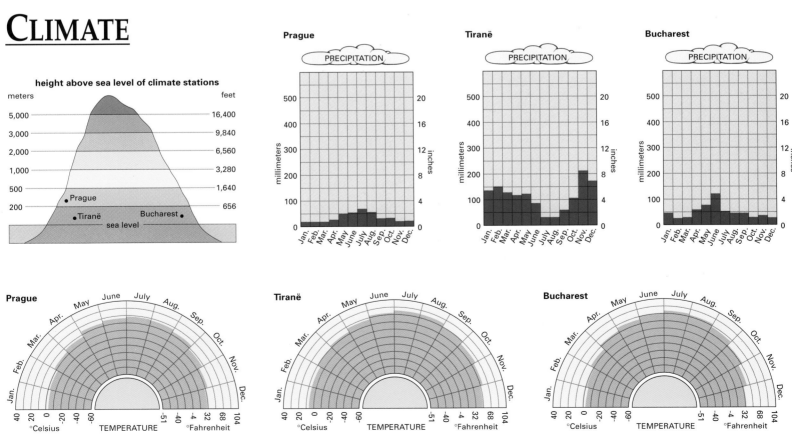

height above sea level of climate stations

meters		feet
5,000		16,400
3,000		9,840
2,000		6,560
1,000		3,280
500		1,640
200	Prague	656
	Tiranë Bucharest	
	sea level	

POPULATION

Industrialization came later to
Eastern Europe than it did to most
other parts of the continent. Even
today the proportion of people in
rural areas is comparatively high,
though urban areas now contain about
65 percent of the population.

POPULATION

Total population of region (millions)			121.3
	Hungary	Poland	Romania
Population density (per sq mi)	286.2	323.7	251.7
Population change (average annual percent 1995–2000)			
Urban	−0.07%	+0.67%	+0.10%
Rural	−0.92%	−1.0%	−0.93%

URBAN POPULATION

As percentage of total population			
2000	64%	66%	56%

TEN LARGEST CITIES

	Country	Population
Bucharest †	Romania	2,027,512
Budapest †	Hungary	1,838,753
Warsaw †	Poland	1,611,800
Belgrade †	Yugoslavia	1,194,878
Prague †	Czech Republic	1,193,270
Sofia †	Bulgaria	1,114,168
Lodz	Poland	789,200
Zagreb †	Croatia	748,500
Kraków	Poland	735,800
Wroclaw	Poland	634,600

† denotes capital city

City population figures are for the city proper.

POPULATION

Population density

urban agglomeration
(National capital is underlined)
- ■ 1,000,000–5,000,000
- ● 500,000–999,999
- ⊙ 250,000–499,999

persons per square mi	persons per square km
520	200
260	100
130	50
26	10

The main concentrations of
population are in the
industrial regions of the
Czech Republic and Poland, and
also around the regions'
national capitals.

INDUSTRY

Apart from Poland's rich coal
deposits and some other minerals,
the region lacks natural resources.
Many industries were set up under
communist rule, and their managers
are now having great difficulties
in converting to private enterprise.

INDUSTRIAL OUTPUT (US $ billion)

Poland	Romania	Hungary
46 (1995)	14 (1996)	13 (1996)

MAJOR PRODUCTS (Poland)

Energy and minerals	Output 1970	1995	Change since 1970
Petroleum products (mil m.t.)	6.1	13	113.1%
Bituminous coal (mil m.t.)	140	137	−2.1%
Lignite/brown coal (mil m.t.)	33	64	93.9%
Natural Gas ('000 terajoules)	186	150	−19.4%
Copper ('000 tons)	72	407	465.3%
Copper ore ('000 tons)	83	384	362.7%
Zinc ('000 tons)	209	167	−20.1%
Zinc ore ('000 tons)	242	154	−36.4%
Silver (tons)	0	60	

AGRICULTURE

While large tracts of Eastern Europe
can be used for arable farming,
irrigation is essential in the south
because of the hot, dry summers.
One-fifth of the land in this region is
mountainous and is only used
for rough grazing.

LAND

Total area 450,519 sq mi (1,166,837 sq km)

Cropland	Pasture	Forest/Woodland
41%	16%	31%
(167,489 sq mi)	(63,829 sq mi)	(125,525 sq mi)

FARMERS	Highest	Middle	Lowest
Agriculture as % of GDP	23% (Bul)	12% (Cro, Mac)	5% (Slvka, Slvna)
% of workforce	49.5% (Alb)	26% (Bul, Cro)	5.6% (CzR)

MAJOR CROPS

Agricultural products: wheat, corn, barley; fruit and
vegetables; sugar beet; olives; grapes; sunflower seeds;
sesame; hops; beef, pigs, poultry; dairy products; tobacco;
forest products

Total cropland ('000 acres)	35,642 (Pol)	11,147 (Bul)	704 (Slvna)
Cropland (acres) per 1,000 people	1,329 (Bul)	818 (Mac)	353 (Slvna)
Irrigated land as % of cropland	31% (Rom)	8% (Mac)	1% (Slvna)
Number of tractors	1,310,500 (Pol)	25,000 (Bul)	2,985 (Cro)
Average cereal crop yields (lbs/acre)	4,431 (Slvna)	3,141 (Yug)	1,970 (BH)
Cereal production ('000 tons)	25,911 (Pol)	6,832 (CzR)	479 (BH)
Change since 1986/88	3%	n/a	n/a

LIVESTOCK & FISHERIES

Meat production ('000 tons)	2,904 (Pol)	841 (CzR)	34 (BH)
Change since 1986/88	1%	n/a	n/a
Marine fish catch ('000 tons)	333.5 (Pol)	18.7 (Rom)	1.1 (Alb)
Change since 1986/88	−40%	−90%	−85%

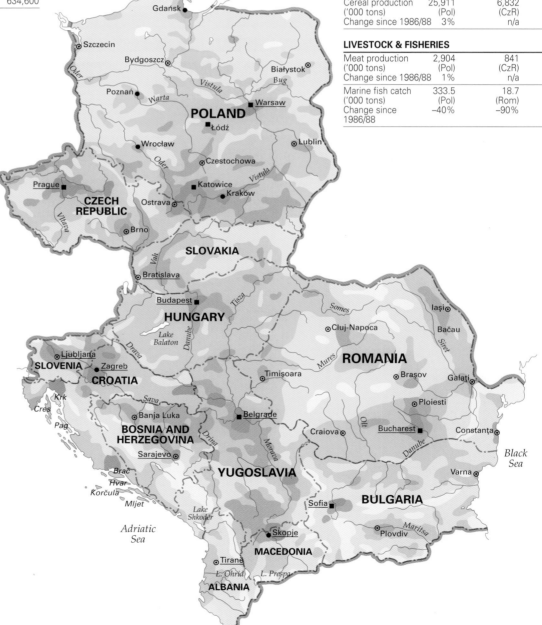

INDUSTRY

Resources and industry

- ◆ industrial center
- ○ port
- • other town
- —— major road
- —— major railroad

mineral resources and fossil fuels

- ◆ iron and other ferroalloy metal ores
- • other metal ores
- ▪ nonmetallic minerals

▨ coal

▨ iron ore

▨ lignite (brown coal)

Before 1945, industry was confined mainly to Poland and what is now the Czech Republic. Under communist rule, many natural resources were exploited, and industries were set up throughout the region.

Baltic Sea

Gulf of Gdańsk

Gdańsk

Szczecin
Stargard

Bydgoszcz

Oder

Poznań

Warta

Vistula

Bug

POLAND

Warsaw

Łódź

Wrocław

Oder

Prague
Plzeň

Vltava

CZECH REPUBLIC

Katowice

Vistula

Ostrava

Kraków

Brno

Žilina

Ruzomberok

SLOVAKIA

Vah

Miskolc

Budapest

Debrecen

Tisza

Somes

HUNGARY

Lake Balaton

Arad

Mures

ROMANIA

Sibiu

Brașov

Siret

Ljubljana

SLOVENIA

Zagreb

Drava

CROATIA

Rijeka

Krk

Cres

Pag

Sava

Sulina

Ploiesti

BOSNIA AND HERZEGOVINA

Belgrade

Drina

Olt

Bucharest

Constanța

Sarajevo

Split

Brač

Hvar

Korčula

Mljet

Krusevac

Morava

Danube

Ruse

Varna

Black Sea

Niš

YUGOSLAVIA

BULGARIA

Lake Shkodër

Bar
Shkodër

Sofia

Skopje

Maritsa

Plovdiv

Burgas

Durrës

Tiranë

MACEDONIA

L. Ohrid

L. Prespa

Adriatic Sea

ALBANIA

AGRICULTURE

Agricultural zones

- ▨ arable and pasture
- ▨ fruit and vegetables
- ▨ pasture
- ▨ rough grazing
- ▨ woods and forest
- ▨ nonagricultural land
- ▲ mountain peak (ft)

The most fertile regions are the North European Plain in Poland and the lowlands of Hungary, Romania, Croatia, and northern Yugoslavia. Livestock are raised in upland areas.

Baltic Sea

Gulf of Gdańsk

Oder

Notec

Warta

Vistula

Bug

POLAND

Sněžka 5,259

Silesian Plain

Oder

Vistula

Erzgebirge

Sudetic Mts.

Bohemian Forest

Vltava

CZECH REPUBLIC

Carpathian Mountains

Tatra Mts.

Gerlachovka 8,711

Slovakian Ore Mts.

SLOVAKIA

Vah

Kékes 3,330

Great Alföld

Tisza

HUNGARY

Lake Balaton

Danube

Somes

Bihor Mts.

Mures

ROMANIA

Carpathian Mts.

Transylvanian Alps

Moldoveanu 2,548

Olt

Siret

Triglav 9,393

SLOVENIA

Kras

CROATIA

Istria

Krk

Cres

Pag

Drava

Sava

Dinaric Alps

Drina

Morava

BOSNIA AND HERZEGOVINA

Danube

Black Sea

Dalmatia

Brač

Hvar

Korčula

Mljet

Bobotov Kuki 8,275

YUGOSLAVIA

Lake Shkodër

Daravica 8,714

Balkan Mountains

Maritsa

Musala 9,597

BULGARIA

Rhodope Mts.

Pirin

Adriatic Sea

L. Ohrid

L. Prespa

MACEDONIA

ALBANIA

RUSSIA AND ITS NEIGHBORS

The region consists of the 15 republics that made up the Soviet Union, together with land-locked Mongolia. In the west is part of the North European Plain, which extends from northern France to the Ural Mountains. East of the Urals is Siberia, a vast landscape of plains and plateaus, with uplands in the east. The far east contains the Kamchatka Peninsula, which has active volcanoes and forms part of the Pacific "ring of fire." In the southwest is the Caucasus Mountain range between the Black and Caspian seas. Further south are two bleak deserts, the Kara Kum and the Kyzyl Kum. On the region's southern flanks are the Pamirs and the Altai Mountains, which extend into Mongolia. Mongolia contains part of the cold Gobi Desert.

The former Soviet government recognized the existence of almost 100 nationalities within its borders. Slavs, including Belarusians, Russians, and Ukrainians, form the largest group. Like most people in the western part of the region, including Latvians and Lithuanians, their languages belong to the Indo-European family.

During the Cold War, the threat of the Soviet Union's military strength was pitted against that of the West. But economic crises in the late 1980s, caused partly by the high expenditure on defense, led to the collapse of communism and the breakup of the country. The newly independent Baltic states restored links with the neighboring Nordic and western European countries. But general political unrest and corruption has troubled Russia throughout the 1990s.

The region covers about one-sixth of the world's land area. It straddles two continents, including the eastern parts of Europe and the northern part of Asia. It contains Russia, which stretches from the Baltic Sea to the Bering Sea, a distance of about 6,000 miles (9,650 km). Russia is also divided between Europe and Asia. The boundary runs down the Ural Mountains, through the Caspian Sea, and along the crest of the Caucasus Mountains.

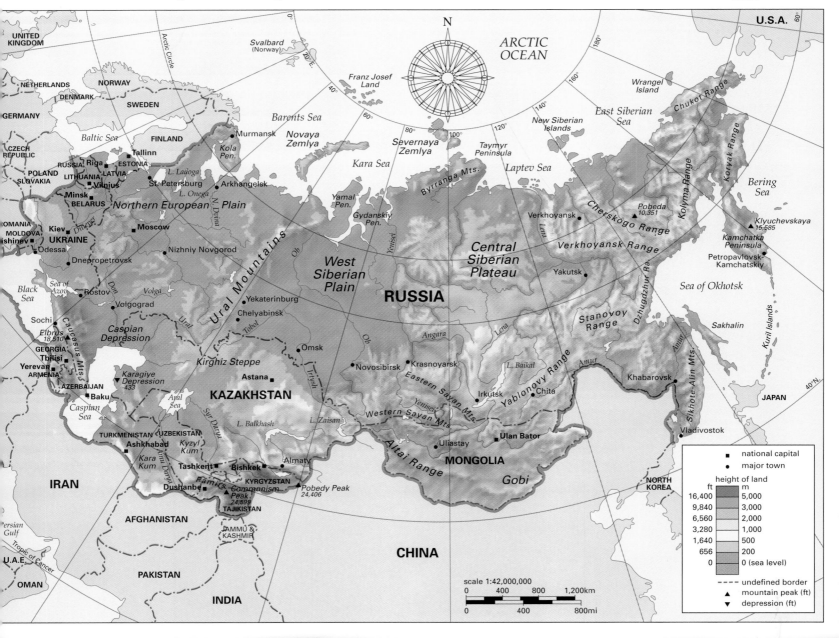

THE POLITICAL AND CULTURAL WORLD

D ramatic changes occurred in the late 1980s, when the leaders of the Soviet Union introduced new policies that involved radical political changes and the introduction of free market trading and private ownership. Estonia, Latvia, and Lithuania, former republics of the Soviet Union, became independent nations in 1991, and at the end of that year, the Soviet Union was formally abolished. The remaining 12 republics became independent states, though they retained contact through a loose structure called the Commonwealth of Independent States (C.I.S.). Mongolia followed the Soviet Union in abandoning communism in 1992.

In May 2000, Russia imposed direct rule on the independent Islamic republic of Chechnya. This followed nearly a decade of fighting during which thousands of people were killed.

COUNTRIES IN THE REGION

Armenia, Azerbaijan, Belarus, Estonia, Georgia, Kazakhstan, Kyrgyzstan, Latvia, Lithuania, Moldova, Mongolia, Russia, Tajikistan, Turkmenistan, Ukraine, Uzbekistan

LANGUAGE

Countries with one official language (Armenian) Armenia, (Azeril) Azerbaijan, (Byelorusian) Belarus, (Estonian) Estonia, (Georgian) Georgia, (Kazakh) Kazakhstan, (Kirghiz) Kyrgyzstan, (Latvian) Latvia, (Lithuanian) Lithuania, (Moldavian) Moldova, (Khalka Mongolian) Mongolia, (Russian) Russia, (Tadzhik) Tajikistan, (Turkmen) Turkmenistan, (Ukrainian) Ukraine, (Uzbek) Uzbekistan

Over 200 languages are spoken in the republics of the former Soviet Union. Russian is the second language in all the non-Russian republics. Other languages include Bashkir, Chuvash, German, Mordvian, Polish, and Tatar.

RELIGION

Countries with one major religion (AAC) Armenia; (GO) Georgia; (M) Azerbaijan, Kazakhstan, Kyrgyzstan, Tajikistan, Turkmenistan, Uzbekistan; (EO) Moldova; (B) Mongolia

Countries with more than one major religion (EO, RC) Belarus, Ukraine; (L, RO, P) Estonia, Latvia; (RC, L, RO) Lithuania; (RO, RC, P, M, J, B) Russia

Key: AAC–Armenian Apostolic Church, B–Buddhism, EO–Eastern Orthodox, GO–Georgian Orthodox, J–Jewish, L–Lutheran, M–Muslim, P–other Protestant, RC–Roman Catholic, RO–Russian Orthodox

STYLES OF GOVERNMENT

Republics All the countries in the region
Multiparty states All the countries in the region
One-chamber assembly Armenia, Azerbaijan, Belarus, Estonia, Georgia, Kazakhstan, Latvia, Lithuania, Mongolia, Moldova, Tajikistan, Ukraine, Uzbekistan
Two-chamber assembly Kyrgyzstan, Russia, Turkmenistan

The newly independent countries in the region include Estonia, Latvia, and Lithuania in the northeast, and Belarus and Ukraine in the west. Moldova lies south of Ukraine. Between the Black Sea and the Caspian Sea lie Georgia, Azerbaijan, and Armenia.

■ national capital
• other town

Area 6,592,786 sq mi (17,075,200 sq km)
Population 146,001,176
Capital Moscow **Russia**

Area 17,462 sq mi (45,226 sq km)
Population 1,431,471
Capital Tallinn **Estonia**

Area 24,938 sq mi (64,589 sq km)
Population 2,404,926
Capital Riga **Latvia**

Area 55,251 sq mi (143,100 sq km)
Population 6,440,732
Capital Dushanbe **Tajikistan**

Area 11,506 sq mi (29,800 sq km)
Population 3,344,336
Armenia Capital Yerevan

Area 26,911 sq mi (69,700 sq km)
Population 5,019,538
Capital Tbilisi **Georgia**

Area 25,174 sq mi (65,200 sq km)
Population 3,620,756
Capital Vilnius **Lithuania**

Area 188,457 sq mi (488,100 sq km)
Population 4,518,268
Capital Ashkhabad **Turkmenistan**

Area 33,437 sq mi (86,600 sq km)
Population 7,748,163
Azerbaijan Capital Baku

Area 1,049,158 sq mi (2,717,300 sq km)
Population 16,733,227
Kazakhstan Capital Astana

Area 13,067 sq mi (33,843 sq km)
Population 4,430,654
Moldova Capital Kishinev

Area 233,090 sq mi (603,700 sq km)
Population 49,153,027
Capital Kiev **Ukraine**

Area 80,155 sq mi (207,600 sq km)
Population 10,366,719
Belarus Capital Minsk

Area 76,641 sq mi (198,500 sq km)
Population 4,685,230
Capital Bishkek **Kyrgyzstan**

Area 604,251 sq mi (1,565,000 sq km)
Population 2,650,952
Mongolia Capital Ulan Bator

Area 172,742 sq mi (447,400 sq km)
Population 24,775,519
Capital Tashkent **Uzbekistan**

HABITATS

The northern part of Russia is tundra, which merges into a vast belt of coniferous forest. Steppes occur in the southeastern parts of Russia and Kazakhstan, with desert in the Aral-Caspian lowland and Mongolia. There are mountains in much of the south.

LAND

Area 9,205,027 sq mi (23,840,858 sq km), including largest country on Earth
Highest point Communism Peak, 24,599 ft (7,498 m)
Lowest point Karagiye Depression on Mangyschlak Peninsula, −433 ft (−132 m)
Major features plains and plateaus of north, Ural Mountains, Caucasus Mountains, Pamirs and Altai ranges, Kara Kum, Kyzyl Kum, and Gobi deserts, Arctic islands

WATER

Longest river Yenisei, 3,650 mi (5,870 km)
Largest basin Yenisei, 1,011,000 sq mi (2,619,000 sq km)
Highest average flow Yenisei, 636,000 cu ft/sec (18,000 cu m/sec)
Largest lake Caspian Sea, 143,240 sq mi (371,000 sq km), largest area of inland water in world; Lake Baikal is world's greatest in volume, at 5,500 cu mi (22,000 cu km) and maximum depth, at 5,184 ft (1,620 m)

NOTABLE THREATENED SPECIES

Mammals Manzbier's marmot (*Marmota menzbieri*), Russian desman (*Desmana moschata*)
Others Amur sturgeon (*Acipenser schrencki*), Balkhash perch (*Perca schrenki*), Caucasian relict ant (*Aulacopone relicta*)
Plants *Astragalus tanaiticus; Elytrigia stipifolia; Eremurus korovinii; Fritillaria eduardii; Iris paradoxa; Lilium caucasicum; Potentilla volgarica; Rhododendron fauriei; Scrophularia cretacea; Tulipa kaufmanniana*

HABITATS

A band of subarctic tundra lies across the north, and huge forested taiga plains lie farther south. In the west are broad regions of dry grasslands called steppes, while semideserts and deserts cover much of the south.

CLIMATE

A subarctic zone called the taiga stretches from northwest Russia to the Pacific Ocean. Summers are short but warm. Winters are long and cold. The west-central areas have a continental climate, while in the far south are deserts and semidesert areas.

CLIMATE

| | Temperature °F (°C) | | Altitude ft (m) |
	January	July	
Moscow	14 (−10)	66 (19)	156 (51.2)
Sochi	45 (7)	73 (23)	31 (102)
Krasnovodsk	36 (2)	82 (28)	89 (292)
Ulan Bator	−15 (−26)	61 (16)	1,337 (4,385)
Verkhoyansk	−53 (−47)	61 (16)	137 (449)
Vladivostok	7 (−14)	63 (17)	138 (453)

| | Precipitation in. (mm) | | |
	January	July	Year
Moscow	1.2 (31)	2.9 (74)	22.6 (575)
Sochi	7.9 (201)	2.4 (60)	57.1 (1,451)
Krasnovodsk	0.4 (11)	0.1 (2)	3.6 (92)
Ulan Bator	0.4 (1)	3.0 (76)	8.2 (209)
Verhoyansk	0.3 (7)	1.3 (33)	6.1 (155)
Vladivostok	0.7 (19)	4.6 (116)	32.4 (824)

ENVIRONMENTAL ISSUES

Rapid industrialization that began after the Russian Revolution of 1917 caused great ecological destruction. Russia's Lake Baikal has been polluted by industrial wastes, and the Aral Sea is shrinking because its water has been used for irrigation.

POPULATION AND WEALTH

	Highest	Middle	Lowest
Population (millions)	146.001 (Russia)	16.733 (Kazakh.)	1.431 (Estonia)
Population increase (% 1990–95)	1.6% (Mongolia)	−0.2% (Russia)	−1.2% (Estonia)
Energy use (lbs/year per person of oil equivalent)	8,838 (Russia)	4,041 (Uzbek.)	988 (Georgia)
Purchasing power parity (Int$/per year)	4,363 (Russia)	2,518 (Armenia)	1,115 (Tajikistan)

ENVIRONMENTAL INDICATORS

	Highest	Middle	Lowest
CO$_2$ emissions ('000 tons year)	1,818,011 (Russia)	438,211 (Ukraine)	3,649 (Armenia)
Car ownership (% of population)	19% (Lithuania)	10% (Georgia)	4% (Moldova)
Protected territory including marine areas	13% (Latvia)	7% (Armenia)	1.5% (Moldova)
Forests as a % of original forest	69% (Russia)	27% (Belarus)	4% (Turkmen.)
Artificial fertilizer use (lbs/acre/year)	130 (Belarus)	68 (Turkmen.)	1.7 (Mongolia)
Access to safe drinking water (% population; rural/urban)	88/99% (Uzbekistan)	49/82% (Tajikistan)	3/73% (Mongolia)

MAJOR ENVIRONMENTAL PROBLEMS AND SOURCES

Air pollution: generally high, urban very high; acid rain prevalent; high greenhouse gas emissions
River/lake pollution: high; *sources*: industry, agriculture, sewage, acid deposition, nuclear, forestry
Land pollution: high; *sources*: industry, agriculture, urban/household, nuclear
Land degradation: *types*: desertification, soil erosion, salinization, deforestation; *causes*: agriculture, industry
Waste disposal issues: domestic; industrial; nuclear
Major events: Chernobyl (1986) and Sosnovyy Bor (1992), nuclear accidents; Kyshtym (1957) hazardous waste spill; Novosibirsk (1979) catastrophic industrial accident; oil spills in Arctic (1994)

Physical zones

- tundra
- mountains/barren land
- forest
- grassland
- semidesert
- desert

- ▲ mountain peak (ft)
- ▼ depression (ft)
- ☆ climate station

ENVIRONMENTAL ISSUES

Key environmental issues

- • major town or city
- ◖ heavily polluted town or city
- ◗ major pollution event
- ⌒ heavily polluted river
- ⬚ area affected by permafrost
- ▨ dead lake

annual air pollution (tons per square mi)

- 8
- 4
- 2
- 0.8

Air and water pollution are greatest in the industrialized west. The 1986 explosion at Chernobyl's nuclear power plant was a disaster that polluted land over much of Europe.

ARCTIC OCEAN

Franz Josef Land

Wrangel Island

Barents Sea

Novaya Zemlya

Severnaya Zemlya

New Siberian Islands

East Siberian Sea

Chukot Range

Baltic Sea

Kola Pen.

L. Ladoga

Kara Sea

Laptev Sea

Koryak Range

Bering Sea

LATVIA

RUSSIA

ESTONIA

LITHUANIA

Sosnovyy Bor

St. Petersburg

L. Onega

N. Dvina

Byrranga Mts.

Taymyr Peninsula

Kolyma Range

Kamchatka Peninsula

Minsk

BELARUS

Northern European Plain

Moscow

Pechora

Yamal Pen.

Gydanskiy Pen.

Norilsk

Cherskogo Range

Verkhoyansk Range

Chernobyl

Kiev

MOLDOVA

UKRAINE

Nizhniy Novgorod

Ob

Yenisey

Lena

Central Siberian Plateau

Sea of Okhotsk

Odessa

Dnepropetrovsk

Kharkov

Kazan

Kama

Perm

West Siberian Plain

Dzhugdzhur Ra.

Sakhalin

Black Sea

Donetsk

Kuznetsk

Samara

Ufa

Nizhniy Tagil

Yekaterinburg

RUSSIA

Angara

Stanovoy Range

Kuril Islands

Sea of Azov

Rostov

Don

Volga

Ural Mountains

Kyshtym

Ob

Lena

Yablonovy Range

Sikhote-Alin Mts.

Caspian Depression

Ural

Kirghiz Steppe

Omsk

Irtysh

Novosibirsk

Eastern Sayan Mts.

L. Baikal

Amur

Sea of Japan

GEORGIA

Tbilisi

Yerevan

ARMENIA

Caucasus Mts.

Kura

KAZAKHSTAN

Yenisey

Western Sayan Mts.

Ulan-Ude

Baikalsk

AZERBAIJAN

Baku

Caspian Sea

Muynak

Aral Sea

Syr Darya

Ust Kamenogorsk

L. Zaisan

Altai Range

MONGOLIA

TURKMENISTAN

UZBEKISTAN

Kyzyl Kum

L. Balkhash

Gobi

Kara Kum

Amu Darya

Tashkent

Almaty

Pamirs

KYRGYZSTAN

TAJIKISTAN

Arctic Circle

CLIMATE

height above sea level of climate stations

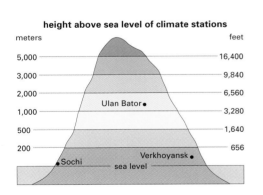

meters		feet
5,000		16,400
3,000		9,840
2,000		6,560
1,000	Ulan Bator	3,280
500		1,640
200	Verkhoyansk	656
	Sochi	sea level

Sochi

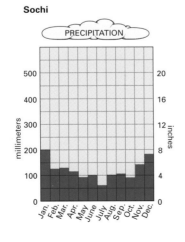

PRECIPITATION

Ulan Bator

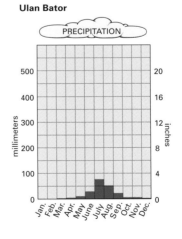

PRECIPITATION

Verkhoyansk

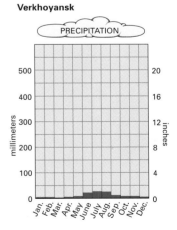

PRECIPITATION

Sochi

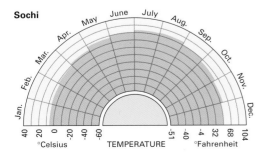

TEMPERATURE

Ulan Bator

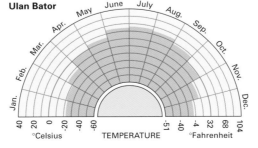

TEMPERATURE

Verkhoyansk

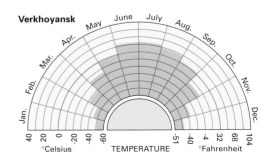

TEMPERATURE

POPULATION

About two-thirds of the population of the region live in the European, western part rather than in the eastern, Asian part. However, under communist rule, the government encouraged the growth of industrial cities in the east, with some success.

POPULATION

Total population of region (millions)			293.3

	Russia	Latvia	Uzbekistan
Population density (persons per sq mi)	23	98	136
Population change (average annual percent 1960–1990)			
Urban	+3%	−1.47%	+0.72%
Rural	−1.68%	−1.47%	+2.09%

URBAN POPULATION

As percentage of total population			
1995–2000	78%	69%	37%

TEN LARGEST CITIES

	Country	Population
Moscow †	Russia	9,389,700
St. Petersburg	Russia	4,169,400
Kiev †	Ukraine	2,616,800
Tashkent †	Uzbekistan	2,079,000
Minsk †	Belarus	1,751,300
Kharkov	Ukraine	1,477,000
Nizhniy Novgorod	Russia	1,418,000
Novosibirsk	Russia	1,402,000
Yekaterinburg	Russia	1,367,000
Tbilisi †	Georgia	1,344,100

† denotes capital city

City population figures are for the city proper.

INDUSTRY

The former Soviet Union built up a huge industrial sector based on its abundant natural resources. It invested in engineering and defense industries rather than the production of consumer goods. These newer industries are now being developed.

TOTAL INDUSTRIAL OUTPUT (US $ billion, 1997)

Ukraine	Russia
17	155

INDUSTRIAL PRODUCTION GROWTH RATE

Russia	8.1% (1999 est.)

INDUSTRIAL WORKERS (millions) for Russia (1995)
(figures in parentheses are percentages of total labor force)

Total	Mining and Manufacturing	Construction
23.7	17.2 (23.5%)	6.5 (8.9%)

MAJOR PRODUCTS (figures in parentheses are percentages of total world supply)

Energy and minerals	Output 1995	
Petroleum products (mil m.t.)	160	(5.40)
Oil (crude, mil m.t., 1980)	301	(9)
Natural gas ('000 terajoules)	21,147	(25.1)
Tin ('000 tons)	5	(2.4)
Copper ('000 tons)	550	(3)
Zinc ('000 tons)	150	(n/a)
Aluminum ('000 tons)	2,700	(10.2)
Steel ('000 tons)	48,816	(6.5)
Phosphates ('000 tons)	7,922	(6.2)
Iron ore (mill tons)	44	(4.3)

AGRICULTURE

Only about 10 percent of the former Soviet Union is suitable for arable farming, while livestock raising is the main occupation in Mongolia. Productivity on the communist state farms and collectives was generally low, and food often had to be imported.

LAND
Total area 9,205,027 sq mi (23,840,858 sq km)

Cropland	Pasture	Forest/Woodland
11%	22%	35%
(1,015,320 sq mi)	(1,659,600 sq mi)	(3,266,834 sq mi)

FARMERS	Highest	Middle	Lowest
Agriculture as % of GDP	45 (Kyrgyzstan)	22 (Azerbaijan)	7 (Lat., Eston.)
% of workforce	over 90 (Mongolia)	55 (Armen., Kirgh.)	11 (Estonia)

MAJOR CROPS: Agricultural products fruit and vegetables; wheat, barley, flax; cotton; sugar beet; sunflower seeds; grapes; tea; beef; sheep and goats; dairy products; fish; tobacco; wool

Total cropland ('000 acres)	316,194 (Russia)	74,464 (Kazakhstan)	1,381 (Armenia)
Cropland (acres) per 1,000 people	4,547 (Kazakhstan)	1,285 (Mongolia)	371 (Tajikistan)
Irrigated land as % of cropland	88% (Uzbekistan)	41% (Georgia)	2% (Lithuania)
Number of tractors	886,490 (Russia)	108,121 (Kazakhstan)	7,000 (Mongolia)
Average cereal crop yields (lbs/acre)	2,366 (Moldova)	1,466 (Armenia)	554 (Kazakhstan)
Cereal production ('000 tons)	67,064 (Russia)	9,985 (Kazakhstan)	218 (Mongolia)

Population density

urban agglomeration
(National capital is underlined)

- ■ over 10,000,000
- ◆ 5,000,000–10,000,000
- ■ 1,000,000–4,999,999
- ● 600,000–999,999
- × national capital less than 600,000

persons per square mi	persons per square km
260	100
130	50
26	10
2.6	1

POPULATION

The tundra and taiga regions are sparsely populated, as also are the southern deserts and mountain areas. The greatest concentrations of population are in the southwestern part of the region.

INDUSTRY

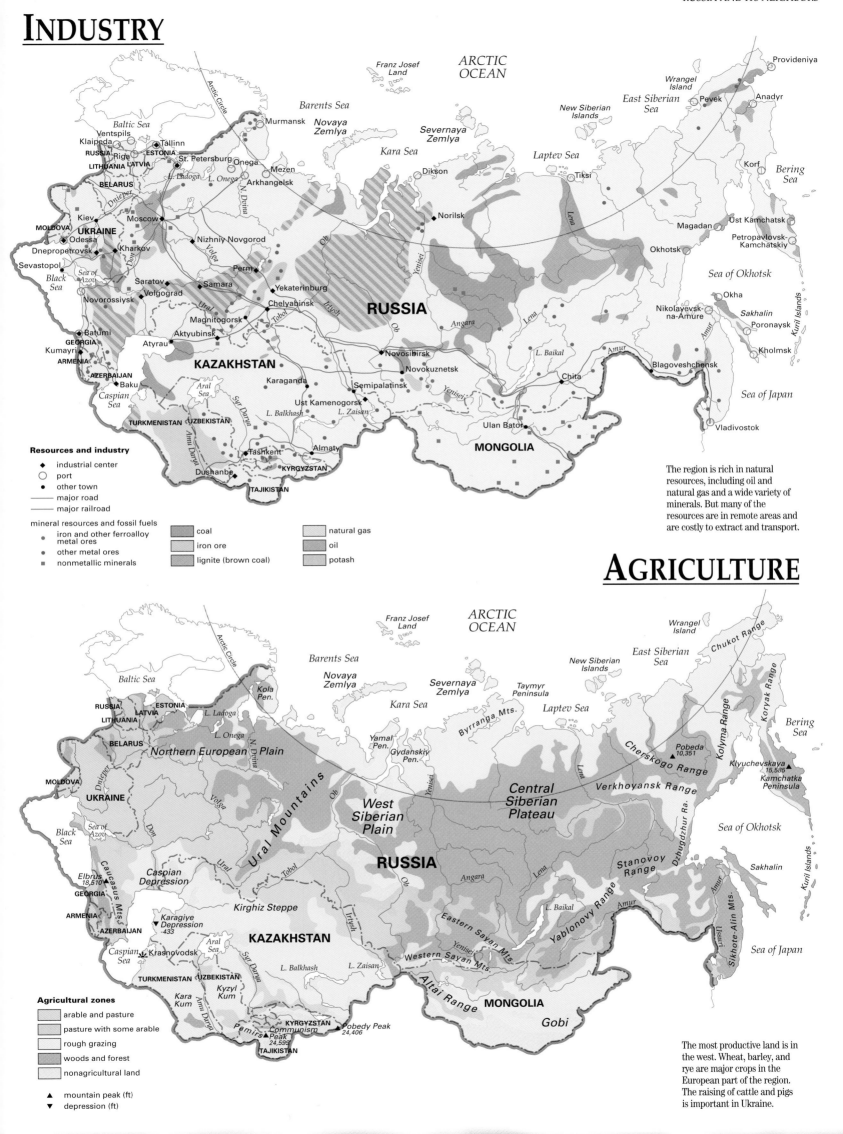

ARCTIC OCEAN

Franz Josef Land

Wrangel Island

East Siberian Sea

Providiniya

Pevek

Anadyr

Bering Sea

Barents Sea

Novaya Zemlya

Severnaya Zemlya

New Siberian Islands

Laptev Sea

Korf

Kara Sea

Dikson

Tiksi

Ust Kamchatsk

Murmansk

Baltic Sea

Ventspils

Klaipeda

RUSSIA Rige

LITHUANIA **LATVIA**

◆ Tallinn

ESTONIA St. Petersburg

Onega

Mezen

Arkhangelsk

L. Ladoga

L. Onega

N. Dvina

BELARUS

Dnieper

Kiev

MOLDOVA

UKRAINE Moscow

Odessa

Dnepropetrovsk Kharkov

Sevastopol

Black Sea

Sea of Azov

Novorossiysk

GEORGIA Batumi

Kumayri

ARMENIA

AZERBAIJAN Baku

Caspian Sea

TURKMENISTAN

Nizhniy Novgorod

Volga

Perm

Saratov

Samara

Volgograd

Don

Ural

Magnitogorsk

Aktyubinsk

Atyrau

KAZAKHSTAN

Yekaterinburg

Chelyabinsk

Tobol

Irtysh

Karaganda

Aral Sea

Syr Darya

L. Balkhash

UZBEKISTAN

Amu Darya

Tashkent

Dushanbe

TAJIKISTAN

KYRGYZSTAN

Almaty

Semipalatinsk

Ust Kamenogorsk

L. Zaisan

Norilsk

Ob

Yenisei

RUSSIA

Novosibirsk

Novokuznetsk

Angara

Lena

Yenisei

L. Baikal

Chita

Amur

Ulan Bator

MONGOLIA

Magadan

Okhotsk

Sea of Okhotsk

Petropavlovsk-Kamchatskiy

Okha

Sakhalin

Nikolayevsk-na-Amure

Poronaysk

Kuril Islands

Blagoveshchensk

Kholmsk

Sea of Japan

Vladivostok

Resources and industry

◆ industrial center
○ port
• other town
— major road
━ major railroad

mineral resources and fossil fuels
• iron and other ferroalloy metal ores
• other metal ores
■ nonmetallic minerals

▨ coal	▨ natural gas
☐ iron ore	▨ oil
▨ lignite (brown coal)	▨ potash

The region is rich in natural resources, including oil and natural gas and a wide variety of minerals. But many of the resources are in remote areas and are costly to extract and transport.

AGRICULTURE

ARCTIC OCEAN

Franz Josef Land

Wrangel Island

East Siberian Sea

Chukot Range

Bering Sea

Barents Sea

Novaya Zemlya

Severnaya Zemlya

New Siberian Islands

Taymyr Peninsula

Laptev Sea

Koryak Range

Kara Sea

Byrranga Mts.

Kolyma Range

Pobeda 10,351

Klyuchevskaya 15,585

Kamchatka Peninsula

Baltic Sea

Kola Pen.

L. Ladoga

L. Onega

N. Dvina

RUSSIA

LATVIA **ESTONIA**

LITHUANIA

BELARUS

Dnieper

MOLDOVA

UKRAINE

Northern European Plain

Black Sea

Sea of Azov

Elbrus 18,510

GEORGIA

Caucasus Mts.

ARMENIA

AZERBAIJAN

Caspian Sea

Karagiye Depression -433

Caspian Depression

Krasnovodsk

TURKMENISTAN

Kara Kum

Volga

Don

Ural Mountains

Ural

Tobol

Kirghiz Steppe

Aral Sea

KAZAKHSTAN

Syr Darya

Kyzyl Kum

UZBEKISTAN

Amu Darya

Pamirs

KYRGYZSTAN

Communism Peak 24,595

TAJIKISTAN

Pobedy Peak 24,406

L. Balkhash

L. Zaisan

Ob

Yenisei

West Siberian Plain

Central Siberian Plateau

RUSSIA

Irtysh

Angara

Lena

L. Baikal

Yablonovy Range

Eastern Sayan Mts.

Western Sayan Mts.

Altai Range

MONGOLIA

Gobi

Verkhoyansk Range

Cherskogo Range

Dzhugdzhur Ra.

Stanovoy Range

Amur

Ussuri

Sikhote-Alin Mts.

Sakhalin

Kuril Islands

Sea of Okhotsk

Sea of Japan

Bering Sea

Agricultural zones

☐ arable and pasture
☐ pasture with some arable
☐ rough grazing
▨ woods and forest
☐ nonagricultural land

▲ mountain peak (ft)
▼ depression (ft)

The most productive land is in the west. Wheat, barley, and rye are major crops in the European part of the region. The raising of cattle and pigs is important in Ukraine.

SOUTHWEST ASIA

Southwest Asia is the meeting place of three continents. Here early peoples began to plant crops, build cities, and found civilizations. Today the region is important economically and strategically because of its large reserves and production of oil and natural gas.

Southwest Asia, also known as the Middle East, contains some of the world's hottest and driest deserts. The two major rivers, the Tigris and Euphrates, rise in the mountains of Turkey and flow across the deserts of Syria and Iraq. The mountains of Turkey are part of a long chain of folded mountains that extends across the northern part of the region to the Hindu Kush in Afghanistan.

Southwest Asia contains several oil-rich nations, but most of the region is economically underdeveloped. It is the home of three religions —Judaism, Christianity, and Islam—but religion has divided people and has been the cause of both international and civil wars. Politically, it is an unstable region, whose conflicts periodically involve the world community.

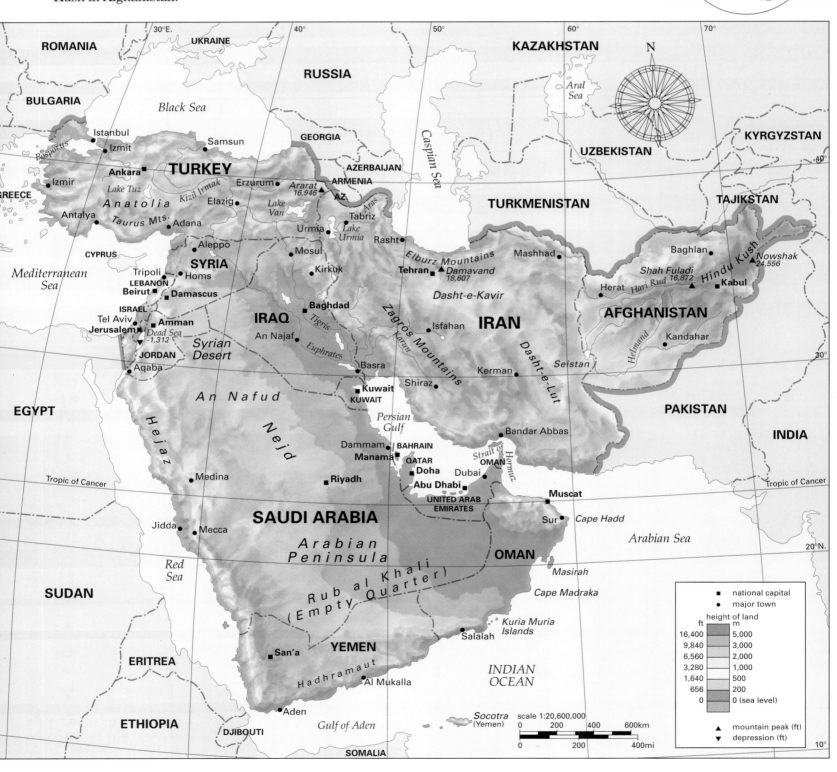

■	national capital	
•	major town	

height of land

ft		m
16,400		5,000
9,840		3,000
6,560		2,000
3,280		1,000
1,640		500
656		200
0		0 (sea level)

▲ mountain peak (ft)
▼ depression (ft)

scale 1:20,600,000
0   200   400   600km
0   200   400mi

THE POLITICAL AND CULTURAL WORLD

Islam, spread throughout the area by Arabs from the seventh century A.D. on, is the dominant religion in Southwest Asia. Israel, the only country in which Muslims are not a majority, has been in conflict with Arab nations since it was created as a homeland for Jews in 1948.

Other conflicts have arisen because of rivalries between ethnic, cultural, and religious groups, as in Lebanon, and the aspirations of minorities, such as the Kurds, who would like to establish their own country in parts of Iraq, Iran, and Turkey. Territorial disputes have led to war between Iraq and Iran (1980–1988) and Iraq's invasion of Kuwait (1990–1991). Islamic forces gained control of Afghanistan in 1992 and established an interim government. Fighting continued and the conservative Islamic group called the Taliban seized power in Afghanistan in the late 1990s.

COUNTRIES IN THE REGION

Afghanistan, Bahrain, Iran, Iraq, Israel, Jordan, Kuwait, Lebanon, Oman, Qatar, Saudi Arabia, Syria, Turkey, United Arab Emirates (U.A.E.), Yemen

LANGUAGE

Countries with one official language (Arabic) Bahrain, Iraq, Jordan, Kuwait, Lebanon, Oman, Qatar, Saudi Arabia, Syria, U.A.E., Yemen; (Farsi) Iran; (Turkish) Turkey
Countries with two official languages (Arabic, Hebrew) Israel; (Dari, Pashtu) Afghanistan

RELIGION

Countries with one major religion (M) Afghanistan, Bahrain, Iran, Iraq, Jordan, Kuwait, Oman, Qatar, Saudi Arabia, Syria, Turkey, U.A.E., Yemen
Countries with more than one major religion (C, J, M) Israel; (C, D, M and other) Lebanon

Key: C-various Christian, D-Druze, J-Jewish, M-Muslim

STYLES OF GOVERNMENT

Republics Afghanistan, Iran, Iraq, Israel, Lebanon, Syria, Turkey, U.A.E., Yemen
Monarchies Bahrain, Jordan, Kuwait, Oman, Qatar, Saudi Arabia
Federal state U.A.E.
Multiparty states Afghanistan, Israel, Lebanon, Turkey
One-party states Iran, Iraq, Syria
States without parties Bahrain, Jordan, Kuwait, Oman, Qatar, Saudi Arabia, U.A.E., Yemen

ECONOMIC INDICATORS

	U.A.E	S.Arabia	Jordan
GDP (US$ billions)	45.1	145.8	7.9
GNP per capita (US$)	21,600	10,870	3,430
Annual rate of growth of GDP, 1980–1990	-4.5%	-1.7%	4.3%
Manufacturing as % of GDP	8.6%	8.7%	16.2%
Central government spending as % of GNP	11.8%	n/a	31.6%
Merchandise exports (US$ billions)	28.0	58.2	1.5
Merchandise imports (US$ billions)	30.3	27.8	4.3
Aid received as % of GNP *	–	–	7.2%

* The United Arab Emirates and Saudi Arabia are aid donors.

WELFARE INDICATORS

	U.A.E	S.Arabia	Jordan
Infant mortality rate (per 1,000 live births)			
1965	103	148	114
2000	16	23	26
Daily food supply available (calories per capita)	3,361	2,746	2,734
Population per physician (1993-4)	715	636	825
Teacher-pupil ratio (primary school, 1995)	1 : 17	1 : 13.3	1 : 21.5

Afghanistan
Area 251,826 sq mi
(652,225 sq km)
Population 25,838,797
Capital Kabul

Bahrain
Area 267 sq mi
(691 sq km)
Population 634,137
Capital Manama

Iran
Area 634,561 sq mi
(1,643,503 sq km)
Population 65,619,636
Capital Tehran

Iraq
Area 169,236 sq mi
(438,317 sq km)
Population 22,675,617
Capital Baghdad

Israel
Area 7,992 sq mi
(20,700 sq km)
Population 5,842,454
Capital Jerusalem

Jordan
Area 34,443 sq mi
(89,206 sq km)
Population 4,998,564
Capital Amman

Kuwait
Area 6,880 sq mi
(17,818 sq km)
Population 1,973,572
Capital Kuwait

Lebanon
Area 3,950 sq mi
(10,230 sq km)
Population 3,578,036
Capital Beirut

Oman
Area 82,031 sq mi
(212,460 sq km)
Population 2,533,389
Capital Muscat

Qatar
Area 4,402 sq mi
(11,400 sq km)
Population 744,483
Capital Doha

Saudi Arabia
Area 864,871 sq mi
(2,240,000 sq km)
Population 22,023,506
Capital Riyadh

Syria
Area 71,499 sq mi
(185,180 sq km)
Population 16,305,659
Capital Damascus

Turkey
Area 300, 949 sq mi
(779,452 sq km)
Population 65,666,677
Capital Ankara

Yemen
Area 203,851 sq mi
(527,970 sq km)
Population 17,479,206
Capital San'a

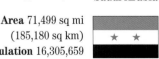

United Arab Emirates (U.A.E.)
Area 30,000 sq mi
(77,700 sq km)
Population 2,369,153
Capital Abu Dhabi

■ national capital
• other town

Southwest Asia has been unstable since 1945. Israel has fought four wars against its Arab foes, while the Palestinians in Israel continue their protests against Israeli rule. The Iran-Iraq war was the longest in the twentieth century, while the expulsion of Iraqi forces from Kuwait in 1991 involved many world powers.

HABITATS

Mountains, plateaus, and deserts dominate Southwest Asia. The Arabian Peninsula is almost completely surrounded by sea, yet much of the peninsula consists of desert and semidesert. The plains of the Tigris and Euphrates are fertile.

LAND
Area 2,666,756 sq mi (6,906,852 sq km)
Highest point Mount Nowshak, 24,556 ft (7,485 m)
Lowest point Dead Sea, –1,312 ft (–400 m), lowest point on land surface on Earth
Major features plateaus of Anatolia and Iran, Hindu Kush, Zagros and Elburz Mountains, deserts of Arabia and Iran

WATER
Longest river Euphrates, 1,700 mi (2,720 km)
Largest basin Euphrates, 427,000 sq mi (1,105,000 sq km)
Highest average flow Euphrates, 101,000 cu ft/sec (2,860 cu m/sec)
Largest lake Caspian Sea, 143,240 sq mi (371,000 sq km), largest area of inland water in the world

NOTABLE THREATENED SPECIES
Mammals Mountain gazelle (Gazella gazella), Arabian oryx (Oryx leucoryx), Arabian tahr (Hemitragus jayakari), Asiatic cheetah (Acinonyx jubatus venaticus), Anatolian leopard (Panthera pardus orientalis)
Birds Yemen thrush (Turdus menachensis)
Plants Alkanna macrophylla; Anthemis brachycarpa; Ceratonia oreothauma subsp. oreothauma; Dionysia mira; Erodium subintegrifolium; Ferulago longistylis; Iris calcarea; Iris lortetii; Rumex rothschildianus; Wissmannia carinensis
Others Latifi's viper (Vipera latifi), Cicek fish (Acanthorutilus handlirschi)

CLIMATE

The coasts of Turkey and the eastern Mediterranean have hot, dry summers and mild, moist winters. Inland is a hot, desert region. The mountains and plateaus of the Turkish interior, Iran, and Afghanistan are subtropical and dry, though it snows in the mountains.

CLIMATE

	Temperature °F (°C)		Altitude
	January	July	ft (m)
Samsun	45 (7)	73 (23)	144 (44)
Haifa	57 (14)	81 (27)	16 (5)
Amman	46 (8)	77 (25)	2,529 (771)
Basra	54 (12)	93 (34)	7 (2)
Riyadh	61 (16)	104 (40)	1,998 (609)
Kandahar	41 (5)	90 (32)	3,313 (1,010)

	Precipitation in. (mm)		
	January	July	Year
Samsun	3.2 (81)	1.5 (39)	28.8 (731)
Haifa	5.1 (129)	0.04 (1)	19.6 (499)
Amman	2.7 (68)	0 (0)	10.7 (273)
Basra	1.0 (26)	0 (0)	6.5 (164)
Riyadh	0.9 (24)	0 (0)	3.2 (82)
Kandahar	0.86 (22)	0 (0)	8.9 (225)

ENVIRONMENTAL ISSUES

Soil erosion and the buildup of salt in the soil caused by poor drainage of irrigated land have damaged the area in the past. There is overgrazing and deforestation. Industrial and urban growth, together with oil extraction and war, have caused recent damage.

POPULATION AND WEALTH

	Highest	Middle	Lowest
Population (millions)	65.667 (Turkey)	4.998 (Jordan)	0.634 (Bahrain)
Population increase (annual growth rate, % 1990–95)	3.7% (Yemen)	2.2% (Israel)	1.4% (Turkey)
Energy use (lbs/year per person of oil equivalent)	29,500 (U.A.E.)	6,618 (Israel)	454 (Yemen)
Purchasing power parity (Int$/per year)	19,181 (U.A.E.)	9,887 (Oman)	795 (Yemen)

ENVIRONMENTAL INDICATORS

CO_2 emissions ('000 tons year)	254,252 (S. Arabia)	99,001 (Iraq)	11,417 (Oman)
Car ownership (% of population)	44% (Kuwait)	18% (S. Arabia)	2% (Yemen)
Protected territory including marine areas	34% (S. Arabia)	13% (Oman)	0% (Syria)
Forests as a % of original forest	11% (Turkey)	6% (Afghan.)	1% (Lebanon)
Artificial fertilizer use (lbs/acre/year)	348 (U.A.E.)	156 (Lebanon)	0.8 (Afghan.)
Access to safe drinking water (% population; rural/urban)	100%/100% (Bahrain)	48%/96% (Iraq)	5%/39% (Afghan.)

MAJOR ENVIRONMENTAL PROBLEMS AND SOURCES

Air pollution: urban high
Coastal pollution: medium/high; *sources:* oil; war
Land degradation: *types:* desertifcation, salinization; oil pollution, *causes:* agriculture; war; drought
Resource issues: fuelwood shortage; inadequate drinking water and sanitation; overgrazing
Population issues: population explosion; war
Major events: Gulf (1991), oil spills and oil well fires during and after the Gulf war

HABITATS

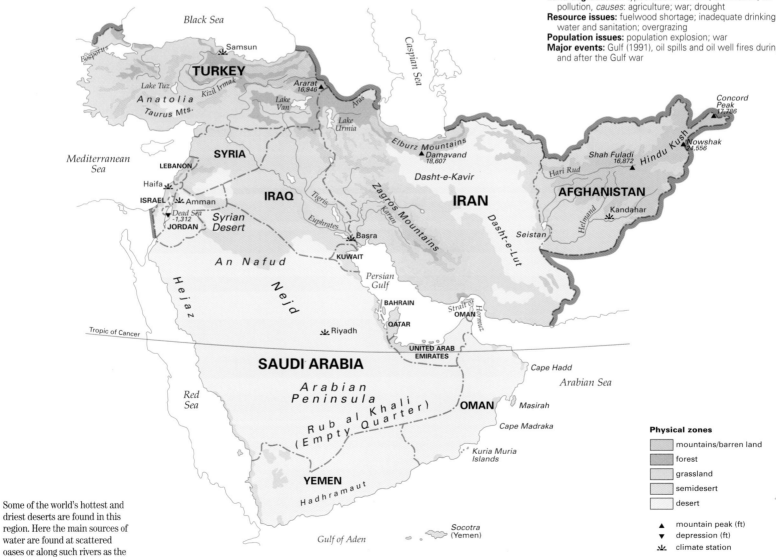

Some of the world's hottest and driest deserts are found in this region. Here the main sources of water are found at scattered oases or along such rivers as the Tigris and Euphrates.

Physical zones
- mountains/barren land
- forest
- grassland
- semidesert
- desert

- ▲ mountain peak (ft)
- ▼ depression (ft)
- ⚲ climate station

ENVIRONMENTAL ISSUES

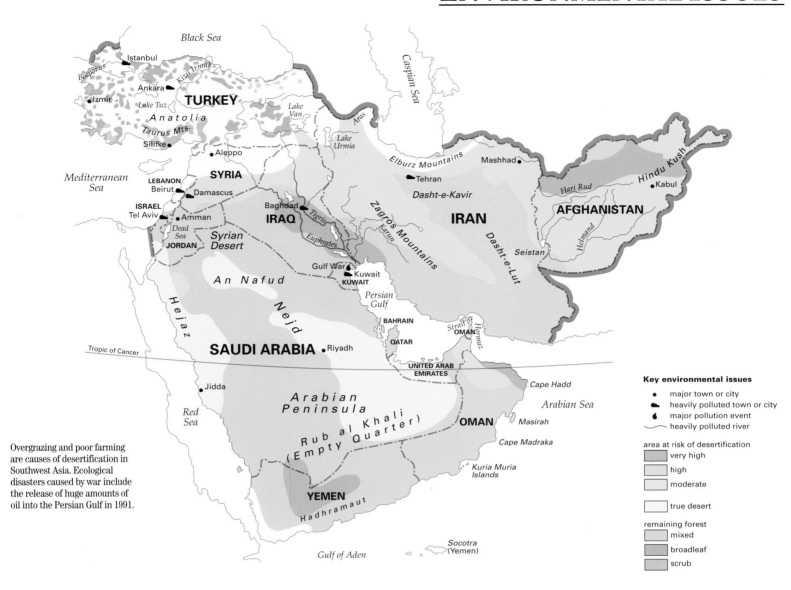

Black Sea

Istanbul

Bosporus

Kızıl Irmak

Ankara

İzmir

Lake Tuz

TURKEY

Anatolia

Taurus Mts.

Silifke

Lake Van

Caspian Sea

Aleppo

Lake Urmia

Aras

Elburz Mountains

Mashhad

Tehran

Dasht-e-Kavir

Hindu Kush

Kabul

Mediterranean Sea

LEBANON
Beirut
Damascus

SYRIA

Hari Rud

AFGHANISTAN

ISRAEL
Tel Aviv

Amman

Baghdad

Tigris

IRAQ

Euphrates

Zagros Mountains

IRAN

Dasht-e-Lut

Helmand

Dead Sea

JORDAN

Syrian Desert

Karun

Seistan

An Nafud

Nejd

Gulf War

Kuwait
KUWAIT

Persian Gulf

Hejaz

SAUDI ARABIA

Riyadh

BAHRAIN

QATAR

Strait of
OMAN

Hormuz

Tropic of Cancer

UNITED ARAB EMIRATES

Cape Hadd

Jidda

Red Sea

Arabian Peninsula

Arabian Sea

OMAN

Masirah

Rub al Khali
(Empty Quarter)

Cape Madraka

Kuria Muria Islands

Overgrazing and poor farming are causes of desertification in Southwest Asia. Ecological disasters caused by war include the release of huge amounts of oil into the Persian Gulf in 1991.

YEMEN

Hadhramaut

Socotra
(Yemen)

Gulf of Aden

Key environmental issues

- • major town or city
- ⬤ heavily polluted town or city
- ⬤ major pollution event
- ∿ heavily polluted river

area at risk of desertification
- ▨ very high
- ▨ high
- ▨ moderate
- ☐ true desert

remaining forest
- ▨ mixed
- ▨ broadleaf
- ▨ scrub

CLIMATE

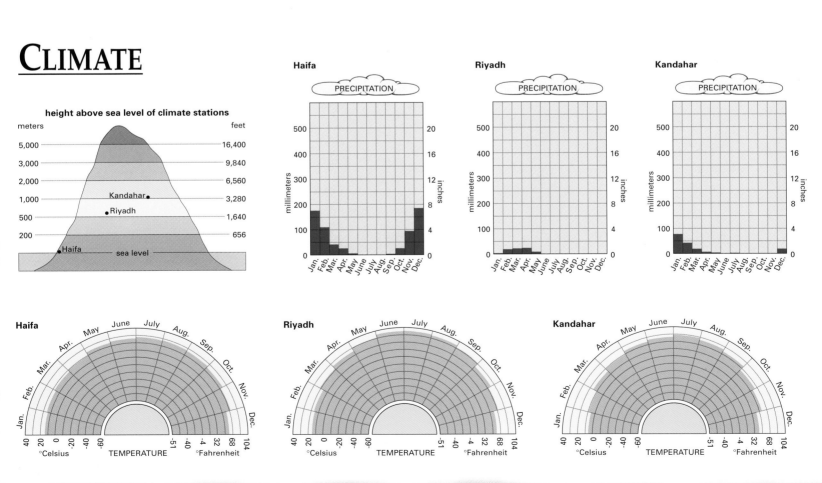

height above sea level of climate stations

meters		feet
5,000		16,400
3,000		9,840
2,000		6,560
1,000	Kandahar	3,280
500	Riyadh	1,640
200		656
	Haifa sea level	

Haifa
PRECIPITATION

millimeters / inches

500 / 20
400 / 16
300 / 12
200 / 8
100 / 4

Jan. Feb. Mar. Apr. May June July Aug. Sep. Oct. Nov. Dec.

Riyadh
PRECIPITATION

millimeters / inches

500 / 20
400 / 16
300 / 12
200 / 8
100 / 4

Jan. Feb. Mar. Apr. May June July Aug. Sep. Oct. Nov. Dec.

Kandahar
PRECIPITATION

millimeters / inches

500 / 20
400 / 16
300 / 12
200 / 8
100 / 4

Jan. Feb. Mar. Apr. May June July Aug. Sep. Oct. Nov. Dec.

Haifa

Jan. Feb. Mar. Apr. May June July Aug. Sep. Oct. Nov. Dec.

°Celsius TEMPERATURE °Fahrenheit

Riyadh

Jan. Feb. Mar. Apr. May June July Aug. Sep. Oct. Nov. Dec.

°Celsius TEMPERATURE °Fahrenheit

Kandahar

Jan. Feb. Mar. Apr. May June July Aug. Sep. Oct. Nov. Dec.

°Celsius TEMPERATURE °Fahrenheit

POPULATION

Cities developed in Southwest Asia more than 5,000 years ago. Today about half of the population is urban, and city populations are rising quickly because of natural increase and the movement of poor people from the countryside, looking for work.

POPULATION

Total population of region (millions)			258.282
	U.A.E.	Saudi Arabia	Jordan
Population density (persons per sq mi)	73	21	125
Population change (average annual percent 1995–2000)			
Urban	+2.48%	+4.08%	+3.80%
Rural	–0.73%	–0.40%	–0.94%

URBAN POPULATION

As percentage of total population			
2000	86%	86%	74%

TEN LARGEST CITIES

	Country	Population
Istanbul	Turkey	8,260,438
Tehran †	Iran	6,758,845
Baghdad †	Iraq	4,869,500
Ankara †	Turkey	2,984,099
Riyadh †	Saudi Arabia	2,776,096
Izmir	Turkey	2,081,556
Jidda	Saudi Arabia	2,046,251
Mashhad	Iran	1,887,405
Kabul †	Afghanistan	1,500,000
Damascus †	Syria	1,394,322

† denotes capital city

City population figures are for the city proper.

INDUSTRY

In Southwest Asia, only Israel and Turkey have built up broad-based manufacturing sectors. Foreign investment and expertise are now helping to build industries in the oil-rich nations, which are seeking to achieve more balanced economies.

INDUSTRIAL OUTPUT (US $ billion)

Saudi Arabia (1995)	63
Iran (1995)	31
Turkey (1997)	48

INDUSTRIAL WORKERS (millions)
(figures in parentheses are percentages of total labor force)

	U.A.E.	Saudi Arabia	Jordan
Manufacturing	0.0634 (9.2%)	0.37 (6.5%)	n/a
Construction	0.119 (17.3%)	0.944 (16.4%)	0.06 (7%)
Mining	n/a	0.0035 (0.1%)	n/a
Petroleum	0.01 (1.5%)	0.0468 (0.8%)	n/a
Total	0.689	5.77	0.859

MAJOR PRODUCTS (TURKEY)

Energy and minerals	Output 1970	1995	Change since 1970
Petroleum products (mil m.t.)	6.8	24	252.9%
Bituminous coal (mil m.t.)	5	6	20.0%
Lignite/brown coal (mil m.t.)	4.5	40	788.9%
Copper ('000 tons)	14	100	614.3%
Coppper ore ('000 tons)	22	38	72.7%
Zinc ('000 tons)	0	20	2,000%
Zinc ore ('000 tons)	24	35	45.8%

AGRICULTURE

Much of the farming in Southwest Asia, when conditions allow it, is still traditional in character. But new high-technology farming now exists in some places, notably Israel, which has used large-scale irrigation systems and new technology to make the deserts bloom.

LAND

Total area 2,666,756 sq mi (6,906,852 sq km)

Cropland	Pasture	Forest/Woodland
11% (280,671 sq mi)	35% (967,039 sq mi)	5% (150,311 sq mi)

FARMERS	Highest	Middle	Lowest
Agriculture as % of GDP	25% (Iran)	12% (Lebanon)	0% (Kuwait)
% of workforce	68% (Afghanistan)	33% (Iran)	1% (Bahrain)

MAJOR CROPS: Agricultural products fruit and vegetables; pulses; nuts; olives; sugar beet; cotton; wheat; wool; mutton; dairy products; poultry; fish, caviar, shrimps; dates; tobacco; camels

Total cropland ('000 acres)	72,059 (Turkey)	13,689 (Iraq)	17 (Kuwait)
Cropland (acres) per 1,000 people	1,137 (Turkey)	487 (Saudi Arabia)	10 (Kuwait)
Irrigated land as % of cropland	98% (Oman)	46% (Israel)	14% (Turkey)
Number of tractors	874,995 (Turkey)	87,442 (Syria)	100 (Kuwait)
Average cereal crop yields (lbs/acre)	3,209 (S. Arabia)	1,469 (Israel)	691 (Iraq)
Cereal production ('000 tons)	30,758 (Turkey)	3,694 (Afghanistan)	1 (U.A.E.)
Change since 1986/88	3%	17%	–19%

LIVESTOCK & FISHERIES

Meat production ('000 tons)	1,437 (Iran)	323 (Israel)	27 (Oman)
Change since 1876–88	n/a	86%	63%
Marine fish catch ('000 tons)	463.7 (Turkey)	100 (Yemen)	2.3 (Syria)
Change since 1986–88	–13%	52%	95%

POPULATION

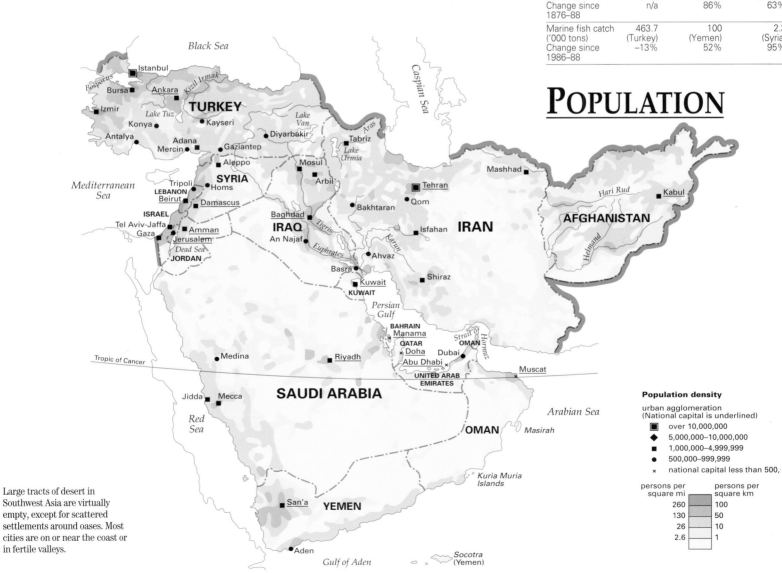

Large tracts of desert in Southwest Asia are virtually empty, except for scattered settlements around oases. Most cities are on or near the coast or in fertile valleys.

Population density

urban agglomeration
(National capital is underlined)

■ over 10,000,000
◆ 5,000,000–10,000,000
▪ 1,000,000–4,999,999
● 500,000–999,999
× national capital less than 500,

persons per square mi	persons per square km
260	100
130	50
26	10
2.6	1

INDUSTRY

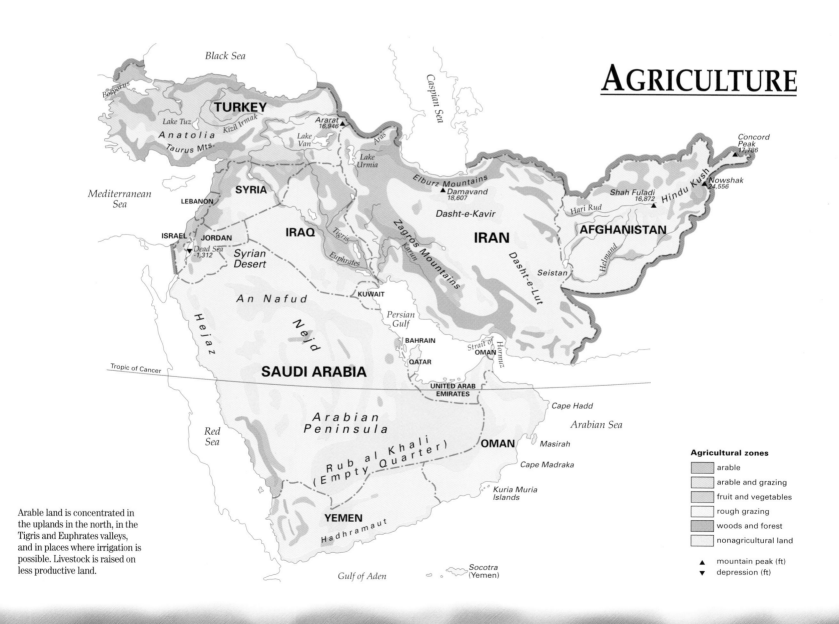

Black Sea

Istanbul
Bosporus
Ankara
Izmir
TURKEY
Lake Tuz
Kizil Irmak
Lake Van
Adana
Aleppo
Mosul
SYRIA
LEBANON
Beirut
ISRAEL
Tel Aviv
Jerusalem
Damascus
Amman
Dead Sea
JORDAN
Baghdad
IRAQ
Tigris
Euphrates
Basra
Abadan
Kuwait
KUWAIT
Persian Gulf
Dammam
BAHRAIN
Manama
QATAR
Doha
Abu Dhabi
UNITED ARAB EMIRATES
Bushire
Bandar Abbas
Strait of Hormuz
OMAN
Muscat
Riyadh
SAUDI ARABIA
Jidda
Mecca
Red Sea
Tropic of Cancer
OMAN
Masirah
Arabian Sea
San'a
Hodeida
YEMEN
Al Mukalla
Salalah
Kuria Muria Islands
Aden
Gulf of Aden
Socotra (Yemen)
Caspian Sea
Lake Urmia
Aras
Karun
Tehran
Isfahan
IRAN
Mashhad
Herat
Hari Rud
AFGHANISTAN
Kabul
Helmand
Seistan
Mediterranean Sea

The region's chief resources are oil and natural gas. Other minerals are scattered throughout the region. The capitals are the main industrial centers.

Resources and industry
- ◆ industrial center
- ○ port
- ● other town
- — major road
- — major railroad

mineral resources and fossil fuels
- • iron and other ferroalloy metal ores
- ● other metal ores
- ■ nonmetallic minerals
- coal
- copper
- iron ore
- natural gas
- oil

AGRICULTURE

Black Sea
Bosporus
TURKEY
Lake Tuz
Anatolia
Taurus Mts.
Kizil Irmak
Ararat 16,946
Lake Van
Lake Urmia
Aras
SYRIA
LEBANON
Mediterranean Sea
ISRAEL
JORDAN
Dead Sea -1,312
Syrian Desert
IRAQ
Tigris
Euphrates
Karun
Zagros Mountains
An Nafud
Nejd
Hejaz
KUWAIT
Persian Gulf
BAHRAIN
QATAR
SAUDI ARABIA
Tropic of Cancer
UNITED ARAB EMIRATES
Arabian Peninsula
Rub al Khali (Empty Quarter)
Red Sea
YEMEN
Hadhramaut
Gulf of Aden
Socotra (Yemen)
Caspian Sea
Elburz Mountains
Damavand 18,607
Dasht-e-Kavir
IRAN
Dasht-e-Lut
Seistan
Hari Rud
Shah Fuladi 16,872
Hindu Kush
Nowshak 24,556
Concord Peak 17,786
AFGHANISTAN
Helmand
OMAN
Strait of Hormuz
OMAN
Cape Hadd
Arabian Sea
Masirah
Cape Madraka
Kuria Muria Islands

Arable land is concentrated in the uplands in the north, in the Tigris and Euphrates valleys, and in places where irrigation is possible. Livestock is raised on less productive land.

Agricultural zones
- arable
- arable and grazing
- fruit and vegetables
- rough grazing
- woods and forest
- nonagricultural land
- ▲ mountain peak (ft)
- ▼ depression (ft)

NORTHERN AFRICA

The northern part of Africa consists largely of a low plateau broken by shallow basins and rugged volcanic highlands. The main land feature in the far northwest is the Atlas Mountain range. The other main highlands are in Ethiopia, though there are also mountain peaks in Algeria, Niger, Chad, and Sudan. Running through these highlands is a section of the Rift Valley, the world's longest geological depression, which runs from Syria, in Southwest Asia, to Mozambique, in Southern Africa.

South of the Mediterranean coastlands and the Atlas Mountains lies the Sahara, the world's largest desert. Only two major rivers, the Nile and the Niger, flow across North Africa throughout the year. But North Africa is not completely arid. South of the Sahara is a dry grassland region called the Sahel, which merges into tropical grassland, or savanna, and forest.

North Africa contains two main groups of people: Arabs and Berbers in the north and black Africans in the lands south of the Sahara. Nomadism is the traditional way of life in the Sahara, though it is now under threat. Most of the people are Muslims, though Christianity, introduced between the fourth and sixth centuries A.D., survived the spread of Islam in the unreachable highlands of Ethiopia. All the countries of the region except Ethiopia were colonized by the French, British, Italians, and Spanish between 1830 and 1914. (Ethiopia was only briefly conquered and ruled by Italy from 1935 to 1941.) Arabic is the official language in the northern states, though some people speak Berber dialects. By contrast, many languages are spoken in the lands south of the Sahara. The former colonial language is used in many countries as an official language or for business and trade.

Northern Africa is part of the ancient landmass of Gondwanaland, which separated between 200 and 100 million years ago. About 70 million years ago, Africa consisted of two land plates: North Africa was tilted downward, while Southern Africa was tilted upward. This divided Africa into a high plateau in the south and a low plateau in the north, which was flooded by the sea. New rocks were formed on the seabed. These rocks now contain water, oil, and natural gas.

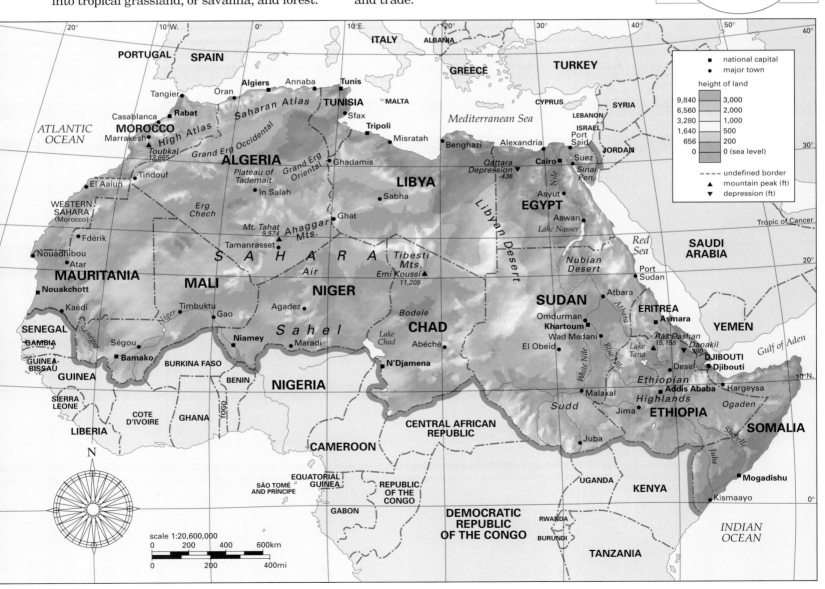

THE POLITICAL AND CULTURAL WORLD

Like many other parts of the developing world, Northern Africa has faced many problems since the countries of the region became independent from colonial rule.

Egypt was in the front line of the Arab-Israeli wars until it agreed to a peace treaty with Israel in 1979. To the south, Chad, Sudan, Ethiopia, and Somalia have suffered bitter civil wars, while Libya has fought with Chad over their disputed border.

Western Sahara (formerly Spanish Sahara), a thinly populated desert territory, was annexed by Morocco in 1991 in the face of opposition from native inhabitants.

COUNTRIES IN THE REGION

Algeria, Chad, Djibouti, Egypt, Eritrea, Ethiopia, Libya, Mali, Mauritania, Morocco, Niger, Somalia, Sudan, Tunisia

MEMBERSHIP OF INTERNATIONAL ORGANIZATIONS

Arab League Algeria, Djibouti, Egypt, Libya, Mauritania, Morocco, Somalia, Sudan, Tunisia
Organization of African Unity (OAU) All countries in the region
Organization of Petroleum Exporting Countries (OPEC) Algeria, Libya

LANGUAGE

Countries with one official language (Amharic) Ethiopia; (Arabic) Algeria, Egypt, Libya, Morocco, Sudan, Tunisia; (French) Mali, Niger
Countries with two official languages (Arabic, French) Chad, Djibouti, Mauritania; (Arabic, Somali) Somalia
Country with more than two official languages (Afar, Amharic, Arabic, Tigre and Kunama, Tigrinya) Eritrea

RELIGION

Countries with one major religion (M) Algeria, Djibouti, Libya, Mauritania, Morocco, Niger, Somalia, Tunisia
Countries with more than one major religion (M, C) Egypt, Eritrea; (M, EO, I) Ethiopia; (M, I, C) Chad, Mali, Sudan

Key: C–Various Christian, EO–Ethiopian Orthodox, I–Indigenous religions, M– Muslim

SYTLES OF GOVERNMENT

Republics All countries in the region except Morocco
Monarchy Morocco
Transitional governments Eritrea, Sudan
Multiparty states Algeria, Chad, Djibouti, Egypt, Ethiopia, Mali, Mauritania, Morocco, Tunisia
One-party states Eritrea, Libya, Somalia,
State without parties Niger
Military influence Algeria, Libya, Mauritania, Sudan
State without effective government (since 1991) Somalia

ECONOMIC INDICATORS

	Algeria	Egypt	Ethiopia
GDP (US$ billions)	45.9	75.5	6.3
GNP per capita (US$)	4,600	2,940	510
Annual rate of growth of GDP, 1990–1997	0.8%	4.0%	4.9%
Manufacturing as % of GDP	8%	24%	6.7%
Central government spending as % of GNP	n/a	37.4	18.1
Merchandise exports (US$ billions)	13.8	5.5	0.5
Merchandise imports (US$ billions)	8.1	14.2	1.0
Aid received as % of GNP	0.9%	2.2%	10.0%
Total external debt as % of GDP	69.0%	39.0%	149.0%

WELFARE INDICATORS

	Algeria	Egypt	Ethiopia
Infant mortality rate (per 1,000 live births)			
1965	154	145	165
2000	44	51	115
Daily food supply available (calories per capita)	3,020	3,289	1,845

Algeria
Area 919,597 sq mi (2,381,741 sq km)
Population 31,193,917

Chad
Area 495,756 sq mi (1,284,000 sq km)
Population 8,424,504

Djibouti
Area 8,958 sq mi (23,200 sq km)
Population 451,442

Egypt
Area 385,230 sq mi (997,739 sq km)
Population 68,359,979

Eritrea
Area 46,842 sq mi (121,320 sq km)
Population 4,135,933

Ethiopia
Area 435,187 sq mi (1,127,127 sq km)
Population 64,117,452

Libya
Area 678,383 sq mi (1,757,000 sq km)
Population 5,115,450

Mali
Area 478,842 sq mi (1,240,192 sq km)
Population 10,685,948

Mauritania
Area 397,956 sq mi (1,030,700 sq km)
Population 2,667,859

Morocco
Area 187,542 sq mi (485,730 sq km)
Population 30,122,350

Niger
Area 458,076 sq mi (1,186,408 sq km)
Population 10,075,511

Somalia
Area 246,201 sq mi (637,657 sq km)
Population 7,253,137

Sudan
Area 966,759 sq mi (2,503,890 sq km)
Population 35,079,814

Tunisia
Area 59,664 sq mi (154,530 sq km)
Population 9,593,402

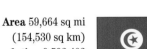

The boundaries of Northern Africa were drawn by the European colonial powers. The boundaries they mandated for many countries have caused friction in recent years. For example, the world's ninth largest country, Sudan, is divided into two cultural regions: the Arab north and the black African south. Tension between the ethnic regions has led to civil war.

■ national capital
• other town

(Map of Northern Africa showing countries: Morocco, Western Sahara (Morocco), Algeria, Tunisia, Libya, Egypt, Mauritania, Mali, Niger, Chad, Sudan, Eritrea, Djibouti, Ethiopia, Somalia with cities including Tangier, Algiers, Annaba, Tunis, Oran, Constantine, Casablanca, Rabat, El Oued, Sfax, Tripoli, Misratah, Benghazi, Alexandria, Port Said, Cairo, Suez, Marrakesh, Ghardaia, Béchar, Ghadamis, El Minya, Timimoun, El Golea, Asyut, Luxor, Tindouf, In Salah, Sabha, Ghat, Aswan, El Aaiún, Djanet, Al Jawf, Fdérik, Tamanrasset, Djado, Nouadhibou, Atar, Kerma, Merowe, Port Sudan, Nouakchott, Timbuktu, Gao, Agadez, Bilma, Faya-Largeau, Atbara, Kaédi, Nioro du Sahel, Niamey, Maradi, Abéché, El Fasher, Omdurman, Khartoum, Asmara, Assab, Mopti, Ségou, Bamako, N'Djamena, Abéché, El Obeid, Wad Medani, Gonder, Desē, Djibouti, Caluula, Berbera, Sarh, Nyala, Debre Markos, Hargeysa, Malakal, Addis Ababa, Wau, Jima, Goba, Juba, Beledweyne, Baydhabo, Mogadishu, Kismaayo)

HABITATS

The desert that dominates Northern Africa is spreading southward into the Sahel region. This is the result of severe droughts and human misuse of the land, including overgrazing by livestock and the cutting down of trees and shrubs for fuel.

LAND

Area 5,764,994 sq mi (14,931,234 sq km)
Highest point Ras Dashan,15,158 ft (4,620 m)
Lowest point Lake Assal, Djibouti, –492 ft (–150 m)
Major features Atlas ranges, Ethiopian Highlands, Sahara, world's greatest desert, northern part of East African Rift Valley

WATER

Longest river most of the Nile's 4,160 mi (6,690 km) length, the world's greatest for a river, and 1,092,000 sq mi (2,802,000 sq km) basin is in the region
Highest average flow Niger, 201,000 cu ft/sec (5,700 cu m/sec) on lower section
Largest lake Chad, 10,000 sq mi (25,900 sq km)

NOTABLE THREATENED SPECIES

Mammals Barbary macaque (*Macaca sylvanus*), Simien jackal (*Canis simensis*), Cuvier's gazelle (*Gazella cuvieri*), Beira (*Dorcatragus megalotis*), Addax (*Addax nasomaculatus*)
Birds Prince Ruspoli's turaco (*Tauraco ruspolii*), Djibouti francolin (*Francolinus ochropectus*), Algerian nuthatch (*Sitta ledanti*)
Plants *Allium crameri; Biscutella elbensis; Centaurea cyrenaica; Cordeauxia edulis* (ye-eb); *Cupressus dupreziana; Cyclamen rohlfsianum; Cyperus papyrus* subsp. *hadidii; Euphorbia cameronii; Gillettiodendron glandulosum; Olea laperrinei*

CLIMATE

Northern Africa contains the Sahara and other deserts in the east. The northern coasts have a Mediterranean climate. To the south is the Sahel, a hot, semiarid zone. The far south has wet and dry seasons. Mountains in the far east have a moderate climate.

CLIMATE

	Temperature °F (°C)		Altitude
	January	July	ft (m)
Ouarzazate	48 (9)	86 (30)	3,726 (1,136)
Timbuktu	73 (23)	90 (32)	895 (273)
Tripoli	52 (11)	81 (27)	276 (84)
Alexandria	59 (15)	79 (26)	23 (7)
Wadi Halfa	55 (13)	90 (32)	508 (155)
Addis Ababa	61 (16)	59 (15)	7,741 (2,360)

	Precipitation in. (mm)		
	January	July	Year
Ouarzazate	0.2 (6)	0.1 (2)	4.8 (123)
Timbuktu	0 (0)	2.6 (65)	8.9 (225)
Tripoli	1.8 (46)	0 (0)	10.0 (253)
Alexandria	1.7 (44)	0 (0)	6.7 (169)
Wadi Halfa	0 (0)	0.04 (1)	0.1 (3)
Addis Ababa	0.9 (24)	9.0 (228)	42.9 (1,089)

World's highest recorded temperature, 136.4°F (58°C), Al Aziziyah, Libya; Wadi Halfa is one of the world's driest places

NATURAL HAZARDS

Drought; earthquakes in mountains of northwest

ENVIRONMENTAL ISSUES

The main environmental issue in the region is water. Intensive agriculture and the rapid expansion of city populations have added to the strain on Northern Africa's limited water resources. Desertification has already taken place in large areas.

POPULATION AND WEALTH

	Highest	Middle	Lowest
Population (millions)	68.359 (Egypt)	9.593 (Tunisia)	0.451 (Djibouti)
Population increase (annual growth rate, 1990–95)	4.2% (Somalia)	2.3% (Algeria)	1.4% (Tunisia)
Energy use (lbs/year per person of oil equivalent)	6,385 (Libya)	1,986 (Algeria)	648 (Ethiopia)
Purchasing power parity (Int$/per year)	5,305 (Tunisia)	2,843 (Egypt)	519 (Ethiopia)

ENVIRONMENTAL INDICATORS

CO2 emissions ('000 tons year)	91,684 (Egypt)	29,294 (Morocco)	11 (Somalia)
Car ownership (% of population)	14% (Libya)	4% (Algeria)	<1% (Mauritania)
Protected territory including marine areas (%)	17% (Ethiopia)	4% (Mali)	0.1% (Libya)
Percentage of original forest remaining	17% (Ethiopia)	12% (Algeria)	5% (Tunisia)
Artificial fertilizer use (lbs/acre/year)	284 (Egypt)	30 (Libya)	0 (Somalia)
Access to safe drinking water (% population; rural/urban)	97/97% (Libya)	55/87% (Mali)	8/60% (Eritrea)

MAJOR ENVIRONMENTAL PROBLEMS AND SOURCES

Air pollution: urban high
Land degradation: *types:* desertification, soil erosion, salinization; *causes:* agriculture, industry, population pressure, flooding
Resource issues: fuelwood shortage; inadequate drinking water and sanitation; inadequate water supply
Population issues: population explosion; urban overcrowding; famine; war; HIV/AIDS

HABITATS

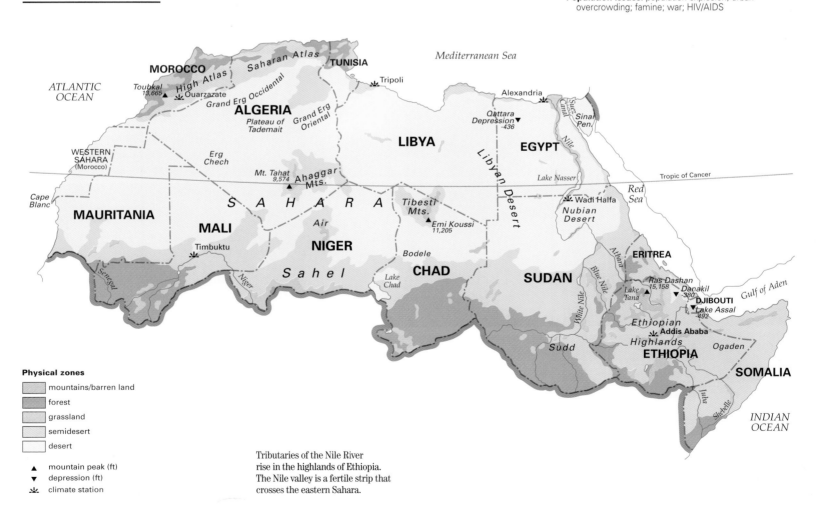

Physical zones
- mountains/barren land
- forest
- grassland
- semidesert
- desert

- ▲ mountain peak (ft)
- ▼ depression (ft)
- �※ climate station

Tributaries of the Nile River rise in the highlands of Ethiopia. The Nile valley is a fertile strip that crosses the eastern Sahara.

ENVIRONMENTAL ISSUES

Key environmental issues

- • major town or city
- ☁ polluted town or city
- ☢ former nuclear test site
- ～ polluted river
- ▬ main area of coastal tourism

area at risk of desertification

- ▓ very high
- ▒ high
- ░ moderate
- ☐ true desert

Mediterranean Sea

ATLANTIC OCEAN

Algiers · Tunis · TUNISIA
Oran · · Saharan Atlas
Rabat · Fès · Tripoli
Casablanca · High Atlas
Marrakesh · Grand Erg Occidental · Benghazi · Alexandria
MOROCCO · Giza · Cairo · Sinai Pen.
WESTERN SAHARA (Morocco) · Grand Erg Oriental
ALGERIA · LIBYA · EGYPT
Reggane ☢ · Erg Chech · Aswan High Dam
In Ekker ☢ · Ahaggar Mts. · Lake Nasser · Tropic of Cancer
Cape Blanc · S A H A R A · Tibesti Mts. · Libyan Desert · Nubian Desert · Red Sea
MAURITANIA · Air · ERITREA
Nouakchott · MALI · NIGER · Bodele
Niger · Agadez · CHAD · Omdurman · Khartoum
Senegal · Niamey · S a h e l · Lake Chad · SUDAN · Lake Tana · DJIBOUTI · Gulf of Aden
Bamako · N'Djamena · White Nile · Blue Nile · Ethiopian Highlands · Addis Ababa · Ogaden
· Sudd · Shebelle · ETHIOPIA · SOMALIA
· Mogadishu
· INDIAN OCEAN

Severe droughts in the Sahel in the 1970s and 1980s have drawn attention to the dangers of desertification and the plight of the people there. Many lost most of their crops and livestock and had to flee their homelands.

CLIMATE

height above sea level of climate stations

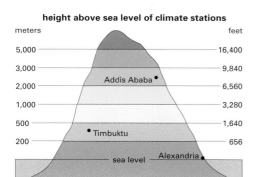

meters		feet
5,000		16,400
3,000	Addis Ababa	9,840
2,000		6,560
1,000		3,280
500	Timbuktu	1,640
200		656
sea level	Alexandria	

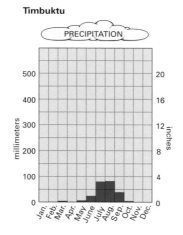

Timbuktu — PRECIPITATION

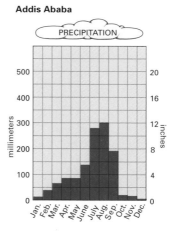

Addis Ababa — PRECIPITATION

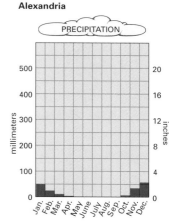

Alexandria — PRECIPITATION

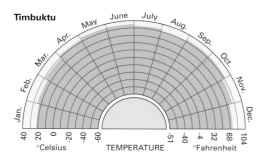

Timbuktu — TEMPERATURE

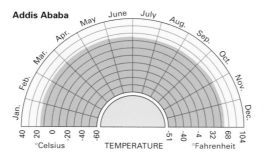

Addis Ababa — TEMPERATURE

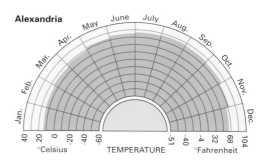

Alexandria — TEMPERATURE

POPULATION

Much of Northern Africa is either uninhabited or sparsely populated. The population is mainly rural, though cities are growing quickly as people move into them from the countryside. Greater Cairo is one of the world's largest conurbations.

POPULATION

Total population of region (millions)			287.27
	Algeria	Egypt	Morocco
Population density (persons per sq mi)	31.1	171.9	159.7
Population change (average annual percent 1960–1990)			
Urban	+3.57%	+2.28%	+3.23%
Rural	+0.51%	+1.59%	+0.02%

URBAN POPULATION

As percentage of total population			
2000	60%	45%	56%

TEN LARGEST CITIES

	Country	Population
Cairo †	Egypt	6,789,479
Alexandria	Egypt	3,328,196
Casablanca	Morocco	2,940,623
Giza	Egypt	2,221,868
Addis Ababa †	Ethiopia	2,112,737
Tripoli †	Libya	1,948,400
Tunis †	Tunisia	1,827,000
Algiers †	Algeria	1,519,570
Omdurman	Sudan	1,271,403
Mogadishu†	Somalia	1,206,700

† denotes capital city

City population figures are for the city proper.

INDUSTRY

Northern Africa's natural resources include oil and gas in Algeria, Egypt, and Libya, uranium in Niger, phosphates in Morocco and Western Sahara, and iron ore in Mauritania. The main industrial areas are in northern Egypt.

INDUSTRIAL OUTPUT (US $)

Morocco	Egypt	Algeria
$11 billion	$22 billion	$19 billion

INDUSTRIAL PRODUCTION GROWTH RATE

Algeria	Egypt	Ethiopia
7%	5%	n/a

INDUSTRIAL WORKERS (millions)

(figures in parentheses are percentages of total labor force)

Total	Mining	Manufacturing	Construction
Algeria	0.05 (1%)	0.65 (11.3%)	0.65 (11.4%)
	Mining/Manufacturing		**Construction**
Egypt	2.0 (12.7%)		0.88 (5.6%)
Ethiopia	0.4 (1.6%)		0.06 (0.3%)

MAJOR PRODUCTS (Egypt)

Energy and minerals	1970	Output 1995	Change since 1960
Oil (mil m.t.)	16	45	181.3
Petroleum products (mil m.t.)	3.2	26	712.5
Natural gas ('000 terajoules)	3.3	436	13,112.1

Manufactures			
Cement ('000 tons)	3,684	14,000	280.0
Steel ('000 tons)	304	2,600	755.3
Photphate ('000 tons)	584	632	8.2
Fertilizers (nitrogenous) ('000 tons)	152	900	492.1
Fertilizers (phosphate) ('000 tons)	116	145	25.0
Television receivers ('000)	64	234	265.6

AGRICULTURE

In the past, most people were subsistence farmers or nomadic herders. But today intensive farming is becoming common. Major products include grain, citrus fruits, cotton, dates, groundnuts, potatoes and other vegetables, and rice.

LAND

Total area 5,764,994 sq mi (14,931,234 sq km)

Cropland	Pasture	Forest/Woodland
4%	27%	10%
(254,115 sq mi)	(1,557,771 sq mi)	(595,443 sq mi)

FARMERS	Highest	Middle	Lowest
Agriculture as % of GDP	55% (Ethiopia)	25% (Mauritania)	9% (Eritrea)
% of workforce	90% (Niger)	50% (Morocco)	17% (Libya)

MAJOR CROPS: Agricultural products fruit and vegetables; cassava; olives; pulses; nuts; grains, wheat, sorghum, millet; sugar beet; sugarcane; gum arabic; oilseed; rice; cotton; sheep, goats, cattle, camels; poultry; dairy products; wine; fish

Total cropland ('000 acres)	41,760 (Sudan)	12,355 (Niger)	971 (Eritrea)
Cropland (acres) per 1,000 people	1,507 (Sudan)	882 (Morocco)	126 (Egypt)
Irrigated land as % of cropland	100% (Egypt)	19% (Somalia)	1% (Niger)
Number of tractors	92,893 (Algeria)	35,100 (Tunisia)	170 (Chad)
Average cereal crop yields (lbs/acre)	5,526 (Egypt)	1,026 (Tunisia)	280 (Niger)
Cereal production ('000 tons)	17,328 (Egypt)	2,934 (Algeria)	131 (Eritrea)
Change since 1986/88	86%	60%	n/a

LIVESTOCK & FISHERIES

Meat production ('000 tons)	1,211 (Egypt)	588 (Sudan)	28 (Eritrea)
Change since 1986–88	116%	71%	n/a
Marine fish catch ('000 tons)	662.8 (Morocco)	98.7 (Algeria)	2.6 (Eritrea)
Change since 1986/88	39%	42%	n/a

POPULATION

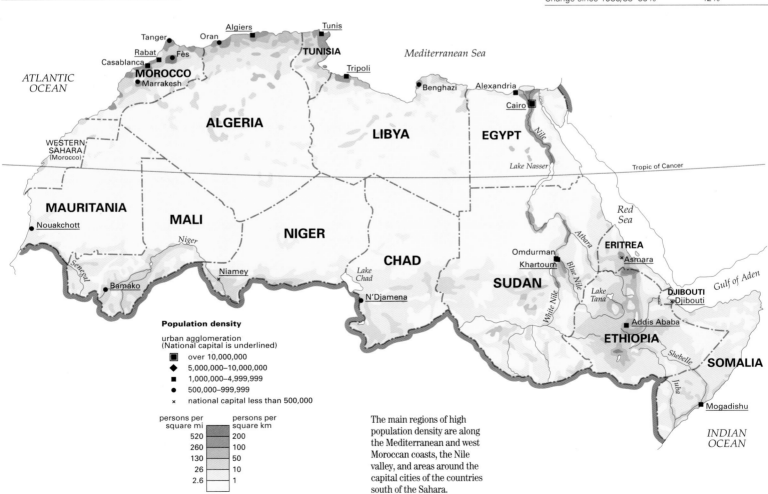

Population density

urban agglomeration
(National capital is underlined)

- ▣ over 10,000,000
- ◆ 5,000,000–10,000,000
- ▪ 1,000,000–4,999,999
- ▪ 500,000–999,999
- × national capital less than 500,000

persons per square mi	persons per square km
520	200
260	100
130	50
26	10
2.6	1

The main regions of high population density are along the Mediterranean and west Moroccan coasts, the Nile valley, and areas around the capital cities of the countries south of the Sahara.

INDUSTRY

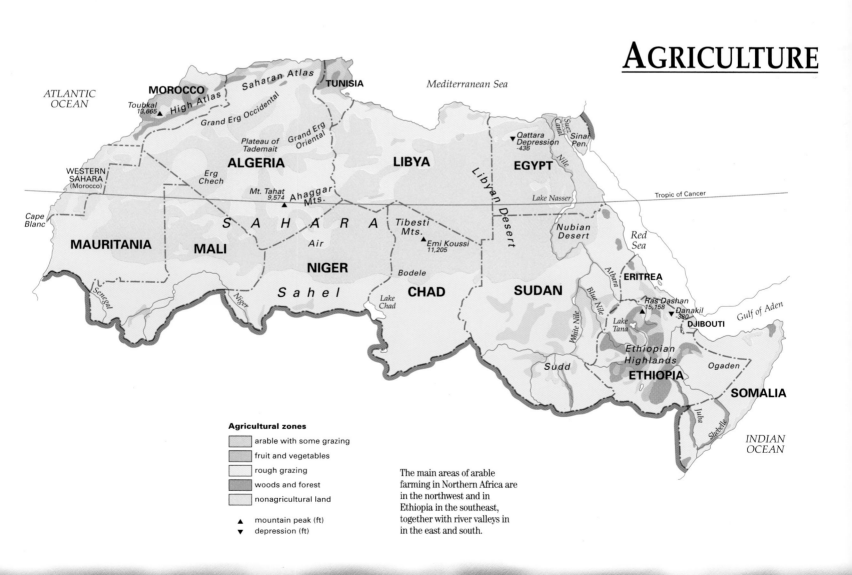

Resources and industry
- ◆ industrial center
- ○ port
- • other town
- —— major road
- —— major railroad

mineral resources and fossil fuels
- ● iron and other ferroalloy metal ores
- ● other metal ores
- ■ nonmetallic minerals
- ▢ natural gas
- ▨ oil
- ▨ phosphates

ATLANTIC OCEAN

Tangier Algiers Annaba Tunis
Oran
Rabat **TUNISIA**
Casablanca Sfax
MOROCCO Tendrara Touggourt Tripoli *Mediterranean Sea*
Marrakesh Benghazi Tobruk Port Said
Agadir Misratah Alexandria
ALGERIA **LIBYA** Cairo Suez
El Aaiun Hun Al Jaghbub **EGYPT**
Boukra El Kharga
WESTERN SAHARA (Morocco) Aswan *Tropic of Cancer*
Lake Nasser

Nouadhibou Wadi Halfa
MAURITANIA Port Sudan *Red Sea*
Nouakchott **MALI** Karima **ERITREA**
NIGER Massawa
Timbuktu *Niger* Agadez Khartoum Asmara
Niamey **CHAD** *Blue Nile* Assab *Gulf of Aden*
Lake Chad **SUDAN** Lake Tana **DJIBOUTI** Djibouti
Bamako N'Djamena Nyala *White Nile* Berbera
Dire Dawa
Addis Ababa *Shebelle*
Wau **ETHIOPIA** **SOMALIA**
Juba
Mogadishu
Kismaayo
INDIAN OCEAN

Manufacturing is increasing in the countries bordering the Mediterranean Sea. Tourism is also important in Egypt, Morocco, and Tunisia.

AGRICULTURE

ATLANTIC OCEAN

MOROCCO *Saharan Atlas* **TUNISIA** *Mediterranean Sea*
Toubkal 13,665 *High Atlas*
Grand Erg Occidental
Plateau of Tademait *Grand Erg Oriental*
WESTERN SAHARA (Morocco) **ALGERIA** **LIBYA** **EGYPT** Qattara Depression -436 *Sinai Pen.*
Erg Chech *Tropic of Cancer* Lake Nasser
Cape Blanc Mt. Tahat 9,574 *Ahaggar Mts.* *Nubian Desert* *Red Sea*
MAURITANIA **MALI** *S A H A R A* *Tibesti Mts.*
Air Emi Koussi 11,205 **ERITREA**
NIGER *Bodele* Ras Dashan 15,158 Danakil -380
Senegal *Sahel* **CHAD** **SUDAN** *Blue Nile* **DJIBOUTI**
Niger Lake Chad *White Nile* Lake Tana *Gulf of Aden*
Ethiopian Highlands *Ogaden*
Sudd **ETHIOPIA** **SOMALIA**
Shebelle
INDIAN OCEAN

Agricultural zones
- ▢ arable with some grazing
- ▨ fruit and vegetables
- ▢ rough grazing
- ▨ woods and forest
- ▢ nonagricultural land
- ▲ mountain peak (ft)
- ▼ depression (ft)

The main areas of arable farming in Northern Africa are in the northwest and in Ethiopia in the southeast, together with river valleys in the east and south.

CENTRAL AFRICA

Central Africa is made up of 26 countries, stretching from Cape Verde, an island nation in the Atlantic Ocean west of Senegal, to the Seychelles, another island nation, east of Kenya in the Indian Ocean.

West Africa, which extends from Senegal to Nigeria, consists of coastal plains that rise inland to low plateaus. Cameroon has some volcanic highlands, but the Congo basin is a shallow depression in the central plateaus. Beyond the Congo basin are mountains that overlook the Rift Valley, which contains Lakes Tanganyika, Edward, and Albert. East of the Rift Valley lie the high plateaus of East Africa. This region contains Africa's largest lake, Victoria, the source of the White Nile. The ancient volcanic mountain, Kilimanjaro, is Africa's highest peak. Such volcanoes were formed while earth movements were fracturing the continent, creating the Rift Valley.

Central Africa straddles the Equator, and the climate is generally hot and humid, though temperatures are much lower in the highlands. The world's second largest rain forest (after the Amazon basin) occupies parts of the Congo basin. Central Africa also contains large areas of savanna, home of much wildlife, especially in the national parks on the plateaus of East Africa.

Most of the people are black Africans, who are divided into many ethnic groups. Each group has its own language, art, customs, and traditional religion, though Islam has made inroads into northern West Africa and also East Africa. Christianity was introduced by European missionaries during the colonial period in the nineteenth and twentieth centuries.

Subsistence farming is the main activity, and manufacturing is generally limited to producing basic items such as cement, clothes, and processed food and drink for the home market.

Central Africa is part of the vast plateau of extremely old rocks that make up the African plateau. In places, the ancient rocks are overlaid by young sedimentary rocks and elsewhere by volcanic rocks. The volcanic rocks in East Africa reached the surface 35 to 25 million years ago through cracks formed when the plateaus were stretched by earth movements. These movements tore open the Rift Valley, which runs north-south through eastern Africa. The ancient rocks of Africa are rich in minerals.

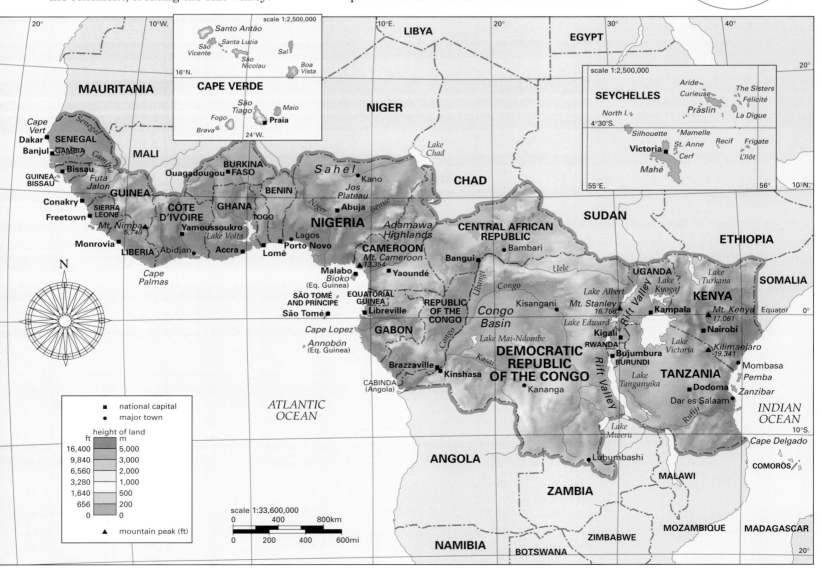

THE POLITICAL AND CULTURAL WORLD

The European colonizers drew Africa's boundaries with little regard for existing ethnic groups. As a result, the nations of Central Africa contain many cultural groups.

Nigeria, for example, has over 200 ethnic groups. As no local language is used enough for it to be the official language, Nigeria, like most countries in the region, has adopted its former colonial language (English) for official purposes.

In 1962 Rwanda became an independent republic. Interethnic clashes between Hutu and Tutsi led to civil war in 1990. The war culminated, in April 1994, in a genocide halted only by international intervention. Civil strife continues into the 2000s.

COUNTRIES IN THE REGION

Benin, Burkina Faso, Burundi, Cameroon, Cape Verde, Central African Republic, Democratic Republic of the Congo, Republic of the Congo, Côte d'Ivoire, Equatorial Guinea, Gabon, Gambia, Ghana, Guinea, Guinea-Bissau, Kenya, Liberia, Nigeria, Rwanda, São Tomé and Príncipe, Senegal, Seychelles, Sierra Leone, Tanzania, Togo, Uganda

Cabinda is a coastal enclave of Angola (see Southern Africa)

LANGUAGE

Countries with one official language (E) Gambia, Ghana, Liberia, Nigeria, Sierra Leone, Uganda; (F) Benin, Burkina Faso, Central African Republic, Congo, Congo (DR), Côte d'Ivoire, Gabon, Guinea, Senegal, Togo ; (P) Cape Verde, Guinea-Bissau, São Tomé and Príncipe; (S) Equatorial Guinea
Countries with two official languages (E, F) Cameroon; (E, Sw) Kenya, Tanzania; (F, K) Burundi; (F, R) Rwanda
Country with three official languages (C, E, F) Seychelles

Key: C–Creole, E–English, F–French, K–Kirundi, P–Portuguese, R–Rwandan, S–Spanish, Sw–Swahili

Numerous indigenous languages are spoken in the region.

Many countries in the region have been subject to one-party or military governments and are in transition toward civilian rule.

In 1997, Zaire's dictator, General Mobutu, was overthrown by a popular rebellion and the country was renamed the Democratic Republic of the Congo. Civil war continued until a cease-fire in 1999, but some fighting still goes on.

RELIGION

Countries with one major religion (M) Gambia; (RC) Cape Verde, Equatorial Guinea
Countries with two major religions (P, RC) São Tomé and Príncipe, Seychelles; (M, C) Nigeria
Countries with three or more major religions (I, M, RC) Benin, Burkina Faso, Côte d'Ivoire, Gabon, Guinea, Guinea-Bissau, Liberia, Senegal; (C, I, M, P, RC) Democratic Republic of the Congo, Kenya; (I, M, P, RC) Cameroon, Burundi, Central African Republic, Republic of the Congo, Ghana, Rwanda, Sierra Leone, Tanzania, Togo, Uganda

Key: C–Various Christian, I–Indigenous religions, M–Muslim, P–Protestant, RC–Roman Catholic

MEMBERSHIP OF INTERNATIONAL ORGANIZATIONS

Economic Community of West African States (ECOWAS) Benin, Burkina Faso, Cape Verde, Côte d'Ivoire, Gambia, Ghana, Guinea, Guinea-Bissau, Liberia, Nigeria, Senegal, Sierra Leone, Togo
Organization of African Unity (OAU)
All countries in the region

STYLES OF GOVERNMENT

Republics All countries in the region
Transitional governments Democratic Republic of the Congo, Nigeria, Togo
Multiparty states All countries in the region except Uganda
One-party state Uganda
Military influence Burundi, Côte d'Ivoire, Democratic Republic of the Congo, Equatorial Guinea, Guinea, Guinea-Bissau, Sierra Leone, Togo

■ national capital
● other town

Benin
Area 43,475 sq mi
(112,600 sq km)
Population
6,395,919

Burkina Faso
Area 105,869 sq mi
(274,200 sq km)
Population
11,946,065

Burundi
Area 10,026 sq mi
(25,967 sq km)
Population
6,054,714

Area 10,830 sq mi
(28,051 sq km)
Population
474,214

Equatorial Guinea

Kenya
Area 220,625 sq mi
(571,416 sq km)
Population
30,339,770

Area 75,955 sq mi
(196,722 sq km)
Population
9,987,494

Senegal

Cameroon
Area 178,963 sq mi
(463,511 sq km)
Population
15,421,937

Area 103,347 sq mi
(267,667 sq km)
Population
1,208,436

Gabon

Liberia
Area 38,250 sq mi
(99,067 sq km)
Population
3,164,156

Area 175 sq mi
(453 sq km)
Population
79,326

Seychelles

Cape Verde
Area 1,557 sq mi
(4,033 sq km)
Population
401,343

Area 4,127 sq mi
(10,689 sq km)
Population
1,367,124

Gambia

Nigeria
Area 356,669 sq mi
(923,768 sq km)
Population
123,337,822

Area 27,699 sq mi
(71,740 sq km)
Population
5,232,624
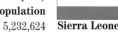
Sierra Leone

Central African Republic
Area 240,324 sq mi
(622,436 sq km)
Population
3,512,751

Area 92,098 sq mi
(238,533 sq km)
Population
19,533,560

Ghana

Republic of the Congo
Area 132,047 sq mi
(342,000 sq km)
Population
2,830,961

Area 342,082 sq mi
(885,987 sq km)
Population
35,306,126
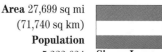
Tanzania

Côte d'Ivoire
Area 123,847 sq mi
(320,763 sq km)
Population
15,980,950

Area 94,926 sq mi
(245,857 sq km)
Population
7,466,200

Guinea

Rwanda
Area 10,169 sq mi
(26,338 sq km)
Population
7,229,129

Area 21,925 sq mi
(56,785 sq km)
Population
5,018,502

Togo

Democratic Republic of the Congo
Area 905,448 sq mi
(2,345,095 sq km)
Population
51,964,999

Area 13,948 sq mi
(36,125 sq km)
Population
1,285,715

Guinea-Bissau

São Tomé and Príncipe
Area 386 sq mi
(1,001 sq km)
Population
159,883

Area 91,134 sq mi
(236,040 sq km)
Population
23,317,560

Uganda

HABITATS

Central Africa contains rain forests and grasslands called savanna. The savanna merges in the north into dry grassland. The altitude, especially on the high plateaus of East Africa, has a marked, moderating influence on the tropical climate.

LAND

Area 3,245,908 sq mi (8,406,844 sq km)
Highest point Kilimanjaro, 19,341 ft (5,895 m)
Lowest point sea level
Major features Jos Plateau and Adamawa Highlands in west, Congo basin, Ruwenzori Range, mountains and Rift Valley in east

WATER

Longest river Congo (DR), 2,880 mi (4,630 km)
Largest basin Congo, 1,467,000 sq mi (3,822,000 sq km)
Highest average flow Congo, 1,377,000 cu ft/sec (39,000 cu m/sec)
Largest lake Victoria, 24,300 sq mi (62,940 sq km)

NOTABLE THREATENED SPECIES

Mammals Nimba otter-shrew (*Micropotamogale lamottei*), Mountain gorilla (*Gorilla gorilla beringei*), chimpanzee (*Pan troglodytes*), Bonobo (*Pan paniscus*), Drill (*Mandrillus leucophaeus*), Pygmy hippopotamus (*Choeropsis liberiensis*), Ader's duiker (*Cephalophus adersi*), Western giant eland (*Tavrotagus derbianus derbianus*)
Birds White-breasted guinea fowl (*Agelastes meleagrides*), Bannerman's turaco (*Tauraco bannermani*), Sokoke scops owl (*Otus ireneae*), Seychelles magpie robin (*Copsychus sechellarum*)
Others Goliath frog (*Conraua goliath*), Lake Victoria cichlid fish (250 species), African blind barbfish (*Caecobarbus geertsi*)
Plants *Aeschynomene batekensis*, *Drypetes singroboensis*, *Justicia hepperi*, *Memecylon fragrans*, *Pitcairnia feliciana*, African violet (*Saintpaulia ionantha*), *Scleria sheilae*, *Temnopteryx sericea*, *Uvariodendron gorgonis*, *Vernonia sechellensis*

HABITATS

West Africa contains low plateaus, which overlook the coastal plains. The high, rolling plateaus in East Africa are broken by huge volcanic massifs, while two arms of the Rift Valley run through the region.

CLIMATE

Central Africa lies on the Equator, and much of the region has a tropical rainy climate, though temperatures vary with altitude. To the east, the mountains have moderate temperatures, giving many places a pleasant, mild climate. To the north is a hot semiarid area.

CLIMATE

| | Temperature °F (°C) | | Altitude |
	January	July	ft (m)
Dakar	70 (21)	81 (27)	75 (23)
Ngaoundéré	72 (22)	70 (21)	3,670 (1,119)
Lisala	77 (25)	75 (24)	1,509 (460)
Bukoba	70 (21)	68 (20)	3,729 (1,137)
Lodwar	84 (29)	82 (28)	1,660 (506)
Mombasa	82 (28)	75 (24)	190 (58)

| | Precipitation in. (mm) | | |
	January	July	Year
Dakar	0 (0)	3.5 (88)	22.8 (578)
Ngaoundéré	0.1 (2)	10.1 (256)	59.5 (1,511)
Lisala	2.5 (63)	7.5 (190)	64.0 (1,626)
Bukoba	5.9 (151)	1.9 (49)	80.4 (2,043)
Lodwar	0.3 (8)	0.6 (15)	6.4 (162)
Mombasa	1.2 (30)	2.8 (72)	45.8 (1,163)

NATURAL HAZARDS

Drought, floods, earthquakes

ENVIRONMENTAL ISSUES

Human adaptation of the environment of Central Africa has been going on for thousands of years. Today, the fast-increasing population and the devastation of wars are adding to the pressure on the region's fragile resources, such as soils and vegetation.

POPULATION AND WEALTH

	Highest	Middle	Lowest
Population (millions)	123.337 (Nigeria)	7.466 (Guinea)	0.079 (Seychelles)
Population increase (annual growth rate, % 1990–95)	7.7% (Rwanda)	2.8% (Uganda)	0.8% (Guinea)
Energy use (lbs per year per person of oil equivalent)	3,170 (Gabon)	1,096 (Kenya)	668 (Zaire)
Purchasing power parity (Int$/per year)	7,655 (Gabon)	1,581 (Ghana)	442 (S. Leone)

ENVIRONMENTAL INDICATORS

CO_2 emissions ('000 tons year)	90,717 (Nigeria)	6,683 (Kenya)	132 (Eq. Guinea)
Car ownership (% of population)	11% (Seychelles)	4% (Gabon)	below 1% (Rwanda)
Proportion of territory protected, including marine areas (%)	111% (Seychelles)	11% (Benin)	0% (Eq. Guinea)
Forests as a % of original forest	90% (Gabon)	38% (Eq. Guinea)	3% (Benin)
Artificial fertilizer use (lbs/acre/year)	22 (Kenya)	8 (Burk. Faso)	0 (Rwanda)
Access to safe drinking water (% population; rural/urban)	100%/88% (Eq. Guinea)	44%/67% (Kenya)	7%/53% (Rep. of Congo)

MAJOR ENVIRONMENTAL PROBLEMS AND SOURCES

Land degradation: *types*: desertification, soil erosion, salinization, deforestation, habitat destruction; *causes*: agriculture, population pressure, war
Resource issues: fuelwood shortage; inadequate drinking water and sanitation; land use competition; oil spills
Population issues: population explosion; urban overcrowding; inadequate health facilities; disease; famine; war; HIV/AIDS
Major event: Lake Nyos (1986), CO_2 cloud released; leakage and explosions from oil pipelines, Nigeria (2000)

Physical zones
- mountains/barren land
- forest
- grassland
- semidesert

▲ mountain peak (ft)
☼ climate station

ENVIRONMENTAL ISSUES

Key environmental issues

- • major town or city
- ⬤ polluted town or city
- + major natural disaster
- ○ port receiving toxic waste
- ⌒ polluted river

remaining tropical rainforest

areas of fuelwood shortage

- severe
- acute
- prospective

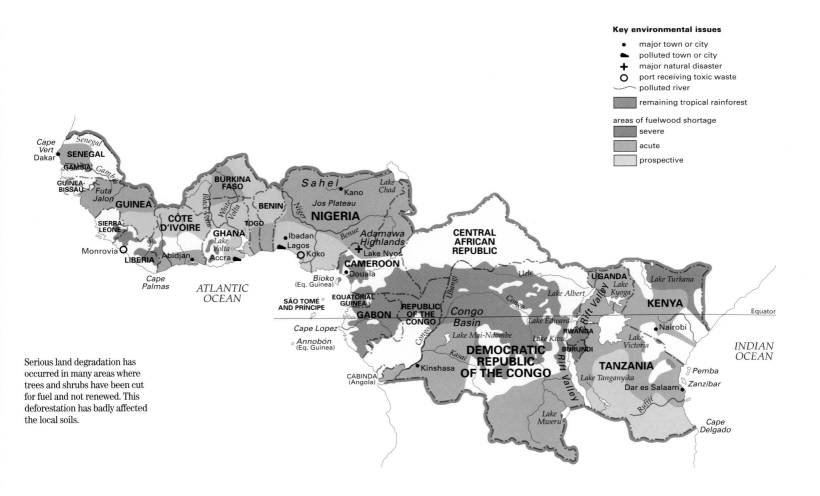

Serious land degradation has occurred in many areas where trees and shrubs have been cut for fuel and not renewed. This deforestation has badly affected the local soils.

CLIMATE

height above sea level of climate stations

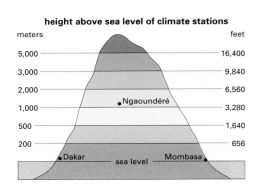

meters		feet
5,000		16,400
3,000		9,840
2,000	Ngaoundéré	6,560
1,000		3,280
500		1,640
200		656
	Dakar Mombasa	
	sea level	

Dakar

PRECIPITATION

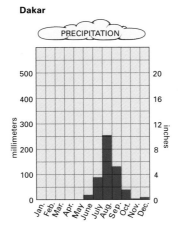

Ngaoundéré

PRECIPITATION

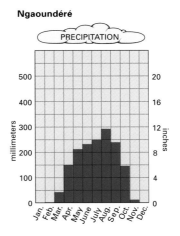

Mombasa

PRECIPITATION

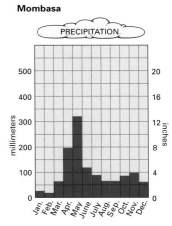

Dakar

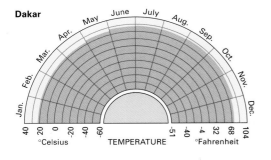

Ngaoundéré

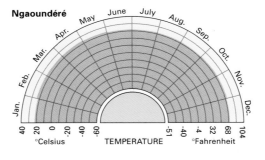

Mombasa

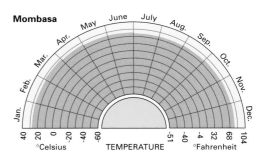

POPULATION

About three out of every four people in Central Africa live in rural areas, in scattered communities or in villages. But during this century, as the countries became independent, the cities have expanded rapidly as people arrive looking for jobs and better education.

POPULATION

Total population of region (millions)			389
	Gabon	Cameroon	Tanzania
Population density (persons per sq mi)	11.4	77.7	80.8
Population change (average annual percent 1960–1990)			
Urban	+3.99%	+4.48%	+6.31%
Rural	−2.59%	+1.12%	+0.55%

URBAN POPULATION

As percentage of total population			
2000	81%	49%	26%

TEN LARGEST CITIES

	Country	Population
Lagos	Nigeria	7,720,200
Kinshasa †	Congo (DR)	6,069,200
Kano	Nigeria	3,169,100
Ibadan	Nigeria	3,018,300
Nairobi †	Kenya	2,391,600
Dar es Salaam	Tanzania	2,372,200
Dakar †	Senegal	2,294,800
Abidjan	Côte d'Ivoire	1,934,342
Accra †	Ghana	1,567,000
Douala	Cameroon	1,204,700

† denotes capital city

City population figures are for the city proper.

INDUSTRY

Central Africa's rich natural resources are mainly exported, because the region lacks manufacturing industries. Most industries are small-scale, except in Kenya and Nigeria, where larger-scale manufacturing is growing. Nigeria and Tanzania have coal deposits.

INDUSTRIAL OUTPUT (US $ billion)

Nigeria (1997)	18

INDUSTRIAL PRODUCTION GROWTH RATE

	Gabon	Cameroon	Tanzania
	2.3%	n/a	8.4%

INDUSTRIAL WORKERS (millions)
(figures in parentheses are percentages of total labor force)

Tanzania*			614,000 (4.7%)
Gabon*			43,000 (11.5%)

	Mining	Manufacturing	Construction
Cameroon	1,793 (0.1%)	174,498 (4.5%)	66,684 (1.7%)

MAJOR PRODUCTS

Energy and minerals	Output change	
	1970	1995
Oil (Gabon)	5.4	18
Natural gas (Nigeria)	4.3	176
Bauxite ('000 tons) (Sierra Leone)	443	729
Diamonds ('000 carats) (Guinea)	74	500
Copper ('000 tons) (Congo, DR)	190	33
Cobalt ('000 tons) (Congo, DR)	13,598	4,100

Manufactures		
Tobacco ('000 tons) (Uganda)	5	7
Coffee ('000 tons) (Congo, DR)	69	76
Cocoa beans ('000 tons) (Ghana)	430	325
Palm oil ('000 tons) (Côte d'Ivoire)	6	249
Cotton seed ('000 tons) (Côte d'Ivoire)	20	109

* Includes utilities

AGRICULTURE

Agriculture employs about 70 percent of the people, with most farmers producing enough to meet the basic needs of their families. There is some nomadic herding. Commercial crops include cocoa, coffee, cotton, groundnuts, palm oil, rubber, and tea.

LAND
Total area 3,245,908 sq mi (8,406,844 sq km)

Cropland	Pasture	Forest/Woodland
11%	22%	52%
(348,702 sq mi)	(710,050 sq mi)	(1,710,130 sq mi)

FARMERS	Highest	Middle	Lowest
Agriculture as % of GDP	58% (Congo, DR)	36% (Ghana)	7% (Gabon)
% of workforce	93% (Burundi)	54% (Nigeria)	10% (Seychelles)

MAJOR CROPS

Agricultural products: fruit, vegetables: yams, pineapples, sweet potatoes, coconuts; millet, rice, corn, sorghum, cassava; copra; spices; nuts; pulses; cotton; palm oil; coffee; tea; cocoa; rubber, sisal; cattle, sheep, goats; quinine

Total cropland ('000 acres)	75,954 (Nigeria)	8,500 (Burkina Faso)	457 (Congo)
Cropland (acres) per 1,000 people	1,460 (C. African R.)	699 (Benin)	168 (Congo)
Irrigated land as % of cropland	6% (Guinea)	3% (Senegal)	0% (Rwanda)
Number of tractors	30,000 (Nigeria)	3,570 (Ghana)	19 (Guinea-Bissau)
Average cereal crop yields (lbs/acre)	1,441 (Gabon)	983 (Rwanda)	585 (Congo)
Cereal production ('000 tons)	22,107 (Nigeria)	2,167 (Burkina Faso)	4 (Congo)
Change since 1986/88	41%	16%	−82%

LIVESTOCK & FISHERIES

Meat production ('000 tons)	1,187 (Nigeria)	159 (Senegal)	7 (Gambia)
Change since 1986/88	89%	96%	29%
Marine fish catch ('000 tons)	351.9 (Senegal)	63.8 (Cameroon)	3.1 (Eq. Guinea)
Change since 1986/88	66%	24%	9%

FOOD SECURITY

Food aid as % of total imports	56% (Rwanda)	13% (Benin)	0% (Gab., Nigeria)
Daily kcal/person	2,735 (Nigeria)	2,232 (Guinea)	1,685 (Burundi)

POPULATION

Areas of high population density include the coastal regions of West Africa and the high plateaus of East Africa. The thinly populated areas are largely rain forests, where there are few towns, except for some river ports.

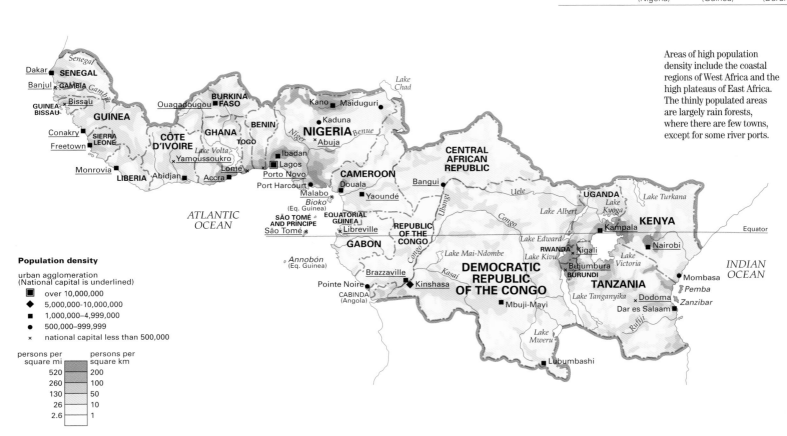

Population density

urban agglomeration
(National capital is underlined)

- ■ over 10,000,000
- ◆ 5,000,000–10,000,000
- ■ 1,000,000–4,999,999
- ● 500,000–999,999
- × national capital less than 500,000

persons per square mi	persons per square km
520	200
260	100
130	50
26	10
2.6	1

INDUSTRY

Resources and industry
- ◆ industrial center
- ○ port
- • other town
- —— major road
- —— major railroad

mineral resources and fossil fuels
- • iron and other ferroalloy metal ores
- • other metal ores
- ▪ nonmetallic minerals
- bauxite
- coal
- copper
- diamonds
- gold
- iron ore
- oil and natural gas

The region is rich in mineral resources. Nigeria, Gabon, and Republic of the Congo produce oil. Ghana has gold mines, the Democratic Republic of the Congo is rich in copper and diamonds, Guinea produces bauxite, and Liberia has large iron ore reserves.

AGRICULTURE

Agricultural zones
- arable and grazing
- fruit, vegetables and tree crops
- rough grazing
- woods and forest with some grazing
- nonagricultural land
- ▲ mountain peak (ft)

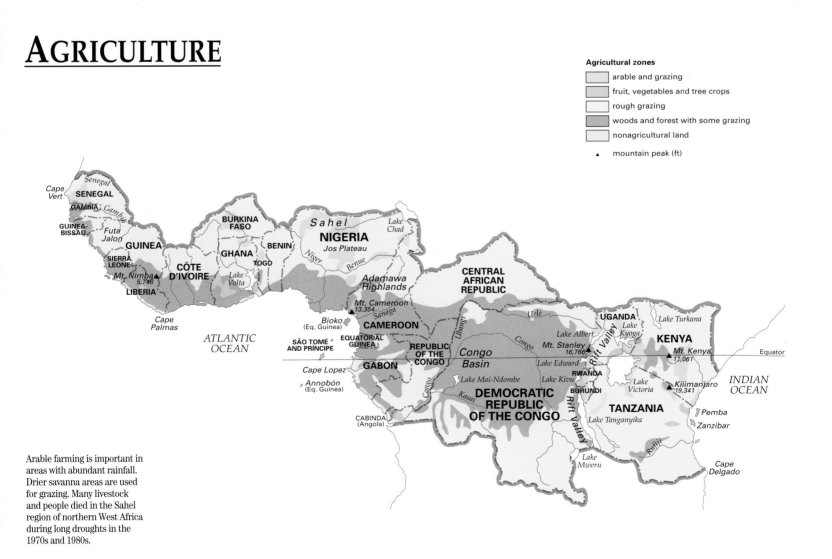

Arable farming is important in areas with abundant rainfall. Drier savanna areas are used for grazing. Many livestock and people died in the Sahel region of northern West Africa during long droughts in the 1970s and 1980s.

SOUTHERN AFRICA

Southern Africa consists of ten mainland countries and three island nations – Madagascar, the Comoros, and Mauritius. The mainland is a high, saucer-shaped plateau bordered by mostly narrow coastal plains. The Drakensberg contains the highest peaks. The region also contains the most southerly part of the Rift Valley, enclosing Lake Malawi.

Forests and savanna are found in the north, but the south is dry grassland, merging into the Kalahari, a semidesert, and the Namib Desert, one of the driest places on the earth.

Colonization, involving the introduction of commercial farming, the exploitation of natural resources and the setting up of manufacturing industries, has made a great impact on the black African cultures of Southern Africa.

Nowhere has the impact been greater than in South Africa. Its history of racial conflict became an international political issue. Talks between the various ethnic groups in the early 1990s led to the adoption of a democratic constitution permitting all adults to vote. South Africa's first ever multiracial elections took place in 1994.

Southern Africa is a region of ancient, often mineral-rich rocks, which once formed part of the supercontinent of Gondwanaland. Younger rocks occur around the central plateau, which have been folded and faulted, notably in the extreme southwest. Apart from the Atlas Mountains, these ranges are Africa's only recently formed fold mountains.

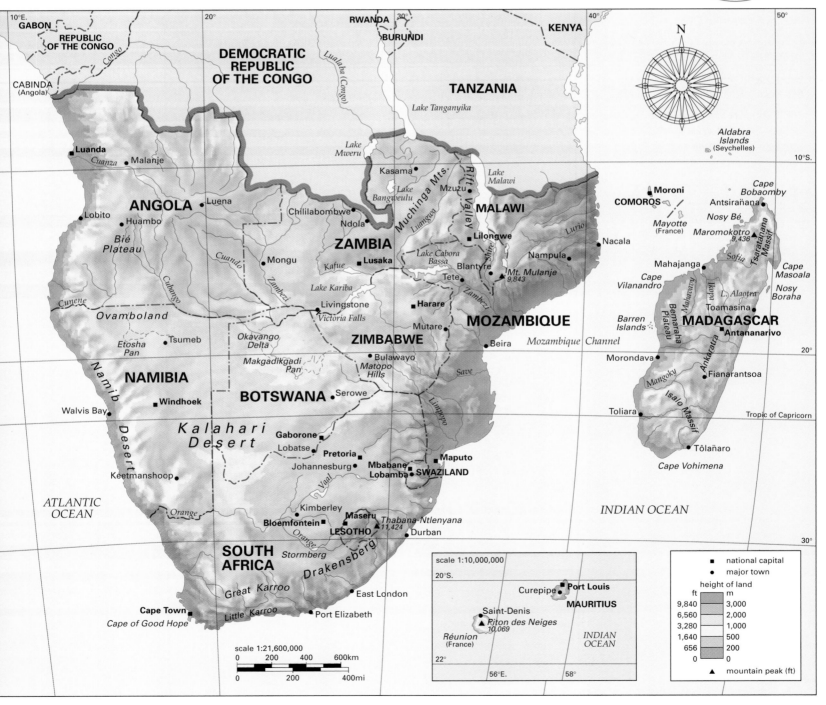

THE POLITICAL AND CULTURAL WORLD

Descendants of the region's earliest people, the Khoi-San (Hottentots and Bushmen), now make up extremely small groups. Most people are black Africans, who speak one of the many Bantu languages, including Tswana and Zulu.

The other main groups are the descendants of European settlers, including the Afrikaaners (descendants of early Dutch settlers in South Africa) and the British. Relationships between European settlers and black Africans have brought political strife to the region. In several countries, including Angola, Namibia, Mozambique, and Zimbabwe, independence was achieved only after long colonial conflicts.

COUNTRIES IN THE REGION
Angola (including Cabinda), Botswana, Comoros, Lesotho, Madagascar, Malawi, Mauritius, Mozambique, Namibia, South Africa, Swaziland, Zambia, Zimbabwe

MEMBERSHIP OF INTERNATIONAL ORGANIZATIONS
Organization of African Unity (OAU)
All countries in the region
Southern Africa Development Community (SADC)
Angola, Botswana, Lesotho, Malawi, Mozambique, Swaziland, Zambia, Zimbabwe

STYLES OF GOVERNMENT
Republics Angola, Botswana, Comoros, Madagascar, Malawi, Mozambique, Namibia, South Africa, Zambia, Zimbabwe
Monarchies Lesotho, Swaziland
Federal state Comoros
Multiparty states Angola, Botswana, Lesotho, Madagascar, Malawi, Mauritius, Mozambique, Namibia, South Africa, Zambia, Zimbabwe
One-party states Comoros, Swaziland
Military influence Comoros

LANGUAGE
Countries with one official language (E) Botswana, Mauritius, Zambia, Zimbabwe; (M) Madagascar; (P) Angola, Mozambique
Countries with two official languages (A, F) Comoros; (Af, E) South Africa, Namibia; (C, E) Malawi; (E, Se) Lesotho; (E, Si) Swaziland
Other significant languages in the region include Comorian (the majority language of the Comoros), ChiSona, Kimbundu, Lunda, Makua, Setwana, Si Ndebele, Tombuka, Umbundu and numerous other indigenous languages.

Key: A–Arabic, Af–Afrikaans, C–Chichewa, E–English, F–French, M–Malagasy, P–Portuguese, Se–Sesotho, Si–siSwati

RELIGION
Countries with one major religion (C) Lesotho, Namibia; (M) Comoros
Countries with two major religions (C, I) Angola, Botswana, Malawi, Swaziland, Zambia, Zimbabwe
Countries with three major religions (C, I, M) Madagascar, Mozambique
Country with more than three major religions (C, DR, H, I, M, RC) South Africa

Key: C–Various Christian, DR–Dutch Reformed, H–Hindu, I–Indigenous religions, M–Muslim, RC–Roman Catholic

Angola **Area** 481,355 sq mi (1,246,700 sq km) **Population** 10,145,267

Botswana **Area** 224,608 sq mi (581,730 sq km) **Population** 1,576,470

Comoros **Area** 719 sq mi (1,862 sq km) **Population** 578,400

Area 11,720 sq mi (30,355 sq km) **Population** 2,143,141

 Lesotho

 Madagascar **Area** 226,658 sq mi (587,041 sq km) **Population** 15,506,472

 Malawi **Area** 45,745 sq mi (118,480 sq km) **Population** 10,385,849

 Mauritius

 Mozambique

 Namibia

Area 788 sq mi (2,040 sq km) **Population** 1,179,368

Area 308,643 sq mi (799,379 sq km) **Population** 19,104,696

Area 317,818 sq mi (823,144 sq km) **Population** 1,771,327

 South Africa **Area** 473,291 sq mi (1,225,815 sq km) **Population** 43,421,021

 Swaziland **Area** 6,704 sq mi (17,364 sq km) **Population** 1,083,289

 **Zambia** **Area** 290,586 sq mi (752,614 sq km) **Population** 9,582,418

 Zimbabwe **Area** 150,873 sq mi (390,759 sq km) **Population** 11,342,521

■ national capital
● other town

In the last 30 years, Southern Africa has been one of the world's most unstable regions. Civil wars occurred in Angola and Mozambique after independence, and a long armed struggle took place in South Africa, with the African National Congress leading the fight against apartheid.

HABITATS

The plateau that forms the heart of Southern Africa is largely enclosed by mountain ranges. Some rivers, such as the Orange and Zambezi, cut through the rim and reach the sea. Others flow into inland drainage basins. In the southwest are desert areas.

LAND

Area 2,539,508 sq mi (6,577,283 sq km)
Highest point Thabana-Ntlenyana, 11,424 ft (3,482 m)
Lowest point sea level
Major features interior plateau, salt pans and deltas, Kalahari and Namib Deserts, Karroo tableland, Cape ranges in southwest, Drakensberg range, Madagascar

WATER

Longest river Zambezi, 1,650 mi (2,650 km)
Largest basin Zambezi, 514,000 sq mi (1,331,000 sq km)
Highest average flow Zambezi, 565,000 cu ft/sec (16,000 cu m/sec)
Largest lake Malawi, 11,400 sq mi (29,600 sq km)

NOTABLE THREATENED SPECIES

Mammals Julian's golden mole (*Amblysomus julianae*), Golden bamboo lemur (*Hapalemur aureus*), Indri (*Indri indri*), Brown hyena (*Hyaena brunnea*), Mauritian flying fox (*Pteropus niger*), Riverine rabbit (*Bunolagus monticularis*), Mountain zebra (*Equus zebra*), Aye-aye (*Daubentonia madagascariensis*)
Birds Madagascar serpent eagle (*Eutriorchis astur*), Cape vulture (*Gyps coprotheres*), Pink pigeon (*Nesoenas mayeri*), Mauritius kestrel (*Falco punctatus*)
Plants *Allophylus chirindensis*, spiral aloe (*Aloe polyphylla*), *Dasylepis burttdavyi*, *Encephalartos chimanimaniensis*, *Hyophorbe amaricaulis*, *Jubaeopsis caffra*, *Kniphofia umbrina*, St. Helena olive (*Nesiota elliptica*), *Protea odorata*, *Ramosmania heterophylla*
Others Angonoka tortoise (*Geochelone yniphora*), Cape platana or clawed toad (*Xenopus gilli*), Fiery refin (*Pseudobarbatus phlegethon*)

CLIMATE

The northern part of the region has a tropical climate, with dry and wet seasons. The southwest is largely desert. The southwestern tip has dry summers and mild, moist winters. The southeastern coasts of South Africa have hot, humid summers and mild, dry winters.

CLIMATE

	Temperature °F (°C)		Altitude
	January	July	ft (m)
Lusaka	72 (22)	61 (16)	4,195 (1,279)
Bulawayo	70 (21)	57 (14)	4,412 (1,345)
Cape Town	72 (22)	55 (13)	39 (12)
Toliara	81 (27)	68 (20)	30 (9)
Antananarivo	66 (19)	55 (13)	4,297 (1,310)

	Precipitation in. (mm)		
	January	July	Year
Lusaka	8.8 (224)	0 (0)	32.6 (829)
Bulawayo	5.3 (134)	0 (0)	23.2 (589)
Cape Town	0.4 (9)	3.8 (96)	25.7 (652)
Toliara	2.8 (72)	0.2 (4)	13.5 (342)
Antananarivo	11.3 (286)	0.4 (10)	32.6 (829)

World's greatest recorded 24-hour rainfall, 73.6 in. (1,870 mm), Réunion island

NATURAL HAZARDS

Drought, flooding

ENVIRONMENTAL ISSUES

Many problems in Southern Africa are related to the population explosion, which puts pressure on habitats and their wildlife. Pollution caused by urbanization and industry are evident in South Africa, while the ravages of war are widespread.

POPULATION AND WEALTH

	Highest	Middle	Lowest
Population (millions)	43.421 (S Africa)	9.582 (Zambia)	0.578 (Comoros)
Population increase (annual growth rate, % 1990–95)	3.2% (Angola)	2.2% (Zambia)	1.4% (Zimbabwe)
Energy use (lbs per year per person of oil equivalent)	6,098 (S Africa)	1,951 (Zimbabwe)	917 (Mozam.)
Purchasing power parity (Int$/per year)	7,729 (S Africa)	2,401 (Zimbabwe)	668 (Mozam.)

ENVIRONMENTAL INDICATORS

CO$_2$ emissions ('000 tons year)	305,805 (S Africa)	9,735 (Zimbabwe)	454 (Swaziland)
Car ownership (% of population)	13% (S Africa)	4% (Lesotho)	below 1% (Angola)
Proportion of territory protected, including marine areas (%)	30% (Zambia)	8% (Mauritius)	0% (Comoros)
Forests as a % of original forest	100% (Botswana)	44% (Madagas.)	0% (S Africa)
Artificial fertilizer use (lbs/acre/year)	42 (S Africa)	16 (Lesotho)	0.8 (Angola)
Access to safe drinking water (% population; rural/urban)	95%/100% (Mauritius)	46%80% (Swaziland)	12%/68% (Madagas.)

MAJOR ENVIRONMENTAL PROBLEMS AND SOURCES

Air pollution: locally high
Land degradation: *types*: desertification, soil erosion, deforestation, habitat destruction; *causes*: agriculture, population pressure, drought, and floods
Resource issues: fuelwood shortage; inadequate drinking water and sanitation; water shortage; poaching game
Population issues: population explosion; urban overcrowding; inadequate health facilities; famine; war; HIV/AIDS
Major events: flooding (2000); oil spill from tanker *Treasure* (2000)

HABITATS

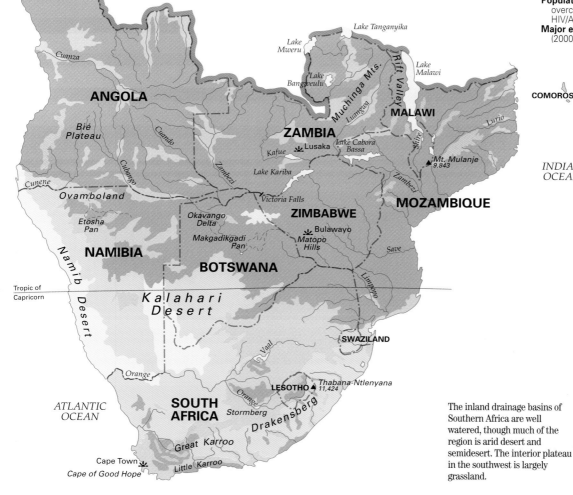

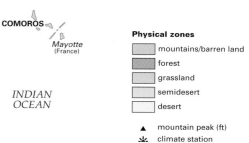

Physical zones

- mountains/barren land
- forest
- grassland
- semidesert
- desert

▲ mountain peak (ft)
☀ climate station

The inland drainage basins of Southern Africa are well watered, though much of the region is arid desert and semidesert. The interior plateau in the southwest is largely grassland.

ENVIRONMENTAL ISSUES

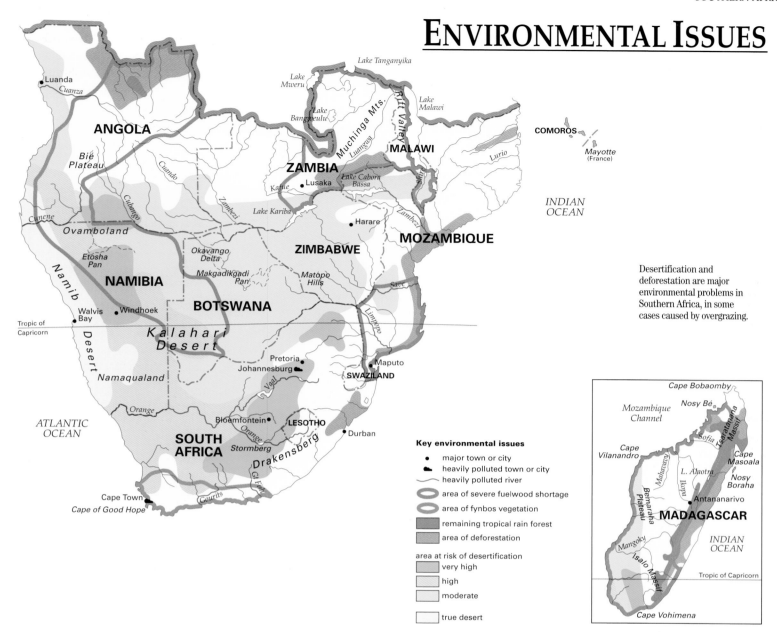

Desertification and deforestation are major environmental problems in Southern Africa, in some cases caused by overgrazing.

Key environmental issues

- • major town or city
- ▬ heavily polluted town or city
- ～ heavily polluted river
- ⬯ area of severe fuelwood shortage
- ⬯ area of fynbos vegetation
- ▰ remaining tropical rain forest
- ▰ area of deforestation

area at risk of desertification
- ▨ very high
- ▨ high
- ▨ moderate
- ☐ true desert

CLIMATE

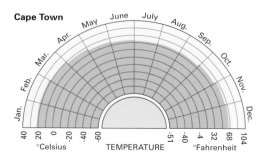

height above sea level of climate stations

meters		feet
5,000		16,400
3,000		9,840
2,000		6,560
1,000	Antananarivo / Lusaka	3,280
500		1,640
200		656
	Cape Town — sea level	

Cape Town

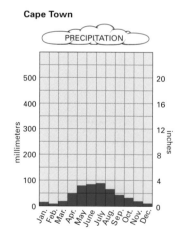
PRECIPITATION

Lusaka

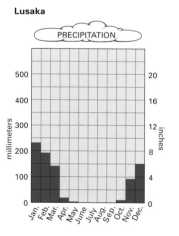
PRECIPITATION

Antananarivo

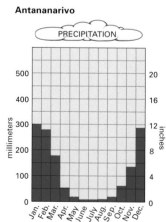
PRECIPITATION

Cape Town

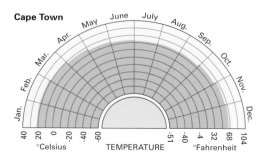
TEMPERATURE

Lusaka

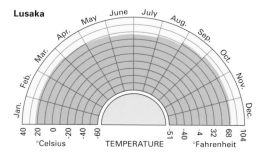
TEMPERATURE

Antananarivo

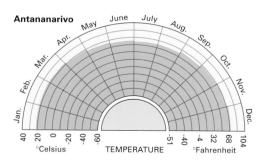
TEMPERATURE

POPULATION

Europeans founded most of the cities in Southern Africa. Today the cities are expanding quickly. They are magnets that attract people from the less populated rural areas who are seeking jobs and better health and education services for their families.

POPULATION

Total population of region (millions)			127.8
	S. Africa	Zimb.	Mozam.
Population density (persons per sq mi)	90.9	74.1	61.6
Population change (average annual percent 1960–1990)			
Urban	+1.90%	+3.53%	+5.93%
Rural	+1.09%	+0.35%	+0.45%

URBAN POPULATION

As percentage of total population			
1990	50%	35%	40%

TEN LARGEST CITIES

	Country	Population
Cape Town †	South Africa	2,639,500
Durban	South Africa	2,314,100
Luanda †	Angola	2,094,200
Harare †	Zimbabwe	1,832,000
Johannesburg	South Africa	1,617,900
Pretoria †	South Africa	1,206,900
Soweto	South Africa	1,200,000
Lusaka †	Zambia	1,173,000
Maputo †	Mozambique	1,062,700
Antananarivo †	Madagascar	855,500

† denotes capital city

City population figures are for the city proper.

INDUSTRY

South Africa is Africa's leading industrialized nation. It attracts migrant workers from the black African states. Some countries, such as Madagascar, have little industry except commercial farming, though Namibia and Botswana export minerals.

INDUSTRIAL OUTPUT (US $ billion)

South Africa (1997)	44

INDUSTRIAL PRODUCTION GROWTH RATES

South Africa	5%
Mozambique	39%
Zimbabwe	n/a

INDUSTRIAL WORKERS (millions) (% of total workforce)

	Mining	Manufacturing	Construction
South Africa (1995)	277,176 (1.9%)	1,614,596 (11.3%)	437,167 (3.1%)
Zimbabwe (1995)	59,000 (4.7%)	185,900 (15.0%)	71,800 (5.8%)
Mozambique (1995)	73,425 (mining and manuf.) (1.3%)		273,369 (4.8%)

MAJOR PRODUCTS (South Africa)

Energy and minerals	Output change	
	1970	1995
Bituminous coal (mil m.t.)	55	206
Oil ('000 tons)	0	393
Copper ('000 tons)	75	140
Nickel ('000 tons)	9	30
Chromium ore ('000 tons)	643	3,590
Manganese ore ('000 tons)	1,182	1,210
Gold (tons)	1,002	522
Diamonds ('000 carats)	8,112	9,100

AGRICULTURE

Subsistence farming is the main occupation in the region. Malawi exports sugarcane. In South Africa and Zimbabwe, there is successful commercial farming. Both of these countries export food, while the other countries are food importers.

LAND

Total area 2,539,508 sq mi (6,577,283 sq km)

Cropland	Pasture	Forest/Woodland
5% (134,906 sq mi)	43% (1,084,528 sq mi)	29% (722,586 sq mi)

FARMERS	Highest	Middle	Lowest
Agriculture as % of GDP	36% (Mal)	16% (Zam)	3% (B)
% of workforce	86% (L, Mal)	66% (Zim)	30% (Sw)

MAJOR CROPS: Agricultural products fruit and vegetables: bananas, coconuts; tea, coffee, cocoa; sisal; corn, manioc, millet, sorghum, rice; cotton, tobacco; pulses; nuts; sunflower seeds; spices; copra; fish; cattle; goats; pigs; poultry; forest products

Total cropland ('000 acres)	40,277	8,649 (A)	803 (L)
Cropland (acres) per 1,000 people	1,515 (Zam)	739 (A)	398 (L)
Irrigated land as % of cropland	35% (Mad)	5% (Zim)	0% (B)
Number of tractors	100,000 (SA)	26,000 (Zim)	1,420 (Mal)
Average cereal crop yields (lbs/acre)	1,836 (SA)	1,012 (Mal)	213 (B)
Cereal production ('000 tons)	12,104 (SA)	2,543 (Zim)	41 (B)
Change since 1986/88	1%	−1%	−18%

LIVESTOCK & FISHERIES

Meat production ('000 tons)	1,212 (SA)	264 (Mad)	29 (L)
Change since 1986/88	−3%	23%	11%
Marine fish catch ('000 tons)	497 (SA)	73 (A)	13.5 (Moz)
Change since 1986-88	−50%	15%	−47%

FOOD SECURITY

Food aid as % of total imports	30 (Moz)	15 (Zam)	0 (SA)
Daily kcal/person	2,990 (SA)	2,145 (Zim)	1,832 (Moz)

POPULATION

The lack of rainfall has greatly influenced the distribution of population in Southern Africa. Inland mining areas and coastal ports are the main zones of high population density.

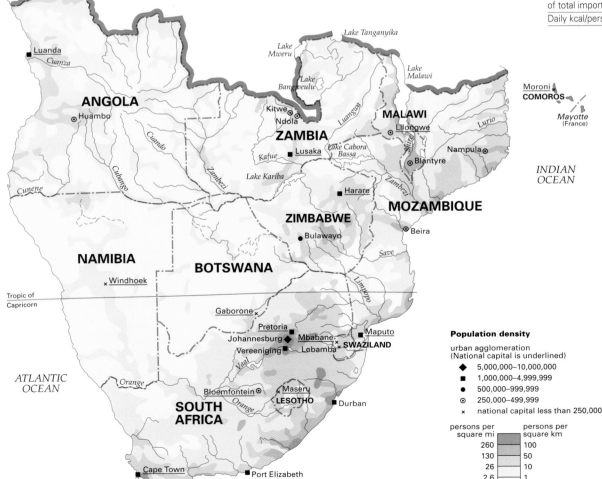

Population density

urban agglomeration (National capital is underlined)

- ◆ 5,000,000–10,000,000
- ■ 1,000,000–4,999,999
- ● 500,000–999,999
- ⊙ 250,000–499,999
- × national capital less than 250,000

persons per square mi	persons per square km
260	100
130	50
26	10
2.6	1

INDUSTRY

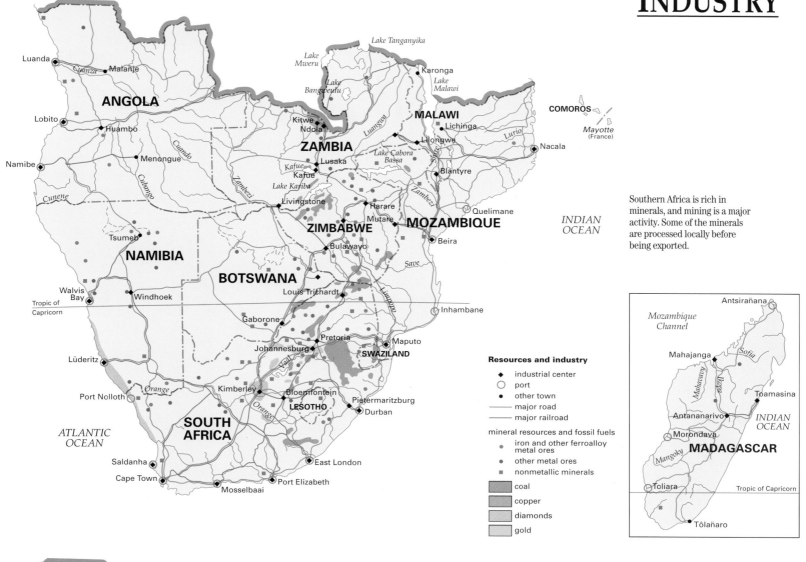

Resources and industry
- ◆ industrial center
- ◯ port
- ● other town
- — major road
- — major railroad

mineral resources and fossil fuels
- ● iron and other ferroalloy metal ores
- ● other metal ores
- ■ nonmetallic minerals
- coal
- copper
- diamonds
- gold

Southern Africa is rich in minerals, and mining is a major activity. Some of the minerals are processed locally before being exported.

Labels on map: Luanda, Malanje, Lobito, Huambo, Menongue, Namibe, Cuanza, Cuando, Cuanza, Cutango, Cunene, Tsumeb, NAMIBIA, Walvis Bay, Tropic of Capricorn, Windhoek, Lüderitz, Port Nolloth, Orange, Saldanha, Cape Town, Mosselbaai, SOUTH AFRICA, Kimberley, Bloemfontein, LESOTHO, Pietermaritzburg, Durban, East London, Port Elizabeth, Johannesburg, Pretoria, Gaborone, BOTSWANA, Louis Trichardt, Limpopo, Inhambane, Maputo, SWAZILAND, Vaal, Orange, Lake Kariba, Kafue, Zambezi, Livingstone, Bulawayo, ZIMBABWE, Harare, Mutare, Save, Beira, MOZAMBIQUE, Quelimane, Lusaka, Kafue, ZAMBIA, Kitwe, Ndola, Luangwa, Lake Cabora Bassa, Zambezi, Blantyre, Lilongwe, MALAWI, Lichinga, Lake Malawi, Karonga, Nacala, Lake Tanganyika, Lake Mweru, Lake Bangweulu, COMOROS, Mayotte (France), INDIAN OCEAN, ATLANTIC OCEAN, ANGOLA

Madagascar inset: Mozambique Channel, Antsirañana, Mahajanga, Sofia, Antananarivo, Toamasina, Morondava, Mangoky, MADAGASCAR, INDIAN OCEAN, Toliara, Tôlañaro, Tropic of Capricorn

AGRICULTURE

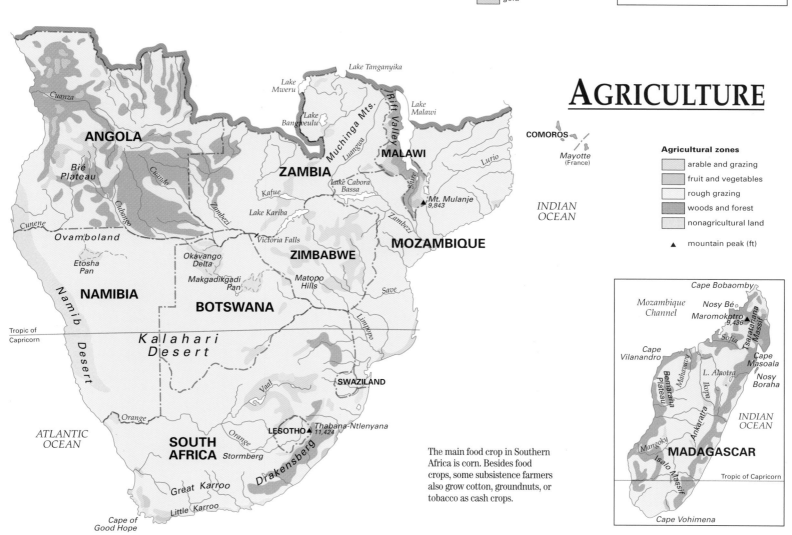

Agricultural zones
- arable and grazing
- fruit and vegetables
- rough grazing
- woods and forest
- nonagricultural land
- ▲ mountain peak (ft)

The main food crop in Southern Africa is corn. Besides food crops, some subsistence farmers also grow cotton, groundnuts, or tobacco as cash crops.

Labels on map: Cuanza, ANGOLA, Bié Plateau, Cuando, Cunene, Ovamboland, Etosha Pan, Namib Desert, NAMIBIA, Tropic of Capricorn, Kalahari Desert, Okavango Delta, Makgadikgadi Pan, BOTSWANA, Vaal, Orange, ATLANTIC OCEAN, SOUTH AFRICA, Stormberg, Great Karroo, Little Karroo, Cape of Good Hope, Drakensberg, LESOTHO, Thabana-Ntlenyana 11,424, SWAZILAND, Limpopo, Save, Matopo Hills, ZIMBABWE, Victoria Falls, Lake Kariba, Kafue, Zambezi, ZAMBIA, Luangwa, Lake Cabora Bassa, Muchinga Mts., Rift Valley, MALAWI, Lake Malawi, Mt. Mulanje 9,843, Shire, MOZAMBIQUE, Lurio, Lake Tanganyika, Lake Mweru, Lake Bangweulu, COMOROS, Mayotte (France), INDIAN OCEAN

Madagascar inset: Cape Bobaomby, Nosy Bé, Maromokotro 9,436, Tsaratañana Massif, Mozambique Channel, Cape Vilanandro, Bemaraha Plateau, Mahajanga, Sofia, L. Alaotra, Ikopa, Cape Masoala, Nosy Boraha, Ankaratra, Isalo Massif, Mangoky, MADAGASCAR, INDIAN OCEAN, Tropic of Capricorn, Cape Vohimena

113

INDIAN SUBCONTINENT

The Indian subcontinent was once part of the ancient continent of Gondwanaland. Plate movements propelled the landmass north until it collided with Eurasia, thrusting up the rocks on the intervening seabed into high fold mountains, the Himalayas, with the world's highest peak.

The region is a pendant-shaped landmass, extending from the world's highest mountain ranges in the north to the islands of Sri Lanka and the Maldives in the south.

The climate ranges from polar conditions on the mountains to hot tropical weather on the plains. The influence of monsoon winds, which bring rain between June and September, are felt throughout much of the region.

Over the centuries, many waves of migrants have settled in the subcontinent. Today the region has many languages and religions, reflecting its complex past. Cultural rivalries and religious differences sometimes cause conflict and violence. Despite such pressures and the poverty in which many people live, India remains the world's most heavily populated parliamentary democracy.

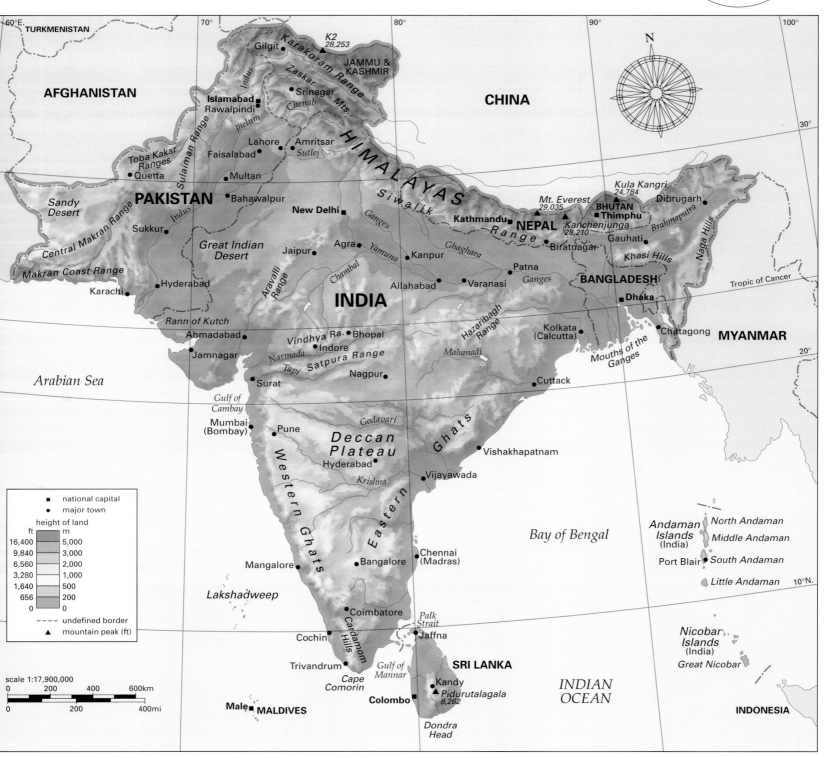

THE POLITICAL AND CULTURAL WORLD

In the mid-nineteenth century, most of the Indian subcontinent, apart from the remote mountain kingdoms of Bhutan and Nepal, was under British rule. But when British India became independent in 1947, the region split into two countries: the mainly Hindu India and Islamic Pakistan. Pakistan consisted of two parts: West and East Pakistan. After a civil war, East Pakistan broke away from West Pakistan in 1971 and proclaimed its independence as Bangladesh.

Tensions between India and the Islamic Republic of Pakistan continue, and the boundary between the two countries in the Jammu and Kashmir region in the northwest is still disputed.

COUNTRIES IN THE REGION

Bangladesh, Bhutan, India, Maldives, Nepal, Pakistan, Sri Lanka
Island territories
Andaman Islands, Nicobar Islands, Lakshadweep (India)

MEMBERSHIP OF INTERNATIONAL ORGANIZATIONS

Colombo Plan Bangladesh, Bhutan, India, Maldives, Nepal, Pakistan, Sri Lanka
South Asia Association for Regional Cooperation Committee (SAARC) All countries of the region

LANGUAGE

Countries with one official language (Bengali) Bangladesh; (Divehi) Maldives; (Nepali) Nepal; (Sinhalese) Sri Lanka; (Urdu) Pakistan
Country with two official languages (English, Hindi) India
Country with three official languages (Dzongkha, English, Lhotsam) Bhutan

India has 14 officially recognized languages. As well as Hindi and Urdu, the most significant languages in the region include Gujarati, Malayalam, Marathi, Punjabi, Tamil and Telugu. There are hundreds of local languages and dialects.

RELIGION

Countries with one major religion (M) Maldives, Pakistan
Countries with two major religions (B, H) Bhutan; (H, M) Bangladesh
Countries with three or more major religions (B, H, M) Nepal; (B, C, H, M) Sri Lanka; (B, C, H, J, M, S) India

Key: B–Buddhist, C–Various Christian, H–Hindu, J–Jain, M–Muslim, S–Sikh

ECONOMIC INDICATORS

	Bangladesh	India	Pakistan
GDP (US$ billions)	32.8	378.6	64.5
GNP per capita (US$)	1,050	1,650	1,590
Annual rate of growth of GDP, 1990–1997	4.7%	6.0%	4.2%
Manufacturing as % of GDP	9.4%	20	16.8%
Central government spending as % of GDP	10%	16.4%	23.2%
Merchandise exports (US$ billions)	4.8	35.4	8.3
Merchandise imports (US$ billions)	6.6	45.7	10.7
Aid received as % of GNP	3.9%	0.6%	1.4%
Total external debt as % of GNP	43%	23%	53%

WELFARE INDICATORS

	Bangladesh	India	Pakistan
Infant mortality rate (per 1,000 live births)			
1965	144	150	149
2000	79	72	74
Daily food supply available (calories per capita)	2,086	2,496	n/a

Pakistan
Area 307,375 sq mi (796,095 sq km)
Population 141,533,775
Capital Islamabad
Currency 1 Pakistan rupee (PRe) = 100 paisa

Bangladesh
Area 55,598 sq mi (143,998 sq km)
Population 129,194,224
Capital Dhaka
Currency 1 Bangladesh taka (Tk) = 100 poisha

Bhutan
Area 18,147 sq mi (47,000 sq km)
Population 2,005,222
Capital Thimphu
Currency 1 ngultrum (Nu) = 100 chetrum

India
Area 1,269,348 sq mi (3,287,590 sq km)
Population 1,014,003,817
Capital New Delhi
Currency 1 Indian rupee (Re) = 100 paise

Maldives
Area 116 sq mi (300 sq km)
Population 301,475
Capital Male
Currency 1 Maldivian rufiyaa (Rf) = 100 laari

Nepal
Area 56,827 sq mi (147,181 sq km)
Population 24,702,119
Capital Kathmandu
Currency 1 Nepalese rupee (NRe) = 100 paisa

Sri Lanka
Area 25,332 sq mi (65,610 sq km)
Population 19,144,875
Capital Colombo
Currency 1 Sri Lankan rupee (SLRe) = 100 cents

■ national capital
● other town

India is a nonaligned state and did not take sides in the Cold War. It possesses nuclear weapons. One family dominated Indian politics for many years. The country was led by the Nehru-Gandhi family from its independence in 1947 until prime minister Rajiv Gandhi was assassinated in May 1991.

HABITATS

The mountains in the north and the deserts in the northwest are barren. The rivers that rise in the mountains, especially the Indus, Ganges, and Brahmaputra, drain the fertile river valleys and deltas south of the mountains.

LAND

Area 1,732,743 sq mi (4,487,774 sq km)
Highest point Mount Everest, 29,035 ft (8,850 m), highest on Earth
Lowest point sea level
Major features Himalayas, world's highest mountain range; plains and deltas in north; Thar Desert; Deccan plateau

WATER

Longest river Brahmaputra and Indus both 1,800 mi (2,900 km)
Largest basin Ganges, 409,000 sq mi (1,059,000 sq km)
Highest average flow Brahmaputra, 678,000 cu ft/sec (19,200 cu m/sec)
Largest lake Manchhar, Pakistan, 100 sq mi (260 sq km); some reservoirs in India are larger

NOTABLE THREATENED SPECIES

Mammals Lion-tailed macaque (*Macaca silenus*), Hispid hare (*Caprolagus hispidus*), Indus river dolphin (*Platanista minor*), Indian rhinoceros (*Rhinoceros unicronis*), Pygmy hog (*Sus salvanius*), Swamp deer (*Cervus duvauceli*), Manipur Brow-antlered deer (*Cervus eldi eldi*)
Birds Lesser florican (*Sypheotides indica*), Jerdon's courser (*Cursorius bitorquatus*), Western tragopan (*Tragopan melanocephalus*), Forest owlet (*Athene blewitii*), Great Indian bustard (*Choriotis nigriceps*)
Others Gharial (*Gavialis gangeticus*), Malabar tree toad (*Pedostibes kempi*), Green labeo (*Labeo fisheri*), Relict Himalayan dragonfly (*Epiophlebia laidlawi*), Scarce red forester (*Lethe distans*)
Examples Beddomes cycad (*Cycas beddomei*), Kin (*Dioscorea deltoidea*), Opposite-leaved ebony (*Diospyros oppositifolia*), Frerea (*Frerea indica*), Shirhoy lily (*Lilium macklineae*), Drury's slipper orchid (*Paphiopedilum druryi*), Himalayan cherry (*Prunus himalaica*), Royle's saussurea (*Saussurea roylei*), Wallich's elm (*Ulmus wallichiana*), Blue vanda (*Vanda coerulea*)

CLIMATE

South of the towering Himalayas, with their polar and subarctic climates, the Indian subcontinent is a warm tropical region. Dry climates include the hot Great Indian Desert on the India-Pakistan border. Other areas have hot monsoon climates with heavy rains between late June and September.

CLIMATE

| | Temperature °F (°C) | | Altitude |
	January	July	ft (m)
Jacobabad	59 (15)	95 (39)	184 (56)
Simla	66 (19)	41 (5)	7,232 (2,205)
New Delhi	57 (14)	90 (32)	216 (708)
Kathmandu	50 (10)	75 (24)	4,376 (1,334)
Chittagong	68 (20)	82 (28)	46 (14)
Trincomalee	79 (26)	86 (30)	10 (3)

| | Precipitation in. (mm) | | |
	January	July	Year
Jacobabad	3.0 (79)	1.0 (27)	3.5 (88)
Simla	2.4 (61)	16.7 (424)	62.1 (1,577)
New Delhi	1.0 (25)	8.3 (211)	28.2 (715)
Kathmandu	0.8 (19)	14.9 (378)	52.3 (1,328)
Chittagong	0.4 (10)	25.3 (642)	112.5 (2,858)
Trincomalee	8.3 (211)	2.1 (54)	68.0 (1,727)

World's highest recorded annual rainfall, 1,042.1 in. (26,470 mm), Cherrapunji, northeast India

NATURAL HAZARDS

Cyclones, storm surges, flooding of great river deltas

ENVIRONMENTAL ISSUES

The Indian subcontinent is subject to such natural disasters as floods, drought, storms, and earthquakes. Population pressures have led to deforestation and soil erosion, while urban and industrial pollution are mounting problems.

POPULATION AND WEALTH

	Highest	Middle	Lowest
Population (millions)	1,014.003 (India)	24.702 (Nepal)	0.301 (Maldives)
Population increase (annual growth rate, 1990–95)	2.8% (Pakistan)	2.4% (Nepal)	1.0% (Sri Lanka)
Energy use (lbs/year per person of oil equivalent)	1,052 (India)	864 (Sri Lanka)	708 (Nepal)
Purchasing power parity (Int$/per year)	2,528 (Sri Lanka)	1,666 (India)	1,057 (Bangl.)

ENVIRONMENTAL INDICATORS

CO₂ emissions ('000 tons year)	908,734 (India)	85,357 (Pakistan)	238 (Bhutan)
Car ownership (% of population)	2% (Sri Lanka)	1% (Bangl.)	<1% (Pakistan)
Protected territory including marine areas	21% (Bhutan)	9% (Nepal)	0% (Maldives)
Forests as a % of original forest	62% (Bhutan)	22% (Nepal)	6% (Pakistan)
Artificial fertilizer use (lbs/acre/year)	114 (Bangladesh)	74 (India)	0.8 (Bhutan)
Access to safe drinking water (rural/urban)	95/99% (Bangladesh)	73/89% (Pakistan)	54/75% (Bhutan)

MAJOR ENVIRONMENTAL PROBLEMS AND SOURCES

Air pollution: high; urban very high; acid rain prevalent
River pollution: medium; *sources:* agriculture, sewage, industry
Land degradation: *types:* desertification, soil erosion, salinization, deforestation, habitat destruction; *causes:* agriculture, industry, population pressure
Resource issues: fuelwood shortage; inadequate drinking water and sanitation; coastal flooding; drought
Population issues: population explosion; urban overcrowding; inadequate health facilities; under nourishment
Major events: Bhopal (1984), leak of poisonous chemicals; Bangladesh (1988, 1991, 1998), major floods; mass arsenic poisoning from groundwater (1990s)

HABITATS

Physical zones

- mountains/barren land
- forest
- grassland
- semidesert
- desert

▲ mountain peak (ft)
☀ climate station

The Deccan, a plateau between two ranges, the Western and Eastern Ghats, is an ancient landmass, unlike the young mountains in the north, which are still rising. Between the two lie broad flood plains.

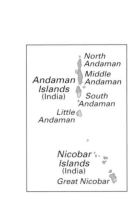

ENVIRONMENTAL ISSUES

The original forests of the Indian subcontinent have largely been destroyed. The arid northwest and the west-central Deccan plateau are at risk of desertification.

Karakoram Range

Zaskar Mountains

Islamabad/Rawalpindi

Chenab

Indus

Jhelum

Lahore

Faisalabad

Ravi

Sutlej

PAKISTAN

Toba Kakar Ranges

Sulaiman Range

HIMALAYAS

Siwalik Range

Kathmandu

NEPAL

BHUTAN
Thimphu

Brahmaputra

Naga Hills

Sandy Desert

Central Makran Range

New Delhi

Ganges

Yamuna

Lucknow

Kanpur

Ghaghara

Khasi Hills

Makran Coast Range

Karachi

Indus

Great Indian Desert

Jaipur

Luni

Chambal

INDIA

Ganges

BANGLADESH
Dhaka

Tropic of Cancer

Arabian Sea

Sabarmati

Rann of Kutch

Ahmadabad

Bhopal

Narmada

Satpura Range

Mahanadi

Hazaribagh Range

Kolkata (Calcutta)

Sundarbans

Mouths of the Ganges

Chittagong

Nagpur

Pranhita

Gulf of Cambay

Godavari

Deccan Plateau

Mumbai (Bombay)

Pune

Koyna Dam

Western Ghats

Hyderabad

Krishna

Ghats

Bay of Bengal

Tunghabadra

Eastern Ghats

Chennai (Madras)

Bangalore

Lakshadweep

Kaveri

Palk Strait

Cardamom Hills

Cape Comorin

Gulf of Mannar

SRI LANKA

Colombo

MALDIVES

Dondra Head

Key environmental issues

- • major town or city
- ➷ heavily polluted town or city
- ⬗ major pollution event
- ✛ major natural disaster
- ∿ heavily polluted river
- ⬭ area liable to flooding
- ▓ remaining tropical rain forest
- ▒ area of deforestation

area at risk of desertification
- ▓ very high
- ▒ high
- ░ moderate
- ☐ true desert

North Andaman
Middle Andaman
Andaman Islands (India)
South Andaman
Little Andaman

Nicobar Islands (India)
Great Nicobar

CLIMATE

height above sea level of climate stations

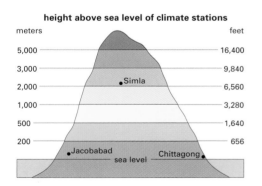

meters		feet
5,000		16,400
3,000		9,840
2,000	Simla	6,560
1,000		3,280
500		1,640
200	Jacobabad Chittagong	656
	sea level	

Jacobabad

PRECIPITATION

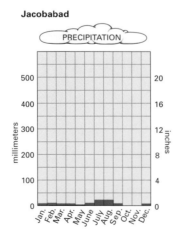

Simla

PRECIPITATION

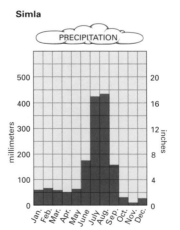

Chittagong

PRECIPITATION

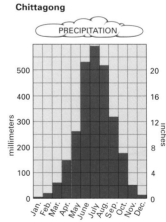

Jacobabad

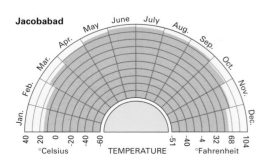

TEMPERATURE

Simla

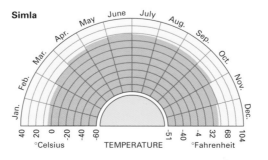

TEMPERATURE

Chittagong

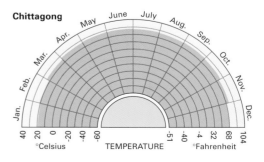

TEMPERATURE

POPULATION

The subcontinent is one of the world's most populous regions. Most people in the subcontinent live in rural areas, but there are many large cities, including some of the world's most crowded, with over 1,200 people per square mile. India alone has more than 200 large cities.

POPULATION

Total population of region			1.330 billion
	India	Pakistan	Bangla.
Population density (persons per sq mi)	857	449	2,467

Population change (average annual percent 1960–1990)

Urban	+2.84%	+4.31%	+4.08%
Rural	+1.19%	+1.92%	+0.99%

URBAN POPULATION

As percentage of total population

1995–2000	28%	37%	25%

TEN LARGEST CITIES

	Country	Population
Mumbai (Bombay)	India	12,903,100
New Delhi †	India	10,089,400
Karachi	Pakistan	10,013,400
Dhaka †	Bangladesh	8,154,100
Lahore	Pakistan	5,470,000
Kolkata (Calcutta)	India	5,061,100
Chennai (Madras)	India	4,470,300
Ahmadabad	India	3,823,400
Hyderabad	India	3,737,500
Bangalore	India	3,636,700

† denotes capital city

City population figures are for the city proper.

INDUSTRY

The countries of the Indian subcontinent are, according to the World Bank, "low-income developing nations." The region has plenty of resources and huge potential, but its industrial development has been extremely slow.

INDUSTRIAL OUTPUT (US $ billion, 1997)

Bangladesh	India	Pakistan
11 bn	104 bn	14 bn

INDUSTRIAL WORKERS (millions)
(figures in parentheses are percentages of total labor force)

	Mining	Manufacturing	Construction
India	1,751,275 (0.6)	28,671,479 (9.1)	5,543,205 (1.8)
Pakistan	2,530,000 (9.6)	2,260,000 (6.2)	n/a
Bangladesh	15,000	5,925,000 (11.6)	525,000 (1)

INDUSTRIAL PRODUCTION GROWTH RATE

Bangladesh	India	Pakistan
2.5% (1997)	6% (1999)	3.8% (1999)

MAJOR PRODUCTS (India)

Energy and minerals	Output 1970	1995	Change since 1970
Bituminous coal (mil m.t.)	74	266	259.5
Iron ore (mil m.t.)	20	42	110.9
Natural gas ('000 terajoules)	19	771	3,957.9
Bauxite ('000 tons)	1,370	5,230	281.8
Manufactures			
Cement ('000 tons)	13,956	66,924	379.5
Automobiles ('000)	45	240	433.3
Commercial vehicles ('000)	41	216	426.8
Fertilizer (phosphate) ('000 tons)	330	2,557	674.8
Fertilizer (nitrogenous) ('000 tons)	1,054	7,944	653.7
Wood (groundwood) (mil cu yards)	119.2	354	258

AGRICULTURE

Farming is the main activity throughout the subcontinent. The best farmland is in the densely populated northern plains. Rice is the main food crop throughout the subcontinent, although wheat is also important in many areas.

LAND

Total area 1,732,743 sq mi (4,487,774 sq km)

Cropland	Pasture	Forest/Woodland
50% (842,564 sq mi)	5% (81,360 sq mi)	21% (346,341 sq mi)

FARMERS	Highest	Middle	Lowest
Agriculture as % of GDP	41% (Nepal)	25% (India, Pak.)	22% (Sri Lanka)
% of workforce	93% (Bhutan)	63% (Bangladesh)	22% (Maldives)

MAJOR CROPS: Agricultural products fruit and vegetables: coconuts; sweet potatoes; wheat, rice; sugarcane; pulses; oilseed; rubber; cotton; jute; tobacco; spices; beef, mutton, goats, water buffalo meat; fish

Total cropland ('000 acre)	419,699 (India)	53,374 (Pakistan)	395 (Bhutan)
Cropland (acre) per 1,000 people	440 (India)	255 (Sri Lanka)	166 (Bangladesh)
Irrigated land as % of cropland	81% (Pakistan)	45% (Bangladesh)	25% (Bhutan)
Number of tractors	1,450,000 (India)	320,500 (Pakistan)	4,600 (Nepal)
Average cereal crop yields (lbs/acre)	2,567 (Sri Lanka)	1,823 (India)	907 (Bhutan)
Cereal production ('000 tons)	220,841 (India)	29,883 (Bangladesh)	112 (Bhutan)
Change since 1986/88	31%	23%	−16%

LIVESTOCK & FISHERIES

Meat production ('000 tons)	4,604 (India)	2,083 (Pakistan)	8 (Bhutan)
Change since 1986/88	57%	133%	21%
Marine fish catch ('000 tons)	2,433 (India)	369.6 (Pakistan)	207.3 (Sri Lanka)
Change since 1986/88	68%	21%	46%

FOOD SECURITY

Food aid as % of total imports	40% (India)	27% (Bangladesh)	3% (Pakistan)
Daily kcal/person	2,496 (India)	2,366 (Nepal)	2,086 (Bangladesh)

POPULATION

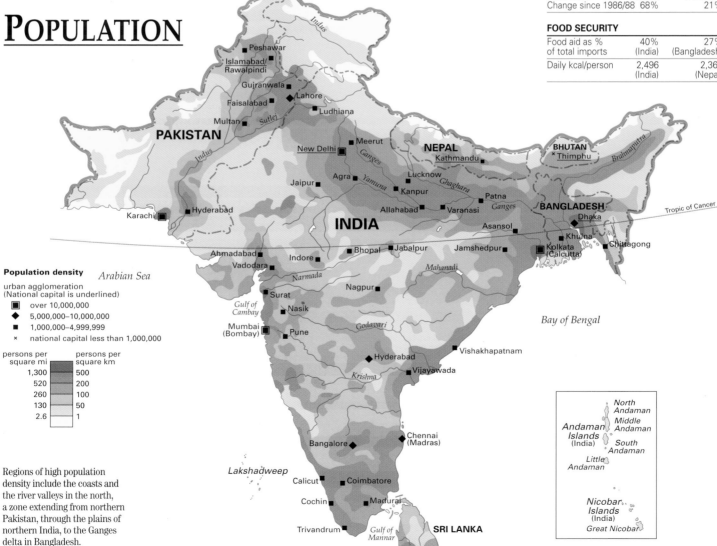

Population density *Arabian Sea*

urban agglomeration
(National capital is underlined)

- ■ over 10,000,000
- ◆ 5,000,000–10,000,000
- ■ 1,000,000–4,999,999
- × national capital less than 1,000,000

persons per square mi	persons per square km
1,300	500
520	200
260	100
130	50
2.6	1

Regions of high population density include the coasts and the river valleys in the north, a zone extending from northern Pakistan, through the plains of northern India, to the Ganges delta in Bangladesh.

INDUSTRY

India has coal and iron reserves, while oil and gas fields are being developed. Pakistan and Bangladesh have large gas reserves.

Resources and industry
- ♦ industrial center
- ○ port
- ● other town
- — major road
- — major railroad

mineral resources and fossil fuels
- ● iron and other ferroalloy metal ores
- ● other metal ores
- ■ nonmetallic minerals

▨	coal
▨	iron ore
▨	natural gas

Indus

Rawalpindi
Jhelum
Chenab
Lahore ● Amritsar
Multan ● ● Simla
Quetta ● *Sutlej*
PAKISTAN
New Delhi
Jaipur
Karachi ● Hyderabad
Bhuj ●
Arabian Sea
Ahmadabad ● Indore
Narmada
Tapi
Gulf of Cambay
Mumbai (Bombay)
INDIA
Chambal
Ganges
Yamuna
Kanpur
Varanasi
Ganges
NEPAL
Kathmandu
BHUTAN ● Thimphu
Brahmaputra
Jamalpur
BANGLADESH
Dhaka
Tropic of Cancer
Khulna ● Chittagong
Kolkata (Calcutta)
Jamshedpur
Mahanadi
Paradwip
Bay of Bengal
Nagpur
Godavari
Hyderabad
Vishakhapatnam
Krishna
Vijayawada
Marmagao
Bangalore ● Chennai (Madras)
Mangalore
Lakshadweep
Cochin ● Madurai ● Jaffna
Trincomalee
Gulf of Mannar
SRI LANKA
Cape Comorin
Colombo
MALDIVES
Dondra Head

Andaman Islands (India)
North Andaman
Middle Andaman
South Andaman
Port Blair
Little Andaman
Nicobar Islands (India)
Great Nicobar

AGRICULTURE

PAKISTAN
Toba Kakar Ranges
Sandy Desert
Central Makran Range
Makran Coast Range
K2 28,253
Karakoram Range
Zaskar Mountains
Indus
Jhelum
Chenab
Sutlej
Sulaiman Range
Great Indian Desert
Aravalli Range
HIMALAYAS
Siwalik Range
NEPAL
Mt. Everest 29,035
Kanchenjunga 28,210
Kula Kangri 24,784
BHUTAN
Brahmaputra
Khasi Hills
Naga Hills
Ganges
Ghaghara
Yamuna
Ganges
BANGLADESH
Tropic of Cancer
INDIA
Chambal
Rann of Kutch
Vindhya Range
Narmada
Tapi
Satpura Range
Hazaribagh Range
Mahanadi
Mouths of the Ganges
Gulf of Cambay
Godavari
Deccan Plateau
Eastern Ghats
Krishna
Arabian Sea
Western Ghats
Bay of Bengal
Lakshadweep
Cardamom Hills
Palk Strait
Cape Comorin
Gulf of Mannar
SRI LANKA
Pidurutalagala 8,262
MALDIVES
Dondra Head

Arable farming is important in most of the region, though irrigation is essential in dry areas. Fruits and fiber crops, including cotton and jute, are widely grown.

Andaman Islands (India)
North Andaman
Middle Andaman
South Andaman
Little Andaman
Nicobar Islands (India)
Great Nicobar

Agricultural zones
- ▨ arable
- ▨ fruit, vegetables and tree crops
- ▨ pasture
- ▨ rough grazing
- ▨ woods and forest
- ▨ nonagricultural land
- ▲ mountain peak (ft)

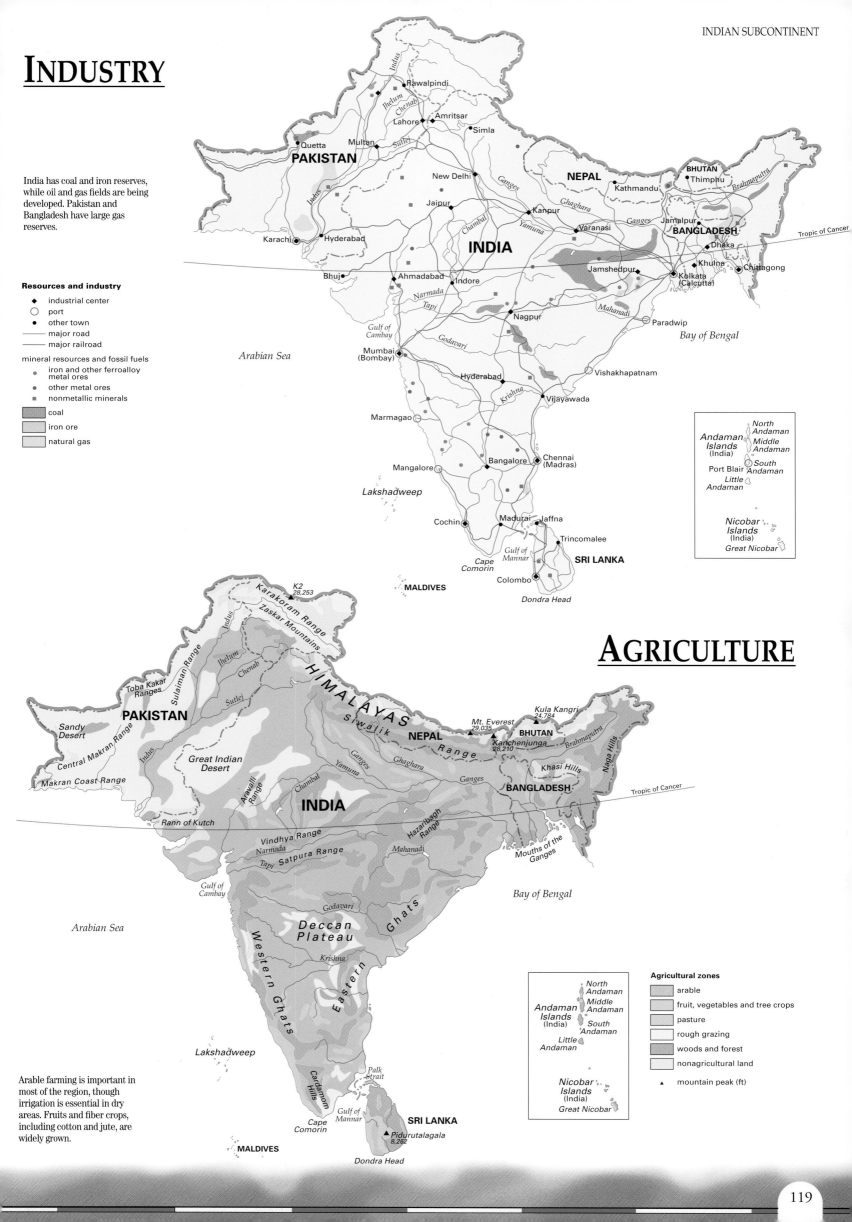

CHINA AND TAIWAN

China is the world's third largest country in area and the largest in population. It contains great mountain ranges, high plateaus, deserts, grasslands, and fertile valleys.

The climate in the southwest Plateau of Tibet is very harsh. The deserts in the northwest have an arid climate with temperatures that may soar to 100°F (38°C) in summer and plunge to −29°F (−34°C) during winter nights. Most people live in the east, where the climate ranges from temperate to subtropical.

About 93 percent of the people in China belong to the Han group, a name that comes from the Han dynasty (206 B.C.–A.D. 220). The other 7 percent belong to minority groups.

Civilization in China dates back around 5,000 years. The Chinese empire became weak in the nineteenth century, and in 1912, the country became a republic. A communist regime has ruled since 1949, though from the late 1980s, the government began to introduce free enterprise economic policies.

China's gross domestic product quadrupled between 1978 and 1998 and, by 1997, China had become the world's second largest economy after the United States.

China is bordered by Mongolia and Russia to the north and the Indian subcontinent and Southeast Asia in the south. It shares Everest, the world's highest mountain, with Nepal. It also has deep basins, one reaching 505 ft (154 m) below sea level. The great plains of China are drained by the great Huang and Chang rivers.

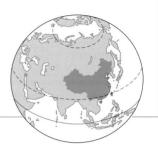

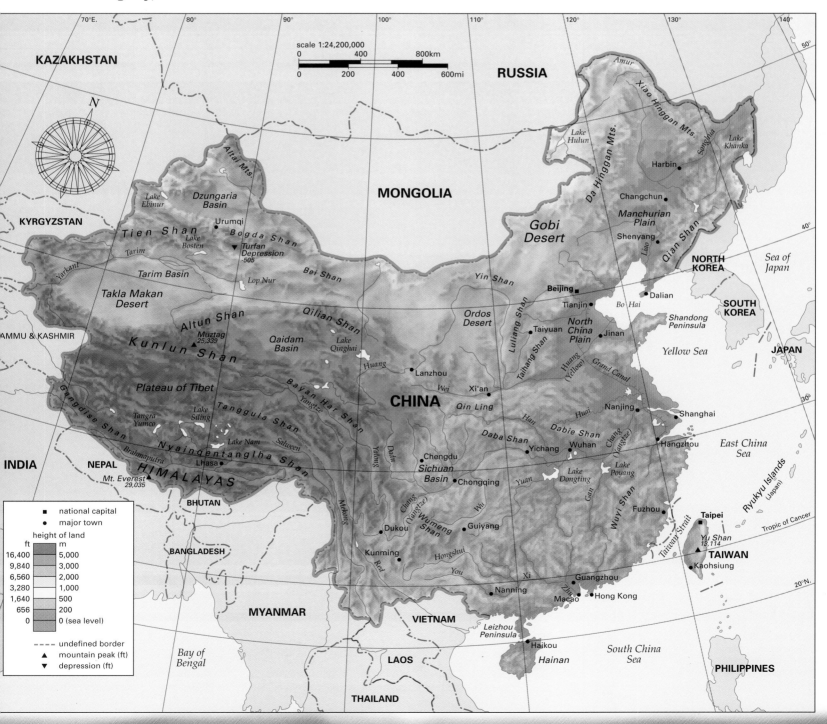

THE POLITICAL AND CULTURAL WORLD

The region includes Hong Kong, an extremely prosperous center for trade and finance on the southeast coast of China. Hong Kong was returned to communist China from British rule in 1997.

Near Hong Kong is the even smaller region of Macao, which Portugal returned to China in 1999, with an autonomous status similar to that of Hong Kong.

The independent island state of Taiwan lies off the southeast coast of China. Taiwan claims to be the sole legitimate Republic of China (its official name), a reflection of the fact that in 1949 it became the last refuge of China's nationalist government after its defeat by the communists on the mainland. Today, the island is discovering an identity of its own while maintaining close relations with China.

Since the death of China's communist leader Mao Zedong (1949–1976), China's leadership has tried to make friendlier relations with other countries, notably Russia and the United States. China was opened to foreign investment and free enterprise, and this led in the late 1980s to demands for political reform. Demonstrators for such changes were brutally suppressed.

COUNTRIES IN THE REGION

The People's Republic of China, Taiwan

Island territories Hainan (China)
Disputed borders China/India, China/Russia

LANGUAGE

Countries with one official language (Mandarin Chinese) China, Taiwan
Other significant languages in the region include Cantonese, Manchu, Miao, Mongol, Portuguese (in Macao), Tibetan, Uighur, and Yi. There are also numerous local languages and dialects.

RELIGION

China Although religion is officially discouraged, many people practice a combination of Confucianist, Taoist, and traditional folk belief. There are smaller groups of Buddhists, Muslims, and Christians.
In Hong Kong and Macao, separate from China for most of the past century until 1997 and 1999 respectively, religious practice is more widespread; in the former the figures are: Buddhist-Confucianist-Taoist (92%), Christian (1.1%), Muslim (0.1%); in the latter, Buddhist (45.1%), nonreligious (43.8%), Roman Catholic (7.4%), Protestant (1.3%)
Taiwan Confucianist-Taoist-traditional (48.5%), Buddhist (43%), Christian (7.4%), Muslim (0.5%)

STYLES OF GOVERNMENT

Republics China, Taiwan
Federal state China
Multiparty state Taiwan
One-party state China
One-chamber assembly China, Taiwan

ECONOMIC INDICATORS

	Taiwan	China
GDP (US$ billions)	357	902
GDP per capita (US$)	16,100	3,800
Annual rate of growth of GDP, 1990–1996	5.5%	11.6%
Manufacturing as % of GDP	n/a	38%
Central government spending as % of GDP	n/a	8.3%
Merchandise exports (US$ billions)	121.6	182.7
Merchandise imports (US$ billions)	101.7	136.4
Aid received as % of GNP	0%	0.3%
Total external debt as % of GDP	9.8%	16.6%

WELFARE INDICATORS

	Taiwan	China
Infant mortality rate (per 1,000 live births)		
1965	n/a	52.6
2000	7.06	41
Daily food supply available (calories per capita, 1995)	3,054	2,741
Population per physician (1995)	873	628
Teacher-pupil ratio (primary school, 1996)	1 : 20.6	1 : 24.3

China

Area 3,705,845 sq mi (9,598,073 sq km)
Population 1,269,394,378
Capital Beijing
Currency 1 yuan (Y) = 10 jiao = 100 fen

Taiwan

Area 13,892 sq mi (35,980 sq km)
Population 22,191,087
Capital Taipei
Currency 1 new Taiwan dollar (NT$) = 100 cents

- ■ national capital
- ▪ provincial, municipal or regional capital
- • other town

- province
- municipality
- autonomous region
- special administrative region

Locales are given in present-day Pinyin spelling.

HABITATS

The landscape of China falls into three main areas. In the west is the immense Plateau of Tibet, the "roof of the world," the highest and largest plateau on earth. Its average height is 13,000 ft (4,000 m). In the far south of the plateau are the Himalayas.

The next main area, to the north and east, is a vast region of plateaus and river basins. It includes the Gobi Desert, and the basin of the Tarim River and the Sichuan Basin. This area is bordered to the west by mountain ranges.

The great plains of China form the third main area, stretching east and southeast from the plateaus to the sea. They were formed from the deposited soils washed down by great rivers flowing from the higher land. The plains are generally below 1,600 ft (500 m), and broken by occasional hills.

The boundaries between these three main areas follow the lines of deep-seated faults in the underlying crust of the earth. Tectonic activity continues— there are frequent earthquakes, particularly in the mountains of the west and on the island of Taiwan.

LAND

Area   3,719,737 sq mi (9,634,053 sq km)
Highest point   Mount Everest, 29,035 ft (8,850 m) highest on earth
Lowest point   Turfan depression, −505 ft (−154 m)
Major features   Plateau of Tibet, Himalayas, world's highest mountain chain, Sichuan and Tarim basins, Takla Makan and Gobi deserts, river plains in east

WATER

Longest river   3,722 mi (Chang, 5,900 km)
Largest basin   Chang, 705,000 sq mi (1,827,000 sq km)
Highest average flow   Chang, 1,137,000 cu ft/sec (32,190 cu m/sec)
Largest lake   Qinghai, 1,721 sq mi (4,460 sq km)

NOTABLE THREATENED SPECIES

Mammals   Kozlov's pika (*Ochtona koslowi*), Golden snub-nosed monkey (*Rhinopithecus roxellana*), Yunnan snub-nosed monkey (*Rhinopithecus bieti*), Baiji (*Lipotes vexillifer*), Giant panda (*Ailuropoda melanoleuca*), Thorold's deer (*Cervus albirostris*)
Birds   White-eared night heron (*Gorsachius magnificus*), Crested ibis (*Nipponia nippon*), Chinese monal pheasant (*Lophophorus lhuysii*)
Others   Chinese alligator (*Alligator chinensis*), Chinese giant salamander (*Andrias davidianus*), Chinese paddlefish (*Psephurus gladius*), Chinese three-tailed swallowtail butterfly (*Bhutanitis thaidina*)
Plants   Baishanzhu mountain fir (*Abies beshanzhuensis*); xianmu (*Burretiodendron hsienmu*); *Camellia granthamiana*; *Coptis teeta*; *Cycas taiwaniana*; dove tree (*Davidia involucrata*); maidenhair tree (*Ginkgo biloba*); *Kirengeshoma palmata*; dawn redwood (*Metasequoia glyptostroboides*); ginseng (*Panax ginseng*)

HABITATS

Physical zones

- mountains/barren land
- forest
- grassland
- semidesert
- desert

▲ mountain peak (ft)
▼ depression (ft)
☀ climate station

China contains barren regions of mountain, desert, and semidesert. There are also grassy plains in the northwest and fertile areas of valleys and plains in the southeast.

CLIMATE

There are three main climatic zones in the region, corresponding to the three major physical regions. The Plateau of Tibet has a harsh, cold, dry climate, and has been called the "earth's third pole." The height of the mountains prevents warmer air from moving north. Above 13,000 ft (4,000 m), it is always freezing. The remote arid steppes and deserts of northwest China are far from the ocean and its rain-bearing winds, and have less than 4 in (100 mm) of rain a year.

The lowlands and hills of eastern China occupy almost half the country and have a great range of climates. The northeast lies in a temperate zone; farther south there are both warm temperate and subtropical zones, while southern Yunnan in the southwest and also the island of Hainan are tropical. Throughout eastern China the monsoon brings high rainfall in summer. Cold, dry, northerly winds (the winter monsoon) blow outward over much of China. When the land warms in spring, a great current of warm, humid air reaches inland from the south and east, bringing rain. This is the wet summer monsoon.

CLIMATE

	Temperature °F (°C) January	July	Altitude ft (m)
Lhasa	28 (–2)	59 (15)	11,988 (3,658)
Hami	10 (–12)	82 (28)	2,421 (738)
Guangzhou	56 (13)	82 (28)	201 (63)
Beijing	23 (–5)	79 (26)	167 (51)
Shanghai	38 (3)	82 (28)	148 (45)
Harbin	–4 (–20)	73 (23)	564 (172)

	Precipitation in. (mm) January	July	Year
Lhasa	0.01 (0.2)	5.6 (142)	17.9 (454)
Hami	0.1 (2)	0.2 (6)	1.3 (33)
Guangzhou	1.5 (39)	8.6 (220)	66.2 (1,681)
Beijing	0.1 (3)	7.7 (197)	26.9 (683)
Shanghai	1.7 (44)	5.6 (142)	44.4 (1,129)
Harbin	0.2 (4)	4.9 (127)	21.8 (554)

NATURAL HAZARDS
Large rivers in flood, earthquakes in interior and on Taiwan, typhoons in coastal areas, landslides

CLIMATE

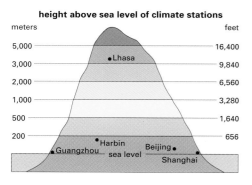
height above sea level of climate stations

Guangzhou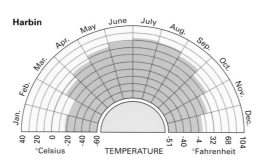

Harbin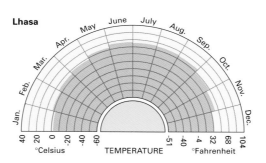

Lhasa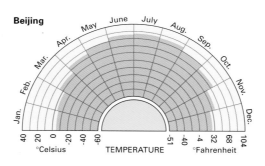

Beijing

Shanghai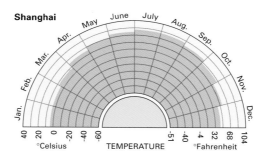

Guangzhou PRECIPITATION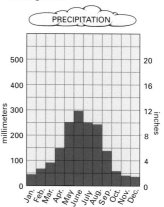

Harbin PRECIPITATION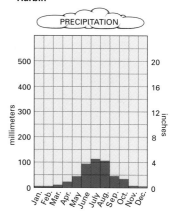

Lhasa PRECIPITATION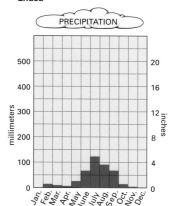

Beijing PRECIPITATION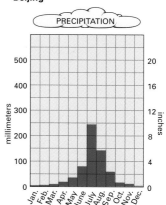

Shanghai PRECIPITATION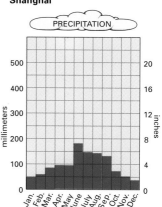

CHINA AND TAIWAN

123

ENVIRONMENTAL ISSUES

The region's environmental problems arise largely from one factor—China's huge and still growing population. Attempts to tackle the problems are linked with the government's policy of reducing the overall population.

In recent decades pressure on the land from farming has contributed to the southward spread of the Gobi Desert. Farming land has been terraced since prehistoric times, but overirrigation in some areas has led to salinization and waterlogging, greatly reducing the productivity of the land. Only about 11 percent of China's forests remain. Also, the country has seen rapid growth of cities and industries since the 1970s, causing severe air and water pollution.

Those industries that still rely on fossil fuels also contribute to pollution. Coal-burning locomotives are still in production and use, and coal is also the chief freight carried by Chinese trains.

The village system of agriculture has encouraged the growth of small-scale environmental projects. These include the recycling of waste water and the conservation of naturally produced methane for domestic use.

For thousands of years there have been repeated flood disasters, particularly on the Huang and Chang rivers. In an effort to control flooding and create much needed hydroelectricity, the government gave the go-ahead for the world's largest dam—the Three Gorges Dam on the Chang river—due to be completed in 2009. The $29 billion project has been described as modern China's largest construction effort since the Great Wall. This expensive and controversial dam will flood 19 counties, 153 towns and 4,500 villages. Nearly 2 million people are being resettled in 13 replacement cities, which are also being constructed.

MAJOR ENVIRONMENTAL PROBLEMS AND SOURCES

Air pollution: generally high, urban very high; acid rain prevalent; high greenhouse gas emissions
River/lake pollution: local/medium; *sources:* agriculture, industry, sewage, soil erosion
Land pollution: local medium; *sources:* industry, agriculture
Land degradation: *types:* desertification, soil erosion, salinization, deforestation, habitat loss; *causes:* agriculture, industry, population pressure
Waste disposal issues: domestic; industrial
Resource issues: inadequate sanitation; land use competition; coastal flooding
Population issues: population explosion; urban overcrowding; inadequate health facilities

ENVIRONMENTAL ISSUES

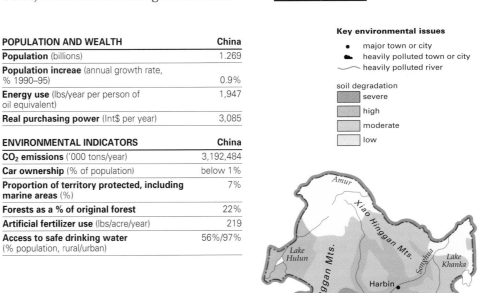

Key environmental issues

- major town or city
- heavily polluted town or city
- heavily polluted river

soil degradation

- severe
- high
- moderate
- low

POPULATION AND WEALTH	China
Population (billions)	1.269
Population increae (annual growth rate, % 1990–95)	0.9%
Energy use (lbs/year per person of oil equivalent)	1,947
Real purchasing power (Int$ per year)	3,085

ENVIRONMENTAL INDICATORS	China
CO$_2$ emissions ('000 tons/year)	3,192,484
Car ownership (% of population)	below 1%
Proportion of territory protected, including marine areas (%)	7%
Forests as a % of original forest	22%
Artificial fertilizer use (lbs/acre/year)	219
Access to safe drinking water (% population, rural/urban)	56%/97%

Over-intensive farming for centuries has caused severe soil erosion in many areas. China's drive to modernize its economy, together with the fast growth of cities, have led to air and water pollution.

POPULATION

China is the world's third largest country and the most populous. As early as 800 B.C., it had a population of nearly 14 million. Most of the people lived in country villages until the late twentieth century. Peasant life was almost unchanged through several thousand years of political change and war, flood, famine, and invasion. European traders boosted the growth of the coastal cities in the eighteenth century, but the interior remained thinly populated. Changing patterns of settlement during the twentieth century have been the result of government policy.

Overpopulation has been China's worst problem since the mid 19th century. The population of China, which doubled between 1949 and 1979, reached 1 billion in the early 1980s. In the early 1960s the growth rate leaped to 3 percent and the population soared again until 1970, when the one-child family planning campaign began to take effect. Annual population growth in the 1990s was around one percent.

The heaviest concentrations of people, and most of the major cities, are found on the east coast and along the Huang and Chang rivers, especially around Shanghai. Western China remains sparsely settled because of its harsh climate and terrain.

POPULATION

Total population of region (billions)	1.292
Population density (China) (persons per sq mi)	332
Population change (average annual percent 1995–2000)	
Urban	+2.47%
Rural	+0.22%

URBAN POPULATION

As percentage of total population	
1960	19.0%
2000 (China)	32%

TEN LARGEST CITIES

	Population
Shanghai	9,536,500
Beijing †	7,336,400
Chongqing	6,140,300
Tianjin	5,213,700
Wuhan	4,284,300
Harbin	4,266,200
Shenyang	4,242,200
Guangzhou	4,173,800
Chengdu	3,272,900
Changchun	2,767,300

† *denotes capital city*

City population figures are for the city proper.

POPULATION

Population density

urban agglomeration
(National capital is underlined)
- ■ over 10,000,000
- ◆ 5,000,000–10,000,000
- ■ 1,000,000–4,999,999

persons per square mi	persons per square km
520	200
260	100
130	50
26	10
2.6	1

Western China, with its harsh climate and rugged terrain, contains few people. The areas of highest population density are on the east coast and along the Huang and Chang rivers, especially around Shanghai.

INDUSTRY

China has huge resources of both fuel and minerals and many industries. On a per capita basis, however, it is one of the world's poorer nations. Many of the resources are underdeveloped. They include coal, petroleum, natural gas, iron ore, bauxite, tin, antimony, and manganese in major reserves. There is great potential for hydroelectric power projects as the country has many large rivers and a hilly landscape.

The economy is centrally planned, with all industries owned by the state until very recently. Some private enterprise is now being encouraged. Petrochemical products account for nearly 25 percent of China's exports. Other major industries include iron and steel, cement, vehicles, fertilizers, food processing, clothing, and textiles.

The most recent government plans have promoted modernization of industry and reform of its organization. Joint ventures with other countries and foreign loans have been encouraged. Much of this overseas investment went into light industry and textiles. Special Economic Zones were created to foster industrial contact with the west.

INDUSTRIAL OUTPUT (US $ billion)

China (1997)	444	Hong Kong (1996)	22

INDUSTRIAL WORKERS (millions) (% of total labor force)

	Total	Mining	Manufacturing	Construction
China (1995)	623.8	10.6 (1.7%)	98 (15.7%)	33 (5.3%)
Taiwan (1996)	9.3	0.01 (0.1%)	2.422 (26%)	0.928 (10%)

MAJOR PRODUCTS

Energy and minerals	Output 1970	1995
Coal, bituminous (mil m.t.)	360	1,250
Coal, lignite and brown	0	48
Natural gas ('000 terajoules)	144	750
Oil, crude (mil m.t.)	25	159
Petroleum products (mil m.t.)	22	114
Iron ore (mil m.t.)	24	153
Tungsten (m.t.)	10,100	17,500
Cement ('000 m.t.)	25,720	400,680
Steel ('000 m.t.)	17,790	93,840

Manufactures		
Ships ('000 m.t.)	0	602
Televisions ('000)	0	32,833
Tires ('000)	4,250	83,484
Fertilizers, nitrogenous ('000 m.t.)	2,245	16,980
Fertilizers, phosphate ('000 m.t.)	1,031	5,041
Magnesite ('000 m.t.)	1,000	1,500
Tobacco ('000 m.t.)	801	2,327
Silk ('000 m.t.)	10,258	80,000
Sisal ('000 m.t.)	9	42
Cotton lint ('000 m.t.)	1,988	4,768

INDUSTRY

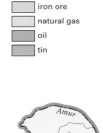

Resources and industry

- ◆ industrial center
- ○ port
- • other town
- —— major road
- —— major railroad

mineral resources and fossil fuels
- ● iron and other ferroalloy metal ores
- ● other metal ores
- ■ nonmetallic minerals

- coal
- copper
- iron ore
- natural gas
- oil
- tin

China's resources include coal, oil, and natural gas, together with many metals and nonmetallic minerals. The smaller territories have few resources but are extremely important for manufacturing.

AGRICULTURE

China covers only 7 percent of the world's land area, but succeeds in feeding its people, amounting to 20 percent of the world's population. Some 80 percent of people belong to peasant or rural households, and traditional farming life continues, despite reforms introduced by communism since 1949.

Much of China, particularly in the north and west, will only grow scrub and provides poor pasture. Only 10 percent of the land can be used for growing crops, mainly in the valleys and plains in the east and south.

The main crops are wheat and rice. Small family plots have always been used to grow vegetables, a key part of the Chinese diet. Pigs, chickens, and ducks are also raised in the villages. Water control is essential to prevent flooding and to provide irrigation in the plains, while in the foothills, terracing conserves both soil and water.

The northern plains also produce corn, millet, and potatoes. South of the Chang River, paddy rice predominates. Tea, tobacco, and mulberry trees (for silkworm production) are also commercially important.

LAND
Total area 3,719,737 sq mi (9,634,053 sq km)

Cropland	Pasture	Forest/Woodland
11%	43%	14%
(374,111 sq mi)	(1,594,049 sq mi)	(526,609 sq mi)

FARMERS
	China
Agriculture as % of GDP	19%
% of workforce	50%

MAJOR CROPS
Agricultural products: rice, wheat, vegetables, sorghum, millet, nuts, tea, cotton; oilseed; pork; fish

Total cropland ('000 acres)	334,487
Cropland (acres) per 1,000 people	269
Irrigated land as percentage of cropland	38%
Annual fertilizer use (lbs per acre of cropland)	219
Number of tractors	703,117
Percentage change since 1987	−21%
Average cereal crop yields (lbs per acre)	4,001
Average production of cereals ('000 tons)	448,904
Percentage change since 1986–88	27%

LIVESTOCK AND FISHERIES
Average meat production ('000 tons)	53,747
Percentage change since 1986–88	191%
Marine fish catch ('000 tons)	8,765
Percentage change since 1986–88	203%
Aquaculture production ('000 tons)	22,054

FOOD SECURITY
Food aid as percentage of total imports	1%
Average daily per capita calories (kilocalories)	2,897

AGRICULTURE

Agricultural zones

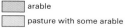

- arable
- pasture with some arable
- rough grazing
- woods and forest
- nonagricultural land

▲ mountain peak (ft)
▼ depression (ft)

The rugged and arid west and north are suitable only for raising livestock. The arable farming regions are in the east, where the densely populated valleys and plains are intensively farmed.

SOUTHEAST ASIA

Southeast Asia includes a peninsula and a vast archipelago, comprising over 20,000 islands. The region contains two zones where volcanic eruptions and earthquakes are caused by collisions between the huge plates that form the earth's crust. One zone runs east-west through southern Indonesia and the other from eastern Indonesia to the Philippines.

The region is humid and tropical. The south has rainfall throughout the year, but the north has a monsoon climate, with most rain coming in the summer months (June through August).

Small groups of Negritos, descendants of the earliest inhabitants, live in remote areas, but most Southeast Asians are of Malay or Chinese descent. The diversity of cultures shows how many outside influences have affected the region. Of the region's ten countries, only Thailand remained free. Wars in Europe marred the area's chances for independence, and the postcolonial years have been marked by civil wars and political instability. Agriculture is the main activity. Industry has been developing rapidly in some areas, including Manila and Singapore.

Southeast Asia lies between the eastern end of the Himalayas and northern Australia. Most of the region lies on the southeastern edge of the huge Eurasian plate and is bordered by deep ocean trenches. As the plates descend into the mantle, their edges melt, forming the molten rock that fuels Southeast Asia's volcanoes.

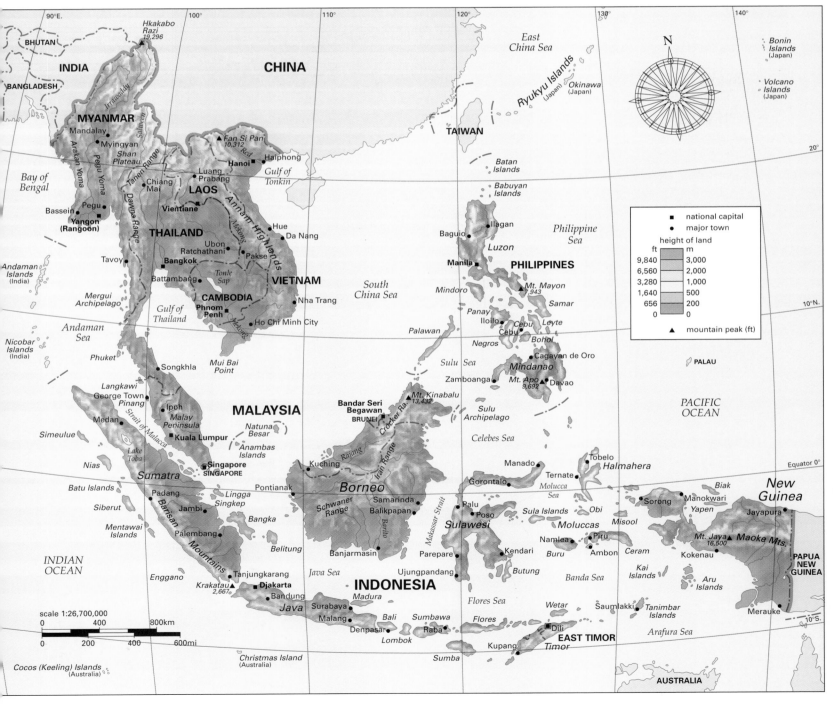

THE POLITICAL AND CULTURAL WORLD

After the defeat of Japan in 1945, communist forces began a long struggle for power in Southeast Asia. The British defeated them in Malaya, but after a long struggle in Vietnam, involving first France and then the United States, the communists emerged victorious in 1975.

In Myanmar (formerly Burma), Indonesia, and Thailand, army rulers have suppressed political parties, while Brunei's sultan has allowed no opposition to his government. The only countries with elements of parliamentary democracy are Cambodia, Malaysia, Singapore, and the Philippines.

East Timor's people voted for independence from Indonesia in 1999. The first free elections were held in 2001.

COUNTRIES IN THE REGION

Brunei, Cambodia, Indonesia, Laos, Malaysia, Myanmar, Philippines, Singapore, Thailand, Vietnam
Disputed borders Cambodia/Thailand, Cambodia/Vietnam, Indonesia/Malaysia, Vietnam/China

LANGUAGE

Countries with one official language (Bahasa Indonesia) Indonesia; (Bahasa Malaysia) Malaysia; (Burmese) Myanmar; (Khmer) Cambodia; (Lao) Laos; (Thai) Thailand; (Vietnamese) Vietnam
Countries with two official languages (English, Malay) Brunei; (English, Filipino) Philippines
Country with four official languages (Bahasa Malaysia, Chinese, English, Tamil) Singapore

RELIGION

Country with one major religion (B) Cambodia
Countries with two major religions (B, I) Laos; (B, M) Thailand
Countries with three or more major religions (B, C, T) Vietnam; (B, C, H, M) Indonesia; (B, C, I, M) Myanmar Brunei; (B, M, P, RC) Philippines; (B, C, H, M, T) Singapore, Malaysia

Key: B-Buddhist, C-various Christian, H-Hindu, I-Indigenous religions, M-Muslim; P-Protestant, RC-Roman Catholic, T-Taoist

ECONOMIC INDICATORS

	Singapore	Thailand	Indonesia
GDP (US$ billions)	96.3	157.2	214.6
GNP per capita (US$)	29,000	6,590	3,450
Annual rate of growth of GDP, 1990–1997	8.5%	7.4%	7.5%
Manufacturing as % of GDP	24.3%	28.4%	25.6%
Central government spending as % of GNP	15.9%	15.8%	14.7%
Merchandise exports (US$ billions)	125.8	56.7	56.3
Merchandise imports (US$ billions)	124.6	55.1	46.2
Aid received as % of GNP	–	0.5%	0.5%
Total external debt as % of GNP	–	62.6%	65.3%
Industrial production growth rate, 1999	14%	12.6%	1.5%

WELFARE INDICATORS

	Singapore	Thailand	Indonesia
Infant mortality rate (per 1,000 live births)			
1965	26	145	128
2000	5	29	48
Daily food supply available (calories per capita, 1995)	3,121	2,296	2,732
Population per physician (1993–4)	709	4,416	7,028
Teacher-pupil ratio (primary school, 1995)	1 : 25.3	1 : 19.3	1 : 22.3

- ■ national capital
- • other town

Area 2,228 sq mi (5,770 sq km)
Population 336,376
Capital Bandar Seri Begawan
Brunei

Area 69,900 sq mi (181,040 sq km)
Population 12,212,306
Capital Phnom Penh
Cambodia

Area 741,101 sq mi (1,919,440 sq km)
Population 224,784,210
Capital Djakarta
Indonesia

Area 91,430 sq mi (236,800 sq km)
Population 5,497,459
Capital Vientiane
Laos

Area 127,317 sq mi (329,750 sq km)
Population 21,793,293
Capital Kuala Lumpur
Malaysia

While the region has a volatile recent political history, the people continue to follow their traditional religious beliefs. The main religions are Buddhism, chiefly on the mainland peninsula; Islam, in Indonesia; and Christianity, in the Philippines. All these religious influences come from outside the region.

Area 198,457 sq mi (514,000 sq km)
Population 61,230,874
Capital Bangkok
Thailand

Area 127,244 sq mi (329,560 sq km)
Population 78,773,873
Capital Hanoi
Vietnam

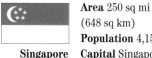

Area 250 sq mi (648 sq km)
Population 4,151,264
Capital Singapore
Singapore

Area 261,971 sq mi (678,500 sq km)
Population 41,734,853
Capital Yangon
Myanmar

Area 115,831 sq mi (300,000 sq km)
Population 81,159,644
Capital Manila
Philippines

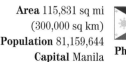

HABITATS

Rain forest flourishes in the south, with deciduous forest and tropical savanna grassland in the north. The fertile lowlands and broad deltas of the great rivers on the mainland peninsula, including the Irrawaddy, Mekong, and Salween, are cultivated.

LAND

Area 1,735,729 sq mi (4,495,508 sq km)
Highest point Hkakabo Razi, 19,296 ft (5,881 m)
Lowest point sea level
Major features mountain chains and flood plains, deltas of great rivers in north region, mountainous and volcanic islands of Malaysia, Indonesia, Philippines, world's largest archipelago

WATER

Longest river Mekong, 2,600 mi (4,180 km)
Largest basin Mekong, 313,000 sq mi (811,000 sq km)
Highest average flow Irrawaddy, 447,000 cu ft/sec (12,660 cu m/sec)
Largest lake Tonle Sap, 3,860 sq mi (10,000 sq km)

NOTABLE THREATENED SPECIES

Mammals Pileated gibbon (*Hylobates pileatus*), orangutan (*Pongo pygmaeus*), Flat-headed cat (*Felis planiceps*), Malayan tapir (*Tapirus indicus*), Javan rhinoceros (*Rhinoceros sondaicus*), Kouprey (*Bos sauveli*), Tamaraw (*Bubalus mindorensis*)
Birds Philippine eagle (*Pithecophaga jefferyi*), Giant ibis (*Pseudibis gigantea*), Gumey's pitta (*Pitta gurneyi*), Salmoncrested cockatoo (*Cacatua moluccensis*)
Others River terrapin (*Batagur baska*), False gharial (*Tomistoma schlegelii*), Komodo dragon (*Varanus komodoensis*)
Plants *Allobunkillia* species; titan arum (*Amorphopallus titanum*); umbrella leaf palm (*Johannesteijsmannia lanceolata*); *Maingaya* species; *Maxburretia rupicola*; pitcher plant (*Nepenthes* – Mount Kinabulu species); Rothschild's slipper orchid (*Paphiopedium rothschildianum*); *Phyllagathis magnifica*; *Rafflesia* species (jade vine (*Strongylodon macrobotrys*)

CLIMATE

Malaysia and Indonesia, which straddle the equator, have a tropical climate, also called a rain-forest climate. The coastal areas in the north of the region have a marked summer monsoon. Other inland areas in the northwest have a distinct dry season in winter.

CLIMATE

| | Temperature °F (°C) | | Altitude |
	January	July	ft (m)
Yangon	77 (25)	81 (27)	75 (23)
Ho Chi Minh City	79 (26)	81 (27)	33 (10)
Manila	77 (25)	82 (28)	49 (15)
Cameron Highlands	64 (18)	64 (18)	4,753 (1,449)
Singapore	79 (26)	81 (27)	33 (10)
Djakarta	79 (26)	81 (27)	26 (8)

| | Precipitation in. (mm) | | |
	January	July	Year
Yangon	0.1 (3)	22.8 (580)	103.1 (2,618)
Ho Chi Minh City	0.2 (6)	9.5 (242)	71.2 (1,808)
Manila	0.7 (18)	10.0 (253)	70.5 (1,791)
Cameron Highlands	6.6 (168)	4.8 (122)	104.0 (2,640)
Singapore	11.2 (285)	6.4 (163)	89.8 (2,282)
Djakarta	13.2 (335)	2.4 (61)	69.1 (1,755)

Rainfall of 46 in. (1,170 mm) in 24 hours has been recorded at Baguio in Luzon, Philippines

ENVIRONMENTAL ISSUES

Natural hazards include earthquakes, hurricanes (locally called typhoons), floods, and volcanic eruptions. But human activity, including the rapid destruction of forests, the population explosion, and urban expansion are causing new problems.

POPULATION AND WEALTH

	Highest	Middle	Lowest
Population (millions)	224.784 (I)	41.734 (My)	0.336 (B)
Population increase (annual growth rate, % 1990–95)	2.6% (L)	1.4% (S)	0.9% (T)
Energy use (lbs per year per person of oil equivalent)	17,291 (S)	5,093 (Ma)	653 (My)
Real purchasing power (Int$/per year)	25,772 (S)	6,790 (T)	1,255 (L)

ENVIRONMENTAL INDICATORS

CO₂ emissions ('000 tons/year)	296,132 (I)	106,604 (Ma)	308 (L)
Car ownership (% of pop.)	49% (B)	14% (Ma)	<1% (My)
Proportion of territory protected, including marine areas (%)	21% (B)	12% (L)	0.3% (My)
Forests as a % of original forest	65% (C)	30% (L)	3% (S)
Artificial fertilizer use (lbs/acre/year)	2,718 (S)	131 (Ma)	1.7 (My)
Access to safe drinking water (% population; rural/urban)	100%/100% (S)	73%/88% (T)	12%/20% (C)

MAJOR ENVIRONMENTAL PROBLEMS AND SOURCES

Air pollution: urban high; high greenhouse gas emissions
Marine/coastal pollution: medium; *sources:* industry, agriculture, sewage, oil, foresty, fish farming
Land degradation: *types:* soil erosion, deforestation, habitat destruction; *causes:* agriculture, industry, population pressure
Resource issues: fuelwood shortage; inadequate drinking water and sanitation
Population issues: population explosion; urban overcrowding; inadequate health facilities
Major events: Burkit Suharto (1982–83), fire in coal seams and peat; Bangkok (1991), chemical explosion and fire; Indonesia forest fires (1997); flooding Mekong (2000); Manila garbage slide (2000)

Southeast Asia is a complex region with rugged peninsulas, islands swathed in forest, and active volcanoes. There are high mountains in the far north and in Borneo.

Physical zones
mountains/barren land
forest
grassland
▲ mountain peak (ft)
☀ climate station

HABITATS

ENVIRONMENTAL ISSUES

As the population expands, more land is needed to produce food. When the land is cleared of trees, the soil fertility declines, and soil erosion becomes a major problem.

Key environmental issues

- • major town or city
- ⬤ polluted town or city
- 🝆 major pollution event
- ✛ major natural disaster
- ▲ active volcano
- polluted river
- ▨ remaining tropical rainforest
- ▨ area of deforestation

Map labels:

MYANMAR
Irrawaddy
Salween
Arakan Yoma
Shan Plateau
Pegu Yoma
Tanen Range
Dawna Range
Ping
Yangon (Rangoon)
LAOS
Hanoi
Haiphong
Gulf of Tonkin
Red
THAILAND
Annam Highlands
Chao Phraya
Bangkok
Tonle Sap
Mekong
VIETNAM
CAMBODIA
Merui Archipelago
Andaman Sea
Gulf of Thailand
Ho Chi Minh City
Phuket
Mui Bai Point
South China Sea

Batan Islands
Babuyan Islands
Cagua
Luzon
Philippine Sea
Pinatubo
Manila
Taal
PHILIPPINES
Mindoro
Mayon
Bulusan
Samar
Panay
Cebu
Leyte
Negros
Bohol
Mindanao
Iligan
Ragang
Apo
Sulu Sea
Sulu Archipelago
Awu
Celebes Sea
PACIFIC OCEAN

Langkawi
Geureudong
Pinang
Medan
Sinabung
Simeulue
Strait of Malacca
Perak
Malay Peninsula
Kuala Lumpur
MALAYSIA
Natuna Besar
Anambas Islands
BRUNEI
Crocker Ra.
Tamabo Ra.
Iran Range
Rajang
Borneo
Schwaner Range
Samarinda
Bukit Suharto
Barito
Kalimantan
Klabat
Ternate
Molucca Sea
Obi
Sula Islands
Halmahera
Equator
Biak
New Guinea
Yapen
Maoke Mts.
Misool
Moluccas
Buru
Ceram
Kai Islands
Aru Islands

Nias
Batu Islands
Merapi
Sumatra
Siberut
Kerinci
Sumbing
Mentawai Islands
Dempo
INDIAN OCEAN
Enggano
Lingga
Singkep
Bangka
Palembang
Belitung
Banjarmasin
Lake Toba
Barisan Mts.
Sumatra
SINGAPORE
Singapore
Makassar Strait
Sulawesi
Butung
Banda Sea
Arafura Sea
Tanimbar Islands

Java Sea
Krakatau
Djakarta
Salak
Bandung
Merapi
Kelud
Bromo
Agung
Lombok
Semarang
Surabaya
Bali
Java
INDONESIA
Flores Sea
Sumbawa
Tamboro
Rinjani
Sumba
Flores
Mandasawu
Ili
Sirung
Wetar
EAST TIMOR
Timor

CLIMATE

height above sea level of climate stations

meters		feet
5,000		16,400
3,000		9,840
2,000	Cameron Highlands	6,560
1,000		3,280
500		1,640
200		656
Yangon (Rangoon)	sea level · Singapore	

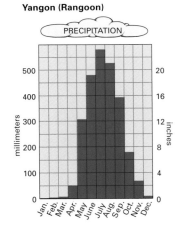

Yangon (Rangoon)
PRECIPITATION
millimeters / inches
Jan. Feb. Mar. Apr. May June July Aug. Sep. Oct. Nov. Dec.

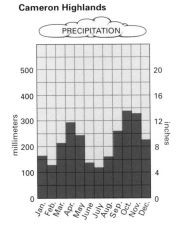

Cameron Highlands
PRECIPITATION
millimeters / inches
Jan. Feb. Mar. Apr. May June July Aug. Sep. Oct. Nov. Dec.

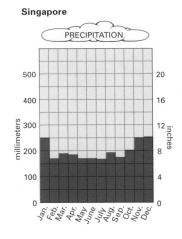

Singapore
PRECIPITATION
millimeters / inches
Jan. Feb. Mar. Apr. May June July Aug. Sep. Oct. Nov. Dec.

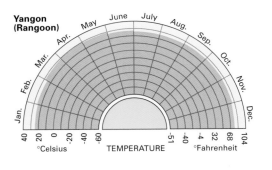

Yangon (Rangoon)
TEMPERATURE
°Celsius / °Fahrenheit

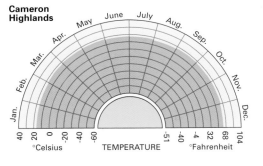

Cameron Highlands
TEMPERATURE
°Celsius / °Fahrenheit

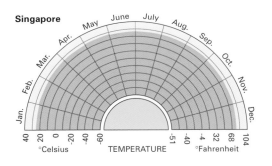

Singapore
TEMPERATURE
°Celsius / °Fahrenheit

POPULATION

The mountains and forest areas in Southeast Asia are thinly populated. Most people live on the cultivated lowlands and around the leading port cities. The percentage of people living in urban areas is low, but the cities are growing at a rapid rate.

POPULATION

Total population of region (millions)			531.67
Population density (persons per sq mi)	**Singapore** 14,939	**Thailand** 300	**Indonesia** 264
Population change (average annual percent 1960–1990)			
Urban	+1.43%	+2.50%	+4.22%
Rural	0.00%	+0.52%	–0.30%

URBAN POPULATION

As percentage of total population (2000)	100%	22%	41%

TEN LARGEST CITIES

	Country	Population
Djakarta †	Indonesia	9,373,900
Bangkok †	Thailand	7,050,000
Ho Chi Minh City	Vietnam	4,322,000
Singapore †	Singapore	4,100,000
Hanoi †	Vietnam	3,056,000
Surabaya	Indonesia	2,900,000
Yangon†	Myanmar	2,513,000
Medan	Indonesia	2,100,000
Quezon City (Manila)	Philippines	1,989,000
Manila †	Philippines	1,673,000

† denotes capital city

City population figures are for the city proper.

INDUSTRY

Political instability has restricted development in Southeast Asia. Some countries, such as Laos and Cambodia, are among the world's poorest. But Malaysia is developing quickly, and Singapore has become a prosperous industrial center.

INDUSTRIAL OUTPUT 1997 (US $ billion)

Thailand	61
Singapore	34
Philippines	26
Malaysia	47
Indonesia	92

MAJOR PRODUCTS (Indonesia)

Energy and minerals	Output change	
	1970	1995
Coal (mil m.t.)	0.1	42
Natural gas ('000 terajoules)	46	2,508
Oil (crude, mil m.t.)	43	77
Tin ('000 m.t.)	5.2	44
Nickel ore ('000 m.t.)	18	87
Cement ('000 m.t.)	515	23,316
Gold (m.t.)	0	74
Silver (m.t.)	9	161

Manufactures		
Radio receivers ('000)	393	3,500
Televisions ('000)	5	1,000
Tires ('000)	358	15,000
Coconuts ('000 m.t.)	5,892	13,868
Palm oil ('000 m.t.)	114	4,480
Coffee ('000 m.t.)	186	485 (1998)

The highest population densities are found on Java, Indonesia. Java contains about one-third of the population of Southeast Asia. The island contains Djakarta, the region's biggest city.

AGRICULTURE

Agriculture employs about half of the people of Southeast Asia. The region has large commercial plantations growing such things as oil palms, pineapples, rubber, and sugarcane, together with small plots worked by subsistence farmers to feed their families.

LAND

Total area 1,735,729 sq mi (4,495,508 sq km)

Cropland	Pasture	Forest/Woodland
20%	4%	53%
(341,060 sq mi)	(74,822 sq mi)	(915,620 sq mi)

FARMERS	Highest	Middle	Lowest
Agriculture as % of GDP	59% (My)	26% (V)	0% (S)
% of workforce	80% (C, L)	45% (I)	<10% (S)

MAJOR CROPS: Agricultural products fruit: bananas, mangoes, coconuts; pineapples; rice, cassava, corn; soybeans; palm oil; sugarcane; rubber; coffee, cocoa, tea; copra; pepper; poultry, pork, water buffalo meat; fish; timber

Total cropland ('000 acres)	76,569 (I)	25,083 (My)	2 (S)
Cropland (acres) per 1,000 people	897 (C)	571 (My)	2 (S)
Irrigated land as % of cropland	25% (T)	16% (I,P)	0% (S)
Number of tractors	149,500 (T)	43,300 (Ma)	65 (S)
Average cereal crop yields (lbs/acre)	3,238 (I)	2,438 (My)	1,476 (C)
Cereal production ('000 tons) Change since 1986/88 27%	59,029 (I)	17,938 (My) 26%	1,670 (L) 32%

LIVESTOCK & FISHERIES

Meat production ('000 tons) Change since 1986–88	1,848 (P) 182%	989 (Ma) 160%	71 (L) 103%
Marine fish catch ('000 tons) Change since 1986/88 72%	2,864.9 (I)	1,503 (P) 20%	7.9 (S) –51%

FOOD SECURITY

Food aid as % of total imports	47% (My)	11% (My)	0% (I, Ma, S)
Daily kcal/person	2,977 (Ma)	2,484 (V)	2,048 (C)

POPULATION

Population density

urban agglomeration
(National capital is underlined)

■	over 10,000,000
◆	5,000,000–10,000,000
■	1,000,000–4,999,999
●	500,000–999,999
×	national capital less than 500,000

persons per square mi	persons per square km
1,300	500
520	200
130	50
26	10

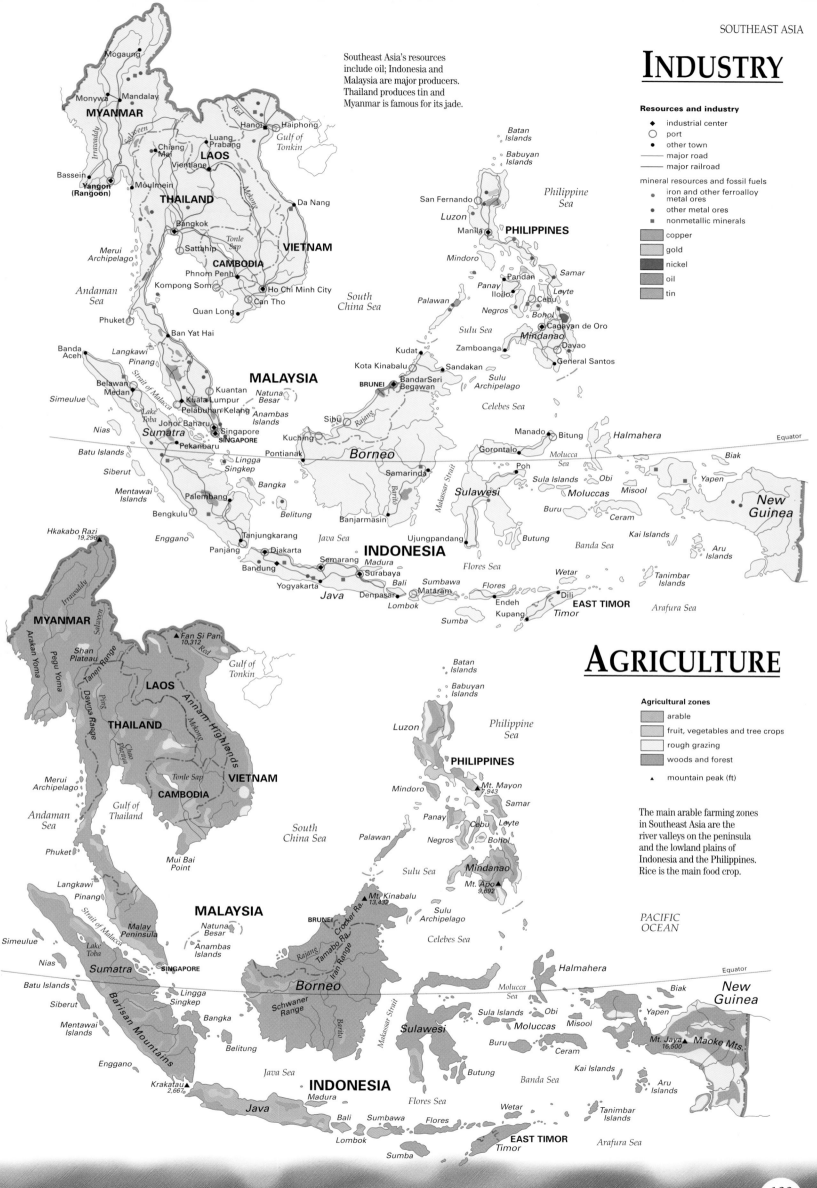

INDUSTRY

Southeast Asia's resources
include oil; Indonesia and
Malaysia are major producers.
Thailand produces tin and
Myanmar is famous for its jade.

Resources and industry

- ◆ industrial center
- ○ port
- • other town
- ── major road
- ── major railroad

mineral resources and fossil fuels
- iron and other ferroalloy metal ores
- • other metal ores
- ■ nonmetallic minerals

	copper
	gold
	nickel
	oil
	tin

MYANMAR

Mogaung
Monywa   Mandalay
Chiang Mai   Luang Prabang   Hanoi   Haiphong
Bassein   LAOS   *Gulf of Tonkin*
Yangon   Vientiane
(Rangoon)   Moulmein
THAILAND   Da Nang
Bangkok
Satahip   *Tonle Sap*   VIETNAM
Merui Archipelago   CAMBODIA
Phnom Penh
Andaman Sea   Kompong Som   Ho Chi Minh City
Can Tho
Phuket   Quan Long   *South China Sea*
Ban Yat Hai

Banda Aceh   *Langkawi Pinang*
Belawan   Kuantan   *Natuna Besar*
Medan   Kuala Lumpur
Simeulue   Pelabuhan Kelang   *Anambas Islands*
Lake Toba   Johor Baharu
Nias   *Sumatra*   Singapore
SINGAPORE   Kuching
Batu Islands   Pekanbaru   Pontianak   *Borneo*
Siberut   *Lingga Singkep*
Bangka   Samarinda
Mentawai Islands   *Palembang*   *Barito*
Belitung
Bengkulu
Enggano   Tanjungkarang   Banjarmasin

Hkakabo Razi 19,296

MALAYSIA

BRUNEI   BandarSeri Begawan
Kudat
Kota Kinabalu   Sandakan
Sulu Archipelago
Celebes Sea

San Fernando   *Philippine Sea*
Luzon   *Batan Islands*
Manila   PHILIPPINES   *Babuyan Islands*
Mindoro   Pandan   *Samar*
Palawan   Panay   Iloilo   *Leyte*
Negros   Cebu   *Bohol*
Zamboanga   Cagayan de Oro
Mindanao   Davao
General Santos
Sulu Sea

Manado   Bitung   *Halmahera*   Equator
Gorontalo   *Molucca Sea*   *Biak*
Poh   *Sula Islands*   Obi   *Yapen*
Sulawesi   *Moluccas*   *Misool*
Buru   *Ceram*   *New Guinea*

Ujungpandang   *Butung*   Kai Islands   *Aru Islands*
Banda Sea

Java Sea   INDONESIA
Djakarta   Semarang   *Madura*   Surabaya   *Wetar*   *Tanimbar Islands*
Bandung   *Bali*   *Sumbawa*   *Flores*   Dili   *Arafura Sea*
Yogyakarta   *Java*   Mataram   Endeh   EAST TIMOR
Denpasar   *Lombok*   Kupang   *Timor*
Flores Sea   *Sumba*

AGRICULTURE

Agricultural zones

	arable
	fruit, vegetables and tree crops
	rough grazing
	woods and forest
- ▲ mountain peak (ft)

The main arable farming zones
in Southeast Asia are the
river valleys on the peninsula
and the lowland plains of
Indonesia and the Philippines.
Rice is the main food crop.

MYANMAR

Irrawaddy   ▲ Fan Si Pan 10,312
Arakan Yoma   *Shan Plateau*   *Red*
Pegu Yoma   *Tanen Range*   LAOS
Dawna Range   *Ping*   THAILAND   *Annam Highlands*
Salween   *Chao Phraya*   *Mekong*   VIETNAM
Merui Archipelago   *Tonle Sap*   CAMBODIA
Andaman Sea   *Gulf of Thailand*
Phuket   Mui Bai Point

Langkawi Pinang   MALAYSIA
Malay Peninsula   *Natuna Besar*
Simeulue   *Lake Toba*   *Anambas Islands*
Nias   *Sumatra*   SINGAPORE   BRUNEI
Batu Islands   *Barisan Mountains*   *Lingga Singkep*
Siberut   *Bangka*   *Borneo*   *Crocker Ra.*
Mentawai Islands   *Belitung*   *Schwaner Range*   *Rajang*   *Tamabo Ra.*   *Iran Range*
Enggano   Krakatau 2,667   *Barito*
Java Sea   INDONESIA

Gulf of Tonkin   *Batan Islands*
Babuyan Islands
Luzon   *Philippine Sea*
PHILIPPINES
Mindoro   ▲ Mt. Mayon 7,943   *Samar*
Panay   *Cebu*   *Leyte*
Palawan   *Negros*   *Bohol*
South China Sea   *Mindanao*
Sulu Sea   Mt. Apo ▲ 9,692
▲ Mt. Kinabalu 13,432   *Sulu Archipelago*
Celebes Sea

PACIFIC OCEAN

Halmahera   Equator
Molucca Sea   *Biak*
Sula Islands   Obi   *New Guinea*
Sulawesi   *Moluccas*   *Misool*   *Yapen*
Buru   *Ceram*   Mt. Jaya 16,500 ▲   *Maoke Mts.*
Butung   *Kai Islands*
Banda Sea   *Aru Islands*

Madura
Bali   *Wetar*   *Tanimbar Islands*
Java   *Sumbawa*   *Flores*
Lombok   EAST TIMOR   *Arafura Sea*
Sumba   *Timor*

JAPAN AND KOREA

Rugged mountains interspersed with lowlands dominate the landscapes of Japan and Korea. The Korean mountains are old and stable, but most of Japan's highest peaks are volcanic. Japan lies in an unstable zone. Earthquakes and tsunamis (powerful sea waves triggered by earth movements) are constant threats. The region has a monsoon climate, with hot, wet summers and cold winters.

Until fairly recent times, Japan and Korea were cut off from the rest of the world. But from the late 1860s, Japan began to modernize and become a world power. Its defeat in World War II proved a challenge. With help from the United States, it has become a major industrial power. Korea, which had been occupied by Japan from 1910 to 1945, is now split into free-enterprise South Korea and the communist North.

Japan and Korea occupy a frontier zone between Eurasia and the Pacific Ocean. Japan forms part of the Pacific "ring of fire," a zone of crustal instability that encircles the Pacific Ocean. Japan has 60 active volcanoes and has over a thousand earthquakes every year.

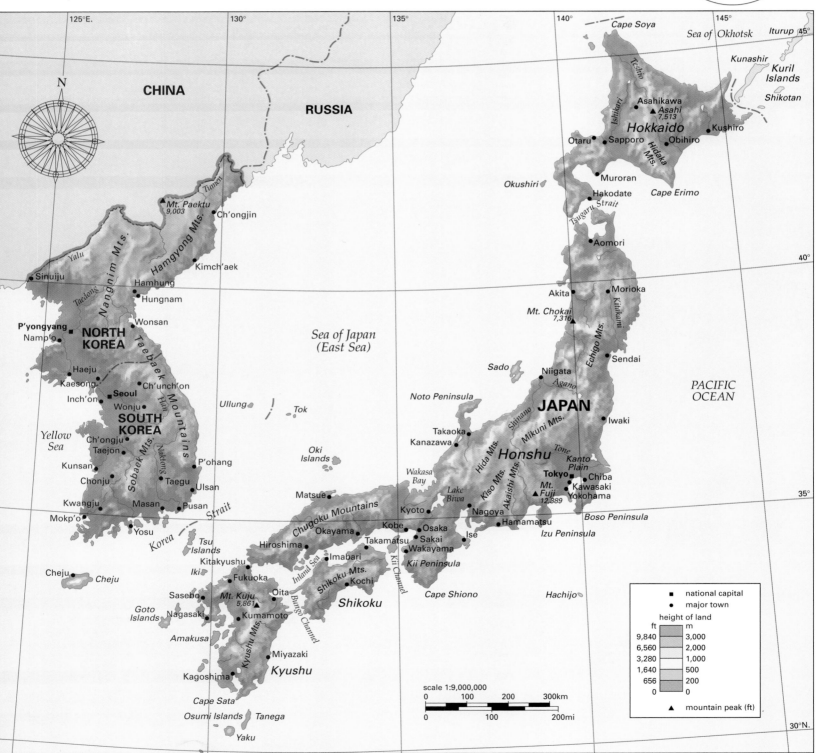

THE POLITICAL AND CULTURAL WORLD

B efore World War II, Japan was a military dictatorship. After the war, the Allied forces occupied the country from 1945 to 1952. During this time a new constitution was adopted in which power was vested in a prime minister and cabinet, who were answerable to the Diet (parliament). The emperor was subsequently given a symbolic role in the country's leadership.

Korea was split into two parts in 1945. Separate governments for North and South Korea were set up in 1947. This action triggered the Korean War (1948–1953). In recent years, talks have been held about reunification, but little progress has been made.

COUNTRIES IN THE REGION

Japan, North Korea, South Korea
Island territories Ryukyu Islands (including Okinawa) (see map on page 128)
Disputed territories Japan/Russia (Kuril Islands and south Sakhalin)

MEMBERSHIP OF INTERNATIONAL ORGANIZATIONS

Colombo Plan Japan
Organization for Economic Cooperation and Development (OECD) Japan

LANGUAGE

Countries with one official language (Japanese) Japan; (Korean) North Korea, South Korea

RELIGION

Japan Most Japanese are adherents both of Shinto (93.1%) and Buddhism (73.9%); Christian (1.4%)
North Korea Nonreligious or atheist (67.9%), traditional beliefs (15.6%), Ch'ondogyo (13.9%), Buddhist (1.7%), Christian (0.9%)
South Korea Nonreligious or atheist (57.4%), Christian (20.7%), Buddhist (19.9%), Confucianist (1.2%), Ch'ondogyo (0.1%), others (0.7%)

STYLES OF GOVERNMENT

Republics North Korea, South Korea
Monarchy Japan
Multiparty states Japan, South Korea
One-party state North Korea
One-chamber assembly North Korea, South Korea
Two-chamber assembly Japan

ECONOMIC INDICATORS

	Japan	S. Korea
GDP (US$ billions)	4,201.6	438.2
GNP per capita (US$)	23,400	13,500
Annual rate of growth of GDP, 1990–1997	1.5%	7.2%
Manufacturing as % of GDP	24.3%	25.7%
Merchandise exports (US$ billions)	409.2	138.5
Merchandise imports (US$ billions)	307.6	141.8
Aid given as % of GNP	0.2%	n/a

WELFARE INDICATORS

	Japan	S. Korea
Infant mortality rate (per 1,000 live births)		
1965	18	62
2000	4	10
Daily food supply available (calories per capita, 1995)	2,887	3,268
Population per physician (1995)	546	784
Teacher-pupil ratio (primary school, 1995)	1 : 19.5	1 : 27.5

North Korea
Area 46,541 sq mi (120,540 sq km)
Population 21,687,550
Capital P'yongyang
Currency 1 won (Wn) = 100 chon

South Korea
Area 38,023 sq mi (98,480 sq km)
Population 47,470,969
Capital Seoul
Currency 1 won (W) = 100 chun

Area 145,883 sq mi (377,835 sq km)
Population 126,549,976
Capital Tokyo
Currency 1 yen ¥= 100 sen

Japan

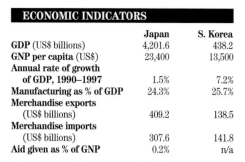

Japan is a constitutional monarchy. An emperor is the ceremonial head of state. The country is divided into 47 prefectures. South Korea is a republic, divided into nine provinces and five cities with the rank of province. North Korea is a communist state, divided into nine provinces and four city areas.

■ national capital
● other town

HABITATS

Both Japan and Korea are largely mountainous, with uplands extending to the sea and with few large coastal lowlands. There are extensive forests throughout the region on the mountain slopes and cultivation of crops in the fertile valleys.

LAND

Area 230,448 sq mi (596,855 sq km)
Highest point Mount Fuji, 12,388 ft (3,776 m)
Lowest point sea level
Major features mountains of moderate height cover most of Japan and Korea; over 3,900 islands in Japan

WATER

Longest river Yalu, 503 mi (810 km)
Largest basin Yalu, 24,000 sq mi (63,000 sq km)
Highest average flow Yalu, 19,000 cu ft/sec (526 cu m/sec)
Largest lake Biwa, 268 sq mi (695 sq km)

NOTABLE THREATENED SPECIES

Mammals Amami rabbit (*Pentalagus furnessi*), Iriomote cat (*Felis iriomotensis*)
Birds Short-tailed albatross (*Diomeda albatrus*), Okinawa rail (*Rallus okinawae*), Amami thrush (*Zoothera amami*). Okinawa woodpecker (*Sapheopipo noguchi*)
Others Japanese giant salamander (*Andrias japonicus*), Tokyo bitterling (*Tanakia tanago*)
Plants Korean fir (*Abies koreana*); *Arisaema heterocephalum*; *Chrysanthemum zawadskii*; *Cyclobalanopsis hondae*; *Cymbidium koran*; *Euphrasia omiensis*; *Fritillaria shikokiana*; *Gentiana yakusimensis*; *Magnolia pseudokobus*; *Rhododendron mucronulatum*

ENVIRONMENTAL ISSUES

Concern about environmental issues is increasing, especially in Japan. Most problems are caused by overcrowding and the rapid development of industry. Minamata disease, for example, is caused by eating seafood that has absorbed mercury from toxic industrial wastes.

POPULATION AND WEALTH

	Japan	N. Korea	S. Korea
Population (millions)	126.549	21.687	47.470
Population increase (annual growth rate 1990–95)	0.2%	1.6%	0.8%
Energy use (lbs/year per person of oil equivalent)	9,006	2,238	8,501
Purchasing power parity (Int$/per year)	24,084	—	13,665

ENVIRONMENTAL INDICATORS

CO₂ emissions (m. tons/year)	1,126,753	256,986	373,592
Car ownership (% of population)	50%	n/a	14%
Proportion of territory protected, including marine areas	7%	3%	7%
Forests as a % of original forest	58%	39%	16%
Artificial fertilizer use (lbs/acre/year)	364	52	573
Access to safe drinking water (% population; rural/urban)	100/100%	100/100%	76/100%

MAJOR ENVIRONMENTAL PROBLEMS AND SOURCES

Air pollution: locally high, urban high; acid rain prevalent; high greenhouse gas emissions
River/lake pollution: medium; *sources:* industry, agriculture, sewage
Marine/coastal pollution: medium; *sources:* industry, agricultural, sewage, oil
Land pollution: local; *sources:* industrial, urban/household
Population issues: urban overcrowding
Major events: Hiroshima (1945), destroyed by atom bomb; Nagasaki (1945), destroyed by atom bomb; Minamata (1940s–60s) leakage of mercury from industry; Taegu (1991), chemicals dumped in river; oil tanker *Nakhodka* spill (1997)
Resource issues: overfishing

CLIMATE

During the winter, North Korea and northern Japan are cooled by polar air, producing low temperatures and heavy snowfalls. In the summer, wet monsoon winds bring hot and humid weather, especially in the south. Typhoons, or hurricanes, often strike eastern Japan.

CLIMATE

	Temperature °F (°C)		Altitude
	January	July	ft (m)
Wonsan	25 (–4)	73 (23)	39 (12)
Seoul	23 (–5)	75 (24)	282 (86)
Sapporo	21 (–6)	68 (20)	59 (18)
Niigata	36 (2)	75 (24)	13 (4)
Tokyo	39 (4)	77 (25)	20 (6)

	Precipitation in. (mm)		
	January	July	Year
Wonsan	1.1 (29)	10.7 (273)	51.6 (1,310)
Seoul	0.7 (17)	14.1 (358)	49.5 (1,258)
Sapporo	4.4 (111)	3.9 (100)	44.7 (1,136)
Niigata	7.6 (194)	7.6 (193)	72.5 (1,841)
Tokyo	1.9 (48)	5.8 (146)	61.5 (1,563)

NATURAL HAZARDS

Earthquakes and associated sea waves (tsunami) in Japan, floods, typhoons, landslides

HABITATS

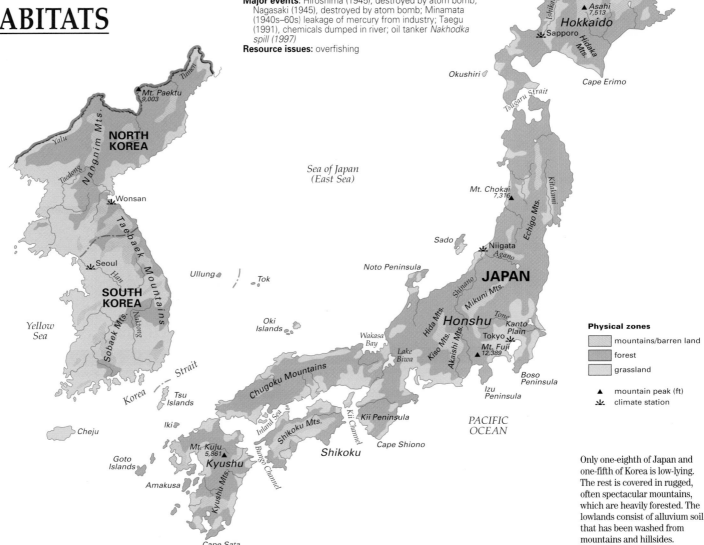

Physical zones
mountains/barren land
forest
grassland
▲ mountain peak (ft)
☼ climate station

Only one-eighth of Japan and one-fifth of Korea is low-lying. The rest is covered in rugged, often spectacular mountains, which are heavily forested. The lowlands consist of alluvium soil that has been washed from mountains and hillsides.

ENVIRONMENTAL ISSUES

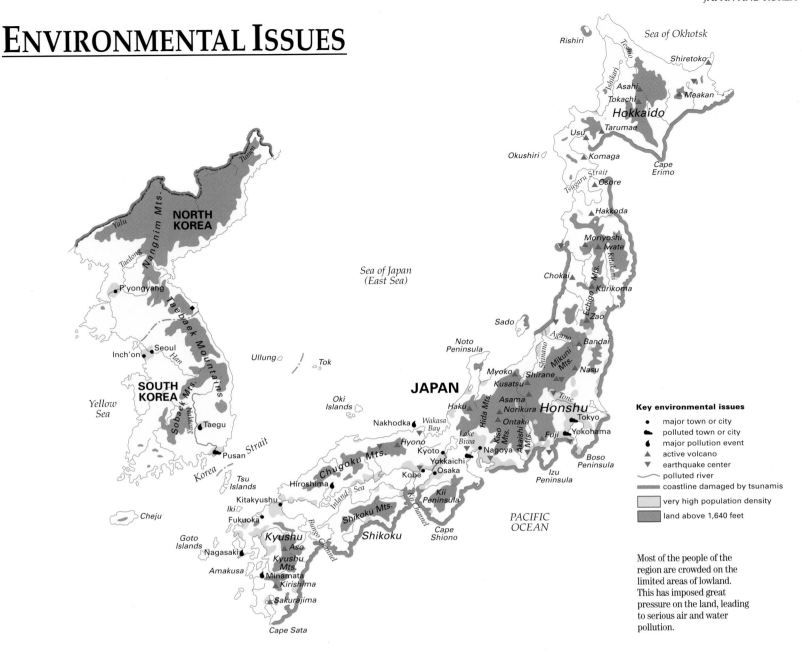

NORTH KOREA

Sea of Okhotsk

Rishiri

Shiretoko

Teshio

Ishikari

Asahi

Tokachi

Meakan

Hokkaido

Usu

Tarumae

Okushiri

Komaga

Cape Erimo

Tsugaru Strait

Osore

Hakkoda

Nangnim Mts.

Yalu

Taedong

P'yongyang

Taebaek Mountains

Sea of Japan (East Sea)

Moriyoshi

Iwate

Kitakami Mts.

Chokai

Kurikoma

Echigo Mts.

Zao

Sado

Agano

Bandai

Inch'on

Seoul

Han

Ullung

Tok

Noto Peninsula

Shinano

Mikuni Mts.

Nasu

SOUTH KOREA

Sobaek Mts.

Naktong

Yellow Sea

JAPAN

Myoko

Kusatsu

Shirane

Asama

Norikura

Haku

Hida Mts.

Ontake

Honshu

Tokyo

Tone

Fuji

Yokohama

Taegu

Nakhodka

Wakasa Bay

Lake Biwa

Kiso Mts.

Akaishi Mts.

Nagoya

Boso Peninsula

Pusan

Korea Strait

Oki Islands

Hyono

Kyoto

Yokkaichi

Osaka

Izu Peninsula

Tsu Islands

Chugoku Mts.

Kobe

Cheju

Hiroshima

Inland Sea

Kii Peninsula

Kii Channel

Kitakyushu

Iki

Fukuoka

Bungo Channel

Shikoku Mts.

Shikoku

Cape Shiono

PACIFIC OCEAN

Goto Islands

Nagasaki

Kyushu

Aso

Kyushu Mts.

Amakusa

Minamata

Kirishima

Sakurajima

Cape Sata

Key environmental issues

- ● major town or city
- ◖ polluted town or city
- ◗ major pollution event
- ▲ active volcano
- ▼ earthquake center
- ～ polluted river
- ▬ coastline damaged by tsunamis
- ▢ very high population density
- ▨ land above 1,640 feet

Most of the people of the region are crowded on the limited areas of lowland. This has imposed great pressure on the land, leading to serious air and water pollution.

CLIMATE

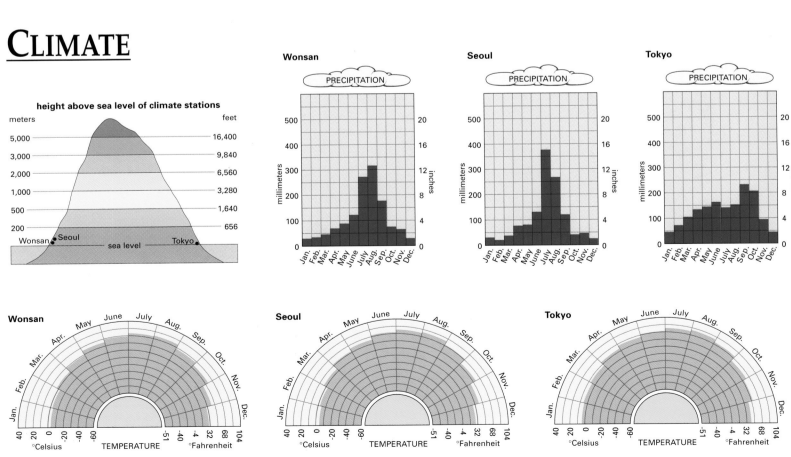

height above sea level of climate stations

meters		feet
5,000		16,400
3,000		9,840
2,000		6,560
1,000		3,280
500		1,640
200		656

Wonsan Seoul   Tokyo

sea level

Wonsan PRECIPITATION

millimeters / inches

Jan. Feb. Mar. Apr. May June July Aug. Sep. Oct. Nov. Dec.

Seoul PRECIPITATION

millimeters / inches

Jan. Feb. Mar. Apr. May June July Aug. Sep. Oct. Nov. Dec.

Tokyo PRECIPITATION

millimeters / inches

Jan. Feb. Mar. Apr. May June July Aug. Sep. Oct. Nov. Dec.

Wonsan

TEMPERATURE

°Celsius   °Fahrenheit

Seoul

TEMPERATURE

°Celsius   °Fahrenheit

Tokyo

TEMPERATURE

°Celsius   °Fahrenheit

POPULATION

Between 1870 and 1970, Japan's population rose from 30 million to over 100 million. The annual growth rate has now dropped, averaging 0.5 percent between 1980 and 1991. The growth rate in North and South Korea is also below the world average of 1.7 percent.

POPULATION

Total population of region (millions)			195.7
	S.Korea	N. Korea	Japan
Population density (persons per sq mi)	1,210	486	873
Population change (average annual percent 1960–1990)			
Urban	+1.73%	+1.93%	+0.37%
Rural	–2.83%	+1.00%	–0.44%

URBAN POPULATION

As percentage of total population (1990)	82%	60%	79%

TEN LARGEST CITIES

	Country	Population
Seoul †	South Korea	10,231,217
Tokyo †	Japan	7,967,614
Pusan	South Korea	3,814,325
Yokohama	Japan	3,307,136
Pyongyang †	North Korea	2,639,000
Osaka	Japan	2,602,421
Taegu	South Korea	2,449,420
Inchon	South Korea	2,308,188
Nagoya	Japan	2,152,184
Sapporo	Japan	1,757,025

† denotes capital city
City population figures are for the city proper.

INDUSTRY

The region has limited natural resources, and the countries import many raw materials. By developing modern technology, they have become world leaders in manufacturing. Their technical expertise ensures the quality and saleability of their products.

INDUSTRIAL OUTPUT (US $)

South Korea (1997)	190 billion
Japan (1996)	1.74 trillion

INDUSTRIAL WORKERS (millions)
(figures in parentheses are percentages of total labor force)

	Total	Mining	Manufacturing	Construction
Japan (1996)	67.1	0.06 (0.1%)	14.45 (21.5%)	6.7 (10.0%)
S. Korea	21.19	0.024 (0.1%)	4.677 (22.1%)	1.97 (9.3%)
N. Korea	3.48 (30%)	n/a	n/a	n/a

MAJOR PRODUCTS

Energy and minerals	Output 1970	1995
Steel (Japan)	93,322	101,640

Manufactures		
Automobiles (Japan)	3,179	7,864
Ships ('000 gross tons)		
Japan	10,476	9,640
S. Korea	0	5,000
Cement ('000 tons)		
Japan	57,189	90,468
S. Korea	5,782	56,100
Copper (Japan) ('000 tons)	705	1,979
Radio receivers (Japan) ('000)	32,618	7,299

AGRICULTURE

Because only 14 percent of the land can be cultivated, farming is generally intensive and scientific, using irrigation, fertilizers, farm machinery, and improved seeds. Mountainous land is terraced along traditional lines to control soil erosion from rain and wind.

LAND
Total area 230,448 sq mi (596,855 sq km)

Cropland	Pasture	Forest/Woodland
14% (32,667 sq mi)	1% (3,235 sq mi)	65% (149,150 sq mi)

MAJOR CROPS: Agricultural products fruit and vegetables; rice, corn; sugar beet; soybeans; pulses; pork, cattle, poultry; dairy produce; fish

	Japan	North Korea	South Korea
Total cropland (m. acres)	10,613	4,942	4,754
Cropland (acres) per 1,000 people	84	215	104
Irrigated land as % of cropland	63%	73%	60%
Number of tractors	2,210,000	75,000	131,358
Average cereal crop yields (lbs/acre)	4,982	1,862	5,450
Cereal production ('000 tons)	12,995	3,142	7,748
Change since 1986–88	–12%	–59%	–12%

LIVESTOCK & FISHERIES

Meat production ('000 tons)	3,081	146	1,614
Change since 1986–88	–20%	–76%	158%
Marine fish catch ('000 tons)	4,524	220	1,635
Change since 1986–88	–53%	–86%	–15%

POPULATION

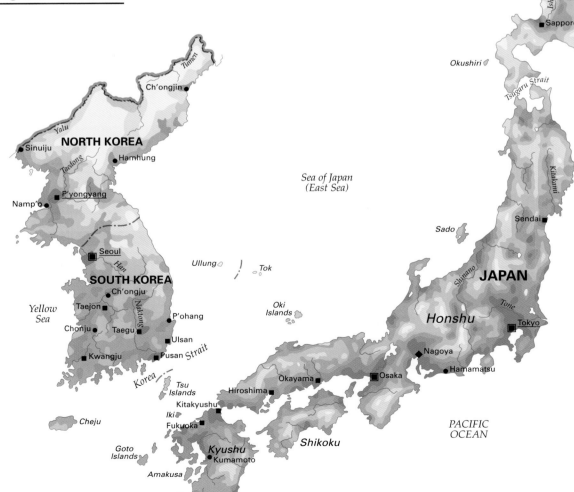

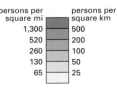

Population density

urban agglomeration
(National capital is underlined)

■	over 10,000,000
◆	5,000,000–10,000,000
■	1,000,000–4,999,999
●	500,000–999,999

persons per square mi	persons per square km
1,300	500
520	200
260	100
130	50
65	25

Since 1950, many people have moved from rural areas into the cities and towns on the coastal lowlands. This migration occurred mainly because of the many jobs available in the new manufacturing industries.

INDUSTRY

North and South Korea have coal resources and hydroelectric power projects. Japan imports most of the fuels it needs for domestic and industrial uses.

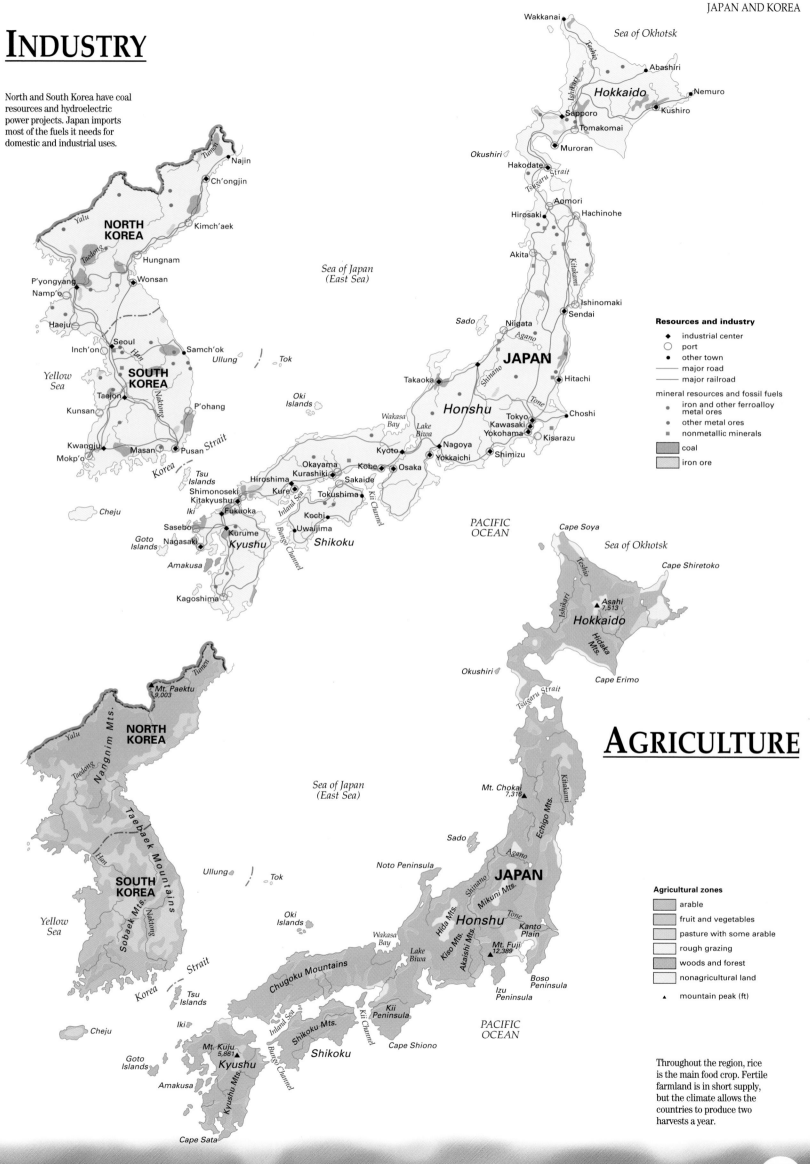

Sea of Okhotsk

Wakkanai
Abashiri
Nemuro
Hokkaido
Sapporo
Kushiro
Tomakomai
Muroran
Okushiri
Hakodate
Tsugaru Strait
Aomori
Hirosaki
Hachinohe
Akita
Ishinomaki
Sendai
Najin
Ch'ongjin
Yalu
NORTH KOREA
Kimch'aek
Taedong
Hungnam
P'yongyang
Wonsan
Namp'o
Sea of Japan (East Sea)
Sado
Niigata
Agano
JAPAN
Shinano
Honshu
Hitachi
Haeju
Seoul
Inch'on
SOUTH KOREA
Samch'ok
Ullung
Tok
Oki Islands
Takaoka
Tokyo
Kawasaki
Yokohama
Choshi
Tone
Wakasa Bay
Lake Biwa
Kyoto
Nagoya
Yokkaichi
Kisarazu
Shimizu
Taejon
Naktong
P'ohang
Kunsan
Kwangju
Mokp'o
Masan
Pusan
Korea Strait
Tsu Islands
Okayama
Kobe
Osaka
Kurashiki
Sakaide
Hiroshima
Kure
Tokushima
Kii Channel
Shimonoseki
Kitakyushu
Iki
Fukuoka
Kochi
Inland Sea
Uwajima
Shikoku
Cheju
Sasebo
Kurume
Nagasaki
Goto Islands
Kyushu
Amakusa
Bungo Channel
Kagoshima
PACIFIC OCEAN

Resources and industry
◆ industrial center
○ port
• other town
— major road
— major railroad

mineral resources and fossil fuels
• iron and other ferroalloy metal ores
• other metal ores
■ nonmetallic minerals
▨ coal
▨ iron ore

AGRICULTURE

Cape Soya
Sea of Okhotsk
Cape Shiretoko
Teshio
Ishikari
▲ Asahi 7,513
Hokkaido
Hidaka Mts.
Cape Erimo
Okushiri
Tsugaru Strait
Mt. Paektu 9,003 ▲
Tumen
Yalu
NORTH KOREA
Nangnim Mts.
Taedong
Taebaek Mountains
SOUTH KOREA
Han
Sobaek Mts.
Naktong
Yellow Sea
Sea of Japan (East Sea)
Ullung
Tok
Oki Islands
Sado
Agano
Noto Peninsula
Mt. Chokai 7,316 ▲
Kitakami
Echigo Mts.
Shinano
JAPAN
Mikuni Mts.
Hida Mts.
Tone
Kanto Plain
Honshu
Wakasa Bay
Lake Biwa
Kiso Mts.
Akaishi Mts.
▲ Mt. Fuji 12,389
Izu Peninsula
Boso Peninsula
Chugoku Mountains
Korea Strait
Tsu Islands
Iki
Inland Sea
Shikoku Mts.
Kii Peninsula
Kii Channel
Cape Shiono
Cheju
Goto Islands
Mt. Kuju 5,861 ▲
Kyushu Mts.
Kyushu
Amakusa
Bungo Channel
Shikoku
Cape Sata
PACIFIC OCEAN

Agricultural zones
▨ arable
▨ fruit and vegetables
▨ pasture with some arable
▨ rough grazing
▨ woods and forest
▨ nonagricultural land
▲ mountain peak (ft)

Throughout the region, rice is the main food crop. Fertile farmland is in short supply, but the climate allows the countries to produce two harvests a year.

AUSTRALIA AND ITS NEIGHBORS

Australia is the world's sixth largest country and its smallest continent. Most of the land is flat—plains or level plateaus make up nine-tenths of Australia. Papua New Guinea is more mountainous but has large lowlands.

The climate ranges from tropical in the north to Mediterranean in the south, though the interior is semiarid or desert. The southeast and Tasmania have a mild temperate climate.

Australia's Aboriginal people arrived from Southeast Asia at least 40,000 years ago. A nomadic people, they developed complex cultural and religious traditions. Most Australians today are of European descent, especially from Britain. Recent arrivals include Asians. Australia is a leading exporter of agricultural products, although the most important part of the economy is manufacturing.

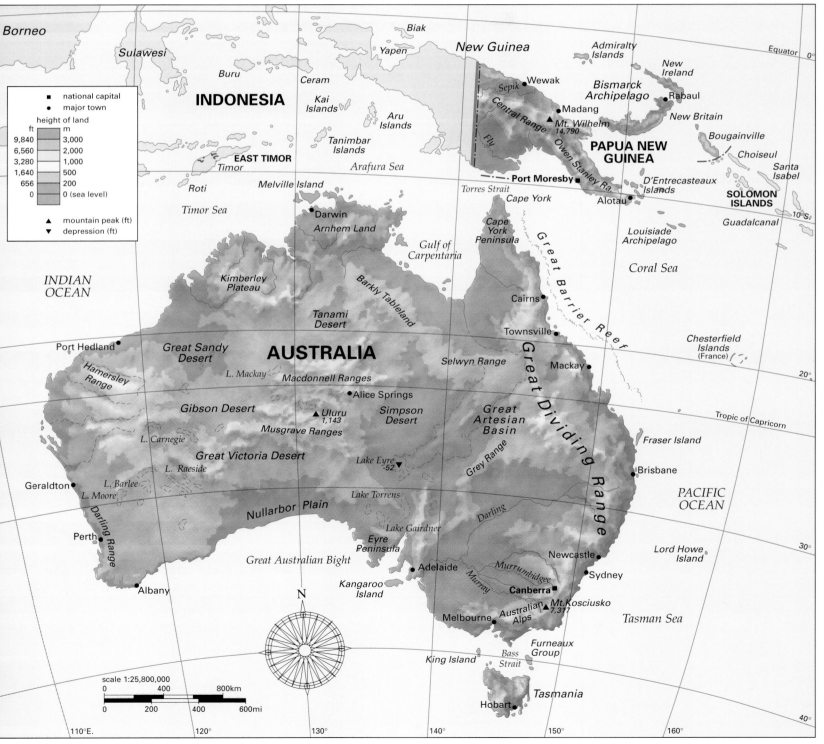

140

THE POLITICAL AND CULTURAL WORLD

In 1901, the former British colonies of New South Wales, Queensland, South Australia, Tasmania, Victoria, and Western Australia became states and federated to become the independent Commonwealth of Australia. Northern Territory was transferred from South Australia as a territory in 1911.

Today Australia remains a constitutional monarchy – its head of state is the British monarch, who is represented by a governor-general. Papua New Guinea, which was under Australian control during the colonial period, is another constitutional monarchy. Both countries are members of the British Commonwealth. In 1999 Australian voters rejected a republic, opting for the continuation of the British monarchy.

- national capital
- state capital
- other town

Area 178,704 sq mi (462,840 sq km)
Population 4,926,984
Capital Port Moresby
Currency 1 Papua New Guinea kina (K) = 100 toea

Papua New Guinea

Area 2,967,916 sq mi (7,686,850 sq km)
Population 19,169,083
Capital Canberra
Currency 1 Australian dollar ($A) = 100 cents

Australia

Although Australia is a constitutional monarchy, political power is vested in the federal government, led by the prime minister. Each state also has its own parliament to deal with such matters as education and public welfare.

Habitats

Northern Australia is tropical, with much savanna grassland that merges into the country's arid center. The east coast has tropical forests, with a range of mountains extending north to south. There are large grassland areas in the southwest and southeast.

LAND

Area 3,146,620 sq mi (8,149,690 sq km)
Highest point Mount Wilhelm, Papua New Guinea 14,790 ft (4,508 m)
Lowest point Lake Eyre, Australia, –52 ft (–16 m)
Major features Australia, 2,967,916 sq mi (7,686,850 sq km), is the world's lowest continent

WATER

Longest river Murray–Darling, 2,330 mi (3,780 km)
Largest basin Murray–Darling, 414,100 sq mi (1,072,000 sq km)
Highest average flow Murray, 14,000 cu ft/sec (400 cu m/sec)
Largest lake Eyre, 3,400 sq mi (8,900 sq km) when flooded

NOTABLE THREATENED SPECIES

Mammals Northern hairy-nosed wombat *(Lasiorhinus krefftii)*, numbat *(Myrmecobius fasciatus)*, Greater bilby *(Macrotis lagotis)*
Birds Paradise parrot *(Psephotus pulcherrimus)*,
Others Western swamp turtle *(Pseudemydura umbrina)*, Baw baw frog *(Philoria frosti)*
Plants Good's banksia (*Banksia goodii*), Huon pine (*Dacrydium franklinii*), caesia (*Eucalyptus caesia*), stag's horn fern (*Platycerium grande*)

Climate

Papua New Guinea and northern Australia have a tropical climate. The interior of Australia is very dry. Mediterranean climates occur in the south. The east is subtropical, while the southeast and Tasmania have warm summers and cool winters.

CLIMATE

	Temperature °F (°C) January	July	Altitude ft (m)
Darwin	82 (28)	77 (25)	89 (27)
Perth	73 (23)	55 (13)	197 (60)
Alice Springs	82 (28)	54 (12)	1,797 (548)
Sydney	72 (22)	54 (12)	138 (42)
Port Moresby	82 (28)	77 (25)	62 (19)

	Precipitation in. (mm) January	July	Year
Darwin	16.1 (409)	0.04 (1)	65.4 (1,661)
Perth	0.3 (8)	7.2 (183)	34.4 (873)
Alice Springs	1.5 (39)	0.4 (10)	9.9 (252)
Sydney	4.0 (102)	4.0 (101)	47.8 (1,214)
Port Moresby	7.1 (178)	1.1 (28)	40 (1,012)

Environmental Issues

While the Aboriginal people generally live in harmony with nature, the rapid population increase in the last 200 years and the spread of livestock farming has led to a depletion of plants and animals. Introduced species, such as rabbits, have caused much damage.

POPULATION AND WEALTH

	Australia
Population (millions)	19.169
Population increase (annual growth rate,% 1990–95)	1.0%
Energy use (lbs per year per person of oil equivalent)	12,220
Purchasing power parity (Int$/year)	20,430

ENVIRONMENTAL INDICATORS

CO_2 emissions ('000 tons/year)	289,808
Car ownership (% of population)	56%
Forests as a % of original forest	64%
Artificial fertilizer use (lbs/acre/year)	16 (Papua New Guinea)
Access to safe drinking water (% population; rural/urban)	100%/100% (Papua New Guinea, 23%/78%)

MAJOR ENVIRONMENTAL PROBLEMS AND SOURCES

Air pollution: urban high
Marine/coastal pollution: medium; *sources*: industry, agriculture, sewage, tourism
Land degradation: *types*: desertification, soil erosion, salinization, deforestation, coastal degradation, habitat destruction; *causes*: agriculture, industry, population pressure, tourism
Resource issues: inadequate drinking water; inadequate sanitation; coastal flooding; coral deaths

Habitats

Physical zones

- mountains/barren land
- forest
- grassland
- semidesert
- desert

▲ mountain peak (ft)
▼ depression (ft)
climate station

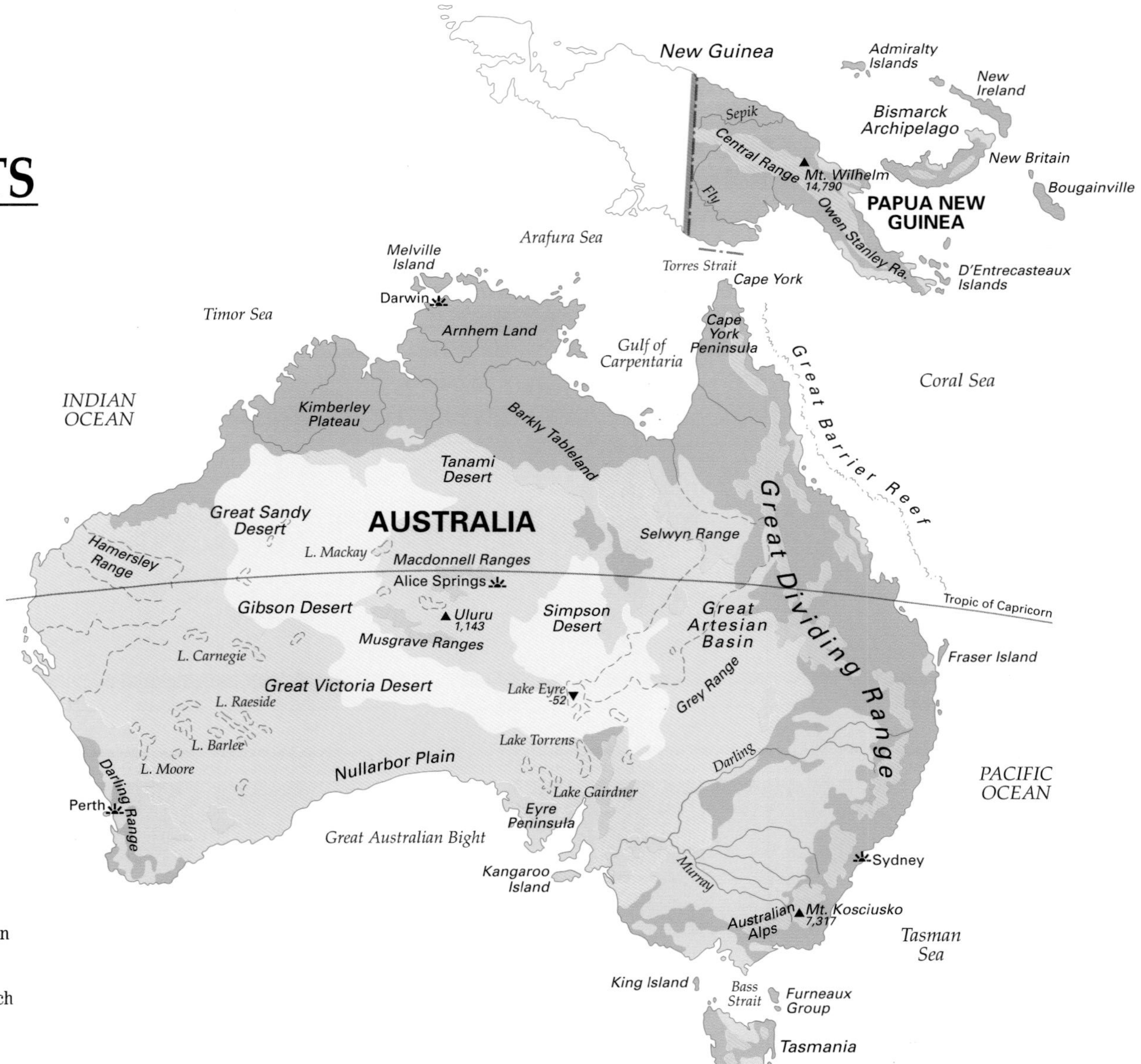

Behind the narrow coastal plain in the east lies the Great Dividing Range of mountains. Beyond lie the grasslands, which merge to the west into the semideserts and deserts of the vast western plateaus.

ENVIRONMENTAL ISSUES

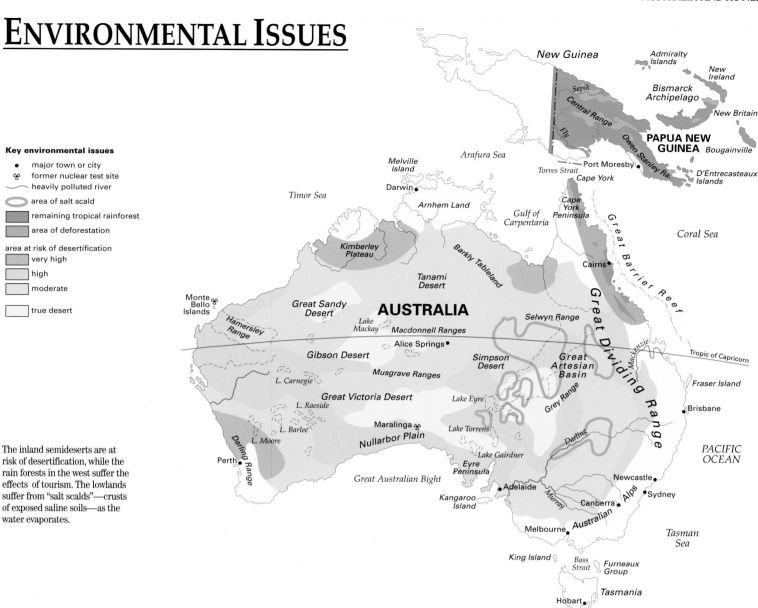

Key environmental issues

- • major town or city
- ✾ former nuclear test site
- ∼ heavily polluted river
- ⬭ area of salt scald
- ▬ remaining tropical rainforest
- ▬ area of deforestation

area at risk of desertification
- ▬ very high
- ▬ high
- ▬ moderate
- □ true desert

The inland semideserts are at risk of desertification, while the rain forests in the west suffer the effects of tourism. The lowlands suffer from "salt scalds"—crusts of exposed saline soils—as the water evaporates.

CLIMATE

height above sea level of climate stations

meters		feet
5,000		16,400
3,000		9,840
2,000		6,560
1,000		3,280
500	• Alice Springs	1,640
200		656
	• Darwin sea level Sydney •	

Darwin — PRECIPITATION

Alice Springs — PRECIPITATION

Sydney — PRECIPITATION

Darwin — TEMPERATURE

Alice Springs — TEMPERATURE

Sydney — TEMPERATURE

POPULATION

Australia has one of the world's lowest average population densities, but 86 percent of its people live in cities and towns on the coasts, making it one of the more urbanized countries. In Papua New Guinea, 84 percent of the people live in rural areas.

POPULATION

Total population of region (millions)	24.1
Population density (persons per sq mi)	6.2 (Australia)

Population change (average annual percent 1995–2000)	
	(Australia)
Urban	+1.02%
Rural	+1.02%

URBAN POPULATION

As percentage of total population 1995	85%

TEN LARGEST CITIES

	Population
Sydney	3,985,800
Melbourne	3,317,300
Brisbane	1,535,300
Perth	1,365,600
Adelaide	1,115,900
Newcastle	479,200
Gold Coast	373,200
Canberra †	320,200
Wollongong	262,900
Port Moresby (Papua New Guinea)	250,000

† denotes capital city

City population figures are for the city proper.

INDUSTRY

Mining is a major industry in Australia. Some raw materials are exported to Japan and elsewhere, but other materials are used in local manufacturing industries. Australia's industries concentrate on producing consumer goods for domestic use and for export.

INDUSTRIAL OUTPUT (US $ billion)

Australia (1996)	106

INDUSTRIAL WORKERS (millions)
(figures in parentheses are percentages of total labor force)

	Total	Mining	Manufacturing	Construction
Australia	9.06	1.11 (12.3%)	0.085 (0.9%)	0.6 (6.6%)

MAJOR PRODUCTS (Australia)

Energy and minerals	Output change	
	1970	1995
Bituminous coal (mil m.t.)	44	193
Copper ('000 m.t.)	146	320
Copper ore ('000 m.t.)	142	365
Zinc ('000 m.t.)	264	320
Zinc ore ('000 m.t.)	496	937
Iron ore (mil m.t.)	29	91
Manganese ('000 m.t.)	397	980
Uranium ('000 m.t.)	299	3,712
Steel ('000 m.t.)	6,874	8,052
Bauxite ('000 m.t.)	3,294	42,660
Gold (m.t.)	19.4	254
Lead ore ('000 m.t.)	459	455

AGRICULTURE

Australia's prosperity was based on farming. Cattle, wheat, and wool are major products, as are dairy products, fruit, and sugarcane. Australia now exports mainly in the Pacific region since its trade with Britain, its main trading partner, declined in the 1970s.

LAND
Total area 3,146,620 (8,149,690 sq km)

FARMERS	Australia
Agriculture as % of GDP	3%
% of workforce	5%

MAJOR CROPS: Agricultural products: fruit and vegetables: sweet potatoes, bananas, breadfruit; potatoes, yams; wheat, barley, rice; sugarcane; coconuts, copra; cassava; pulses; taro; coffee, tea, cocoa; palm kernels; rubber; timber; spices; cattle, sheep, goats, poultry; dairy products; wine; fish

Total cropland ('000 acres)	131,210
Cropland (acres) per 1,000 people	7,156
Irrigated land as % of cropland	5%
Number of tractors	315,000
Average cereal crop yields (lbs/acre)	1,650
Cereal production ('000 tons) Change since 1986/88	32,534 48%

LIVESTOCK & FISHERIES

Meat production ('000 tons) Change since 1986/88	3,335 31%
Marine fish catch ('000 tons) Change since 1986/88	126.8 21%

FOOD SECURITY

Food aid as % of total imports	n/a
Daily kcal/person	3,224

POPULATION

Population density

urban agglomeration
(National capital is underlined)

- ■ 1,000,000–5,000,000
- ● 500,000–999,999
- ◉ 250,000–499,999
- ○ 100,000–249,999

persons per square mi		persons per square km
260		100
130		50
26		10
2.6		1

The cities of Sydney, Melbourne, Brisbane, Perth, and Adelaide together contain about 60 percent of Australia's population. Most of the interior is uninhabited. Papua New Guinea is also thinly populated.

INDUSTRY

Australia has many valuable reserves of metals, coal, oil, and precious stones, including opals. Papua New Guinea has some gold and copper.

Resources and industry

- ◆ industrial center
- ○ port
- ● other town
- major road
- major railroad

mineral resources and fossil fuels

- ● iron and other ferroalloy metal ores
- ● other metal ores
- ■ nonmetallic minerals

- bauxite
- coal
- diamonds
- iron ore
- lignite (brown coal)
- natural gas
- oil

AGRICULTURE

Agricultural zones

- arable and grazing
- fruit, vines and vegetables
- pasture with some arable
- rough grazing
- woods and forest
- nonagricultural land

- ▲ mountain peak (feet)
- ▼ depression (feet)

The main farming zones are in the southeast and southwest, including the Murray-Darling river basin. Sheep and cattle are raised in the Great Artesian Basin.

NEW ZEALAND AND ITS NEIGHBORS

Neew Zealand is an island nation with snow-capped mountains, fertile green plains, forested hills, and volcanic regions famous for their bubbling hot springs and explosive geysers. The climate varies from subtropical in North Island to wet temperate on South Island. The Southern Alps on South Island have a severe mountain climate.

The Maoris, a Polynesian people, settled in New Zealand (called Aotearoa, or "Land of the Long White Cloud") about A.D. 750. Dutch sailors reached the islands in 1642, but Europeans did not settle there until the early 1800s. Most New Zealanders are descendants of British immigrants. The country's economy was founded on farming and foreign trade.

New Zealand lies in the southwestern Pacific Ocean, 994 miles (1,600 km) southeast of Australia. It is in an unstable zone, characterized by earthquakes and volcanic eruptions. Glacial action has carved scenic fjords into the southwest coast of South Island.

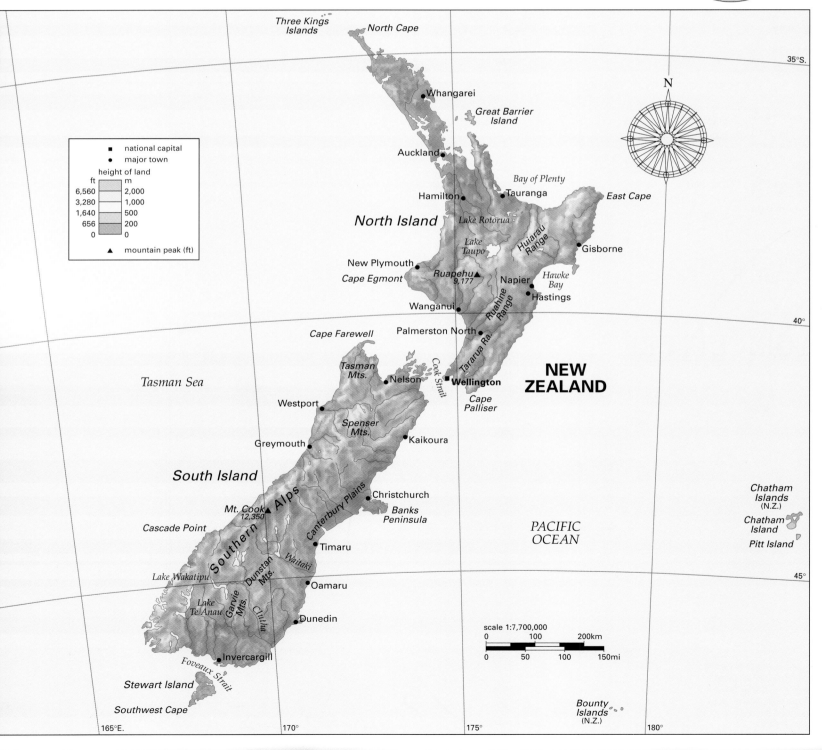

THE POLITICAL AND CULTURAL WORLD

With its Maori population, New Zealand is regarded as part of Polynesia, which also includes the independent island nations of Tonga, Tuvalu, and Samoa, as well as the American state of Hawaii.

Micronesia lies mainly in the North Pacific and includes Kiribati, Nauru, the Marshall Islands, Palau and the Federated States of Micronesia. Kiribati contains both Polynesians and Micronesians. Melanesia includes Papua New Guinea, the Solomon Islands, Vanuatu, and Fiji.

Fiji
Area 7,054 sq mi (18,270 sq km)
Population 832,494
Capital Suva

Kiribati
Area 277 sq mi (717 sq km)
Population 91,985
Capital Tarawa

Marshall Islands
Area 70 sq mi (181.3 sq km)
Population 68,126
Capital Majuro

Micronesia
Area 271 sq mi (702 sq km)
Population 133,144
Capital Palikir

Nauru
Area 8 sq mi (21 sq km)
Population 11,845
Capital Yaren

New Zealand
Area 103,738 sq mi (268,680 sq km)
Population 3,819,762
Capital Wellington

Palau
Area 177 sq mi (458 sq km)
Population 18,766
Capital Koror

Samoa
Area 1,104 sq mi (2,860 sq km)
Population 179,466
Capital Apia

Solomon Islands
Area 10,985 sq mi (28,450 sq km)
Population 466,194
Capital Honiara

Tonga
Area 289 sq mi (748 sq km)
Population 102,321
Capital Nuku'alofa

Tuvalu
Area 10 sq mi (26 sq km)
Population 10,838
Capital Funafuti

Vanuatu
Area 5,699 sq mi (14,760 sq km)
Population 189,618
Capital Port-Vila

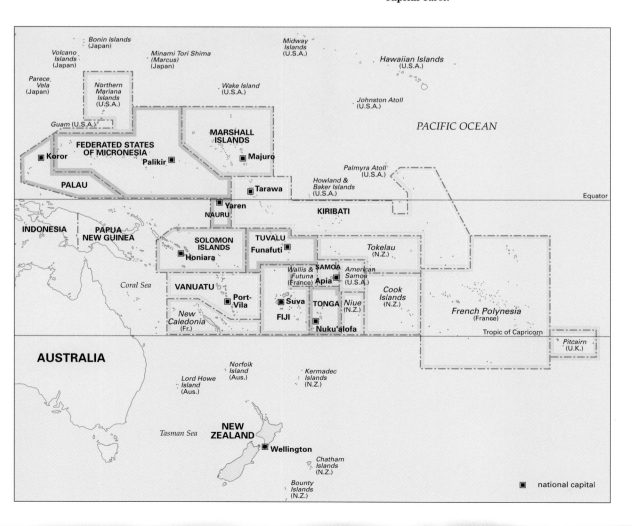

Oceania contains thousands of islands scattered across the Pacific Ocean. Some are mountainous and volcanic, while others are made up of coral that has accumulated on the tops of submerged volcanoes.

HABITATS

Scenic mountains and wilderness cover much of the country, providing habitats for New Zealand's wildlife. Forests run the length of the country from northeast to southwest. There are volcanoes, fjords, and geysers. The island countries have a range of tropical habitats.

LAND

Area 335,873 sq km (129,682 sq mi)
Highest point Mount Cook, New Zealand, 12,350 ft (3,764 m)
Major features Volcanic activity and mountain ranges in New Zealand, coral atolls and volcanic islands in Pacific

WATER

Longest river Waikato, New Zealand 270 mi (434 km)
Largest lake Lake Taupo, New Zealand 234 sq mi (606 sq km)

NOTABLE THREATENED SPECIES

Mammals Woodlark Island cuscus (*Phalanger lullulae*), Pohnpei flying fox (*Pteropus molossinus*), Samoan flying fox (*Pteropus samoensis*)
Birds Kagu (*Rhynochetos jubatus*), Black stilt (*Himantopus novaezelandiae*), Rapa fruit-dove (*Ptilinopus huttoni*), Kakapo (*Strigops habroptilus*), Guam flycatcher (*Myiagra freycineti*)
Plants Kau silverwood (*Argyroxiphium kauense*), Lobster claw (*Clianthus puniceus*), Philip Island hibiscus (*Hibiscus insularis*), Chatham Island forget-me-not (*Myosotium hortensia*), Vuleito (*Neoveitchia storckii*), Toromiro (*Sophora toromiro*), *Tecomanthe speciosa*
Others Tuatara (*Sphenodon punctatus*), Short Samoan tree snail (*Samoana abbreviata*), Stephens Island weta beetle (*Deinacrida rugosa*), Queen Alexandra's birdwing butterfly (*Ornithoptera alexandrae*)

CLIMATE

New Zealand has a mild, wet climate. North Island is warm and humid in the north, but the central plateau has frosts. South Island is cooler, and the Southern Alps contain large snowfields and glaciers. The west is rainy, while the eastern plains are much drier.

CLIMATE

| | Temperature °F (°C) | | Altitude |
	January	July	ft (m)
Auckland	66 (19)	51 (10)	85 (26)
Hokitika	59 (15)	45 (7)	12 (4)
Wellington	62 (17)	47 (9)	415 (127)
Dunedin	58 (14)	42 (6)	240 (73)
Christchurch	61 (16)	42 (6)	32 (10)

| | Precipitation in. (mm) | | |
	January	July	Year
Auckland	3.1 (79)	5.7 (145)	49.1 (1,249)
Hokitika	10.3 (262)	8.6 (218)	114.4 (2,907)
Wellington	3.2 (81)	5.4 (137)	47.4 (1,205)
Dunedin	3.4 (86)	3.1 (79)	36.9 (936)
Christchurch	2.2 (56)	2.7 (69)	25.1 (637)

ENVIRONMENTAL ISSUES

New Zealanders are concerned that local trees are being replaced by imported species. The country has its own supply of energy from hot water geysers. Many people oppose the testing of nuclear weapons on Pacific islands, where deforestation also occurs.

POPULATION AND WEALTH

Population (millions)	3.819 (NZ)
	0.011 (Nauru)
Population increase (annual growth rate, % 1990–95)	3.1% (Solomon Is.)
	1.2% (Fiji)
Energy use (lbs per year per person of oil equivalent)	9,775 (NZ)
Purchasing power parity (Int$/year)	4,132 (Fiji)
	2,306 (Solomon Is.)

ENVIRONMENTAL INDICATORS

CO₂ emissions ('000 tons/year)	27,440 (NZ)
	161 (Solomon Is.)
Car ownership (% of population)	10% (Fiji)
Proportion of territory protected, including marine areas (%)	24% (NZ)
	0.2% (Vanuatu)
Forests as a % of original forest	94% (Solomon Is.)
	29% (NZ)
Artificial fertilizer use (lbs/acre/year)	179 (NZ)
	55 (Fiji)
Access to safe drinking water (% population; rural/urban)	82%/100% (NZ)

MAJOR ENVIRONMENTAL PROBLEMS AND SOURCES

Air pollution: urban high
Marine/coastal pollution: medium; *sources*: industry, agriculture, sewage, tourism
Land degradation: *types*: desertification, soil erosion, salinization, deforestation, coastal degradation, habitat destruction; *causes*: agriculture, industry, population pressure, tourism
Resource issues: inadequate drinking water; inadequate sanitation; coastal flooding; coral deaths

HABITATS

North Island contains the long, mountainous northern peninsula and a volcanic region around lakes Taupo and Rotorua. The mountain range extends southwest across South Island, though both islands have fertile coastal plains.

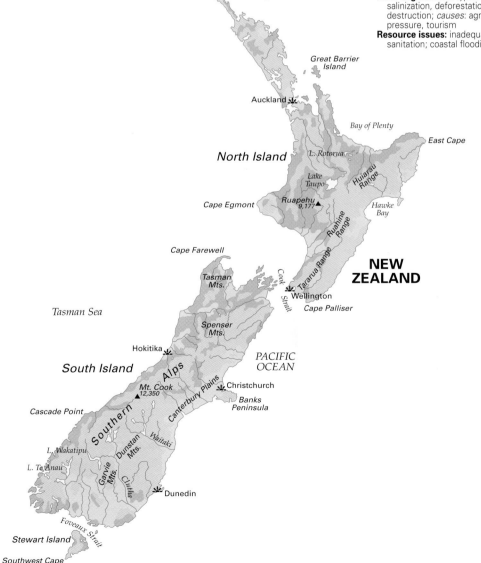

Physical zones

- mountains/barren land
- forest
- grassland

▲ mountain peak (ft)
☀ climate station

ENVIRONMENTAL ISSUES

Key environmental issues

- ● major town or city
- ▲ active volcano
- ▭ main area of coastal erosion
- ⬭ main area affected by soil erosion
- ▨ remaining forest
- ▧ area of deforestation

New Zealand has strong conservationist groups concerned with protecting national parks and nature reserves. Plans to build hydroelectric projects have been opposed because they may damage the environment.

North Cape
Great Barrier Island
Auckland
Bay of Plenty
Tauranga · White Island
Hamilton
North Island
L. Rotarua
Tarawera
East Cape
Lake Taupo
Huiarau Range
New Plymouth · Ngauruhoe · Tongariro
Cape Egmont
Ruapehu
Hawke Bay
Ruahine Range
Wanganui
Palmerston North
Cape Farewell
Cook Strait
Tasman Sea
Tasman Mts.
Wellington
Cape Palliser
NEW ZEALAND
Spenser Mts.
South Island
Southern Alps
Christchurch
Canterbury Plains
Banks Peninsula
PACIFIC OCEAN
Cascade Point
Waitaki
L. Wakatipu
Dunstan Mts.
L. Te Anau
Garvie Mts.
Clutha
Dunedin
Foveaux Strait
Invercargill
Stewart Island
Southwest Cape

CLIMATE

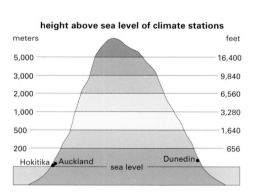

height above sea level of climate stations

meters		feet
5,000		16,400
3,000		9,840
2,000		6,560
1,000		3,280
500		1,640
200		656

Hokitika · Auckland — sea level — Dunedin

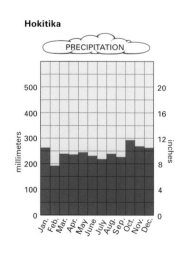

Hokitika
PRECIPITATION

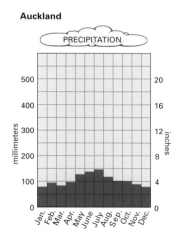

Auckland
PRECIPITATION

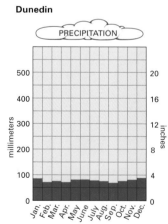

Dunedin
PRECIPITATION

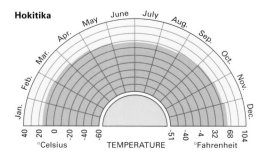

Hokitika
TEMPERATURE
°Celsius   °Fahrenheit

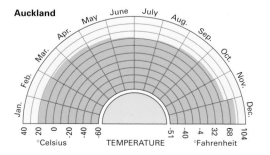

Auckland
TEMPERATURE
°Celsius   °Fahrenheit

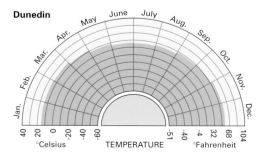

Dunedin
TEMPERATURE
°Celsius   °Fahrenheit

POPULATION

North Island has more than 70 percent of the population of New Zealand and the two largest cities, Auckland and Wellington. South Island has attracted fewer people. Populations in the Pacific Islands tend to be small but concentrated.

POPULATION

Total population of region (in millions)	5.9
Population density (persons per sq mi)	35
Population change	+1.13%/+0.34%
(average annual percent, 1995–2000, urban/rural)	

URBAN POPULATION

As percentage of total population	
1995	86%

TEN LARGEST CITIES

	Country	Population
Auckland	New Zealand	381,800
Christchurch	New Zealand	324,200
Manukau	New Zealand	281,800
North Shore	New Zealand	187,700
Waitakere	New Zealand	170,600
Wellington †	New Zealand	166,700
Dunedin	New Zealand	118,400
Hamilton	New Zealand	103,000
Suva †	Fiji	69,665
Palmerston North	New Zealand	69,300

† denotes national capital

City population figures are for city proper.

INDUSTRY

Water power used in hydroelectric power plants is the main source of electricity. Many industries process agricultural products, but New Zealand's cities have many other industries. Auckland is the leading industrial city. There is little other industry in the region.

INDUSTRIAL OUTPUT (US$ billion)

Total	Mining	Manufacturing
21.6	5.93	15.32

INDUSTRIAL WORKERS (millions)
(figures in parentheses are percentages of total labor force)

	Total	Mining	Manufacturing	Construction
New Zealand	1.8	0.004 (0.2%)	0.285 (15.8%)	0.111 (6.2%)

MAJOR PRODUCTS

Energy and mineral	output
Gold (m.t.)	6.9

Manufactures	
Cement (mil m.t.)	0.6
Aluminum (mil m.t.)	0.24

AGRICULTURE

New Zealand has plenty of grazing land, and sheep and cattle farming are still the chief agricultural activities. But forestry, fruit growing, and other kinds of farming have become increasingly important in recent years. The other countries export few farm products.

LAND
Total area   129,682 sq mi (335,873 sq km)

FARMERS	Fiji	New Zealand
Agriculture as % of GDP	18%	7%
% of workforce	67%	10%

MAJOR CROPS   Agricultural products: fruit and vegetables: sweet potatoes, bananas, breadfruit; potatoes, yams; wheat, barley, rice; sugarcane; coconuts, copra; cassava; pulses; taro; coffee, tea, cocoa; palm kernels; rubber; timber; spices; cattle, sheep, goats, poultry; dairy products; wine; fish

	Fiji	New Zealand
Total cropland ('000 acres)	704	8,105
Cropland (acres) per 1,000 people	895	2,155
Irrigated land as % of cropland	1%	9%
Number of tractors	7,000	76,000
Average cereal crop yields (lbs/acre)	1,732	4,663
Cereal production ('000 tons)	19	930
Change since 1986/88	−32%	−6%

LIVESTOCK & FISHERIES

	Fiji	New Zealand
Meat production ('000 tons)	24	1,334
Change since 1986/88	57%	11%
Marine fish catch ('000 tons)	24.2	458.8
Change since 1986/88	0%	141%

FOOD SECURITY

	Fiji	New Zealand
Food aid as % of total imports	0%	n/a
Daily kcal/person	2,865	3,395

POPULATION

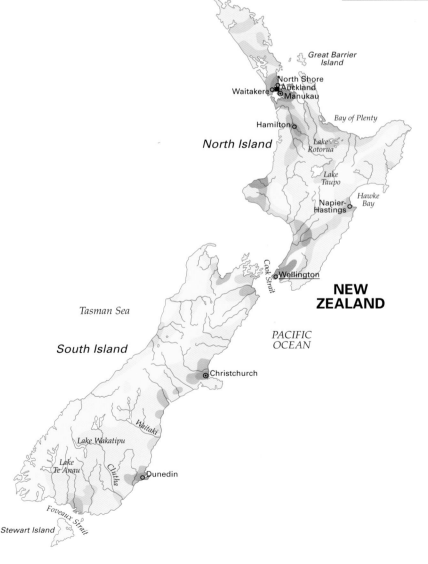

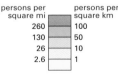

Population density

urban agglomeration
(National capital is underlined)

- ■ 1,000,000–5,000,000
- ● 500,000–999,999
- ◉ 250,000–499,999
- ○ 100,000–249,999

persons per square mi	persons per square km
260	100
130	50
26	10
2.6	1

More than 80 percent of the people of New Zealand live in urban areas. Nearly 50 percent live in one of three cities: Auckland, Wellington, and Christchurch. Large areas are thinly populated.

INDUSTRY

New Zealand's mineral resources include coal, natural gas, iron ore, and gold. Steam from geysers in North Island's volcanic area is used as a source of power.

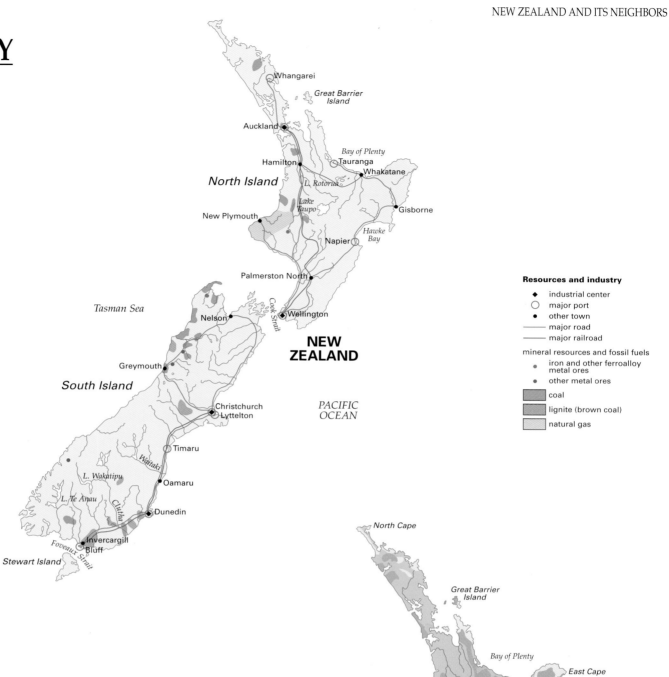

Resources and industry

- ◆ industrial center
- ○ major port
- • other town
- —— major road
- —— major railroad

mineral resources and fossil fuels

- • iron and other ferroalloy metal ores
- • other metal ores
- coal
- lignite (brown coal)
- natural gas

AGRICULTURE

Agricultural zones

- arable and pasture
- fruit and vegetables
- pasture with some arable
- pasture
- rough grazing
- woods and forest
- nonagricultural land

- ▲ mountain peak (ft)

The Canterbury Plains are the chief grain-growing region. Livestock farming is important in the southeast corner of South Island. Sheep are bred on both South Island and North Island.

ANTARCTICA

Antarctica is the coldest place on earth. It is a mountainous and mostly ice-covered continent surrounding the South Pole. It is also the driest continent, though it holds almost nine-tenths of the planet's ice. Much of the region is poorly mapped because it is difficult to reach and has a very harsh climate. But research on Antarctica has helped in the understanding of the way the southern continents have reached their present positions. Its climate influences weather systems all over the world. The ice sheet over Antarctica holds a record of recent climatic change and of pollution, including the presence of greenhouse gases. The ice sheet comprises so much of the world's ice and snow, that were it to melt, the world mean sea level would rise by 200 ft (60 m).

Antarctica has no permanent population although scientists carry out research there. In 1982, scientists located a hole in the ozone layer of the atmosphere over Antarctica. The ozone layer screens out 90 percent of the sun's ultraviolet radiation. Damage to it has been attributed to chlorofluorocarbons, chemicals used as propellants in some aerosol spray cans. These chemicals are also used in industry and in the coolant system of refrigerators.

The ozone hole is seasonal, developing only in the Antarctic winter and spring, and its size also changes. An increase in ultraviolet radiation would decrease the yield of farmers' crops, change climates around the world, and also lead to an increase in the number of cases of skin cancer.

Antarctica was once part of the ancient supercontinent of Gondwanaland, which also comprised Australia, New Zealand, and the southwest Pacific islands. About 500 million years ago, it was near the equator and had a warm, wet climate. Coal deposits give evidence of this. As Gondwanaland broke up, the part that became Antarctica drifted toward the South Pole and remained there, while the other continents drifted away to the warmer north.

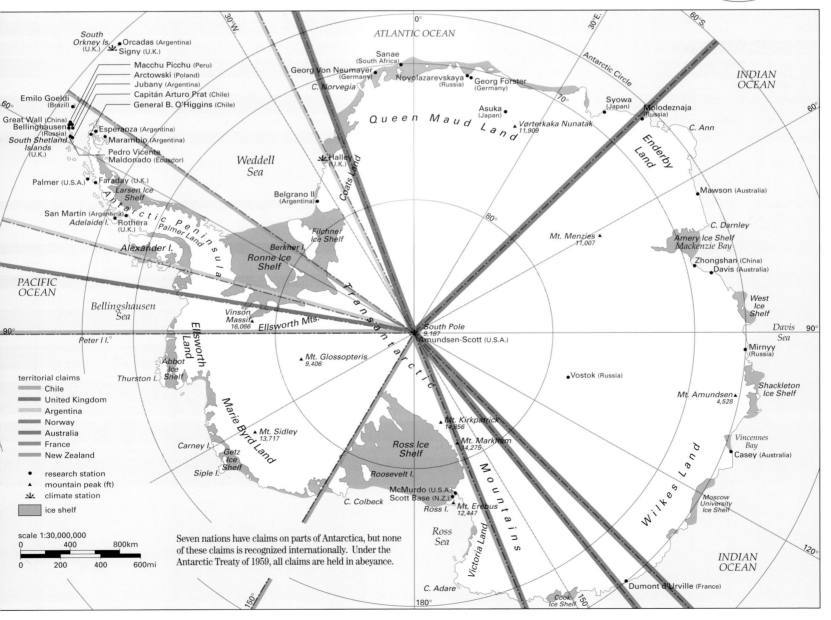

Seven nations have claims on parts of Antarctica, but none of these claims is recognized internationally. Under the Antarctic Treaty of 1959, all claims are held in abeyance.

territorial claims
- Chile
- United Kingdom
- Argentina
- Norway
- Australia
- France
- New Zealand

- • research station
- ▲ mountain peak (ft)
- ☀ climate station
- ▨ ice shelf

scale 1:30,000,000

THE POLITICAL AND CULTURAL WORLD

Despite claims to parts of Antarctica by various nations, people from any part of the world can go anywhere in Antarctica, providing their purpose is peaceful, because under international agreement, Antarctica is a demilitarized, nuclear-free zone.

Under recent agreements, restrictions have been placed on the development of the continent. Under the 1991 Environmental Protocol, for example, mining was banned for a period of 50 years. Some campaigning conservationists would like to go further and declare that Antarctica should become a world park, dedicated to science and the preservation of this fragile wilderness. Early this century several sledge expeditions set out to reach the South Pole at the heart of the interior. A Norwegian, Roald Amundsen (1872–1928), was the first to arrive on December 14, 1911. He was followed a month later by Robert F. Scott (1868–1912), and a team of British explorers, who perished in a blizzard on the return journey. In 1929 the American Richard E. Byrd (1888–1957) became the first man to fly over the South Pole.

LAND

Area of exposed rock 18,650 sq mi (48,310 sq km)
Highest point Vinson Massif 16,066 ft (4,897 m)
Height of surface at South Pole 9,187 ft (2,800 m)
Maximum thickness of ice 15,669 ft (4,776 m)

World's lowest recorded temperature, –128°F (–89.2°C) Vostok, Antarctica

HABITATS

The long chain of the Transantarctic Mountains runs across the whole of Antarctica, passing close to the South Pole and dividing the continent into two unequal parts: Lesser Antarctica and the massive semicircle of Greater Antarctica. From Lesser Antarctica the mountainous Antarctic Peninsula snakes northeast toward the southern tip of South America to the west of the Weddell Sea. The Ross Sea is a smaller gulf south of New Zealand. The southern end of both these seas is covered by permanent ice shelves.

The hostile conditions in Antarctica, combined with long months of darkness, limit plant life to lichens, mosses, algae, and molds in the few ice-free areas. There are no land mammals in Antarctica, but whales and seals feed on masses of tiny, shrimplike krill, while porpoises and dolphins are attracted by shoals of fish, especially Atlantic perch. With no land predators, the Antarctic coast is a haven for birds. Emperor penguins, Antarctic petrels, and South Polar skuas breed here and nowhere else, and more than 40 other species of birds live in Antarctica.

CLIMATE

Temperatures in Antarctica rarely rise above 32°F (0°C) in summer, and they plummet in winter from -40 to -94°F (-40 to -70°C). Strong winds sweep outward from the plateau at 43 mph (70 km/h), with gusts reaching 118 mph (190 km/h). The wind chill factor makes conditions even worse. On the Antarctic Peninsula, milder winds from neighboring oceans raise summer temperatures slightly. High atmospheric pressure, giving clear winter skies, dominates the interior of the continent.

The winds blow loose snow across the surface, creating blinding blizzards. Yet Antarctica has little precipitation. With about 2 in (50 mm) of snow a year, it is classified as a desert. Only trace amounts of precipitation are recorded at climate stations in the region. By the end of March, the sun sets on Antarctica, and the continent is in freezing darkness for six months. Although the summer is very short, the land receives more sunlight than equatorial regions do throughout the year. However, the ice sheet reflects most of the sun's energy back into the atmosphere.

CLIMATE

height above sea level of climate stations

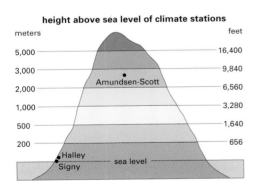

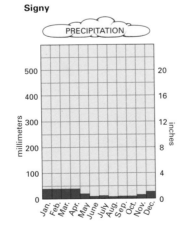

Signy — PRECIPITATION

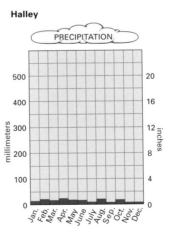

Halley — PRECIPITATION

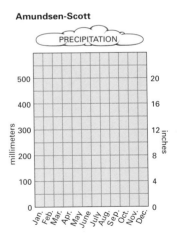

Amundsen-Scott — PRECIPITATION

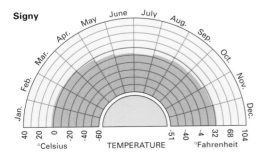

Signy — TEMPERATURE

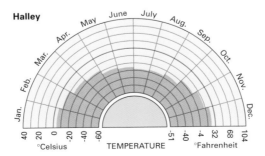

Halley — TEMPERATURE

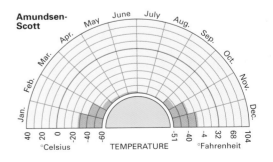

Amundsen-Scott — TEMPERATURE

GLOSSARY

acid rain Rain that has become more acid by combining with waste gases discharged into the atmosphere.

Arctic The region lying north of latitude 66 32N, where for a time in summer the sun never sets and in winter it never rises.

arid dry Arid areas generally have less than 10 in. (250 mm) of rain a year.

atoll A coral reef enclosing a lagoon.

bauxite The ore that is smelted to make the metal aluminum.

biome A major global unit in ecology, with its own plants and animals, e.g. savanna grassland.

bituminous coal Black coal with less carbon than anthracite but more than lignite.

cash crop A crop grown for sale rather than subsistence.

cereal A food crop and member of the grass family.

colony A territory under the control of another country.

Commonwealth A loose association of countries that are former members of the British empire.

communism A social, political, and economic system based on the communal ownership of property.

coniferous forest One of cone-bearing, usually evergreen trees.

conservation The management and protection of natural resources.

constitutional monarchy A form of government with a hereditary monarch and a constitution.

consumer goods Goods bought for people's needs, rather than for manufacturing uses.

continental climate A climate with a wide daily and seasonal variation of temperature and low rainfall, usually occurring in the interior of continents.

continental drift The complex process by which the continents move their positions relative to each other on the plates of the earth's crust. Also known as plate tectonics.

coral reef An underwater ridge or mound composed mostly of dead and living coral.

deciduous Shedding leaves annually.

deforestation Cutting down and clearing of forested land.

delta A usually triangular deposit of sand and soil at the mouth of a river.

democracy A form of government in which decisions are made by the people or those elected by them.

dependency A territory subject to the laws of another country but not formally part of it.

desert An arid area with less than 10 in (250 mm) of rain a year.

desertification The creation of desert by overgrazing, soil erosion, or climate change.

dictator A ruler with absolute power.

empire Political organization of countries and territories in which one dominates the rest.

endemic species A species that is native to a specific area.

erosion The process by which exposed land is broken down into small pieces or worn away by water, wind, or ice.

evergreen Having green leaves throughout the year.

exports Goods and services sold to other countries.

fault A fracture in the earth's crust.

federalism A form of constitutional government in which power is shared between a central, or federal, government and state or provincial governments.

ferroalloy metals Metals blended with iron in the manufacture of steel.

fjord A steep-sided inlet formed when a U-shaped valley is drowned by the sea.

fossil fuel A fuel such as oil, coal, peat, or natural gas, formed from ancient organic remains.

global warming An increase in the earth's average temperature, which some scientists believe will result from the greenhouse effect.

greenhouse effect The process in which radiation from the sun passes through the atmosphere, is reflected off the surface of the earth, and is then trapped by gases in the atmosphere. The buildup of carbon dioxide and other gases increases the effect.

Gross Domestic Product (GDP) The total value of a country's annual output of goods and services.

Gross National Product (GNP) A country's GDP plus income from abroad.

habitat The native environment in which a plant or animal lives.

hardwood The wood from trees other than conifers, which produce softwood. Hardwoods are generally stronger and more resistant to rot.

ice age A geological period during which glaciers covered large parts of the earth.

imports Goods and services bought from other countries.

indigenous people The original inhabitants of a region.

international dollar (Int $) Standardized international dollar values are used to measure purchasing power parity. Using a standardized unit provides the best available starting point for comparisons of economic strength and well-being between countries without being influenced by currency exchange rates.

lava Molten rock from a volcano; also its solid form when cooled.

lignite A dark brownish coal that is softer than anthracite.

llanos Tropical grasslands in South America.

maritime climate A moist climate generally found in areas near the sea.

Mediterranean climate One with warm, wet winters and hot, dry summers.

military regime A government controlled by the armed forces.

monarchy A form of rule where there is a hereditary head of state.

monsoon Tropical wind systems that reverse direction with the seasons; also, the rain brought by these winds.

multiparty system A system of rule in which parties compete for votes in elections.

nomad A member of a group of people who migrate seasonally in search of food, water, or grazing for their animals.

official language The language used by governments, schools, courts, and other official institutions in countries where there is no single common language.

one-party system A system of rule where there is no competition at elections, and all but the government party is banned.

pampas Temperate grasslands in South America.

peat A thick layer of partly decomposed plant remains found in wetlands. High acidity, low temperatures, and low nutrient and oxygen levels prevent total decomposition.

per capita For each person.

permafrost A permanently frozen layer of soil beneath the topsoil.

plateau A large area of level, high land.

polar regions Regions extending from the poles to the lines of latitude known as the Arctic and Antarctic circles. At these high latitudes the sun does not set in midsummer.

polder Low-lying land reclaimed from the sea by the building of dikes, particularly in the Netherlands.

prairie The flat grassland in the interior of North America, used for cereal crops.

precipitation Moisture reaching the earth from the atmosphere in the form of mist, dew, rain, sleet, snow, and hail.

province An administrative division of a country.

purchasing power parity (PPP) A way of measuring GDP based on standardized international dollar values (Int $). Using Int $ values means that the PPP is less prone to fluctuations in exchange rates that may distort the comparisons between countries.

radioactivity The radiation emitted from atomic nuclei. This is greatest when the atom is split, as in a nuclear reactor.

rain forest Forest where there is abundant rainfall all year. Tropical rain forests are rich in plant and animal species, and growth is lush and very rapid.

republic A form of government with a head of state that is elected or nominated.

rift valley A long valley formed when a block of land between two faults subsides.

Romance languages Family of languages derived from Latin.

savanna A habitat of open grassland with scattered trees in tropical and subtropical areas.

scrub vegetation Area of low trees and shrubs with tough evergreen leaves, found where there is drought in summer.

sediment Material, such as gravel, sand, or silt, that has been deposited by water, ice, or wind.

semiarid Having little rainfall. Semiarid areas have enough moisture to support a little more vegetation than a desert can.

softwood The wood from coniferous trees.

soil erosion The removal of the topsoil from land, mainly by the action of wind and rain.

steppe An open grassy plain with few trees or shrubs. It has low, sporadic rainfall, and wide ranges of annual temperature.

subsistence The minimum level of providing for one's needs, such as food and shelter.

subtropical zone Either of the two zones between the tropical and temperate zones. The subtropical zones have marked seasonal changes of temperature but are never very cold.

sustainable development Use of the earth's resources to improve people's lives without diminishing the ability of the earth to support life today and in the future.

taiga The coniferous, evergreen forests of subarctic lands, covering large areas of northern North America and Eurasia.

temperate zone Either of the two zones in the middle latitudes. Such zones lie between the warm tropics and cold polar regions.

tropics The area between the Tropic of Cancer and the Tropic of Capricorn. The lines mark latitudes farthest from the equator where the sun is still found directly overhead at midday in midsummer.

tundra Level, treeless land lying in the very cold northern parts of Europe, Asia, and North America.

wetland Land having wet and spongy soil, such as a swamp, bog, or marsh.

Gazetteer and Index